A GENERAL
THEORY OF
COMPETITION

Marketing for a New Century

A Sage Publication Series

Series Editor
Naresh K. Malhotra

The **Marketing for a New Century** series examines current and emerging issues in the field of marketing. Written by researchers who are widely acknowledged subject area experts, the books provide an authoritative, up-to-date review of the conceptual, research, and practical implications of the major issues in the marketing discipline.

A GENERAL THEORY OF COMPETITION by Shelby Hunt is the first volume in the series. Future volumes now in development will create a library of current, state-of-the-art texts and supplements for advanced courses in the marketing curriculum.

A General Theory of Competition

Resources,

Competences,

Productivity,

Economic Growth

Shelby D. Hunt

Marketing for a New Century

 Sage Publications, Inc.
International Educational and Professional Publisher
Thousand Oaks ■ London ■ New Delhi

For information:

Sage Publications, Inc.
2455 Teller Road
Thousand Oaks, California 91320
E-mail: order@sagepub.com

Sage Publications Ltd.
6 Bonhill Street
London EC2A 4PU
United Kingdom

Sage Publications India Pvt. Ltd.
M-32 Market
Greater Kailash I
New Delhi 110 048 India

Printed in the United States of America

Library of Congress Cataloging-in-Publication Data

Hunt, Shelby D.
    A general theory of competition : Resources, competences, productivity, economic growth / by Shelby D. Hunt.
      p. cm. — (Marketing for a new century)
    Includes bibliographical references and index.
    ISBN 0-7619-1728-4 (cloth: acid-free paper)
    ISBN 0-7619-1729-2 (pbk. : acid-free paper)
    1. Competition. I. Title. II. Series.
    HB238 .H86 2000
    338.6'048—dc21   99-6724

00 01 02 03 04 05 10 9 8 7 6 5 4 3 2

Acquiring Editor:	Harry Briggs
Editorial Assistant:	MaryAnn Vail
Production Editor:	Denise Santoyo
Editorial Assistant:	Cindy Bear
Typesetter/Designer:	Danielle Dillahunt
Indexer:	Teri Greenberg
Cover Designer:	Candice Harman

This book is dedicated to
my absolutely marvelous grandchildren,
Megan and Collin

Contents

Preface

This book develops the structure, foundations, and implications of the resource-advantage ("R-A") theory of competition. This new theory, it is argued, is a general, interdisciplinary, evolutionary, disequilibrium-provoking, process theory of competition. R-A theory has been developed in a sequence of more than a dozen journal articles that my friend and coauthor, Robert M. Morgan, and I have written for journals in economics, management, marketing, and public policy. The original idea for this book was to integrate and summarize the dozen articles in a monograph. However, as readers familiar with the separate articles will attest, this book extends the topics that R-A theory addresses substantially beyond the published articles, especially in such areas as economic growth and public policy.

Readers should be alert to three stylistic features of this book that differentiate it from most monographs. First, because R-A theory is a genuinely interdisciplinary theory, much more space is allocated to "literature review" than one finds in most books. Indeed, three chapters out of ten are specifically devoted to the "antecedents and affinities" of resource-advantage theory. Some readers may find the attention devoted to the research traditions on which resource-advantage theory draws (or shares affinities with) to exceed their comfort level. Nonetheless, I believe it to be a scientific and moral imperative to give credit to those works in the "pedigree" of resource-advantage theory. I ask readers' indulgence for the extensive review of traditions with which they are unfamiliar.

The second difference stems from the first. Even for an academic book, approximately six hundred references are a lot. Given that academic disciplines are rapidly becoming disciplinary "silos," for publishing purposes one normally must cite *only* those sources in the specific research tradition in which one writes. Because resource-advantage theory is genuinely interdisciplinary, works in different research traditions must be cited, even when such works involve similar treatments of similar topics. Again, I ask readers' indulgence.

The third stylistic difference concerns the extensive use of direct quotations. Regrettably, it is becoming commonplace, even in academic books, to simply paraphrase the works of others. In contrast, this book makes *extensive* use of direct quotations. I believe one has a scientific and moral imperative to accurately characterize the works of authors discussed, *especially* when one can be viewed as being critical of such works. The extensive use of direct quotations shows readers and original authors where to look for attributed views; they can then determine whether there might possibly be some misinterpretation or mischaracterization.

Most readers will disagree with some parts of resource-advantage theory. Some readers will disagree with most of it. Such disagreement is welcomed, since a major objective of this monograph is to stimulate thoughtful discussion and empirical research concerning the nature of competition. I only hope that I have made the structure and foundations of the theory clear enough to assist critics in their efforts to show where it is in error or poorly developed. I would rather be found wrong than obtuse.

Many scholars are working on developing process theories of competition. Indeed, many are referenced in this book. I invite all scholars developing process theories in economics, economic sociology, management, and marketing to (1) explicate their theories' structures and foundational premises and (2) compare and contrast them with R-A theory's structure (see Figures 6.1 and 6.2) and foundations (see Table 5.1). Then, we can evaluate how and why the theories are consistent or inconsistent, are saying different things or saying the same things differently, are genuinely rival or actually complementary.

First on my list of acknowledgments must be Robert M. Morgan at the University of Alabama. A longtime friend and coauthor, Rob has provided significant input to developing the structure and foundations of R-A theory. Without him, it is fair to say, the theory would never have been developed. Rob, thank you.

Numerous scholars here at Texas Tech University have provided significant input to the theory's development, including Dennis B. Arnett, Larry M. Austin, Kim Boal, Dale F. Duhan, Patrick Dunne, Roy D. Howell, James Jonish,

C. Jay Lambe, Deborah Laverie, Jamie Oliver, Robert L. Phillips, R. Stephen Sears, Samuel Spralls, Alex Stewart, James B. Wilcox, and Robert E. Wilkes. I appreciate very much not only their technical assistance on many issues but also their encouraging me to undertake this task.

A host of scholars in economics, management, marketing, and sociology have had a significant input to the development of the theory and the preparation of this book. I would like to specifically acknowledge the help of Jay Barney, Sundar G. Bharadwaj, S. Tamer Cavusgil, William W. Cooper, K. Chris Cox, Peter R. Dickson, Tom Donaldson, Henrik J. Duus, Steve Edison, Amitai Etzioni, Andreas Falkenberg, O. C. Ferrell, Nicolai J. Foss, Steve German, Aimé Heene, Geoffrey Hodgson, Bob Hopkins, Robert Jacobson, Israel M. Kirzner, Peter Klein, John Legge, Robert F. Lusch, William McKinley, Anil Menon, Richard R. Nelson, Paul Ngobo, Michael O'Keeffe, William D. Perrault, Robert A. Peterson, Peter Roberts, Paul Robertson, Ron Sanchez, Ronald Savitt, William R. Schroder, Robert M. Solow, John R. Sparks, P. Rajan Varadarajan, and Ulrich Witt. Of course, all the customary caveats apply.

All those who have attempted to find publishers for works that have small markets know the difficulty of the task. Therefore, I should like to thank Sage Publications for agreeing to publish this work and, in particular, to thank Harry M. Briggs and Naresh K. Malhotra for their work as editors.

Finally, but very important, thanks go to Mary Bishop and Robin Kirkland for their excellent typing assistance.

S. D. HUNT

Introduction

Assume competition. On thousands of occasions each day, in lectures, discussions, books, and journals, one finds the expression *assume competition*. And on each such occasion, the expression is taken to mean that one is being asked to assume the foundational premises, structure, and implications of the theory of *perfect* competition. Good communication is economical; to place the adjective "perfect" before the noun "competition" is simply redundant. That it frames the language, hence the discourse, of mainstream economics testifies as to the dominance of the theory of perfect competition.[1]

All disciplines have research traditions.[2] In economics, for example, one finds the neoclassical, institutional, evolutionary, historical, "Austrian," Keynesian, and Marxist traditions. Research traditions have a knowledge content (i.e., concepts and theories), a methodology (i.e., a set of norms and procedures for developing new content), and an epistemology (i.e., a set of norms and procedures for evaluating new content).

Perfect competition theory is a central part of the knowledge content of the neoclassical research tradition in economics. Demand theory, general equilibrium theory, and the theory of the firm are other key components.[3] The neoclassical tradition's methodological norms include the predisposition toward equilibrium analyses, the requirement that firms and consumers be maximizers, and the preference for mathematics as the preferred language of discourse. The neoclassical tradition's epistemology favors formal proofs and statistical tests on third-party generated data. Disfavored, for example, are historical evidence and statistical tests on primary data from surveys. (Data from census questionnaires are good; data from researcher questionnaires are bad.)

Research traditions have both their positive and negative sides. On the positive side, they are economical and guide debate and research. Each time one uses "competition" or "significant at the 0.5 level," one need not take time to defend *perfect* competition or the appropriateness of using a particular statistical test. Also on the positive side, researchers have some assurance that a research project that "follows the rules" of the tradition will have its results be publishable and its findings taken seriously.

On the negative side, concepts, theories, methods, and evidence not consistent with a research tradition, though they may be conceptually and empirically meritorious, may be wrongly, even summarily, dismissed by the tradition's adherents.[4] Also on the negative side, the strictures of a tradition may prevent its adherents from asking important questions or researching important issues and, by creating research "silos," may inhibit, even prevent, intradisciplinary communication (as well as *inter*disciplinary dialogue, of course). Therefore, because the essence of science is the recognition that a discipline's concepts and theories may be incomplete, wrong, or downright false, healthy disciplines have multiple research traditions. Furthermore, those working within a tradition are admonished to maintain an openness toward scholarship with nonconforming content, methods, and epistemologies.

This book develops—in a preliminary manner to be sure—a new theory of competition. This theory—labeled "resource-advantage theory"—stems from no single research tradition. Rather it draws on, shares affinities with, several different research traditions in several different disciplines. Specifically, it draws on several traditions in the disciplines of economics, management, marketing, and sociology. Evidence for its claim to being both intertradition and interdisciplinary is the fact that articles developing the theory have appeared in an extraordinarily diverse set of journals in economics (Hunt 1997b,c,d, 1999c), management (Hunt 1995, 1999a), public policy (Hunt 1998), and marketing (Hunt 1997a, 1999b; Hunt and Morgan 1995, 1996, 1997). The goal of this monograph is to develop resource-advantage theory—hereafter, for the sake of brevity, often referred to as "R-A theory"—in more detail than can be done in journal format.

As to research traditions, Table 1.1 displays the "pedigree" of resource-advantage theory. Specifically, it shows (1) eleven different research traditions or programs, (2) works representative of those traditions, and (3) examples of affinities the traditions have with R-A theory. For example, both transaction cost economics and R-A theory agree that opportunism occurs and that many resources important for explaining economic phenomena are firm-specific.

Although R-A theory has affinities with the traditions shown in Table 1.1, it is not a *composite* of the various theories in those traditions. Because the elements of a theory must be internally coherent, R-A theory draws only on those aspects of the traditions in Table 1.1 that *fit*. Indeed, R-A theory differs significantly from each tradition in its pedigree on numerous issues. For example, unlike transaction cost economics, R-A theory denies the assumption of *universal* opportunism and rejects the assumption that firms maximize.

Perfect competition theory is advanced by the neoclassical tradition as a positive theory that purports to explain and predict economic phenomena. Friedman's (1953) famous essay puts it this way:

> A hypothesis is important if it "explains" much by little, that is, if it abstracts the common and crucial elements from the mass of complex and detailed circumstances surrounding the phenomena to be explained and permits valid predictions on the basis of them alone. . . . [T]he relevant question to ask about the "assumptions" of a theory is not whether they are descriptively "realistic," but whether they are *sufficiently good approximations* for the purpose in hand. (pp. 14-15; italics added)

For the neoclassical tradition, therefore, good theories are those that explain and predict phenomena *well*. Why, then, do some theories predict better than others? For the tradition, some theories predict well and others do not because the foundational premises of good theories are *close enough* to approximate real-world economic conditions. Perfect competition, for example, predicts well when it is "close enough"—an expression we will return to on numerous occasions in this monograph.[5]

Resource-advantage theory, like perfect competition, is also advanced as a positive theory that purports to explain and predict economic phenomena. Indeed, R-A theory is argued to explain and predict certain phenomena better than perfect competition. It does so, it is further argued, because R-A theory's foundational premises are descriptively realistic. That is, compared with perfect competition theory, R-A theory's premises are *closer* approximations of real-world conditions.

However, let there be no misunderstanding: *R-A theory does not criticize neoclassical theory for its "unrealistic" assumptions.* Indeed, it accepts the view that good theories, among other things, should explain and predict phe-

TABLE 1.1   The Pedigree of Resource-Advantage Theory*

Research Tradition	Representative Works	Affinities with R-A Theory
1. Evolutionary economics	Marshall (1890) Schumpeter (1934, 1950) Alchian (1950) Nelson & Winter (1982) Langlois (1986) Dosi et al. (1988) Witt (1992) Foss (1993), Hodgson (1993)	Competition is an evolutionary, disequilibrating process. Firms have heterogeneous competences. Path dependencies can occur.
2. Austrian economics	Mises (1920, 1949) Hayek (1935c, 1948) Rothbard (1962) Kirzner (1979, 1982) Lachmann (1986)	Competition is a knowledge-discovery process. Markets are in disequilibrium. Enterpreneurship is important. Value is subjective. Intangibles can be resources.
3. Heterogeneous demand theory	Chamberlin (1933) Smith (1956) Alderson (1957, 1965) McCarthy (1960) Myers (1996)	Intra-industry demand is substantially heterogeneous. Heterogeneous supply is natural. "Product" should be defined broadly.
4. Differential advantage theory	Clark (1954, 1961) Alderson (1957, 1965)	Competition (a) is dynamic, (b) is both initiatory and defensive, and (c) involves a struggle for advantages. General equilibrium is an inappropriate welfare ideal.
5. Historical tradition	North (1981, 1990) Chandler (1990) Landes (1998)	History "counts." Firms are entities that are historically situated in space and time. Institutions influence economic performance.
6. Industrial-organization economies	Mason (1939) Bain (1954, 1956) Porter (1980, 1985)	Firm's objective is superior financial performance. Marketplace positions determine relative performance. Competitors, suppliers, and customers influence performance.
7. Resource-based tradition	Penrose (1959) Lippman & Rumelt (1982) Rumelt (1984) Wernerfelt (1984) Dierickx & Cool (1989) Barney (1991, 1992) Conner (1991), Grant (1991)	Resources may be tangible or intangible. Firms are historically situated combiners of heterogeneous, imperfectly mobile resources.

TABLE 1.1   *Continued*

Research Tradition	Representative Works	Affinities with R-A Theory
8. Competence-based tradition	Selznick (1957), Andrews (1971) Hofer & Schendel (1978) Hamel & Prahalad (1989, 1994a,b) Prahalad & Hamel (1990, 1993) Teece & Pisano (1994) Day & Nedungadi (1994), Aaker (1995) Sanchez, Heene, & Thomas (1996) Heene & Sanchez (1996) Sanchez & Heene (1997)	Competition is disequilibrating. Competences are resources. Renewal competences prompt proactive innovation. Firms learn from competing. Firms are embedded.
9. Institutional economics	Veblen (1899, 1904) Commons (1924, 1934) Hamilton (1932) Kapp (1976) Neale (1987) Mayhew (1987) DeGregori (1987) Ranson (1987) Hodgson (1994)	Competition is disequilibrating. "Capital" is more than just physical resources. Resources have "capabilities."
10. Transaction cost economies	Coase (1937) Williamson (1975, 1985, 1996)	Opportunism occurs. Many resources are firm-specific. Firm-specific resources are important.
11. Economic sociology	Parsons & Smelser (1956) Granovetter (1985, 1994) Etzioni (1988), Coleman (1990) Zukin & DiMaggio (1990) Powell & Smith-Doerr (1994) Smelser & Swedberg (1994) Scott (1995), Uzzi (1996) Fligstein (1996)	Institutions can be independent variables. Social relations may be resources. Economic systems are embedded.

* The order of the traditions is the order they are discussed in the book. No order of importance is implied.

nomena. Instead, the claims advanced here are that (1) R-A theory explains and predicts certain economic phenomena better than neoclassical theory and (2) R-A theory explains its empirical successes on the basis of its more descriptively realistic premises, that is, its foundations are *closer.*

Some philosophers of science (e.g., Rosenberg 1992) who specialize in economics characterize the neoclassical research program as an empirical failure. Many economists are also keenly disappointed with the tradition's record as to predictive accuracy. For example, in his 1970 presidential address to the American Economic Association, Nobel laureate Wassily Leontief (1970/1985) lamented: "In no other field of empirical enquiry has so massive and sophisticated a statistical machinery been used with such indifferent results" (p. 275). And twelve years later, he concluded:

> Year after year economic theorists continue to produce scores of mathematical models and to explore in great detail their formal properties; and the econometricians fit algebraic functions of all possible shapes to essentially the same sets of data without being able to advance, in any perceptible way, a systematic understanding of the structure and operations of a real economy. (1982, p. xii)

However, the task of this book, I stress in the strongest possible terms, is not to join the chorus in criticizing perfect competition and the neoclassical tradition for their empirical failures. Indeed, the tradition's scorecard has many empirical successes, and *all* traditions in the social sciences have empirical failures aplenty. Neither, I stress, is the objective to propose a *replacement* for perfect competition. Rather than criticize or replace perfect competition theory, R-A theory is offered as—and is argued to be—a general theory of competition that incorporates perfect competition as a special case. As a consequence, R-A theory incorporates the predictive successes of perfect competition and preserves the cumulativeness of economic science. Thus, R-A theory is a conserving theory.

If theories are to explain and predict phenomena, what should a theory of competition explain and predict? Undoubtedly, the single, most important, macroeconomic phenomenon of the twentieth century was the collapse of the planned or "command" economies and the concomitant empirical success of market-based economies. The central economic lesson of the twentieth century is that, compared with command economies, market-based economies are more productive, more innovative, and have higher-quality goods and services.

Note, however, that (1) command economies are premised on cooperation among state-owned firms under the direction of a central planning board and (2) market-based economies are premised on *competition* among privately owned firms that are self-directed. For starters, therefore, a good theory of competition, it would seem, should explain or contribute to explaining why economies *premised* on competition, when compared with command economies, are more productive, more innovative, and have higher-quality goods and services. This book argues, among other things, that R-A theory is superior to neoclassical theory in explaining the observed differences between market-based and command economies on productivity, innovation, and quality.

Perfect competition theory is advanced by the neoclassical tradition as not just a positive theory but a normative, public policy theory as well. That is, certain aspects of the positive theory have normative implications. Thus, the theory has been used for decades to frame discussions and guide public policy in such areas as antitrust legislation and the promotion of productivity and economic growth. Similarly, resource-advantage theory is also advanced as a positive theory with normative, public policy implications.[6] Furthermore, the implications of R-A theory for such areas as antitrust, productivity, and economic growth are very different from those of perfect competition.

The objective of this book is to articulate R-A theory, use the theory to explain and predict economic phenomena, show how (and why) it explains and predicts such phenomena, and begin the process of developing the theory's implications for public policy. This introductory chapter (1) discusses certain aspects of perfect competition theory that are central to understanding R-A theory, then (2) provides an overview of R-A theory, before (3) discussing the plan of the book. To begin: why is perfect competition *perfect?*

1.1 THE PERFECTION OF PERFECT COMPETITION

Stigler (1957) states succinctly a ground for viewing perfect competition as perfect: "The normative role of the [perfectly] competitive concept arises from the fact that the equality of rate of return on each resource in all uses which defines competition is also the condition for maximum output from given resources" (p. 16).[7] Because the readers of this book are likely to have heterogeneous backgrounds and because the claimed perfection of perfect competition is so important to understanding the claims of R-A theory, a brief review of how Stigler comes to his conclusion is desirable.

Table 5.1 in Chapter 5 displays the foundational premises of the theory of perfect competition. As to consumer behavior, the theory assumes that demand is homogeneous for every industry's product. That is, though consumers are allowed to prefer different quantities of each industry's product (heterogeneity across generic products), their tastes and preferences are assumed to be identical with respect to desired product features and characteristics (homogeneous within industries). Consumers also have perfect information, which is costless to them, about the availability, characteristics, benefits, and prices of all products. Consumer motivation, one dimension of human motivation, is self-interest or "utility" maximization.

The firm's objective is profit maximization or, more accurately stated, wealth maximization, that is, the maximization of the net present value of future profits. Acting under conditions of perfect and costless information, perfect competition theory focuses on the firm producing a single product using the resources of capital, labor, and (sometimes) land. These "factors" of production are assumed to be homogeneous and perfectly mobile, that is, each unit of labor or capital equipment is assumed to be identical with other units and can "flow" from firm to firm without restrictions. Because all innovation is exogenous, the only role of management is to respond to changes in the environment by determining the quantity of product to produce and then implementing a production function that is identical across all firms in each industry.

Competition, then, in perfect competition theory is each firm in each industry (1) in the "short-run" adjusting its quantity of product produced in reaction to changes in the market price of its product and the prices (costs) of its resources and other inputs, and (2) in the "long-run" adjusting the scale of its plant. Therefore, the firm's environment strictly determines its conduct. In particular, all firms in an industry will inexorably produce at an output rate where marginal cost equals marginal revenue (the product's market price). In the short-run, where such resources as plant and equipment are relatively "fixed," each firm will incur profits (or losses) depending on whether price exceeds (or is less than) the average total cost of producing the profit-maximizing quantity.

However, in long-run equilibrium in a perfectly competitive market, all resources are "variable," and each firm produces the quantity where market price equals long-run marginal cost, which itself equals the *minimum* long-run average cost. The position of long-run equilibrium is a "no profit" situation—firms have neither a pure profit (or "rent") nor a pure loss, only an accounting profit equal to the rate of return obtainable in other perfectly competitive industries. Therefore, the firm's environment strictly determines its performance (i.e., its profits).

The welfare economics literature investigates the normative implications of the conditions prevailing at the position of long-run, *general* equilibrium. Hence, neoclassical welfare economics is referred to as a "static efficiency" welfare analysis. (In contrast, the expression "dynamic efficiency" is often used to refer to analyses that focus on economic growth.)

If all industries in an economy are perfectly competitive and no further adjustments in quantity produced are made by any firm in any industry, then at this general equilibrium position every firm has the optimum-sized plant and operates it at the point of minimum cost. Furthermore, every resource or "factor" employed is allocated to its most productive use and receives the value of its marginal product. Moreover, the distribution of products produced is (Pareto) optimal at general equilibrium because the price of each product (reflecting what consumers are *willing* to pay for an additional unit) and its marginal cost (the extra resource cost society *has* to pay for an additional unit) will be exactly equal. On the preceding, static efficiency grounds, therefore, the adjective "perfect" is taken literally in neoclassical theory. Perfect competition is *perfect* and should guide public policy.

R-A theory's normative implications contrast strikingly with those of perfect competition's welfare analysis. For example, R-A theory argues that the process of competition—resource-advantage competition, that is—produces both gains in static efficiency and increases in dynamic efficiency, that is, economic growth. How the process of R-A competition produces productivity, economic growth, and the wealth of nations is addressed in Chapters 7, 8, and 9. This introductory chapter provides a brief overview of certain aspects of R-A theory as a "taste" of things to come.

1.2 AN OVERVIEW OF R-A THEORY

As an evolutionary, process theory of competition, R-A theory views (1) innovation and organizational learning as endogenous to competition, (2) firms and consumers as having imperfect information, and (3) institutions and public policy as affecting economic performance. Specifically, firms and resources are proposed as the heritable, durable units of evolutionary selection, with competition for a comparative advantage in resources constituting the selection process. Because the selection process focuses on firms and resources that are locally fitter, not maximally fittest, R-A theory is nonconsummatory (i.e., there is no predetermined end point for the process of competition) and, therefore, the theory accommodates path dependencies. Thus, though R-A competition is a process that is *moving,* it is not moving toward some ideal point (such as a Pareto-optimal, general equilibrium). My brief overview of R-A theory focuses on its pedigree and structure.

1.2.1 Pedigree

As shown in Table 1.1, the pedigree of R-A theory traces to eleven different traditions.[8] First, it traces to the historical tradition, the resource-based view of the firm, and the competence-based tradition. Contrasted with the neoclassical tradition's view that firms are time-independent, mathematical abstractions that combine homogeneous, perfectly mobile resources, the resource-based view posits that firms are entities that (1) are historically situated in space and time and (2) combine heterogeneous, imperfectly mobile resources. Contrasted with the neoclassical position that competition is equilibrating, the competence view is that competition is disequilibrating. Second, R-A theory draws on marketing's heterogeneous demand theory. This theory holds that because intra-industry demand is significantly heterogeneous, different market offerings are required for different market segments in the same industry. Third, R-A theory draws on industrial-organization economics and differential advantage theory. In this view, marketplace positions of competitive advantage (disadvantage) determine superior (inferior) financial performance. Thus, firms can have (1) an efficiency advantage, that is, *more* efficiently producing value, (2) an effectiveness advantage, that is, efficiently producing *more* value, or (3) an efficiency-effectiveness advantage, that is, *more* efficiently producing *more* value (see cells 2, 3, and 6 in Figure 6.2 in Chapter 6).

Fourth, R-A theory draws on evolutionary economics. Evolutionary economics views competition as a selection process, a *struggle*. It is this process of competition that produces innovations, Schumpeter's (1950) "creative destruction," increases in productivity, and economic growth. Fifth, R-A theory draws on "Austrian" economics. Stressing the importance of entrepreneurship and economic institutions, Austrian economics views competition as a process of competitive rivalry in which information is dispersed and tacit. Therefore, competition is a knowledge-discovery process. Sixth, R-A theory draws on economic sociology and institutional economics. R-A theory recognizes that societal institutions, such as laws, customs, taboos, traditions, and moral codes, produce order by structuring political, economic, and social interaction. The kind of order produced by societal institutions influences the process of R-A competition and, thereby, influences such outcomes as productivity and economic growth.

Although R-A theory draws on the previously cited streams of literatures, I again emphasize that the theory is neither the same thing as any of the works in its pedigree nor is it a composite of such works. For example, Schumpeter (1934, 1950) starts from equilibrium and focuses exclusively on major innovations in his theory of economic growth. In contrast, R-A theory does not start from equilibrium, includes both major and incremental innovations, and shows how *both* kinds of innovations drive economic growth. R-A theory's structure shows other differences.

1.2.2 Structure

Figures 6.1 and 6.2 in Chapter 6 provide a schematic depiction of the relationships among R-A theory's key constructs; Table 5.1 in Chapter 5 shows its foundational premises. Because R-A theory draws heavily on Austrian and evolutionary economics, (1) innovation and organizational learning are endogenous to R-A competition, (2) firms and consumers have imperfect information, and (3) entrepreneurial competence and institutions affect economic performance. Because it incorporates marketing's heterogeneous demand theory, intra-industry demand is viewed as significantly heterogeneous as to consumers' tastes and preferences. Therefore, different market offerings are required for different market segments in the same industry.

Because R-A theory adopts a resource-based view of the firm, firms are theorized to be historically situated combiners of heterogeneous, imperfectly mobile resources. Combining the resource-based view of the firm with heterogeneous demand and imperfect information results in diversity in the sizes, scopes, and levels of profitability of firms. This diversity exists not only across industries but for firms within the same industry.

R-A theory stresses the importance of market segments, a comparative advantage (disadvantage) in resources, and marketplace positions of competitive advantage (disadvantage). Market segments are intra-industry groups of consumers whose tastes and preferences for an industry's output are relatively homogeneous. (The ultimate segment is, of course, a segment of one.) Resources are the tangible and intangible entities available to the firm that enable it to produce efficiently and/or effectively a market offering that has value for some market segment(s). Because many of the resources of firms within an industry are significantly heterogeneous and relatively immobile, some firms will have a comparative advantage and others a comparative disadvantage in efficiently and/or effectively producing market offerings that have value for particular market segments.

International trade theory has long recognized that nations have heterogeneous, immobile resources. Therefore, it focuses on the implications of comparative advantages in societal resources on trade. Similarly, R-A theory recognizes that many of the resources of firms within the same industry are significantly heterogeneous and relatively immobile. Therefore, it focuses on the implications of comparative advantages in firm-level resources on competition, productivity, and economic growth.

Analogous to nations, some firms will have a comparative advantage and others a comparative disadvantage in efficiently and/or effectively producing particular market offerings that have value for particular marketing segments. Specifically, when firms have a comparative advantage (or disadvantage) in resources, they will occupy marketplace positions of competitive advantage (or disadvantage), as shown in Figure 6.1 and further explicated in the nine marketplace positions in Figure 6.2. Marketplace positions of competitive advantage (or disadvantage) then result in superior (or inferior) financial performance.

Firms occupying positions of competitive advantage (cells 2, 3, and 6 in Figure 6.2) can continue to do so if (1) they engage in proactive innovation, (2) they continually reinvest in the resources that produced the competitive advantage, and/or (3) rivals' acquisition and reactive innovation efforts fail. Rivals will fail (or take a long time to succeed) when an advantage-producing resource when it is protected by such societal institutions as patents; when it is causally ambiguous, socially complex, highly interconnected, or tacit; or when it has time compression diseconomies or mass efficiencies.

Competition, for R-A theory, is the disequilibrating process that consists of the constant struggle among firms for comparative advantages in resources that will yield marketplace positions of competitive advantage for some market segment(s) and, thereby, superior financial performance. The nature of competitive processes and how well they work (e.g., how effectively competition increases productivity and produces economic growth) are significantly influenced by five environmental factors: the societal resources on which firms draw, the societal institutions that structure economic actions, the actions of competitors and suppliers, the behaviors of consumers, and public policy.

1.3 A LOOK AHEAD

This monograph may be viewed as having four sections. The first is composed of Chapters 2, 3, and 4, which discuss the eleven research traditions (a) on which R-A theory draws, that is, its antecedents, and (b) to which it has aspects in common, that is, its affinities. The second section, composed of Chapters 5 and 6, develops the foundational premises and structure of R-A theory. The first and second sections of the book are written so that they are "freestanding." Indeed, some readers may choose to read Chapters 5 and 6 first and then read Chapters 2, 3, and 4.

The third section of the book, composed of Chapters 7, 8 and 9, explores how R-A theory addresses issues of productivity, economic growth, and the wealth of nations. These chapters show how R-A theory contributes to explaining why some nations are very productive, grow rapidly, and are wealthy, whereas others are low in productivity, grow slowly, and are poor. The fourth section, Chapter 10, advances the argument that R-A theory is a general theory of competition and, in a preliminary manner, examines the public policy implications of R-A theory.

More specifically, as to the structure, explanatory power, predictive accuracy, and normative implications of R-A theory, I shall argue in the four sections that R-A theory (1) contributes to explaining firm diversity (Section 6.3), (2) makes the correct prediction concerning financial performance diversity (Section 6.3.1), (3) contributes to explaining observed differences in quality, innovativeness, and productivity between market-based and command economies (Section 7.3), and (4) shows why competition in market-based economies is dynamic (Section 5.7.1).

Furthermore, I shall argue in this book that R-A theory (1) incorporates the resource-based view of the firm (Section 4.1.5), (2) incorporates the competence view of the firm (Sections 2.1.3 and 4.1.5), (3) has the requisites of a phylogenetic, nonconsummatory, disequilibrium-provoking, theory of competition (Section 2.1.3), (4) explicates the view that competition is a process of knowledge-discovery (Sections 2.2.3 and 6.1.4), (5) contributes to explaining why social relations constitute a resource only contingently (Section 4.2.4), (6) has the requisites of a moderately socialized theory of competition (Section 4.2.4), and (7) shows how path-dependence effects can occur (Sections 6.2.4 and 6.2.5).

Finally, I shall argue that R-A theory (1) expands the concept of *capital* (Section 8.2.1), (2) contributes to explaining the growth pattern of the (former) Soviet Union (Section 8.6.1), (3) provides a theoretical foundation for why formal institutions promoting property rights and economic freedom also promote economic growth (Section 9.2), (4) provides a theoretical foundation for why informal institutions promoting social trust also promote economic growth (Section 9.3.3), (5) has the requisites of a general theory of competition that incorporates perfect competition as a limiting, special case, thereby incorporating the predictive successes of neoclassical theory and preserving the cumulativeness of economic science (Section 10.1), (6) shows why the debate over antitrust legislation and implementation has been so misguided (Section 10.2.2), and (7) provides some—preliminary, to be sure—recommendations for public policy (Section 10.3).

The preceding agenda is an ambitious one. Let's get started.

NOTES

1. See Stigler (1957) for a history of perfect competition theory. See McNulty (1968) for a classic critique of the theory. See Foss (1994a) for the view that Chamberlin (1933) and Robinson (1933) deserve more credit for developing perfect competition theory than they are customarily accorded: "In the process of taking the theory of perfect competition as a critical starting point, Chamberlin and Robinson constructed their own target, bringing together hitherto dispersed elements—e.g., full mobility (J. M. Clark, Frank Knight), perfect information (Knight), the equilibrium firm (Pigou), firms as price-takers (Pigou), etc.—under a rigorous geometrical treatment" (p. 1124).

2. I prefer "research program" or "research tradition" over "paradigm" because the latter denotes (or connotes) for many that all research in science takes place within rigid, encapsulated, self-justifying, incommensurable, paradigmatic cocoons—as the cognitive relativism of Kuhn (1962) argued. "Research program" and "research tradition," to their credit, do not have this denotation or connotation. See Hunt (1991a, pp. 320-49) for a critique of Kuhnian relativism.

3. See Nelson and Winter (1982) for a discussion of the components of the neoclassical research tradition.

4. Nelson and Winter (1982) explore whether the neoclassical tradition has become an "orthodoxy," that is, whether it provides a "narrow set of criteria that are conventionally used as a cheap and simple test for whether an expressed point of view on certain economic questions is worthy of respect." They conclude: "Our own thought and experience leave us thoroughly persuaded that an orthodoxy exists . . . and that it is quite widely enforced" (p. 6).

5. Friedman (1953) draws on the logical positivist view that theories and their constituent terms are to be interpreted in a Machian *instrumentalist* fashion. For instrumentalism, "theories are only instruments for making predictions" (Blaug 1980, p. 105). Scientific realism, in contrast, maintains—among other things—that theories may contain theoretical terms that are in principle unobservable and which cannot be reduced through correspondence rules or definitions to observable terms (Manicas 1987). As McMullin (1984) succinctly puts it: "The basic claim made by scientific realism . . . is that the long-term success of a scientific theory gives reason to believe that something like the entities and structure postulated by the theory actually exists" (p.26).

Truth plays an important role in scientific realism. The empirical successes of a theory are explained on the basis of *approximate* (not absolute) truth. That is, the empirical successes of a theory give us reason to believe that *something like* (not necessarily exactly like) the theory's concepts and structure do exist. When Friedman (1953) explains the empirical successes of a theory by its being "close enough," he appears to be using a realist argument to justify an instrumentalist view of theories. In any respect, R-A theory adopts scientific realism, not logical positivism, or logical empiricism, or relativism, as a philosophical position. See Hunt (1989, 1990b, 1991a,b, 1992, 1993, 1994), Leplin (1984), Manicas (1987), and Suppe (1977) for discussions of logical positivism, logical empiricism, relativism, and scientific realism.

6. Resource-advantage theory is also claimed to have normative implications for business strategy. However, strategic issues are not the focus of this book. See the works cited in Section 4.1 on the "resource-based view" and competence-based strategy for representative strategic implications that are incorporated into R-A theory.

7. Note that as early as 1957, Stigler (1957) saw it as redundant to put the adjective "perfect" before "competitive concept."

8. Although I have labored to include all traditions that have affinities with R-A theory and though this monograph has approximately six hundred references, there are (no doubt) theories, traditions, and references omitted. Readers are asked to advise me of omissions.

Antecedents and Affinities

Evolutionary and "Austrian" Economics

A s an interdisciplinary theory of competition, resource-advantage the-ory draws on—shares affinities with—diverse theories, research programs, and traditions. In particular, R-A theory draws on evolutionary economics, "Austrian" economics, heterogeneous demand theory, differential advantage theory, business strategy, and institutional theory (see Table 1.1 for a summary). A comprehensive review of each of these theories, programs, and research traditions is beyond the scope of this work. Instead, I review only those portions that are directly relevant to R-A theory and point readers toward more comprehensive reviews. This chapter examines evolutionary economics and "Austrian" economics. Chapter 3 focuses on the theories of heterogeneous demand and differential advantage. Chapter 4 reviews business strategy and institutional theory.

As to evolutionary economics, I discuss (1) its status at the end of the nine-teenth century and its suppression thereafter, (2) its revival in the 1980s, and (3) its theory of the firm. Finally, I discuss the affinities between evolutionary economics and R-A theory.

2.1 EVOLUTIONARY ECONOMICS

Should economies be viewed through the lens of mechanistic metaphors or biological? That is, are economies best analyzed by viewing them as similar to Newtonian, mechanical systems at equilibrium or evolutionary, dynamic systems in motion? At the end of the nineteenth century, both the Newtonian, static-equilibrium and biological, evolutionary views were prominent (Hodgson 1993).[1] Indeed, Alfred Marshall (1842-1924) is customarily accorded the status of being the "father" of neoclassical economics on the grounds that he developed in detail the marginal conditions of partial equilibrium analysis. Yet Marshall (1890/1949), who relegated all mathematics to footnotes and appendices, believed that "economics has no near kinship with any physical science" and "economics is a branch of biology broadly considered" (p. 772). Of the many biological metaphors he employed, his trees in the forest metaphor is arguably the most famous:

> But here we may read a lesson from the young trees of the forest as they struggle upwards through the benumbing shade of their older rivals. Many succumb on the way, and a few only survive; those few become stronger with every year, they get a larger share of light and air with every increase of their height, and at last in their turn they tower above their neighbors, and seem as though they would grow on for ever, and for ever become stronger as they grow. But they do not. One tree will last longer in full vigour and attain a greater size than another; but sooner or later age tells on them all. Though the taller ones have a better access to light and air than their rivals, they gradually lose vitality; and one after another they give place to others, which, though of less material strength, have on their side the vigour of youth. (pp. 315-16)

Marshall then likened the growth of firms to the growth of trees:

> Nature still presses on the private business by limiting the length of the life of its original founders, and by limiting even more narrowly that part of their lives in which their faculties retain full vigour. And so, after a while, the guidance of the business falls into the hands of people with less energy and less creative genius, if not with less active interest in its prosperity. (p. 316)

Of course, Marshall's dynamic, "life-cycle" view of individual *firms* conflicted with his static-equilibrium analysis of *industries*. He attempted to resolve the conflict by the heuristic fiction of the "representative firm"—which, for Marshall, was not in equilibrium. That is, the Marshallian representative firm, rather than existing in a state that equated marginal cost with average revenue and price, actively sought incremental cost reductions (Foss 1991).

In the decades since Marshall gave prominence to both evolutionary and mechanistic metaphors, the neoclassical tradition "hardened" around profit-maximizing firms in static equilibrium. Marshall's representative firm and his view that firms actively sought cost reductions through innovations gave way to Pigou's (1928) equilibrium firm that faces a known production function and equates marginal cost, average revenue, and price. Mainstream economics and its journals came to view Marshall's life-cycle perspective of firms as "biological folklore" and "fantasia" (Levine 1980). As Colander (1995) puts it, the standard view in the neoclassical tradition is: "Marshall is for kids and liberal arts professors; real economists (professors at universities) do Walras" (p. 281). Works in economics that attempted to start from evolutionary, process-oriented, biological metaphors were, in the words of Foss (1991), *suppressed.*

2.1.1 The Revival

The use of biological metaphors resurfaced with Alchian's (1950) often-cited article on the epistemic standing of the profit maximization assumption in neoclassical theory. To counter the argument of neoclassical theory's critics that firms do not have, either explicitly or implicitly, the objective of maximizing profits, Alchian (1950) argued that evolutionary processes would ensure that the "fit" firms, that is, those that actually maximize, will survive and prosper. Friedman (1953) then used a "survival of the fittest" argument in his famous defense of assuming firms and agents to be optimizers. For him, either neoclassical assumptions are "close enough" or evolutionary processes work "as if" firms maximized.

Many economists, though advocating an evolutionary approach to economic change, criticize works such as Friedman's (1953) as simplistic because they do not provide a *theory* of the very evolutionary, competitive processes invoked to justify (allegedly) the optimal, static-equilibrium outcomes of neoclassical economics. For example:

> Natural selection does not lead to the superlative fittest, only the tolerably fit. But even in a weaker sense, evolution is not necessarily a grand or natural road leading generally towards perfection. Change can be idiosyncratic, error can be reproduced and imitated, and a path to improvement can be missed. Furthermore, an evolutionary process involving selection cannot be an optimizing one, at least in the strict sense, because for evolution to work there must always be a variety of forms from which to select. (Hodgson 1993, pp. 200-201)

In the 1960s and 1970s, philosophers of science reexamined the role of metaphors in science. This reexamination distinguished purely literary metaphors from theoretical metaphors and showed the importance of the latter for theory development in science (Black 1962; Ortony 1979). Concomitantly, many economists began to reevaluate the possibility of using biological metaphors as models for theory construction. By the 1980s, many heterodoxical research programs in evolutionary economics began to take shape.

Witt's (1992) review identifies several, ongoing programs in evolutionary economics: (1) the Schumpeterian stream (e.g., R. H. Day 1984; Dosi et al. 1988; Nelson and Winter 1982), which focuses on technical progress, innovation, industrial development, business cycles, and growth; (2) the Austrian-subjectivist works (e.g., Hayek 1978; Lachmann 1986; Loasby 1991b), which emphasize subjective knowledge and competition as a discovery process; (3) the institutionalist stream (e.g., Dopfer 1986; Gordon and Adams 1989; Hodgson 1993), which focuses on how routinized patterns of behavior and habits of thought affect economic change; and (4) the neo-Darwinian works (e.g., Boulding 1981; Faber and Proops 1990; Hirshleifer 1982; Metcalfe and Saviotti 1991), which rely on explicit biological analogies to explain change. Witt (1992) argues that, though extraordinarily diverse, "a coherent research program is gaining shape in evolutionary economics" (p. 405).

The impetus for research programs in evolutionary economics has been the general recognition that the equilibrium tradition cannot account satisfactorily for economic change, for example, changes in technology, productivity, and economic growth. Therefore, evolutionary theorizing tends to view economic systems as disequilibrating and process oriented. But to just be process oriented is not sufficient for a theory to be evolutionary. For Dosi and Nelson (1994), evolutionary theories in economics should explain the movement of economic variables through time by means of "elements which generate or renew some variation of the variables in question, and mechanisms that systematically winnow on extant variation" (p. 154). They identify (1) units of selection; (2) mechanisms that do the selecting; and (3) the criteria of selection, adaptation, and variation as the "building blocks" of evolutionary economic theories.

Hodgson (1993) provides the most detailed analysis yet of the characteristics of the various kinds of evolutionary theories possible in economics. His taxonomy distinguishes developmental theories that focus on "stages" (e.g., Marxism) from genetic theories that concentrate on a set of fairly durable human entities and a detailed causal explanation of their interactions. Within genetic theories, he distinguishes ontogenetic theories that focus on "a set of given and unchanging" entities (e.g., Schumpeter's [1950] "creative destruction") from phylogenetic theories that focus on the "complete and ongoing evolution of the population, including changes in its composition." He then distinguishes phylogenetic, consummatory theories that have end stages of "finality or consummation" (e.g., perfect competition's, Pareto-optimal position) from phylogenetic, nonconsummatory theories that permit neverending evolution (pp. 39-51).

Although not all phylogenetic, nonconsummatory theories sort through natural selection, the key requirements for those that do so, Hodgson (1993) maintains, are that (1) they must have units of selection that are fairly durable (i.e., the units can exist, at least potentially, through long periods of time) and heritable (i.e., the units can be transmitted to successors), and (2) there must be a selection process that involves a struggle for existence that encompasses a renewable source of variety and change, where the struggle results in the survival of the "fitter," not necessarily the "fittest."

2.1.2 Evolutionary Economics and the Theory of the Firm

The seminal work for many of the research programs in evolutionary economics is Nelson and Winter's (1982) *Evolutionary Theory of Economic Change.* In this work, Nelson and Winter introduce the concept of organizational routine, which they define as "all regular and predictable behavioral patterns of firms" (p. 14) and which they view to be analogous to genes in biological theory. As durable, heritable, guides to firm behavior, routines include characteristics of firms that range from "well-specified technical routines for producing things, through procedures for hiring and firing, ordering new inventory, or stepping up production of items in high demand, to policies regarding investment, research and development (R&D), or advertising, and business strategies about product diversification and overseas investment" (p. 14). The concept of routines, which "represent the skills of an organization" (p. 124), provides a major step toward developing a genuinely evolutionary theory of the firm. Foss (1993) contrasts this emerging, evolutionary theory with the neoclassical tradition's contractual theory of the firm.

Consider the two versions of the contractual theory of the firm and their respective answers to the question: why do firms exist? First, in the nexus of contracts view, one finds maximizing managers who face moral hazard. Therefore, firms result from the incentive problems that arise when team-production is combined with opportunism (e.g., Jensen and Meckling 1976). Second, in the incomplete contracting view, one finds boundedly rational managers who face opportunism. Therefore, firms arise from efforts to secure the rents that flow from transaction-specific assets (e.g., Williamson 1985). Indeed, in this view, a firm is a "contractual instrument, a continuation of market relations, by other means" (Williamson 1991b, p. 162). Such an instrument is used as a "last resort, to be employed when all else fails" (Williamson 1991a, p. 279).

As Foss (1993) points out, however, both contractual perspectives imply a static analysis in which "technology—as well as the menu of inputs and outputs more generally—is given through some process that is historically and logically prior to the issue of the organization of economic activities" (p. 131). Indeed, he notes that taking the transaction as the analytical unit and viewing "the firm" as nothing more than shorthand for a set of contracts among transacting individuals implies that the *firm's* strategy is a meaningless concept and "it comes as no big surprise that . . . nexus of contracts theorists . . . call for the abandonment of the concepts of 'the entrepreneur' and 'the firm,' respectively" (p. 130).

In contrast, Foss (1993) argues for an evolutionary, competence perspective, which views the firm as a repository of tacit knowledge. Associated with the works of Demsetz (1988), Klein (1988), Langlois (1986), and Nelson and Winter (1982), Foss (1993) traces the competence perspective to the long-neglected work of Edith Penrose (1959). Her work maintained that not only are firms pools of intangible resources, but also: "Businessmen commonly refer to the managerial group as a 'team' and the use of this word implies that management in some sense works as a unit" (p. 45). Building on her prescient work, Carlsson and Eliasson (1991), Eliasson (1990 a,b), and Pelikan (1988, 1989a,b) have developed an evolutionary, *competence* perspective of the firm. Following Pelikan's (1989b) treatment, Foss (1993) characterizes the epistemic and economic content of the concept of competence:

> (1) Competence is an information capital which tells its owner how to understand and use information to solve economic problems, how to make economic decisions and how to further expand existing competence; (2) it is agent-specific and it is tacit; (3) it is distributed asymmetrically over individuals and firms; and (4) stocks of economic competence are difficult to measure and compare with each other. (p. 134)

Under this perspective, what gives birth to firms and determines their boundaries? Foss (1993) argues that it is the idiosyncrasy of entrepreneurship: "Utilization of entrepreneurial competence . . . requires a *firm* with the entrepreneur as residual claimant" (p. 136, italics in original). Furthermore, the tacit nature of competence implies that firms integrate because, at times, "it is practically impossible for . . . integrating firms to convey—at least at reasonable cost—information to their suppliers about what precisely they want from them" (p. 138). Therefore, "integration arises from the largely non-communicable, idiosyncratic, and non-contractible nature of competence" (p. 139).

Langlois and Robertson (1995) further develop the competence perspective in their evolutionary theory of firm capabilities. Identifying the *capabilities* of an organization or network of organizations as the repertoire of routines that an organization (or network) possesses, they contend: "Those business organizations that can create and utilize superior capabilities tend to perform better" (p. 3). For them:

> Our basic argument is that firms and other types of organizations consist of two distinct but changing parts. The first part, the *intrinsic core,* comprises elements that are idiosyncratically synergistic, inimitable, and noncontestable. That is, the capabilities in the intrinsic core cannot be duplicated, bought, or sold, and they combine to generate unique outcomes that are more valuable than the outcomes that the core elements could produce separately. The remainder of the organization consists of *ancillary capabilities* that are contestable and may not be unique. (p. 7, italics in original)

2.1.3 Evolutionary Economics and R-A Theory

Resource-advantage theory has strong affinities with evolutionary economics. As a first affinity, R-A theory is argued to be an evolutionary, phylogenetic, nonconsummatory, disequilibrium-provoking, theory of competition (Hunt 1997c). In brief, defining resources as the tangible and intangible entities available to firms that enable them to produce efficiently and/or effectively market offerings that have value to some market segment(s), R-A theory proposes that both resources and firms are the heritable, durable units of evolutionary selection. Furthermore, R-A theory identifies the selection process as *competition,* which is viewed as the disequilibrating, ongoing process that consists of the constant struggle among firms for comparative advantages in resources that will yield marketplace positions of competitive advantage and, thereby, superior financial performance. (See Chapter 6, Figures 6.1 and 6.2.)

Because the selection process in R-A theory deals with extant firms employing known (or knowable) resources competing in the face of imperfect information (instead of idealized firms using hypothetical resources and perfect information), the process results in the survival of firms and resources that are locally fitter. Because the surviving, locally fitter firms and resources may be different from some hypothetical entities that are maximally fittest, R-A theory is nonconsummatory. Because R-A theory is nonconsummatory, path dependencies are possible. That is, though R-A competition is a disequilibrating process that is moving, it is not moving toward some ideal point (such as a Pareto-optimal, general equilibrium; see Section 6.2).

As a second affinity, R-A theory accommodates, complements, and incorporates the evolutionary, competence perspective of the firm. R-A theory incorporates by subsumption the competence perspective by viewing competences as higher-order resources that are composed of distinct packages or bundles of basic resources. Competences are viewed as socially complex, interconnected combinations of tangible (e.g., specific machinery) and intangible (e.g., specific organizational policies and procedures and the skills and knowledge of specific employees) basic resources that fit coherently together in a synergistic manner. Competences, then, play a major role in enabling firms to produce efficiently and/or effectively valued market offerings.

Competences take center stage in R-A theory because many resources are proposed—see Section 5.5—to be significantly heterogeneous and asymmetrically distributed across competitors. Furthermore, many resources are proposed as imperfectly mobile, that is, not commonly, easily, or readily bought and sold in the "factor" markets. For example, an organizational competence for building high-quality automobile engines is not something that an organization can ordinarily purchase in the marketplace. Competences are *distinct* resources because they are entities that contribute as distinct packages to the firm's ability to produce efficiently and/or effectively market offerings that have value for some market segment(s). Thus, when a firm has a competence (or any other resource) that is rare among competitors, it has the potential for producing a comparative advantage for that firm.

2.2 AUSTRIAN ECONOMICS

The appellation "Austrian" signifies a school of economics that traces to the nineteenth-century Austrian economists Carl Menger (1840-1921), Friedrich von Wieser (1851-1926), and Eugen Bohm-Bawerk (1851-1914). Menger was one of the trio of economists—the others being the Englishman William Stanley Jevons (1835-1882) and the Frenchman Leon Walras (1834-1910)—who initiated the "marginalist revolution" in economics in the 1870s. Rejecting the view that objective factors, such as the quantity of labor, determined a commodity's value, Menger, Jevons, and Walras—each working independently—articulated a subjectivist theory of value. In this view, the key to understanding the exchange value of a commodity was the subjective increment to utility attributed by the consumer to the last unit added to or subtracted from the consumer's stock of the commodity. This incremental or *marginal* utility, which they argued declined monotonically with each additional unit, enabled them to resolve Adam Smith's paradox that (1) water is very useful but has low exchange value, whereas (2) diamonds have little use value but high exchange value.

The concept of marginal utility enabled Jevons and Walras to import differential calculus into economics. For them, utility was a continuous function and marginal utility was its first derivative, that is, $MU_x = dU/dx$. The current practice of expressing key economics constructs in mathematical equations that can then be solved for their maxima and minima using the calculus began with the marginal utility construct developed in the 1870s for analyzing demand. For the next seven decades, the mathematization of *all* areas comprising the neoclassical research tradition proceeded steadily.

After the publication of Samuelson's (1947) *Foundations of Economic Analysis,* the mathematization of neoclassical economics accelerated; by 1990, it was complete (Debreu 1990). The prestigious John Bates Clark medal was first awarded by the American Economics Association in 1947. Of the first 21 awards, 20 went to Fellows of the Econometric Society. Similarly, of the 30 Nobel awards for economics made between 1969 and 1990, 25 went to ES Fellows (Debreu 1990). Not only had equation solving become the preferred language of discourse in the journals of mainstream economics by 1990, but "economic theory" and "mathematical equations" had become synonymous.[2] Although Carl Menger contributed to developing the marginal utility construct, he interpreted it in discrete, nonmathematical terms. Indeed, both he and his successors (who later became known as the Austrian School) resisted the mathematization of economics.

Modern Austrian economics, associated with the works of Mises (1920, 1949), Hayek (1935c, 1948, 1960, 1978), Lachmann (1986), Kirzner (1979, 1982, 1985, 1988, 1992, 1996), and Rothbard (1962), among others, retains Menger's belief that mathematics and statistics should have a modest, at best, role in economic analysis. Indeed, Hayek (1952/1979) labels as "scientism" the indiscriminate use of mathematics and statistics in mainstream economics. In addition to a severely circumscribed role for mathematics and statistics, Baird (1994) isolates four other characteristics that distinguish Austrian from neoclassical economics: (1) expanding subjectivism to costs (contrasted with limiting subjectivism to consumer demand), (2) adopting methodological individualism (contrasted with attributing causal powers to economic aggregates), (3) emphasizing exchange (contrasted with emphasizing economizing and optimizing), and (4) focusing on market processes (contrasted with emphasizing equilibrium states).[3]

The defining event for the development of Austrian economics was the "socialist calculation debate" that took place in the 1920s, 1930s, and 1940s. This debate pitted Austrian economists against socialist economists on the issue of the relative efficiency of socialist versus market-based economies. Prior to the socialist calculation debate, Austrian economists believed that their views were compatible with, indeed had been incorporated into, the neoclassical tradition (Mises 1969). After the debate, however, it was clear that the Austrian and neoclassical traditions differed significantly. Because the debate is chronicled in Chapter 7, our review of Austrian economics focuses on (1) market processes, (2) entrepreneurship, and (3) competition as knowledge-discovery, before turning to (4) the affinities between Austrian economics and R-A theory.

2.2.1 Market Processes

If there is one thing, above all others, that separates the Austrian and neoclassical traditions, it is the Austrian insistence that competition is a process:

> The market is not a place, a thing, or a collective entity. The market is a process, actuated by the interplay of the actions of the various individuals cooperating under the division of labor. The forces determining the—continually changing—state of the market are the value judgments of these individuals and their actions as directed by these value judgments. The state of the market at any instant is the price structure, i.e., the totality of the exchange ratios as established by the interaction of those eager to buy and those eager to sell. There is nothing inhuman or mystical with regard to the market. The market process is entirely a resultant of human actions. Every market phenomenon can be traced back to definite choices of the members of the market society.
>
> The market process is the adjustment of the individual actions of the various members of the market society to the requirements of mutual cooperation. The market prices tell the producers what to produce, how to produce, and in what quantity. The market is the focal point to which the activities of the individuals converge. It is the center from which the activities of the individuals radiate. (Mises 1949, pp. 258-59)

The preceding quote from Mises highlights several of the foundations of the Austrian tradition. First, harking back to Adam Smith's *Wealth of Nations,* Mises emphasizes that understanding the nature of firms requires recognizing that firms consist of "individuals cooperating under the division of labor." Second, existing prices at any point in time have an information or knowledge function in that they "tell the producers what to produce, how to produce, and in what quantity." Third, because a market is not a "collective entity," to understand markets one must forswear the use of economic aggregates. Indeed, Austrian methodological individualism ("MI") should be adopted because all market phenomena "can be traced back to definite choices of the members of the market society."[4] Fourth, the natural state of the market is one that is "continually changing," that is, in disequilibrium.

If markets are "continually changing," what motivates change? For Mises (1949), answering this question was a major focus of *praxeology,* his science of human action. Human action, defined by Mises as all purposeful behaviors, requires three conditions.[5] First, the person must not be "perfectly content with the state of his affairs" but have "some uneasiness." Second, the person must "imagine conditions which suit him better." And third, the person must have the expectation that action can bring about the more desirable state, that is, "the expectation that purposeful behavior has the power to alleviate the felt uneasiness" (pp. 13-14). The purposeful behaviors of human action are always future oriented. That is, they "aim . . . always to render future conditions more satisfactory than they would be without the interference of action" (p. 100).

2.2.2 Entrepreneurship

If human action, motivated by "uneasiness," makes markets continually changing, which economic actors bring change about? For Austrian economics, the principal actors are consumers and entrepreneurs: "One cannot deal with the market of consumers' goods and disregard the actions of the consumers. One cannot deal with the market of the goods of higher orders while disregarding the actions of the entrepreneurs" (Mises 1949, p. 332). The alertness of entrepreneurs to profitable opportunities, then, drives changes in market offerings and prices:

> The entrepreneur is the agency that prevents the persistence of a state of production unsuitable to fill the most urgent wants of the consumers in the cheapest way. All people are anxious for the best possible satisfaction of their wants and are in this sense striving after the highest profit they can reap. . . . [Entrepreneurs] guess what the consumers would like to have and are intent upon providing them with these things. In the pursuit of such plans they bid higher prices for some factors of production and lower the prices of other factors of production by restricting their demand for them. In supplying the market with those consumers' goods in the sale of which the highest profits can be earned, they create a tendency toward a fall in their prices. In restricting the output of those consumers' goods the production of which does not offer chances for reaping profit, they bring about a tendency toward a rise in their prices. All these transformations go on ceaselessly

and could stop only if the unrealizable conditions of the evenly rotating economy and of static equilibrium were to be attained . . .

The essential fact is that it is the competition of profit-seeking entrepreneurs that does not tolerate the preservation of false prices of the factors of production. The activities of the entrepreneurs are the element that would bring about the unrealizable state of the evenly rotating economy if no further changes were to occur. (Mises 1949, pp. 332, 35)

Note that entrepreneurs do not *know* what alternative goods and services consumers would like to have, they "guess" in the face of uncertainty. Note also that the actions of entrepreneurs bring about a "tendency" for various prices to rise or fall. Note finally, that even though an evenly rotating, static-equilibrium economy is an "unrealizable state," the actions of entrepreneurs tend to move prices *toward* equilibrium, absent "further changes."

If the Austrian position is that markets are in a state of continual change or disequilibrium, how can the actions of entrepreneurs *tend* to move prices toward equilibrium? Kirzner (1979) addresses this question by focusing, first, on why neoclassical theory requires a specific theory of market processes. He asks that we consider the standard classroom exercise in which the instructor draws the Marshallian supply and demand curves and explains how the market is cleared only at the price corresponding to the curves' intersection. If the actual price happens to be above the intersection, there will be unsold inventories that will tend to depress price. A price lower than the market clearing, equilibrium price will result in excess demand "forcing up" price. Such classroom exercises, Kirzner notes, take place assuming the full panoply of conditions requisite for perfect competition, that is, a homogeneous product, perfect information, and price-taking firms.

However, if firms are price-takers, "it is not clear how unsold inventories or unmet demand effect price changes. If no one raises or lowers price bids, *how* do prices rise or fall?" (Kirzner 1979, p. 4; italics in original). That is, there is no mechanism in neoclassical theory by which price-taking firms can *find* the equilibrium price.[6] Clearly, if there is such an entity as an equilibrium price, finding it requires postulating the existence of firms that are not price-takers. What is needed, argues Kirzner, "is a theory of the market process that takes notice of the way systematic changes in the information and expectations upon which market participants act lead them in the direction of the postulated equilibrium solution" (p. 5).

For Austrian economics, it is entrepreneurial alertness that is key for understanding market processes. Humans are not just calculating agents who choose from *given* opportunities, but agents who are alert to and *discover* the opportunities from which they choose. When entrepreneurs note that prices are not clearing the market, they revise (up or down) the prices of their market offerings and their bids for various resources. Thus, "entrepreneurship converts the theory of market equilibrium into a theory of market process" (Kirzner 1979, p. 7). Exit perfect competition; enter the Austrian conception of competition as knowledge-discovery.

2.2.3 Competition as Knowledge-Discovery

What is the economic problem facing society? Kirzner (1988, p. 12) points out that Hayek, as late as 1935, was arguing the view that the economic problem facing society was the "distribution of available resources between different uses" (Hayek 1935a/1948, p. 121). By 1945, however, Hayek was asserting that the major economic problem was a *knowledge* problem:

> The peculiar character of the problem of a rational economic order is determined precisely by the fact that the knowledge of the circumstances of which we must make use never exists in concentrated or integrated form but solely as the dispersed bits of incomplete and frequently contradictory knowledge which all the separate individuals possess. The economic problem of society is thus not merely a problem of how to allocate "given" resources—if "given" is taken to mean given to a single mind which deliberately solves the problem set by these "data." It is rather a problem of how to secure the best use of resources known to any of the members of society, for ends whose relative importance only these individuals know. Or, to put it briefly, it is a problem of the utilization of knowledge which is not given to anyone in its totality. (Hayek 1945/1948, pp. 77-78)

For Hayek (1945/1948), the assumption of perfect knowledge in neoclassical theory assumes away the very problem that the process of competition must solve. Consumers' tastes and preferences are not given to firms; through competing, firms discover them. The costs of producing goods by various technologies are not provided to firms; such costs must be learned.

What, then, is the meaning of equilibrium in Austrian economics, and what does it mean to state that the process of competing *tends* toward equilibrium? Hayek (1937/1948) argues that the common practice of conceptualizing equilibrium as an unchanging or "stationary state" should be abandoned. Rather: "For a society, then, we can speak of a state of equilibrium at a point of time—but it means only that the different plans which the individuals composing it have made for action in time are mutually compatible" (p. 41). In other words, equilibrium is "the state of affairs characterized by universally correct anticipation of the actions of other people" (Kirzner 1979, p. 20). A process will tend toward equilibrium, therefore, if it tends to reduce errors in expectations. For Hayek (1937/1948), "a tendency toward equilibrium . . . means . . . that, under certain conditions, the knowledge and intentions of the different members of society . . . come more and more into agreement or, . . . in less general and less exact but more concrete terms, that the expectations of the people and particularly of the entrepreneurs will become more and more correct" (p. 45).

2.2.4 Austrian Economics and R-A Theory

The affinities between Austrian economics and R-A theory are many. Here, I focus on (1) competition as a process, (2) competition as knowledge-discovery, (3) the concept of value, and (4) the nature of resources.

First, like Austrian economics, R-A theory views competition as a process, not a state. For example, Addleson (1994) states the Austrian view that "competition has nothing to do with market structures" (p. 101). For him:

> Firms compete in many ways. One of these is through the products or the services they sell in order to attract customers and to improve the position of the business. . . . [T]his type of competition [can] be interpreted as the attempt by the business to provide an offer to potential buyers which they will regard as better, or more attractive, than other offers from which they might choose. (p. 100)

Likewise, for R-A theory, competition is the ongoing process that consists of the constant struggle among firms for comparative advantages in resources that will yield marketplace positions of competitive advantage and, thereby, superior financial performance (see Figures 6.1 and 6.2 in Chapter 6). Therefore, R-A theory incorporates Addleson's *offering* competition.

As discussed in Section 2.1.3, R-A theory views the process of competing as an evolutionary, selection process—a struggle. Similarly, for Austrian economics, financial performance stimulates the selection process of competition:

> [An] element that contributes to sound judgment in pricing is the selection process of profit and loss. Those who are skilled at estimating which products to manufacturer, which resources to use and which prices to offer will prosper; their firms will succeed and the sphere of their influence will widen. Those who are poorer judges will struggle and perhaps fail; their firms will not grow and their judgment will be restricted to a relatively narrow sphere. (Baird 1994, p. 154)

R-A theory and Austrian economics also concur that disequilibrium is the normal state of any market-based economy. However, unlike Austrian economics, R-A theory views the process of competition as disequilibrating, not equilibrating. Do these views conflict?

R-A theory means by *equilibrium* the view—common in economics despite the protestations of Hayek and others—of a stationary state in which all change comes from factors exogenous to competition. Therefore, *disequilibrating* for R-A theory means that factors endogenous to the process of competition provoke changes in any stationary state in the marketplace that might temporarily occur. Consequently, R-A theory's disequilibrating view of competition does not conflict necessarily with the Austrian equilibrating position because *equilibrating* is used differently. Indeed, I argue that the two positions are compatible when differences in terminology are taken into account.

R-A theory's justification that competition is disequilibrating—in the sense of status quo disturbing—stems from both its premise that the primary objective of firms is to seek *superior* financial performance and its posit that such performance results from firms' occupying marketplace positions of competitive advantage (see Table 5.1 and Figures 6.1 and 6.2). Here, "superior" equates with *better than* and *more than*. Because all firms cannot be simultaneously superior, strong forces always exist to disrupt any temporary status quo. That is, any temporary equilibrium in which all rivals earn parity returns will tend to be unstable because of rivals' drive for superiority.

Recall that Mises (1949) stressed the importance of "uneasiness" as the ultimate source of human action. Similarly, in R-A theory the drive for superior performance posited by R-A theory stems from firms' "uneasiness" with situations in which they make inferior or parity returns. Because all rivals cannot be simultaneously superior, all status quo situations must have firms that are uneasy with their financial performance. Recall also Mises' emphasis on methodological individualism. Because R-A theory justifies firms' seeking superior financial performance as a primary objective on the grounds that individuals (i.e., firm owners, managers, and employees) will then tend to receive superior financial and nonfinancial rewards, not only is it consistent with the disequilibrium implications of Mises' theory of human action but it justifies its disequilibrating view using Austrian methodological individualism.

As a second affinity, both Austrian economics and R-A theory view competition as a knowledge-discovery process. Whereas Austrian economics focuses on the information contained in the price of a market offering, R-A theory maintains that firms learn through competition as a result of feedback from relative financial performance signaling relative marketplace positions, which in turn signal relative resources (Figure 6.1). Therefore, the economic problem to be solved by firms is how to achieve, through time, superior financial performance (by whatever financial measure and compared with whatever referent). For R-A theory, the firm's problem of superior performance is "solved" by firms learning how they can occupy marketplace positions of competitive advantage (cells 2, 3, and 6 in Figure 6). That is, superior performance through time results from firms' learning how to create (and then sustain) an efficiency advantage (cell 2), an effectiveness advantage (cell 6), or an efficiency-effectiveness advantage (cell 3).

The preceding sketch shows how the solving of individual and firm problems fuses, in the aggregate, with the solving of society's knowledge problem, at least as that problem is viewed by Austrian economics. That is, it is through the process of firms attempting to solve their individual knowledge problems (i.e., learning how to achieve superior performance through being more efficient and/or effective) that firms will, in the aggregate, solve society's knowledge problem (i.e., learning how to use and create knowledge so as to be more efficient, more effective, and thereby more productive).

Third, there are parallels between R-A theory and Austrian economics on *value.* Figure 6.2 shows nine possible competitive positions for the various combinations of a firm's relative, resource-produced value for some market segment(s) and relative resource costs for producing such value. As used in R-A theory, *value* refers to the sum total of all benefits that consumers perceive they will receive if they accept a particular firm's market offering. *Relative superior value,* therefore, equates with *perceived to be worth more.* Perceived value may or may not be systematically related to any third party's assessments of "objective" value. It is not that R-A theory denigrates third-party assessments. Rather, it is that perceptions of value are posited to drive consumer preferences and choices in the marketplace.

As to the Austrian view of value, Yeager (1987) asks: "Why Subjectivism?" Although he defends Austrian subjectivism on numerous grounds, he attacks the "pure subjectivism" (p. 23) of the "ultrasubjectivists," which he associates with Rothbard (1962), Taylor (1980), Shand (1984), and Garrison (1979). A major example of ultrasubjectivism, for Yeager, is:

> The point repeatedly turns up in Austrian discussions that goods that people consider different from each other are indeed different goods, no matter how closely they resemble each other physically. This point is not downright fallacious, but the significance attributed to it is excessive, and its use in question-begging ways is likely to repel mainstream economists. An example is the contention that when a manufacturer sells essentially the same good under different labels at different prices, he is nevertheless not practicing price discrimination; for the goods bear-

ing the different labels are considered by the consumers to be different goods, which *makes* them different goods in all economically relevant senses. The manufacturer is supposedly just charging different prices for different things. (p. 23; italics in original)

Now, R-A theory does not propose that perceived value is the *only* conceptualization of value that is in all cases "economically relevant." Nonetheless, it does hold that the value of a market offering as perceived by a market segment is central to understanding how the process of competition actually works. Indeed, if a market segment perceives more value in an offering of "essentially the same good" that has one label (say, "Mitsubishi" or "Arrow") than another (say, "Plymouth" or "JCPenney"), it is these perceptions, not third-party assessments, that drive marketplace behavior. Therefore, R-A theory's perceived value might be viewed by some as ultrasubjectivist and "likely to repel mainstream economists."

On the other hand, Block (1988) disagrees both with Yeager's concern for placating mainstream colleagues and with his categorization of types of subjectivism. Contrasted with Yeager (1987), Block argues for four categories: (1) nonsubjectivists (e.g., neoclassicists), (2) moderate subjectivists (e.g., Yeager), (3) Austrian subjectivists (e.g., Rothbard and Kirzner) and (4) ultrasubjectivists (e.g., Wiseman, Shackle, and Lachmann). Therefore, argues Block (1988), the ultrasubjectivist view, though sometimes associated with Austrian economics, is not (or he believes should not be considered) genuinely *Austrian.* As Block (1988), quoting portions of Yeager (1987), puts it:

[The] Austrian view does not mean that the "realities of nature, science, and technology have *nothing* to do with determining prices and interest rates" (p. 22, emphasis in original). On the contrary, as Yeager himself later seems to grant to the Austrians, "physical reality counts only *through* people's subjective perceptions of it" (p. 22, emphasis in original). In contrast, it is only the ultrasubjectivists, category D, not the Austrians, category C, who speak almost as if they wish to "banish the influence of objective reality" (p. 22). (p. 202)

Block (1988) then defends Austrian subjectivism for insisting that goods that people consider different from each other are indeed different goods by pointing out the import of the word "essentially" in Yeager's (1987) phrase "essentially the same good" (p. 23). Block asks: "In whose mind is the determination of sameness to be made?" And he suggests: "The Austrians' answer 'In the mind of the economic actor,' and this would appear to make good sense" (p. 204).

Two conclusions on *value* are warranted. First, the perceived value view of R-A theory accords well with category C in Block's (1988) schema because it is perceptions of value that drive marketplace behavior. As Hayek (1948) puts it, "no superior knowledge the observer may possess about . . . [an] object, but which is not possessed by the acting person, can help us in understanding the motives of their actions" (p. 60). And, as Rothbard (1962) concludes:

> Here again, it is very important to recognize that what is significant for human action is not the physical property of a good, but the evaluation of the good by the actor. Thus, physically there may be no discernible difference between one pound of butter and another, or one cow and another. But if the actor chooses to evaluate them differently, they are no longer part of the supply of the same good. (p. 19)

Second, R-A theory is, most assuredly and emphatically, not ultrasubjectivist in the sense of seeking to "banish the influence of objective reality" (Yeager 1987, p. 22). Banishing objective reality implies epistemological relativism. In contrast, the epistemology of R-A theory is scientific realism (Hunt and Morgan 1995), which is decidedly antirelativist. Scientific realism's core tenets are (1) the world exists independently of its being perceived; (2) the job of science is to develop genuine knowledge about that world, even though such knowledge will never be known with certainty; (3) all knowledge claims must be critically evaluated and tested to determine the extent to which they do, or do not, represent or correspond to that world; and (4) the long-term success of a theory gives reason to believe that something like the entities and structure postulated by the theory actually exists (Hunt 1990b, 1991a, 1994). Rather than banish objective reality, scientific realism—uniquely among philosophies—shows how science can be objective, when in fact it is (Hunt 1994).[7]

As a fourth affinity, consider the concept of *resources*. Rather than restricting resources to a firm's tangible factors of production or even to its tangible assets plus human capital, R-A theory defines resources as the tangible and intangible entities available to the firm that enable it to produce efficiently and/or effectively a market offering that has value for some market segment(s). Thus, as shown in Table 5.1, resources can be categorized as financial (e.g., cash reserves and access to financial markets); physical (e.g., plant, raw materials, and equipment); legal (e.g., trademarks and licenses); human (e.g., the skills and knowledge of *individual* employees, including, importantly, their entrepreneurial skills); organizational (e.g., controls, routines, cultures, and competences—including, importantly, a competence for entrepreneurship); informational (e.g., knowledge about market segments, competitors, and technology); and relational (e.g., relationships with competitors, suppliers, and customers).

Hayek (1948) points out that "practically every individual has some advantage over all others because he possesses unique information of which beneficial use can be made only if the decisions depending on it are left to him or are made with his active co-operation" (p. 80). Likewise, for R-A theory, resources are both significantly heterogeneous and imperfectly mobile across firms. Viewing firms as entities historically situated in space and time, resource heterogeneity implies that every firm has an assortment of resources that is (at least in some ways) unique. *Imperfectly mobile* implies that many firm resources, to varying degrees, are not commonly, easily, or readily bought and sold in the marketplace. Because of resource immobility, resource heterogeneity can persist through time despite attempts by firms to acquire the same resources of particularly successful competitors.

Note that even intangible entities can be resources, as long as they have an *enabling* capacity. Note also that a resource need not be owned by a firm, but only available to it. For example, a strategic alliance between firms A and B may contribute to their efficiency and/or effectiveness and, thus, constitute a resource for both. Yet neither A nor B *own* the resource, for neither can sell it.

R-A theory's view of resources not only differs from that of neoclassical economics but also diverges from a long-standing position in business strategy. For example, Day and Wensley (1988) distinguish between the "skills" and "resources" of a firm on the basis that the former are "the distinctive capabilities of personnel" and the latter are the "more tangible requirements for advantage" (pp. 2-3). In contrast, R-A theory maintains that intangibles can be resources and views the skills of individuals and the competences of firms as *kinds* of resources. Austrian economics, I argue, supports this view.

In evaluating the methodology of Simon's (1981) *The Ultimate Resource,* Sinnett (1987) explores the nature of resources by turning to Hayek's (1948) discussion of the nature of "facts" in the social sciences. Hayek investigates how it is that social science classifies the objects ("facts") to be explained and asks: "[Are] the human actions which we observe, and the objects of these actions, things of the same kind because they appear as physically the same or different to us, the observers—or for some other reason?" (p. 59).

Using such concepts as "tools," "medicine," "weapons," and "acts of production" as examples, Hayek (1948) rejects the view that social science classifies things into or out of these conceptual categories based on "some objective properties possessed by the things . . . [for] there is no single physical property which any one member of a class must possess" (p. 54). Indeed, social science "concepts are also not merely abstractions of the kind we use in all physical sciences; they abstract from *all* the physical properties of the things themselves" (p. 59, italics in original). Therefore, for Hayek, social science concepts used to categorize the "facts" are "teleological concepts" and "can be defined only by indicating relations between three terms: a purpose, somebody who holds that purpose, and an object which that person thinks to be a suitable means for that purpose" (pp. 59-60). In the social sciences: "Money is money, a word is a word, a cosmetic is a cosmetic because somebody thinks they are" (p. 60).

R-A theory's view of resources, I argue, accords well with the human purpose view of Austrian economics. The human purpose of firms, for R-A theory, involves producing market offerings that have value for market segments. Consequently, *any* entity, tangible or intangible, that contributes to a firm's ability to produce efficiently and/or effectively a market offering that has value for some market segment(s) can be considered a resource for that firm. Therefore, restricting the concept of resources only to tangible entities would be, for both the Austrians and R-A theory, artificial.

NOTES

1. Hodgson (1993) provides the most comprehensive analysis of the role of biological metaphors in economics. Witt (1992) and Nelson (1995) provide excellent reviews of current work in evolutionary economics. The *Journal of Evolutionary Economics* is the major journal in this research tradition.

2. Boettke (1994a) points out that because the language of Austrian economics is "verbal," rather than mathematical, Austrian works have been "systematically eliminated from the top journals" (p. 605). Therefore, Austrian economics is a "book culture," not a journal-oriented school of thought. Rosenberg (1992) argues that mainstream economics has become so mathematized that it has ceased to be an empirical science at all. Rather, he argues, it is a branch of applied mathematics.

3. See Boettke (1994b) for an overview and introduction to Austrian economics. See Jacobson (1992) for a discussion of the insights of Austrian economics for strategic management. See Foss (1994c) for an "Austrian" theory of the firm.

4. Austrian economics views neoclassical macroeconomics as containing aggregate constructs that are artificial in the sense that though perhaps correlated, they do not (and cannot) have causal powers. See Block (1980) for a discussion of methodological individualism (i.e., MI).

5. The praxeology of Mises (1949) assumes that if one starts a science of human action with true axioms, one can deduce absolutely certain conclusions. Therefore, the goal of his praxeology was an apodictically certain science of human action in which empirical testing would (could) play no important role. Although many Austrian

economists subscribe to the epistemology of apodictic certainty, Prychitko (1994) urges its abandonment. Similarly, for R-A theory, *certainty* is a theological concept, not a scientific one (Hunt 1991a). Furthermore, empirical testing has a valuable role in R-A theory, which distinguishes R-A theory from the views of (at least many) Austrian economists.

6. Kirzner (1979, pp. 4-5) also shows how the Marshallian approach of marking off demand prices and supply prices for different quantities cannot result in market participants in perfect competition "finding" the equilibrium price-quantity.

7. See, also, Leplin (1984) and Manicas (1987) for more on scientific realism.

3

Antecedents and Affinities

*Heterogeneous Demand
and Differential Advantage*

This chapter continues the process of reviewing the theories, research programs, and traditions that resource-advantage theory either draws on or shares affinities with. In particular, this chapter discusses heterogeneous demand theory and differential advantage theory. Again, I review only those portions of each theory relevant to R-A theory and point readers toward more comprehensive reviews.

3.1 HETEROGENEOUS DEMAND THEORY

The neoclassical tradition assumes both homogeneous, intra-industry demand and homogeneous, intra-industry supply. That is, neoclassical theory focuses on, strictly speaking, the demand for and production of *commodities*. As Stigler (1957) puts it: "The formal condition [in perfect competition] that there be many producers of *a* commodity assumes homogeneity of this commodity" (p. 13; italics in original). The assumptions of homogeneity of demand and supply are necessary for drawing the industry demand and supply curves required for determining the market clearing, equilibrium price. Absent homogeneous demand, the concept of *an* industry demand curve makes no sense. For example, the category of "Transportation equipment," which is Standard Industrial Classification (SIC) number 37, is not homogeneous for the purpose of estimating an industry demand or supply curve. Neither is "Motor vehicles and equipment" (SIC #371) sufficiently homogeneous, nor "Motor vehicles and car bodies" (SIC #3711).

In practice, however, the neoclassical tradition routinely extends the concept of *commodity* significantly beyond its everyday English meaning. That is, it extends it from such commodities as corn, tea, and coal to goods such as footwear, computers, and automobiles. For example, consider the—now classic—work of Joan Robinson (1903-1983). She defines a "commodity" as a "consumable good, arbitrarily demarcated from other kinds of goods, but which may be regarded for *practical purposes* as homogeneous within itself" (Robinson 1933, p. 17; italics added). She then defines demand and supply curves:

> A *demand curve* represents a list of prices at which various amounts of a certain commodity will be bought in a market during a given period of time. Such conceptions as the amount of raw cotton bought in the world per year, or the number of motor cars bought in England per month, or the number of silk stockings bought in Berwick Market per day, may be represented by a demand curve.
>
> Similarly a *supply curve* represents the amounts of output of a commodity, during a given period of time, which will be associated with different prices. (p. 17; italics in original)

Beg pardon? The tastes, preferences, and use requirements of consumers for *automobiles,* as well as the actual output of various automobile manufacturers, may be regarded for "practical purposes" as homogeneous? Rolls Royces, Ford "Model Ts," Jaguars, Chevrolets, and Packards are all the same commodity for the purpose of drawing a single demand curve, a single supply curve, and thereby determining *the* market clearing price? There are practical purposes for which it is meaningful to speak of an *automobile industry.* However, for drawing industry demand and supply curves is not such a purpose. The recognition that there exist many industries—including automobiles—for which it makes no sense to claim that demand and supply are homogeneous prompted Edward H. Chamberlin (1899-1967) to develop his *Theory of Monopolistic Competition* (1933).

For Chamberlin (1933), theories of pure and perfect competition simply do not apply to most industries because most industries are characterized by heterogeneous demand and supply. Indeed, he uses automobiles (an industry claimed by Robinson to be an example of an industry that for "practical purposes" is homogeneous) to argue that industry demand curves often make no sense:

> Consider, for instance, the competitive analysis as applied to the automobile industry. How is one to conceive of demand and supply curves for "automobiles in general" when, owing to variations in quality, design, and type, the prices of individual units range from several hundred to many thousands of dollars? How define the number of units which would be taken from or put upon the market at any particular price? How fit into the analysis a wide variety of costs based mostly upon a correspondingly wide variety of product? . . . Competitive theory does not fit because competition throughout the group is only partial and is highly uneven. The competition between sport roadsters and ten-ton trucks must be virtually zero; and there is probably more justification for drawing up a joint demand schedule for Fords and house room than for Fords and Locomobiles. (1933/1962, p. 9)

What is needed, argued Chamberlin, is a theory of competition that recognizes that most industries have elements of both monopoly and competition—hence his label "monopolistic competition." My review focuses on (1) the early, neoclassical Chamberlin; (2) the later, "quasi-Austrian" Chamberlin; (3) mainstream economics and heterogeneity of demand; and (4) marketing and heterogeneity of demand. I conclude by discussing the affinities between R-A theory and heterogeneous demand theory.

3.1.1 The Early, Neoclassical Chamberlin

Chamberlin's (1933) *Theory of Monopolistic Competition* was written as a Ph.D. thesis at Harvard under Professor Allyn Young in 1927.[1] He shortened his thesis to book form in 1933 and revised it in 1937, 1938, 1942, 1946, 1948, 1956, and 1962. Throughout its many revisions, Chamberlin lamented the many mischaracterizations of the theory (see Chapter 9 and Appendix H of the 1962 edition). Most notably, Chamberlin decried those who lumped his theory together with Robinson's (1933) *Economics of Imperfect Competition* because, he argued, her theory assumed away the very problem that his theory was developed to address. That is, whereas Robinson (1933) assumes industry demand and supply to be homogeneous, Chamberlin's theory examines the implications of—what for him was the obvious economic fact of—industry heterogeneity. What, then, are the implications of industry heterogeneity?

For Chamberlin (1933), pure competition exists when there are (1) a large number of sellers and (2) a homogeneous product (he defines "product" broadly to include location in space and other conditions of sale).[2] Under pure competition, each competitor faces a horizontal demand curve, and the equilibrium price is the same as the market clearing price. A monopolist, in contrast, has control over the supply of some product and, thus, faces a downward-sloping demand curve. Prior to Chamberlin's work, monopoly theory had focused on those who control the total supply of some generic commodity. In contrast, he addresses the noncommodity situation that results from heterogeneous demand. In his terms, he examines the implications of *product differentiation:*

> A general class of product is differentiated if any significant basis exists for distinguishing the goods (or services) of one seller from those of another. Such a basis may be real or fancied, so long as it is of any importance whatever to buyers, and leads to a preference for one variety of the product over another. Where such differentiation exists, even though it be slight, buyers will be paired with sellers, not by chance and at random (as under pure competition), but according to their preferences. (1933/1962, p. 56)

Note that Chamberlin indicates that differences among goods may be "real or fancied," as long as they lead to differences in preferences, a downward-sloping demand curve, and the nonrandom pairing of buyers and sellers. Note also that product differentiation results from both heterogeneous demand, that is, differences in preferences, and heterogeneous supply, that is, differences in what firms choose to produce or are capable of producing. Heterogeneous demand alone is not sufficient to result in product differentiation. Firms may be unaware of demand heterogeneity, collude so as to ignore such heterogeneity, or be required by state fiat to produce a homogeneous product.

Chamberlin uses the example of a monopoly of "Lucky Strike" cigarettes to drive home the point that competition in most industries is characterized as monopolistic, that is, as a blend of monopoly and competition. Because American Tobacco Company has total control of the supply of "Lucky Strikes," it faces a sloping demand curve and, hence, has a monopoly of its brand. But American Tobacco has no control over the supply of the grade of tobacco used in Lucky Strikes and faces competition from close substitutes. Likewise, American Tobacco has no control over the overall supply of tobacco in general and faces competition from other tobacco products, for example, pipe tobacco. For

Chamberlin (1933/1962), therefore, "[d]ifferentiation implies gradations, and it is compatible with perfect monopoly of one product that control stop short of some more general class of which this product is a part, and within which there is competition" (p. 65).

If monopolistic competition has elements of monopoly at one level, for example, Lucky Strikes and Rolls Royces, which it blends with elements of competition at another, for example, cigarettes and luxury automobiles, what are its welfare implications? What impact does monopolistic competition have on the prices consumers pay, the quantities firms produce, product quality, scales of production, and overall economic efficiency? Being squarely in the neoclassical tradition, Chamberlin (1933) answers these questions using the (now-standard) geometry of static equilibrium analysis.

Chamberlin (1933/1962, pp. 74-81) begins by analyzing the circumstances that must prevail for an individual monopolistic firm to be in equilibrium. He draws a downward-sloping demand curve, a U-shaped total cost curve, a downward-sloping marginal cost (MC) curve, and a U-shaped marginal revenue (MR) curve. He next assumes firms to be profit maximizers and points out that the profit-maximizing quantity occurs where MC = MR. He then directs the reader to the demand curve and shows that the profit-maximizing quantity occurs at a price that exceeds MR. Because under pure (as well as perfect) competition, MC = MR = Price, he concludes:

> [T]he effect of monopoly elements on the individual's adjustment . . . is characteristically to render his price higher and his scale of production smaller than under pure competition. This is the result of the sloping demand curve, as compared with the perfectly horizontal one of pure competition. No matter in what position the demand curve is drawn, its negative slope will define maximum profits at a point further to the left than if it were horizontal, as under pure competition. This means, in general, higher production costs and higher prices. (pp. 77-78)

Chamberlin (1933/1962, pp. 81-100) next turns to the issue of competition from substitutes and, again, focuses on the static equilibrium situation. He posits that there exist groups of competitors to which each monopolistic firm belongs, and he seeks to determine the nature of such *group* equilibria (which parallel the customary industry equilibria). However, determining a group equilibrium poses a challenge because the product of each firm in monopolistic competition "has distinctive features and is adapted to the tastes and needs of those who buy it. Qualitative differences lead to wide divergences in the curves of cost of production, and buyers' preferences account for a corresponding variety of demand curves" (p. 81). His "solution" is to assume that the demand curves and cost curves for all group members are identical, which he characterizes as a "heroic assumption" (p. 82).

Given identical demand and cost curves for a group of monopolistically competitive firms, the surplus profit of the group's members that stems from their higher prices (compared with pure competition) attracts new entrants to the group. The total quantity sold by the group must then be divided among more producers, which shifts each firm's demand curve to the left. Consequently, for each firm the profit-maximizing quantity decreases and its price increases. Chamberlin (1933/1962) then shows that group equilibrium (no further entry or exit of firms or price-quantity adjustments) occurs where each firm's demand curve is tangent to its total cost curve. At this group equilibrium price and quantity, all surplus profits have been competed away, but "the price is inevitably higher and the scale of production inevitably smaller under monopolistic competition than under pure competition" (p. 88).

Chamberlin (1933/1962) then extends his analysis to other welfare implications of monopolistic competition. As to product quality, he argues that it will be "inevitably somewhat inferior" (p. 99) at all equilibrium prices. As to factors of production, because excess productive capacity has no "automatic corrective," the "surplus capacity is never cast off and the result is high prices and waste" (p. 109). Whether labor is exploited in the sense of receiving less than the value of its marginal product, as argued by Robinson (1933), "all factors are necessarily 'exploited' . . . [for] it would be impossible for employers to avoid the charge of 'exploitation' without going into bankruptcy" (p. 183).

Chamberlin's (1933/1962) neoclassical analysis paints a dismal picture of the welfare implications of the monopolistic competition spawned by heterogeneous demand and supply. Compared with pure competition's homogeneous demand and supply, prices are higher, quantities produced are lower, excess capacity is permanent, products produced are inferior, and all factors of production are exploited. Clearly then, for Chamberlin, public policy should *mandate* the homogeneity of demand and supply for all products—or should it?

3.1.2 The Later "Quasi-Austrian" Chamberlin

Both Chamberlin's theory and Robinson's (1933) *Economics of Imperfect Competition* were much debated in the 1930s and 1940s.[3] By the 1950s, Robinson (1951) was lamenting that instead of the Marshallian, evolutionary process approach that she *could* have adopted, her static equilibrium analyses represented a "wrong turning" (pp. vii-viii). Because, she lamented, the neoclassical approach lacked a "comprehensible treatment of historical time," the "theoretical apparatus [was] useless for the analysis of contemporary problems in the micro and macro spheres" (1979, p. 58). Accordingly, she pleaded for "getting economic theory out of the desert of equilibrium and into fruitful fields" (1980, p. xiv).[4]

Like Robinson, the debate led Chamberlin to question his theory's welfare implications (if not its static equilibrium methodology). The "later" Chamberlin summarized his views of the debate in a new and final Chapter 9 in the 1946 edition of his book. Notwithstanding that the "early" Chamberlin had consistently used pure competition as a standard against which monopolistic competition would be compared, the "later" Chamberlin states: "The explicit recognition that product is differentiated brings into the open the problem of variety and makes it clear that *pure competition may no longer be regarded as in any sense an 'ideal' for purposes of welfare economics*" (p. 214; italics in original). Indeed, he pleads *mea culpa:* "I must plead guilty myself to having done what is here held to be meaningless" (1951, p. 349). In Chapter 9 and his subsequent works (1950, 1951, 1954), he develops numerous arguments to justify not just his conclusion that pure competition is in no sense ideal but also that the very concepts *industry* and *commodity* represent nothing less than a "snare and delusion" (1950, p. 86).

The later Chamberlin's arguments against using pure competition as a competitive ideal can be placed into two general categories: (1) heterogeneous, intra-industry supply is natural, not artificial; and (2) heterogeneous, intra-industry demand is natural, not artificial. First, as to the heterogeneity of intra-industry supply being natural, Chamberlin (1933/1962) points out that every supplier is necessarily unique in its physical location: "Retail shops, for example, could not all be located on the same spot" (p. 214). Second, he argues that there are natural "[p]eculiarities of any individual establishment which cannot be duplicated . . . [such as] reputation, skill, and special ability . . . [that result in] returns which cannot be reduced by others moving in to share them" (p. 112).

Third, he argues that heterogeneity of supply is natural because it is a direct response to heterogeneity of demand: "Commodities are differentiated . . . partly in response to differences in buyers' tastes, preferences, locations, etc., which are as much a part of the order of things *within* any broad class of product as they are *between* one class of product and another" (Chamberlin 1933/1962, p. 213; italics in original). That is, one reason for the differences between Rolls Royces and Ford Model Ts is that some consumers have the desire for luxury automobiles and the incomes to buy them. Indeed, "if we are to imagine a purely competitive automobile industry, will its homogeneous product be Packards, Plymouths, or Peugeots?" (1954, p. 259).

As to heterogeneous, intra-industry demand being natural: "Differences in tastes, desires, incomes, and locations of buyers, and differences in the uses which they wish to make of commodities all indicate the need for variety" (Chamberlin 1933/1962, p. 214). Such differences are natural because "human beings are individuals" (1950, p. 86). Therefore, product differentiation is neither "the reprehensible creation by businessmen of purely fictitious differences between products which are by nature fundamentally uniform" (1950, p. 87), nor "an optical illusion based upon ignorance" and "imperfect knowledge," nor a result of "irrational" preferences (1950, p. 88). Instead, the belief by neoclassical economists that consumers would prefer homogeneous, intra-industry goods but for consumers' ignorance, irrationality, and susceptibility to the wiles of advertising is economic arrogance of the most condescending form:

> Diversity is the natural consequence of the system of demands, in the same sense as is any variety whatever in the output of the economic system. I do not mean to assert that no qualifications are needed to the general proposition that 'demand guides production', but only that . . . [the] qualifications are not peculiar to the intra-industry problem. A preference for the *New York Times* over the *Daily Record* is not to be dismissed as irrational or of no consequence merely because they are both a part of the 'newspaper industry'. The general principle of free choice in the spending of one's income includes not only freedom to vary the proportions between the larger categories of food, shelter, etc., but freedom also to express a market demand for Smith's sausages if one believes them superior to Jones's. (1954, p. 260)

Readers should note that the later Chamberlin's stress on economic freedom imparts a distinctly "Austrian" flavor to his arguments for the heterogeneity of demand. Consider his argument that "since what people want—an elaborate system of consumer preferences—is the starting point in welfare economics, their wants for a heterogeneous product would seem to be as fundamental as anything could be" (1950, p. 86). This position accords well with Austrian economics:

> The belief in the advantages of perfect competition frequently leads enthusiasts even to argue that a more advantageous use of resources would be achieved if the existing variety of products were reduced by *compulsory* standardization. Now, there is undoubtedly much to be said in many fields for assisting standardization by agreed recommendations or standards which are to apply unless different re-

quirements are explicitly stipulated in contracts. But this is something very different from the demands of those who believe that the variety of people's tastes should be disregarded and the constant experimentation with improvements should be suppressed in order to obtain the advantages of perfect competition. It would clearly not be an improvement to build all houses exactly alike in order to create a perfect market for houses, and the same is true of most other fields where differences between the individual products prevent competition from ever being perfect. (Hayek 1948, pp. 98-99; italics in original)

Given that Chamberlin argues that tastes and preferences involve economic freedom and are fundamental for welfare purposes, why does this section label his arguments "quasi-Austrian," not *Austrian?* Chamberlin's arguments are properly *quasi*-Austrian because of (1) his view that the natural heterogeneity of demand poses a problem for some collective entity to solve and (2) his view of how the collective entity should solve the problem.

For Chamberlin (1950), the problem of incorporating heterogeneity into the welfare ideal forces a trade-off: "How are the two to be compared—a larger, less heterogeneous output as against a smaller, more heterogeneous one?" (pp. 89-90). For him, "In some cases it seems clear that increased standardization of certain products by public authority is indicated, as when oligopolistic forces are supporting an unduly large number of producers, or when the gain in efficiency is judged by proper authorities to be more important than the losses in consumers' surplus through abandoning certain products" (pp. 88-89).[5] Therefore, he concludes that if heterogeneity were included in the welfare ideal: "There would be less heterogeneity than we find at present" (p. 90). (Note that the "present" for Chamberlin would be the range of consumer choice in the late 1940s.)

In contrast, the preceding quote from Hayek (1948) stresses the view that standards should be agreed to by the parties involved in the transaction. Thus, the emphasis on economic freedom in Austrian subjectivism denies that there can exist any Chamberlinian "proper authority" to judge the optimal amount of product diversity in an industry. The state, of course, has the power to coerce, but the Austrians maintain that such compulsion is not *proper.* Note also how Hayek (1948) argues against compulsory standardization because it would inhibit "the constant experimentation with improvements" (p. 98). Therefore, the static equilibrium welfare ideal—contrasted with a dynamic welfare ideal—is itself deficient because it does not include the experimentation in new products that leads to improvements in welfare. Thus, the later Chamberlin is labeled *quasi*-Austrian.

3.1.3 Mainstream Economics
and Heterogeneity of Demand

In the 1940s and 1950s, mainstream economics had the choice of interpreting product differentiation in the manner of the early (neoclassical) or later (quasi-Austrian) Chamberlin. That is, product differentiation could have been viewed as uniformly pernicious because it leads to higher prices, lower quantities, excess capacity, inferior products, and the exploitation of the factors of production. Alternatively, product differentiation could have been seen to have (at least some) redeeming value because intra-industry demand and supply are natural, economic freedom has value, and dynamic improvements in welfare must be considered. Given that the pernicious option was argued by Chamberlin on resource-efficiency grounds in the language of equilibrium equations and the redeeming value view was argued on economic freedom grounds in English, it was no contest. By the middle 1950s, Stigler (1957) could confidently assert that the radical aspects of monopolistic competition theory had been "defeated" by perfect competition (p. 17). Indeed, the standard treatment of product differentiation in mainstream textbooks and research is that it is wasteful.

As textbook examples, consider Samuelson and Nordhaus (1995, pp. 155, 168-70) and Mankiw (1998, pp. 364-70). Using such exemplars as breakfast cereals, automobiles, and novels, both texts do the now-standard, Chamberlinian, neoclassical analysis that shows how excess capacity, monopoly profits, and overall waste results from heterogeneous demand and supply. Although Samuelson and Nordhaus (1995) conclude that the inefficiency "argument against monopolistic competition has real appeal," they do, however, provide the reader with the following, quasi-Austrian caveat: "Centrally planned socialist countries tried to standardize output on a small number of varieties, and this left their consumers highly dissatisfied" (p. 170).[6] Mankiw (1998), in contrast, does not admit even the existence of either the Austrian or quasi-Austrian view:

> In the end, we can conclude only that monopolistically competitive markets do not have all the desirable welfare properties of perfectly competitive markets. That is, the invisible hand does not ensure that total surplus is maximized under monopolistic competition. Yet because the inefficiencies are subtle, hard to measure, and hard to fix, there is no easy way for public policy to improve the market outcome. (p. 370)

Although, for Mankiw (1998), the inefficiency problems posed by heterogeneity of demand and supply are subtle and hard to measure, many researchers have tried. Such works as Bergson (1973), Cowling and Mueller (1978), Harberger (1954), and Siegfried and Tieman (1974) attempt to measure the social costs of the deviations from perfect competition that result from the heterogeneity of demand and supply. Estimates of waste commonly range from 0.1% to 13% of GDP.

For example, Cowling and Mueller (1978) explore the welfare losses attributable to the "monopoly power" of large corporations using several, highly illuminating assumptions. First, "monopoly power" for them means that the firms face Chamberlinian, downward-sloping demand curves (not that firms have a monopoly of the supply of a generic commodity). Second, as a comparison reference, they assume that the "competitive" return on capital invested is 12% (which they argue would be the expected return of a widely diversified portfolio of stocks). Third, they assume that the profit in any year of any firm in excess of the 12% competitive return signifies economic waste (which implies, for example, if the higher profits result from a firm producing higher-quality products, the firm's efforts to produce quality products represent *waste*). Fourth, all firms with profits less than 12%—more than half their sample of firms—were set to zero (which means that losses of the less profitable firms are not allowed to offset the "waste" of the more profitable firms). They argue that "these firms would not survive in the long run and hence represent no long run welfare loss to society" (p. 740). And fifth, all advertising expenditures were added to monopoly profits because "the argument for advertising as a provider of information should not be taken too seriously" (p. 734).

With the preceding five assumptions, Cowling and Mueller (1978) use partial equilibrium analysis to estimate the social welfare losses of "monopoly power" in the United States at 4% to 13% of gross corporate product. Indeed, "General Motors leads the list with an annual welfare loss of over 1\frac{3}{4}$ billion, which alone is over $\frac{1}{4}$ of 1% of average GNP during the period" (p. 738). Adhering strictly to the neoclassical tradition, Cowling and Mueller—like the other empirical works cited in this section—never discuss the Austrian or quasi-Austrian arguments that consumer choice has value. For the neoclassical tradition, it appears that there are welfare costs, but no benefits, to intra-industry freedom of choice. That is, no welfare benefits accrue from allowing firms the freedom to choose to produce variety or consumers the freedom to choose from among variety. Stated in the obverse: there are no welfare costs in restricting intra-industry freedom of choice.[7]

3.1.4 Marketing and Heterogeneity of Demand

Chamberlin's (1933) argument that intra-industry heterogeneity of supply and demand is natural was much discussed in the marketing literature in the 1950s and 1960s.[8] Smith (1956), in what is now considered a seminal marketing article, argued that the natural heterogeneity of supply in the marketplace results from differences among firms in five areas: (1) production processes, (2) resources, (3) product development capabilities, (4) quality control procedures, and (5) perceptions of the market. Similarly, for him, five factors make intra-industry demand natural: (1) differences in customs, (2) the desire for variety, (3) the desire for exclusiveness, (4) differences in user needs, and (5) shopping errors. He considered product differentiation and market segmentation to be two strategies that firms could employ to respond to heterogeneous demand.

While Smith's (1956) conceptualization of product differentiation differs from that of the neoclassical tradition, it still captures that belief that differentiation is fundamentally pernicious. For him, a firm practices "product differentiation" when, in the face of heterogeneous demand, it produces one standard product (or one trivially different from its competitors) and uses advertising and promotion to convince consumers to buy it, rather than competitors' (essentially the same) products. Firms pursue product differentiation because they reap production economies: "In its simplest terms, *product differentiation* is concerned with the bending of [the natural heterogeneity of] demand to the will of supply. . . . It may be classified as a *promotional* strategy" (pp. 4-5; italics in original). In contrast:

> Market segmentation . . . consists of viewing a heterogeneous market . . . as a number of smaller homogeneous markets in response to differing product preferences. . . . It is attributable to the desires of consumers or users for more precise satisfaction of their varying wants. Like differentiation, segmentation often involves substantial use of advertising and promotion. This is to inform market segments of the availability of goods or services produced for . . . their needs with precision. . . . Market segmentation is essentially a *merchandising* strategy, merchandising being used here in its technical sense as representing the adjustment of market offerings to consumer or user requirements. (p. 5; italics in original)

For Smith (1956), though firms may continue to practice differentiation and ignore the heterogeneity of demand, "market segmentation may be regarded as a force in the market that will not be denied" (p. 6). He argues that three trends (that he saw in the 1950s) make market segmentation an increasingly attractive strategy: (1) the decreasing size of the minimum efficient plant enables small production runs to be profitable, (2) the increasing trend toward self-service retailing necessitates products more precisely adapted to consumers' preferences, and (3) the prosperous times enable consumers to afford the increased cost of products adapted more precisely to their needs.

Smith's (1956) advocacy of market segmentation complemented well the position of General Electric in the 1950s concerning what it called the marketing management concept or, in short, the *marketing concept.*[9] Historically, GE and other major corporations had limited the marketing function to sales, advertising, pricing decisions, and relationships with distributors. GE restructured its organization in the 1950s so that it would be more customer oriented.

Specifically, in GE's customer-oriented, marketing concept philosophy of management, the marketing function was to take an active role in new product development, production scheduling, and finished goods inventory. Rather than marketing's responsibility beginning after products are made, it would be an integrating function that focused all firm activities on satisfying the needs, wants, and desires of GE's customers. Through its marketing research department, marketing was charged with understanding the nature and reasons for customer preferences and then using such preferences to guide product development. As one GE vice president put it: "So the principal task of the marketing function in a management concept is not so much to be skillful in making the customer do what suits the interests of the business as to be skillful in conceiving and then making the business do what suits the interests of the customer" (McKitterick 1957, p. 78). Market segmentation analysis as a response to heterogeneous demand, therefore, became a major tool for GE and a host of other companies in the 1950s.

Heterogeneity of demand became firmly ensconced as a major component of marketing thought and practice with Alderson's theoretical works (1957, 1965) and the publication of McCarthy's (1960) lucid exposition of the new marketing management philosophy.[10] For McCarthy, intra-industry demand is not only heterogeneous but imperfectly understood. Therefore, the starting point for marketing management is the analysis of consumer behavior: why do people buy what they do, where they do, when they do, and how they do? After analyzing consumer behavior, firms should use segmentation analysis to choose one or more "target markets" (or target segments) for which to develop precisely tailored market offerings.

Each market offering for each target segment was to be composed of a distinct marketing "mix."[11] This mix was to include, at the minimum, a product (with specific attributes tailored to the segment), promotion (with specific appeals and media tailored to the segment), a channel of distribution (with specific wholesalers and retailers to reach the segment), and a price (with specific regard to the segment's perceptions of the offering's value).[12] The elements of the market offering or "mix" were to fit together in a coherent package to appeal precisely to each chosen target market.

Since 1960, both consumer behavior and procedures for segmentation have been studied intensively in marketing and such allied disciplines as consumer psychology. The *Journal of Consumer Research*, cosponsored by the American Marketing Association and nine other academic associations, was founded in 1974 and quickly became the premier academic journal focusing on consumer behavior.[13] Works on segmentation analysis have focused on the "basis variables" for segmenting markets and on data analysis techniques for generating segments empirically. Common basis variables include demographics, psychographics, social class, stage in the family life cycle, personality, consumption patterns, and benefits sought. Common data analysis techniques include factor analysis, cluster analysis, latent class modeling, the automatic interaction detector, and multidimensional scaling.[14]

3.1.5 Heterogeneous Demand Theory and R-A Theory

R-A theory shares five affinities with the heterogeneous demand theory argued for by Chamberlin (1933/1962) and further developed in marketing. First, R-A theory agrees that demand in the overwhelming majority of industries is *substantially* heterogeneous. Hence, it makes no sense to draw demand curves for most industries. There are far more industries like motor vehicles (SIC #3711), women's footwear (#3144), and book publishing (#2731) than there are industries like corn (SIC #0115), gold ores (#1041), and industrial sand (#1446). Hence, the path of general equilibrium analysis was a wrong turn. Mainstream economics should have taken the Marshallian, dynamic path (Robinson 1951, 1979).

Second, R-A theory agrees with the (later) Chamberlin (1933/1962) that the concepts of commodity and industry have been a "snare and delusion" for the neoclassical tradition (p. 86). They became a snare because there are indeed some products, for example, certain agricultural products, for which (1) demand is relatively homogeneous, (2) the appellation *commodity* is appropriate, and (3) the group of suppliers of such products may be viewed as an *industry*. For such products and industries, the derivation of both industry supply and demand curves, as well as the deployment of the other tools of partial equilibrium analysis, provides useful information in an elegant, mathematical, Newtoniandeterministic manner. For example, if there are numerous firms in the industry, perfect information, and no barriers to entry, then partial equilibrium analysis can show mathematically that resources in such an industry will be efficiently allocated. Thus, the usefulness of partial equilibrium analysis in *some* industries sets Chamberlin's snare.

If only all products, both consumer and intermediate, were "close enough" (Friedman 1953) to commodities, then all industries could be analyzed in the elegant, mathematical, partial equilibrium manner. Indeed, if demand in such industries as automobiles were, like corn, close enough for "practical purposes" (Robinson 1933) to being homogeneous, then—given the other conditions of perfect competition—one could develop an elegant, mathematical, general equilibrium model of an entire economy.

The temptation of the snare was just too great. The neoclassical tradition embraced Chamberlin's "delusion" that demand in *all* industries was close enough to being homogeneous in order to (1) analyze all industries with the tools of partial equilibrium analysis, (2) develop the elegant equations of general equilibrium, and (3) use static assumptions to address the social welfare issues of a modern, dynamic economy. Hence, we have the sorrowful situation of scholars in the neoclassical tradition doing analyses that imply that (1) there are welfare costs, but no benefits, to intra-industry freedom of choice and (2) social welfare analysis is primarily, if not exclusively, a static, efficiency issue, rather than a dynamic, welfare-improving, economic growth problem.

As a third affinity, R-A theory agrees that the problem that heterogeneous, intra-industry demand poses for the neoclassical tradition cannot be solved by the simple expedient of further subdividing industry, four-digit codes into finer categories. No matter how finely the categories are defined, most firms in most industries will still be quantity-takers and price-makers, rather than price-takers and quantity-makers. Therefore, the use of partial equilibrium analysis and the achievement of its alleged welfare ideal require that homogeneous-industries-with-demand-curves would have to be created by government mandate. Such government intervention then poses the question, as Chamberlin (1933/1962, p. 259) put it, should the government mandate that the automobile industry produce Packards, Plymouths, or Peugeots? If downward-sloping demand curves for novels (Mankiw 1998, p. 363) represent waste that is "subtle" and "hard to measure" (p. 370), but waste nonetheless, which novel should government mandate? If each principles of economics textbook has a downward-sloping demand curve, which text should government require? Indeed, if mandating homogeneity produced disastrous consequences in the command economies (Samuelson and Nordhaus 1995, p. 170), why would it be desirable in societies that value freedom?

Fourth, R-A theory agrees that the concept of *product* or what R-A theory refers to as *market offering* should be defined broadly. For R-A theory, a market offering is a distinct entity that (1) is composed of a bundle of attributes, which (2) may be tangible or intangible, objective or subjective, and which (3) may be viewed by some potential buyer(s) as a want-satisfier.[15]

Most market offerings have blends of tangible (e.g., an automobile's engine, tires, and transmission) and intangible attributes (e.g., an automobile's warranty, reliability, and prestige). If tangible attributes predominate, market offerings are referred to as goods; if intangibles predominate, they are services. Attributes are relatively more objective or subjective depending on the degree of uniformity across buyers as to (1) the importance weights given to different attributes, (2) the extent to which different market offerings have or do not have different attributes, and (3) the extent to which different offerings have different levels of attributes. In all cases, consumer perceptions are dispositive. Market offerings perceived by consumers to be closer to their ideal constellation of attributes and their ideal levels of same are perceived to be more relatively valuable.

R-A theory's acceptance that intra-industry demand in most industries is substantially heterogeneous implies that firms have a major strategic and informational problem, as well as a major opportunity. That is, how many market offerings, composed of which attributes, at what attribute levels, targeted at which market segments should it produce? Different firms in the same industry are likely to solve this problem differently (based on, among other things, their differing resources). Accordingly, those firms that solve the problem well, relative to rivals competing for the same segment(s), are likely to have superior financial performance. Thus, the heterogeneity of intra-industry demand poses both a problem for firms to solve and an opportunity for them to achieve superior financial performance.

Fifth, R-A theory agrees that heterogeneous, intra-industry *supply* is natural. R-A theory attributes heterogeneous supply to the fact that many intra-industry firm resources are heterogeneous and imperfectly mobile. Specifically, R-A theory views resources as the tangible and intangible entities available to firms that enable them to efficiently and/or effectively produce market offerings that have value for some market segment(s). Therefore, the natural heterogeneity of supply is explained on the basis that many resources are heterogeneous (hence, asymmetrically distributed among rivals) and not readily, commonly, or easily bought and sold in the factor markets (i.e., imperfectly mobile).

The preceding five affinities with Chamberlin (1933) notwithstanding, and as a major point of differentiation, R-A theory rejects both the view that competition is equilibrium-seeking and the view that static equilibrium analysis is useful or appropriate for most firms, industries, and Chamberlinian "groups." For R-A theory, competition is disequilibrium-provoking (see Sections 2.2.4, 5.4.1, and 6.1.3). Because both intra-industry supply and demand are naturally heterogeneous, static equilibrium analysis ignores firm and industry dynamics. The implication of partial equilibrium analysis being inappropriate for most firms and industries is clear: general equilibrium analysis is misguided and assuredly inappropriate for social welfare analysis. Chamberlin (1933) was forced to use partial equilibrium analysis because at that time there was no dynamic theory of competition. This book offers R-A theory to fill this gap.

3.2 DIFFERENTIAL ADVANTAGE THEORY

As discussed in Section 3.1, the high prices, low quantities of goods produced, permanent excess capacity, inferior products, and exploited factors of production implied by Chamberlin's (1933) and Robinson's (1933) neoclassical analyses implied a dismal picture of the welfare implications of the monopolistic competition that is spawned by heterogeneous demand and supply. Indeed, Robinson (1954) argued that competition is an anomaly, if not "impossible." For her, "three tendencies—the tendency for competition to make markets imperfect by product differentiation, the tendency towards oligopoly where advantages of scale exist, and the tendency for excess capacity to lead to collusion—between them leave only narrow areas where conditions are such that [perfect] competition can normally prevail" (p. 254).[16] If perfect competition, the welfare ideal, is an unnatural anomaly, then the state should intervene in the most forceful manner in all nonperfect industries to mandate homogeneity of demand and supply.

Some scholars in the 1940s, 1950s, and 1960s began questioning whether perfect competition is the appropriate welfare ideal. Most notable, for our purposes, are John Maurice Clark's (1884-1963) theories of workable competition (1940) and effective competition (1954, 1961) and Wroe Alderson's (1905-1965) functionalist theory of market behavior (1957, 1965). Because the concept of differential advantage is prominent in both Clark's and Alderson's works, I group them under the label "differential advantage theory."

3.2.1 Workable Competition

Clark (1940) notes that Chamberlin's (1933) and Robinson's (1933) efforts had resulted in the detailed explication of both the nature of perfect competition and its use as a welfare ideal.[17] On perfect competition, Clark states, "I am not quarreling with proper use of this standard as an ideal" (p. 241). He worries, though, that "it has seemed at times to lead to undesirable results, in that it does not afford reliable guidance to the factors which are favorable to the closest available working approximation to that ideal, under actual conditions" (p. 241). In particular, he argues that perfect competition should not *always* serve as the welfare ideal because "where one of the conditions of perfect competition is absent, the presence of others may lead to greater rather than less imperfection" (p. 241). Thus, government intervention that focused on changing one element of an industry might not benefit social welfare but simply result in a "sick industry" characterized by "a cut-throat price war, driving prices below an efficient producer's total cost of production" (p. 243).

Clark's (1940) concept of workable competition, contrasted with perfect competition, attempts to avoid instances of the extremes of competition, that is, ones that are both too strong and too weak. He begins his development of workable competition by defining generic competition:

> Competition is rivalry in selling goods, in which each selling unit normally seeks maximum net revenue, under conditions such that the price or prices each seller can charge are effectively limited by the free option of the buyer to buy from a rival seller or sellers of what we think of as "the same" product, necessitating an effort by each seller to equal or exceed the attractiveness of the others' offerings to a sufficient number of sellers to accomplish the end in view. (p. 243)

Three aspects of Clark's (1940) generic competition merit special attention. First, competition is not a random pairing of anonymous buyers and sellers, as in perfect competition, but a *rivalry* among competitors. Second, the ability of firms to charge high prices is limited to the extent that buyers have the option of obtaining similar products from rivals in the marketplace. And third, sellers seek to "equal or exceed the attractiveness of the others' offerings." Although the first two characteristics are in Chamberlin (1933), the dynamics implied by "equal or exceed" in the third are not.

Clark (1940) then discusses the kinds of conditions under which competition takes place and develops a typology of forms of competition. The major categories and requisites of his forms of competition are:[18]

I. *Pure (rigorous, unmitigated) competition.* Requisites: standard product, known price, many sellers available at any locality, free entry. Price may be quoted or supply-governed and tends to equal marginal cost.

A. *Perfect competition.* Requisites: above plus perfect two-way mobility of the factors of production. Current control of output is probably implied. Price covers average cost, which equals marginal cost.

B. *Imperfect pure competition.* Lacking perfect mobility, marginal cost is less than average cost when demand at average-cost prices falls below capacity.

II. *Modified, intermediate, or hybrid competition.* ("Monopolistic competition" in the broader sense.)

A. *Standard products, few producers.* The most important cases involve formally free entry, but no exit without loss.

B. *Unstandardized or quality products: "monopolistic competition."* Individual demand schedules sloping, but more elastic than general demand schedule. Competition hinges on the extent to which quality differences are open to imitation. Schedule of response to selling outlay is a complicating factor.

With his framework in place, Clark (1940) discusses numerous factors in the forms of competition that mitigate the harmful effects of their departures from perfect competition. For example, the long-run demand curves of firms in monopolistic competition are much flatter than short-run curves. Thus, the entry of new firms offering ever closer substitutes mitigates monopoly profits and prices. Second, long-run cost curves are flatter than short-run curves. In fact, rather than there being a single, optimum size for a manufacturing plant, there appears to be a broad range of optimally sized plants. Thus, "economies due to size are far from being such a vitally important factor as is suggested by the type of theoretical cost curve now in general use" (p. 249). Third, firms offering higher-quality products at prices higher than their rivals are not *always* a problem for society. Through time, technological progress, the increased use of product specifications, and more consumer information are likely to wipe out quality differentials and the harmful effects of same. He concludes his article by stating that these factors:

> would increase the number of industries which, despite large-scale production, have the characteristics of fairly healthy and workable imperfect competition, rather than those of slightly-qualified monopoly. In such cases, one may hope that government need not assume the burden of doing something about every departure from the model of perfect competition. (p. 256)

Note that even though Clark's definition of generic competition has dynamic elements, his analysis of workable competition is still static equilibrium in nature. In workable competition, "dynamic" is not an ongoing process but what happens between short-run and long-run equilibrium. In the 1950s, he turned from static, *workable* competition to dynamic, *effective* competition. In doing so, he introduced the concept of differential advantage.

3.2.2 Effective Competition and Differential Advantage

In the 1950s and 1960s, Clark (1954, 1961) abandoned the label *workable* and replaced it with *effective* for reasons he states clearly:

> I am shifting the emphasis from "workable" to "effective competition" because "workable" stresses mere feasibility and is consistent with the verdict that feasible forms of competition, while tolerable, are still inferior substitutes for that "pure and perfect" competition which has been so widely accepted as a normative ideal. And I have become increasingly impressed that the kind of competition we have, with all its defects—and these are serious—is better than the "pure and perfect" norm, because it makes for progress. Some departures from "pure and perfect" competition are not only inseparable from progress, but necessary to it. The theory of effective competition is dynamic theory. (1961, p. ix)

Because a dynamic theory of competition would have different standards of appraisal, he inquires as to the objectives society would want competition to accomplish. He suggests that competition should provide or promote an adequate variety of products (including low-priced products, high-quality products, and new products), economic opportunity, social mobility, a productive economy, rewards to innovators, low search costs, a diffusion of the gains of progress, high and stable employment, business freedom, the elimination of process inefficiencies, and an appropriate balance of desirable and undesirable effects on individuals (Clark 1954, pp. 323-24; 1961, pp. 63, 74, 77, 78, 81, 82, 86).

Taken collectively, the desirable outputs of competition would seem to be a tall order. Yet Clark maintains that effective, dynamic competition could come tolerably close to achieving all his suggested goals. But effective, dynamic competition does not imply that firms would be price-takers, or that they would seek to maximize profits, or that competition is a struggle with only one winner (1961, p. 18). What, then, does effective competition imply? Acknowledging his "kinship" with Schumpeter's "creative destruction," Clark (1954) defines competition as:[19]

> a form of independent action by business units in pursuit of increased profits . . .
> by offering others inducements to deal with them, the others being free to accept

the alternative inducements offered by rival business units. Active competition consists of a combination of (1) initiatory actions by a business unit, and (2) a complex of responses by those with whom it deals, and by rivals. (p. 326)

Clark's definition of dynamic competition is remarkably compact. Indeed, his entire 1961 book is devoted to "unpacking" it. A good starting point for us is his view that firms pursue increased profits rather than maximum profits.

Clark (1961, p. 9) specifically alerts readers that his "profit minded" firms are not profit maximizers. He argues that firms do not maximize profit because (1) all firms at all times face such conditions of uncertainty as to consumers' and rivals' actions that they lack the necessary information to maximize (pp. 93, 471), (2) some firms at some times sacrifice profits for growth (p. 96), (3) some firms at some times sacrifice profits in favor of community responsibilities (p. 91), and (4) some firms at some times sacrifice profits because of following the "morals of trade" (p. 479). By substituting "increased profits in the face of uncertainty" for the neoclassical "maximum profits in the face of perfect information," Clark makes competition dynamic. That is, the continuing pursuit of increased profits, *more* profits, prompts changes in the "inducements to deal."

When firms are successful in effecting changes in inducements targeted at specific customers, for example, by providing market offerings of higher quality or lower prices, such firms have a "differential advantage" over rivals (Clark 1954, p. 327). It is the pursuit of differential advantages over rivals that prompts the innovations that constitute "aggressive competition" (1961, p. 14). For Clark, the sum of innovations that result in differential advantages over rivals constitutes the technological progress required for a "dynamically progressive system," that is, economic growth (1961, p. 70). Therefore, mandating the homogeneity of demand and supply would necessitate the "stoppage of growth and progress, a price we should be unwilling to pay (1961, p. 70). Indeed, "perfect competition . . . define[s] a model from which competitive progress would be ruled out; progress could come only by government fiat" (1954, p. 329).

For Clark, the innovations resulting from aggressive competition can come from small firms, as stressed by Marshall (1890), or from large firms, as stressed by Schumpeter (1950). Contrasted with Schumpeter (1950), however, the innovations can be small ones that improve quality or lower costs only modestly. Clark (1961) points out, however, that small innovations, cumulatively, are important to the firm and economy. Whether an innovation is brought about by small firms or large ones, whether it is industry-shaking or only a modest improvement, "the life history of a successful innovation is a cycle. It is developed, profitably utilized, and ultimately loses its value as a source of special profit" (p. 189).

An innovation loses its value to produce superior profits when it is either superseded by something better (i.e., Schumpeter's "creative destruction") or when it is diffused among rivals and becomes standard practice by "defensive competition." Thus, when an innovation is diffused among rivals, it becomes—rather than a differential advantage for the originator—much like the "ante" in a poker game. Both aggressive and defensive competition are required for *effective* competition: "without initiatory moves, competition does not begin, without defensive responses, it does not spread" (Clark 1961, p. 429). Aggressive competition creates innovations and differential advantages; defensive competition diffuses innovations and neutralizes such advantages. As to the speed of neutralization:

> If a potential innovator expects neutralization to be complete before he has recovered the costs of innovation, his incentive vanishes. . . . On the other hand, if neutralizing action were permanently blocked, the initiator would have a limited monopoly, in the sense of a permanent differential advantage. . . . The desirable case lies somewhere between too prompt and too slow neutralization. I will not call it an "optimum," because that term suggests a precision which no actual system could attain. (1954, pp. 327-28)

Clark's hope was that his dynamic theory of effective competition would provide a framework for understanding actual forms of competition and for fostering the ones most conducive to a dynamic welfare ideal. He knew, however, that "the threat of failure looms large, in that readers whose conception of theory is identified with models of determinate equilibrium are likely to decide that no theory has been produced" (1961, p. x). He was prescient, to say the least. His 500-page 1961 book—having not a single differential equation or geometrical representation—was not incorporated into mainstream economics. However, it did have a significant impact on the marketing discipline through Alderson's (1957, 1965) functionalist theory of market behavior.

3.2.3 A Functionalist Theory of Market Behavior

Alderson (1957, 1965) was strongly influenced by Chamberlin's (1933) heterogeneous demand theory and by Clark's (1954, 1961) theory of effective, dynamic competition. Also, he was impressed by Merton's (1949) functionalist, systems approach to theory development. Furthermore, his background in marketing, with its historical interest in groups of manufacturers, wholesalers, and retailers that form channels of distribution, pointed him toward developing a theory of marketing systems. Accordingly, his functionalist theory of market behavior may be viewed as a functionalist, systems approach to integrating theories of heterogeneous demand, differential advantage, and channels of distribution.[20]

Alderson (1957) views functionalism as "that approach to science which begins by identifying a system of action, and then tries to determine how and why it works as it does" (p. 16). He identifies (1) firms as the subsystems that produce goods and (2) households as the subsystems that constitute the basic consuming units. He (1965) notes that firms evolve in a society when specialization of labor results in removing the production function for some goods from the household (p. 39). Extending Chamberlin's (1933) view that intra-industry demand is substantially heterogeneous, he notes that the particular assortment of goods that is viewed as meaningful or desirable by any one household is likely to differ greatly from that of others. Thus, the macrosystems that he seeks to understand and explain are those that involve firms taking resources from their natural state and transforming them into a variety of marketplace goods that ultimately wind up as meaningful assortments of goods in the hands of particular households.

Although firms pursue profit, Alderson (1957) maintains that they do so *as if* they had a primary goal of survival (p. 54). The survival goal results from firm owners and employees believing that they can obtain more in terms of financial and nonfinancial rewards by working toward the survival of their existing firms than by acting individually or by becoming members of other firms. Firm growth, therefore, is sought because of the conviction that growth is necessary for survival (pp. 103-8). In a market-based economy, however, survival depends crucially on a firm's ability to compete with other firms in seeking the patronage of specific intermediate buyers and/or ultimate households.

A firm can be assured of the patronage of intermediate buyers and/or groups of households only when buyers have reasons to prefer its output over that of competing firms. Therefore, each competing firm will seek some advantage over other firms to ensure the patronage of some group of either intermediate buyers or ultimate households. Citing the work of Clark (1954), Alderson (1957) labels the process "competition for differential advantage" (p. 101). Indeed, "no one enters business except in the expectation of some degree of differential advantage in serving his customers, and . . . competition consists of the constant struggle to develop, maintain, or increase such advantages" (p. 106). Therefore:

The functionalist or ecological approach to competition begins with the assumption that every firm must seek and find a function in order to maintain itself in the market place. Every business firm occupies a position which is in some respects unique. Its location, the product it sells, its operating methods, or the customers it serves tend to set it off in some degree from every other firm. Each firm competes by making the most of its individuality and its special character. It is constantly seeking to establish some competitive advantage . . . [because] an advanced method of operation is not enough if all competitors live up to the same high standards. What is important in competition is differential advantage, which can give a firm an edge over what others in the field are offering. (pp. 101-2)

Alderson (1957, pp. 184-97) identifies six bases of differential advantage for a manufacturing firm: market segmentation, selection of appeals, transvection, product improvement, process improvement, and product innovation. While product improvement, process improvement, and product innovation require no elaboration, the other three do. By market segmentation having the potential for a differential advantage, Alderson means that firms may have an advantage over competitors when (1) they identify segments of demand that competitors are not servicing (or rivals are servicing poorly), and (2) they subsequently develop market offerings that will appeal strongly to those particular segments. On the other hand, selection of appeals recognizes that some firms can achieve advantage by the images that are conveyed to consumers through advertising and other promotional means. Similarly, transvection implies an advantage in reaching a market segment through a unique channel of distribution.

The existence of a differential advantage gives the firm a position in the marketplace known as an "ecological niche" (Alderson 1957, p. 56). The "core" and "fringe" of a firm's ecological niche consists of the market segments for which the firm's differential advantage is (1) ideally suited for and (2) satisfactorily suited for, respectively. A firm can survive attacks by competitors on its "fringe" as long as its "core" remains intact; it can survive attacks on its "core" as long as it has the will and ability to find another differential advantage and another core (pp. 56-57). Therefore, given heterogeneity of demand and competition for differential advantage, heterogeneity of supply is a natural phenomenon. That is, manufacturers will respond to heterogeneity of demand by producing a variety of different goods and many variations of the same generic kind of good (p. 103).

To reach households, however, manufacturing firms require market intermediaries, that is, channels of distribution. Market processes involving intermediaries are essentially "matching" processes, that is, matching segments of demand with segments of supply. In a perfectly heterogeneous market, each small segment of demand, that is, each household, could be satisfied by just one unique segment of supply, that is, one firm (Alderson 1965, p. 29). In most markets, however, there are partial homogeneities. That is, there are groups or segments of households *desiring* substantially similar products, and there are groups of firms *supplying* substantially similar products.

The major job of marketing intermediaries is to effect exchange by matching segments of demand with segments of supply. The matching process comes about as a result of a sequence of sorts and transformations (Alderson 1965, p. 26). A sort is the assignment of goods, materials, or components to the appropriate facilities. A transformation is the change in the physical form of a good or its location in time or space.

With the preceding as backdrop, Alderson (1965, p. 26) can answer the question that prompted his functionalist theory. Given heterogeneity of demand, heterogeneity of supply, and the requisite institutions (intermediaries) to effect the sorts and transformations necessary to match segments of demand with segments of supply, market processes will take resources in the natural state and bring about meaningful assortments of goods in the hands of households.

3.2.4 Differential Advantage Theory and R-A Theory

Resource-advantage theory draws more strongly from differential advantage theory than from any other research tradition. First, both differential advantage ("DA") theory and R-A theory maintain that competition is dynamic. Indeed, they share a similar propulsion mechanism. For DA theory, the mechanism is increased profits; for R-A theory, it is superior financial performance, that is, *more* than and *better* than (see Section 5.4.1). Thus, both DA theory and R-A theory deny that firms have the requisite information to maximize profits, and both affirm that institutional factors (such as moral codes) at times will mitigate profit seeking. The substitution of "superior financial performance in the face of uncertainty" for "profit maximization in the face of certainty" or even for "profit maximization in the face of estimable probability distributions" is a critical distinction between R-A theory and the neoclassical tradition.

Second, neither DA theory nor R-A theory is defended on the ground that such theories of competition represent "second best" or "workable" approximations of perfect competition. Instead, both theories deny that the equations of general equilibrium, relying as they do on perfect competition, represent the appropriate welfare ideal. For both DA and R-A theory, the appropriate wel-

fare ideal must accommodate, at the minimum, competition-induced technological progress.

Third, both DA and R-A theory share the view that competition involves
both initiatory and defensive actions. The "aggressive competition" and "defensive competition" of DA theory parallel the "proactive innovation" and "reactive innovation" of R-A theory (see Chapter 4 and Section 9.1.3). Thus,
competition-induced innovations, whether large or small, by huge corporations or solitary entrepreneurs, play a major role in both theories.

Fourth, both DA and R-A theory share the view that competition involves
the struggle among rivals for *advantages*. For DA theory, the concept of the
kinds of advantages that firms pursue are of a general nature. For R-A theory,
adopting the resource-based view of the firm (see Section 4.1.3), firms pursue
comparative advantages in resources that will yield marketplace positions of
competitive advantage and, thereby, superior financial performance. Furthermore, R-A theory explicates the nature of resources that will make effective
neutralization by rivals less likely or at least more time-consuming: when resources are imperfectly mobile, inimitable, and imperfectly substitutable, they
are more likely to thwart effective neutralization. That is, when resources are
tacit, causally ambiguous, socially complex, or interconnected or they exhibit
mass efficiencies or time-compression diseconomies, they are *less* likely to be
quickly and effectively neutralized and *more* likely to produce a sustainable
competitive advantage (see Section 6.1.2).

Finally, both DA theory and R-A theory are developed in English, not in the
language of mathematical equations. But R-A theory's preference for natural-
language exposition should not be interpreted as being anti-equation. Rather, it
is argued to be a general theory of competition that incorporates perfect competition theory as a special case and, thereby, explains when the equations in
the neoclassical tradition will predict accurately (see Sections 9.1 and 10.1).

NOTES

1. Thus, as Chamberlin (1933/1962, Appendix H) points out, his theory was not
developed—as was Robinson's (1933)—in the context of, or as a response to, the depression of the 1930s.

2. For Chamberlin, "perfect" competition has the two requisites of pure competition plus such conditions as perfect information.

3. See the bibliography in the 1962 edition of Chamberlin's book for works debat-
ing the merits of Chamberlin's theory. Triffin (1940) is a good starting point.

4. See Loasby (1991b) for an analysis of the "wrong turning." As Mongiovi (1992)
points out: "The despair that marked the final years of her [Robinson's] life was due not

only to the discipline's indifference to her message [that equilibrium analysis is a desert], but also to her rising doubts about whether the method she endorsed could in fact help to explain processes in historical time" (p. 964).

5. In the sentence quoted, Chamberlin refers the reader to pages 100-109 in his (1933/1962) book. In this section he uses—with unintended irony—pure competition as an ideal to argue that heterogeneity of demand and supply lead "with impunity" (p. 109) to the wastes of excess capacity.

6. The quasi-Austrian caveat does not appear in the 1989, pre-command-economy-collapse edition of the text.

7. Lancaster's (1991) work is a departure from the conventional approach to product variety. He assumes goods to be bundles of objective characteristics and intra-industry demand to be heterogeneous in order to explore the issue of whether there is a socially optimal degree of product differentiation. On the basis of a static equilibrium welfare ideal, he concludes that there is a theoretical optimum but that the actual amount appears empirically inestimable because "there are no easily recognizable conditions with respect to the actual number of goods" (p. 179). As to whether perfect competition would generate the optimum amount and, thus, should be the policy ideal, he concludes that it would not be optimal under increasing returns to scale, which is the "most important and most interesting" case (p. 179). Therefore, "we cannot look to perfect competition to solve the optimum differentiation problem" (p. 179). See, also, Spence (1976), Dixit and Stiglitz (1977), and Itoh (1983) for other analyses using the static equilibrium welfare ideal on the issue of product variety.

8. Chamberlin's works were so highly regarded in marketing that the American Marketing Association awarded him the Paul D. Converse Award in 1953. At that time, it was the highest award that the association conferred.

9. See Baker, Black, and Hart (1994); Barksdale and Darden (1971); Hooley, Lynch, and Shepherd (1990); and Houston (1986) for a history of the marketing concept and its implications. See McKay (1954) for an early and influential treatment.

10. For efficiency in exposition, a review of Alderson's (1957, 1965) views on the heterogeneity of demand and segmentation is deferred to Chapter 4. See Reekie and Savitt (1982) for the relationship between Alderson's theory and "Austrian" economics.

11. See Borden (1964) for how the concept of a marketing "mix" was developed.

12. McCarthy (1960) referred to the elements of the marketing mix as the "four Ps" of product, price, promotion, and place. Hence, his theory is often referred to as the "four Ps model" of marketing.

13. See Robertson and Kassarjian (1991) for a review of consumer behavior.

14. See Myers (1996) for a review. See Allenby, Noeroj, and Ginter (1998) for arguments that even market segments that are presumed to be homogeneous are still significantly heterogeneous.

15. Note that Lancaster (1991) differs from the approach here in that he restricts his analysis to objective attributes and he uses equilibrium analysis.

16. Note that Robinson (1954) saw it as redundant to have the adjective "perfect" before the noun "competition" (see first paragraph of Chapter 1).

17. See Foss (1991) for a discussion of the contributions of Chamberlin (1933) and Robinson (1933) to formalizing the concept of perfect competition. As Foss points out:

It was the theorists of monopolistic competition who supplied the neo-classical theory of the firm with its Kuhnian exemplar, the theory of firm behavior under perfect competition. In the process of polemicizing against perfect competition, Chamberlin and Robinson constructed their own target, bringing together hitherto dispersed elements—e.g., full mobility (J. M. Clark, Knight), perfect information (Knight), the equilibrium firm (Pigou), firms as price-takers (Pigou), etc.—under a rigorous geometrical treatment. (p. 70)

18. See Clark (1940, pp. 244-45) for the complete taxonomy.

19. Throughout his 1961 book, Clark (pp. 9, 13, 18, 213) gives definitions of "competition." Although each is consistent with his 1954 work, none appears to be as complete, yet still succinct.

20. Surveys of marketing scholars identify Alderson as the scholar who has most contributed to the development of marketing theory (Chonko and Dunne 1982). See Hunt, Muncy, and Ray (1981) for a detailed explication of Alderson's functionalist theory of market behavior.

Antecedents and Affinities

Business Strategy and
Institutional Theory

This chapter continues our discussion of the theories, research programs, and traditions that resource-advantage theory draws on and
shares affinities with. Here, the focus is on business strategy and institutional
theory. Again, I review only those portions that are directly relevant to R-A theory and point readers toward more comprehensive reviews.

4.1 BUSINESS STRATEGY

Modern business strategy traces to the works on administrative policy of Kenneth Andrews and his colleagues at Harvard (Andrews 1971/1980/1987;
Christensen et al. 1982; Learned et al. 1965). Viewing business strategy as the
match a business makes between its internal resources and skills and the opportunities and risks created by its external environment, they developed the
SWOT framework: *S*trengths, *W*eakness, *O*pportunities, *T*hreats. In this framework, the chief executive officer is in charge of the process of strategy forma-

tion, and the main task of corporate-level strategy is identifying businesses in which the firm will compete (Andrews 1971).

Alternative strategies for the firm are developed through an appraisal of the opportunities and threats it faces in various markets, that is, *external* factors, and an evaluation of its strengths and weaknesses, that is, *internal* factors. Good strategies are those that are explicit (for effective implementation) and effect a good match or "fit." Such strategies avoid environmental threats, circumvent internal weaknesses, and exploit opportunities through the strengths or distinctive competences of the firm. The process of choosing the final strategy for implementation will be guided by the differences in fit of the alternatives, the values of the managers, and societal constraints.

Since the development of the SWOT model of business strategy, an enormous literature on strategy and strategic planning has developed, much of which has appeared in *Strategic Management Journal, Journal of Business Strategy, Long Range Planning,* and the *Journal of Strategic Marketing,* among others. Modern business strategy maintains (1) that the strategic imperative of a firm should be sustained, superior financial performance and (2) the belief that this goal can be achieved through a sustainable competitive advantage in the marketplace (Aaker 1995; Barney 1991; Bharadwaj, Varadarajan, and Fahy 1993; Cecil and Goldstein 1990; Coyne 1985; G. S. Day 1984; Day and Nedungadi 1994; Day and Wensley 1988; Ghemawat 1986; Lado, Boyd, and Wright 1992; Porter 1985; Reed and DeFillippi 1990).[1] Again, the discussion here focuses only on issues directly relevant to R-A theory. In particular, I examine two questions that have sparked much debate. First, to what extent should strategic planning be formalized? Second, if a sustainable competitive advantage is paramount, should external factors (i.e., opportunities and threats) or internal factors (i.e., strengths and weaknesses) be the primary focus of strategy development?

As to the first question, the strategic planners (e.g., Ansoff 1965; Steiner 1969) argue for a high level of formalization and the creation of freestanding, strategic planning departments. As to the second, industrial organization theorists (Porter 1980, 1985) argue for the primacy of external (industry) factors in the pursuit of sustainable competitive advantage, whereas resource-based theorists (Barney 1991, 1992; Conner 1991; Dierickx and Cool 1989; Grant 1991; Lippman and Rumelt 1982; Rumelt 1984; Wernerfelt 1984) and competence-based theorists (Hamel and Prahalad 1989, 1994a; Prahalad and Hamel 1990, 1993; Sanchez and Heene 1997; Sanchez, Heene, and Thomas 1996) argue for internal factors. I begin with formal strategic planning and its derivative, portfolio analysis.

4.1.1 Formal Strategic Planning and Portfolio Analysis

Strategic planning as a formal process entered corporate America in the 1960s (Ansoff 1965; Steiner 1969).[2] Although the CEO was always acknowledged as having ultimate responsibility for the corporate plan, planning should take place, it was argued, in a freestanding planning department because line managers were simply too busy to plan effectively. A basic premise of strategic planners was that "[s]trategy formation should be controlled and conscious as well as a formalized and elaborated process, decomposed into distinct steps, each delineated by checklists and supported by techniques" (Mintzberg 1994, p. 42).

Ansoff's (1965, pp. 202-3) detailed model of the strategic planning process, with fifty-seven boxes, was influential. In it, the decision process flows from preliminary diversification decisions to more detailed decisions based on much greater information. At each stage, "gaps" between the firm's objectives and its current position are estimated. Also explored at each stage are opportunities for *synergy,* which is defined as any "effect which can produce a combined return on the firm's resources greater than the sum of its parts" (p. 75) and which "is similar in many ways to what is frequently called 'evaluation of strengths and weaknesses' " (p. 76). The output of Ansoff's model is a diversification strategy:

> The end product of strategic decisions is deceptively simple; a combination of products and markets is selected for the firm. This combination is arrived at by addition of new product-markets, divestment from some old ones, and expansion of the present position. (p. 12)

Formal strategic planning swept through corporate America in the 1960s and 1970s. As strategic planning departments proliferated and growth through diversification intensified, conglomerates became a prominent organizational form. Indeed, the conglomerate form of organization was argued to be efficient for well-run, multidivisional ("M-form") firms (Williamson 1975). By 1980, more than half of all *Fortune 500* firms operated in three or more 2-digit SIC industries (Davis, Diekmann, and Tinsley 1994).

But there was a curious omission in all the formal, strategic planning models: the formation of the actual strategies themselves. As one of the foremost advocates of formal strategic planning acknowledged, "although a good bit of progress has been made in developing analytical tools to identify and evaluate strategies, the process [of strategy formation] is still mostly an art" (Steiner 1979, p. 178). The strategy formation "gap" was argued to be closed, or at least addressed, by the product portfolio models. Although several firm-as-portfolio planning models were developed in the 1960s and 1970s, the two most prominent were the Boston Consulting Group (BCG) growth-share matrix and the General Electric-McKinsey market attractiveness-business position matrix.[3] I illustrate the approach using the BCG model.

The key working concept in the BCG model is a product's or strategic business unit's (SBU's) market share, that is, product or SBU sales divided by industry sales. Market share is key because empirical studies show a strong correlation between market share and return on investment (ROI) (Buzzell, Gale, and Sultan 1975; Gale and Branch 1982; Ravenscraft 1983). Furthermore, a high market share relative to one's largest competitor indicates that one will have a lower relative cost because of the *experience effect*. That is, as a firm develops experience in manufacturing a product, its costs per unit are thought to decline at a fixed rate. For example, an "85% experience curve" suggests that cost per unit will decline 15% with every doubling of total units produced. Therefore, a high market share through time will result in lower relative costs per unit and higher relative ROI.

BCG's growth-share matrix is constructed by plotting each of the firm's products or SBUs on a matrix where the Y axis is the market sales growth rate and the X axis is the product's *relative* market share (i.e., market share divided by largest competitor's market share). High (low) growth markets are customarily defined as those greater (less) than 10% per year; high (low) relative share products are greater (less) than 1.0. Using 10% growth per year and 1.0 relative share to divide the matrix into quadrants results in the possible product positions being (1) high share-high growth products, which are labeled "stars," (2) high share-low growth ones, labeled "cash cows," (3) low share-high growth, labeled "problem children," and (4) low share-low growth, labeled "dogs."

The strategic analysis of a firm's portfolio proceeds through several stages. First, one checks for balance. Balanced portfolios have few problem children and dogs, and most of the firm's sales come from market-leading cash cows. Second, one investigates for trends. Trends are identified by comparing the present matrix with both a matrix constructed for a period three to five years earlier and a projected, three-to-five year one (the projection of which assumes no changes in strategy). Third, one develops a three-to-five year *target* matrix and chooses a strategy for each product. The customary strategies of choice are (1) hold market share, (2) build market share, (3) harvest, and (4) withdrawal. Hold share is appropriate for cash cows. Indeed, they throw off the cash necessary for new investment. Build share is appropriate for stars and (at least some targeted) problem children. Harvesting and withdrawal are appropriate for some problem children and most dogs.

Portfolio planning was rhetorically colorful ("dogs," "cash cows"), was easily understood (no fifty-seven boxes and detailed checklists), and yielded actual strategies for each product or SBU. Furthermore, it was formal, yet unlikely to result in the massive, leather-bound, intricate plans of other strategic planning approaches. For many firms, an implication of relative market share being the key to profitability was to slash prices to build share quickly and thus gain the advantages of the experience effect. Surveys showed that by 1979 almost half of *Fortune 500* companies—including 75% of the diversified ones—were using portfolio planning to guide strategy (Haspeslagh 1982).

In the 1980s, the pendulum swung against formal strategic planning, corporate planning departments, diversification, conglomerates, and the firm-as-portfolio view of planning strategy. As planning was increasingly shifted toward line managers and scores of corporate planning groups were totally eliminated, even General Electric—the acknowledged exemplar of corporate planning—drastically cut its staff of "planocrats" (*Business Week* 1984). Complained the chairman of General Motors, "We got these great plans together, put them on the shelf, and marched off to do what we would be doing anyway. It took us a little while to realize that wasn't getting us anywhere" (*Business Week* 1984, p. 62). And, lamented a vice-president in charge of strategic planning at Eaton, "If there is a hell for planners, over the portal will be carved the term 'cash cow' " (*Business Week* 1984, p. 63). By the mid-1980s, strategy theorists could assert confidently both that "synergy has become widely regarded as passe" (Porter 1985, p. 317) and that "the days when portfolio management was a valid concept of corporate strategy are past" (Porter 1987, p. 51).

The formal planning and portfolio analysis approaches to strategy led to what has been described as "the biggest collective error ever made by American business" (*Economist* 1991, p. 44). Their decline has been attributed to numerous factors.[4] Prominent among them, it is claimed, are (1) their reliance on "top down" planning, (2) their artificial separation of strategy and implementation, (3) their wrongheaded substitution of number-crunching exercises for creativity, managerial experience, and intuition, (4) their focus on incremental change, (5) the morale problems that resulted from SBU's being labeled "dogs" and "cash cows," (6) the fact that product life cycles are becoming so short (especially in high-technology products) that the hypothesized experience effects never kick in, (7) the failure of so many planning-motivated mergers to effect synergy, (8) the failure of "general management expertise" to transfer and add value across diverse lines of businesses, and (9) the failure to recognize that many successful strategies, rather than being rationally planned and chosen, *emerge* from day-to-day decision making (Davis, Diekmann, and Tinsley 1994; Goold and Luchs 1993; Mintzberg 1994; Porter 1985, 1987). Important for our purposes here is another factor: the findings of empirical works that reexamined the relationship between market share and profitability.

The fundamental premise of the portfolio approaches stemmed from cross-sectional, empirical works that showed a strong correlation between market share and ROI. In particular, studies using the Profit Impact of Marketing Strategies (PIMS) data suggested that every 1% increase in market share resulted in a 0.5% increase in ROI (Buzzell, Gale, and Sultan 1975; Gale and Branch 1982; Ravenscraft 1983). The question remains: is the observed relationship spurious or causal? If it is spurious, then the unremitting pursuit of market share—as implied by portfolio planning—may not raise ROI.

Using the same PIMS data that established the market share-ROI relationship and analysis techniques that controlled for the effects of unobservable factors (as signaled by serial correlation), studies by David Aaker and Robert Jacobson show the relationship to be spurious (Jacobson 1988; Jacobson and Aaker 1985). Indeed, "a reduced form representation of profitability produces estimated coefficients for market share that are indistinguishable from zero" (Jacobson 1988, p. 77). In short, portfolio planning approaches failed in part because the fundamental proposition underlying such analyses is false: market share and ROI are correlated positively because both are caused by some other factor(s)—not because increases in market share cause increases in ROI.

Of course, the criticisms of formal strategic planning do not imply that firms do not have strategies or that strategic decisions need not be made. Nor do they imply that at least some kinds of systematic planning might not be useful at times. The necessity of strategy and the pursuit of a sustainable competitive advantage, therefore, prompt our second question: should external factors or internal factors be the focus of strategy? Industry-based theory suggests that external factors are key.

4.1.2 Industry-Based Theory

As discussed in Section 3.1.3, mainstream economics did not adopt the "quasi-Austrian" Chamberlin. Instead, it incorporated the view that product differentiation leads to higher prices, lower quantities, excess capacity, inferior products, and the exploitation of the factors of production. Similarly, as discussed in Section 3.1, it did not adopt the dynamic, differential advantage theory of competition. Instead, mainstream economics stood steadfastly with equilibrium theory. Indeed, at the very conference in which Clark (1954) was arguing for dynamic theory and Chamberlin (1954) was maintaining that no simple index could possibly measure the degree of monopoly or "imperfection" in an industry, Bain (1954) was arguing that the four-firm concentration ratio is an index that effectively measures the monopoly power in an industry. Furthermore, he was arguing that product differentiation and scale economies constituted barriers to entry and, therefore, Chamberlin's conclusion that monopoly profits would be competed away was unfounded. For Bain (1954):

> A small margin of long-run excess profit coupled with "a little monopoly" may be a reasonable price to pay for diminishing the force and effectiveness of pressures for State-sponsored cartelization. But the limits of "a little monopoly" should be carefully drawn. (p. 240)

Bain's (1956, 1968) books, when joined with the works of Mason (1939), formed the basis of industrial-organization economics ("IO") and its SCP model, which maintains that industry *S*tructure determines *C*onduct, which determines *P*erformance. Because barriers to entry enable firms in concentrated industries to collude, superior financial performance results from collusion and the exercise of monopoly power in concentrated industries. For IO theory, public policy should be aimed at decreasing the monopoly element in concentrated industries by restricting mergers, breaking up large corporations, and reducing barriers to entry.

The industry-based theory of strategy, as exemplified by Porter (1980, 1985), turns IO economics "upside down" (Barney and Ouchi 1986, p. 374). If superior financial performance results primarily from industry factors, choosing the industries in which to compete and/or altering the structure of chosen industries to increase monopoly power should be the focus of strategy:

> Present research [i.e., Schmalensee (1985)] continues to affirm the important role industry conditions play in the performance of individual firms. Seeking to explain performance differences across firms, recent studies have repeatedly shown that average industry profitability is, by far, the most significant predictor of firm performance. . . . In short, it is now uncontestable that industry analysis should play a vital role in strategy formation. (Montgomery and Porter 1991, pp. xiv-xv)

Porter's (1980) "five forces" framework maintains that the profitability of a firm in an industry is determined by (1) the threat of new entrants to the industry, (2) the threat of substitute products or services, (3) the bargaining power of its suppliers, (4) the bargaining power of its customers, and (5) the intensity of rivalry amongst its existing competitors. These forces—the first two, as previously discussed, being those addressed by Chamberlain (1933)—constitute industry competition, which "continually works to drive down the rate of return on invested capital toward the competitive floor rate of return, or the return that would be earned by the economist's 'perfectly competitive' industry" (Porter 1980, p. 5). "Because, however, a firm is not a prisoner of its industry's structure" (p. 7), strategy should aim at altering industry structure by raising barriers to entry and increasing one's bargaining power over suppliers and customers.

After choosing industries and/or altering their structure, Porter (1980) advocates choosing one of three "generic" strategies: (1) cost leadership, (2) differentiation, or (3) focus. That is, superior performance can result from a competitive advantage brought about by a firm, relative to others in its industry, having a lower cost position, having its offering being perceived industrywide as unique, or having a focus on one particular market segment and developing a market offering specifically tailored to it. Although it is possible to pursue successfully more than one strategy at a time (and the rewards are great for doing so), "usually a firm must make a choice among them, or it will become stuck in the middle" (Porter 1985, p. 17).

Argues Porter (1985), only after the firm chooses one of the three generic strategies do internal factors come into play. Specifically, he argues that the firm should implement its strategy by managing well the activities in its "value chain." Indeed, "[t]he basic unit of competitive advantage . . . is the discrete activity" (1991, p. 102). If value is defined as "what buyers are willing to pay," then "superior value stems from offering lower prices than competitors for equivalent benefits or providing unique benefits that more than offset a higher price" (1985, p. 4).

For Porter (1985), activities in the firm's value chain are categorized as either primary or support. Primary activities include inbound logistics, operations, outbound logistics, marketing and sales, and service. Support activities include procurement, technology development (improvement of product and process), human resource management, and firm infrastructure (e.g., general management, planning, finance). Doing these activities well improves gross margin, promotes competitive advantage, and thereby produces superior financial performance.

Being masterfully crafted, filled with prescriptions for strategists, and based on a theory of competition that has guided public policy for decades, Porter's (1980, 1985) works have been very influential on business strategy. However, because (1) empirical studies show that highly concentrated industries are no more profitable than their less concentrated counterparts (Buzzell, Gale, and Sultan 1975; Gale and Branch 1982; Ravenscraft 1983), (2) other studies show that the industry market share-profitability relationship is spurious (Jacobson 1988; Jacobson and Aaker 1985), and (3) many industry-based prescriptions appear anti-competitive (Fried and Oviatt 1989; O'Keeffe, Mavondo, and Schroder 1996), many business strategy theorists have questioned the external focus of industry-based theory. In particular, those labeled "resource-based" theorists argue for the primacy of heterogeneous and imperfectly mobile resources.

4.1.3 Resource-Based Theory

For neoclassical theory, firm resources (labor and capital) are factors of production, and all resources are perfectly homogeneous and mobile. That is, each unit of labor and capital is identical with other units, and all units can move without restriction among firms within and across industries in the factor markets. Firms are viewed as combiners of homogeneous resources by means of a known, standardized production function.

In contrast, the fundamental thesis of resource-based theory is that resources (to varying degrees) are both significantly heterogeneous across firms and imperfectly mobile.[5] Resource heterogeneity means that each and every firm has an assortment of resources that is at least in some ways unique. Imperfectly mobile implies that firm resources, to varying degrees, are not commonly, easily, or readily bought and sold in the marketplace (the neoclassical factor markets). Because of resource immobility, resource heterogeneity can persist through time despite attempts by firms to acquire the same resources of particularly successful competitors.

As with the evolutionary theory of the firm (see Section 2.1.2), resource-based theory in business strategy traces to the long-neglected work of Penrose (1959). Consciously avoiding the term "factor of production" because of its ambiguity, she viewed the firm as a "collection of productive resources" and pointed out that "it is never *resources* themselves that are the 'inputs' to the production process, but only the *services* that the resources can render" (pp. 24-25; italics in original). Viewing resources as bundles of possible services that an entity can provide, she argues that it "is the heterogeneity . . . of the productive services available or potentially available from its resources that gives each firm its unique character" (pp. 75, 77). Therefore, contrasted with the neoclassical notion of an *optimum* size of firm, "the expansion of firms is largely based on opportunities to use their existing productive resources more efficiently than they are being used" (p. 88).

Works drawing on Penrose (1959) to explicate resource-based theory in business strategy include the seminal articles of Lippman and Rumelt (1982), Rumelt (1984), and Wernerfelt (1984) in the early 1980s. They were followed by the efforts of Dierickx and Cool (1989), Barney (1991, 1992), and Conner (1991) to further articulate the nature and foundations of the theory. Since then, tests, applications, and implications of resource-based theory have been developed by Barney and Hansen (1994); Black and Boal (1994); Brumagim (1994); Conner and Prahalad (1996); Collis (1991, 1994); Collis and Montgomery (1995); Foss (1997); Foss, Knudsen, and Montgomery (1995); Grant (1991); Lado and Wilson (1994); Madhok (1997); Mahoney and Pandian (1992); Mehra (1994); Miller and Shamsie (1996); Montgomery (1995); Peteraf (1993); Pringle and Kroll (1997); Schendel (1994); Schulze (1994); and Schoemaker and Amit (1994). Again, my review must be restricted to the theory's nature and foundations, as developed by Lippman and Rumelt (1982), Rumelt (1984), Wernerfelt (1984), Dierickx and Cool (1989), Barney (1991, 1992), and Conner (1991).

Lippman and Rumelt (1982) examine why some firms differ from their industry rivals in efficiency. For them, entrepreneurs produce new production functions that increase efficiency. However, "causal ambiguity"—how do they do that?—about production technologies often results in rivals finding it difficult to imitate their more efficient competitors. That is, abandoning the assumption of perfect information about production technologies, Lippman and Rumelt's uncertain imitability approach ascribes intra-industry efficiency differentials to the causal ambiguity inherent in many factors of production.

Rumelt (1984) extends the basic idea of uncertain imitability by positing that causal ambiguity is one of many "isolating mechanisms," others being specialized assets, team-embodied skills, patents, trademarks, and reputation. Introducing the concept of the "strategic firm," which he characterizes as a "bundle of linked and idiosyncratic resources and resource conversion activities" (p. 561), he adopts the Schumpeterian view that "[w]ithout resource heterogeneity (and the equivalent of property rights to unique resources), there is little incentive for investing in the risky exploration of new methods and the search for new value" (p. 561). Therefore, as to competition:

> Firms in the same industry compete with substantially different bundles of resources using disparate approaches. These firms differ because of differing histories of strategic choice and performance and because managements appear to seek asymmetric competitive positions. (p. 559)

Wernerfelt (1984) positions his resource-based view of the firm as complementing the external focus of the product portfolio approach. For him, resources are analogous to a firm's strengths and weaknesses and are "defined as (tangible and intangible) assets which are tied semi-permanently to the firms" (p. 172). Identifying brand names, employee skills, machinery, and trade contacts as examples, he asks: "Under what circumstances will a resource lead to high returns over longer periods of time?" (p. 172). His answer is that superior profitability results only when there is something about the resource that constitutes a barrier to rivals' attempts at resource acquisition, imitation, or substitution. Therefore, "firms need to find those resources which can sustain a resource position barrier" (p. 175).

Dierickx and Cool (1989) point out that firm resources can be usefully categorized into those that are tradable (e.g., unskilled labor, raw materials, and standard pieces of machinery) and nontradable (e.g., firm-specific skills, reputations for quality, dealer loyalty, R&D capability, brand loyalty, and customers' trust). Whereas tradable resources can be acquired quickly and easily in the factor markets (i.e., they are mobile), the "stocks" of nontradable resources must be developed, accumulated, and maintained through time (i.e., they are immobile). The resources critical for competitive advantage, they argue, are always those that are nontradable.

Dierickx and Cool (1989) then maintain that a sustainable competitive advantage is associated with five particular characteristics of nontradable resources: (1) time compression diseconomies, (2) asset mass efficiencies, (3) interconnectedness of asset stocks, (4) asset erosion, and (5) causal ambiguity. That is, critical resources providing a competitive advantage are less likely to be successfully and quickly imitated by rivals to the extent that (1) the time required to develop the resource cannot be easily compressed (e.g., "crash" R&D programs are typically less effective than lower annual expenditures that are spread out over a longer time), (2) adding increments to a stock of a resource is facilitated by having high levels of it (e.g., often "success breeds success" in areas such as advertising and channels of distribution), (3) adding new increments of a resource depends on having a complementary resource (e.g., getting distributors to carry a firm's product may require an existing service network), (4) the holder of the resource prevents asset stock decay through maintenance expenditures (e.g., an emphasis on training programs to maintain the skills of the sales force), and (5) the resource is causally ambiguous in the sense of Lippman and Rumelt (1982).

Barney (1986, 1991, 1992, 1995) explicates resource-based concepts and their interrelationships in greater detail than had hitherto been done. First, he defines firm resources to "include all assets, capabilities, organizational processes, firm attributes, information, knowledge, etc., controlled by a firm that enable the firm to conceive of and implement strategies that improve its efficiency and effectiveness" (1991, p. 101). (Note that his definition is very broad and focuses on an entity's ability to efficiently and/or effectively create value.) He points out that if all firms in an industry have homogeneous, perfectly mobile resources, then all firms will implement the same strategies equally well and no firm can have a competitive advantage. Therefore, only resources that are heterogeneous, imperfectly mobile, and asymmetrically distributed among rivals, that is, are *rare*, can generate competitive advantage and superior financial performance.

Second, Barney (1991) points out that heterogeneity and immobility alone do not guarantee a *sustained* competitive advantage. Sustainability occurs only when rivals find it difficult to both imitate the competitive advantage-producing resource and develop or acquire strategic substitutes for it. Imperfect imitability results from (1) unique historical circumstances (e.g., buying a piece of property that later provides a locational advantage), (2) causally ambiguous resources, and (3) socially complex resources.

Third, Barney (1992) describes socially complex resources as those "that enable an organization to conceive, choose, and implement strategies because of the values, beliefs, symbols, and interpersonal relationships possessed by individuals or groups in a firm" (p. 45). Examples include organizational culture, trust, reputation among customers, and managerial teamwork. As to physical technology, it is customarily imitable. However, the ability to exploit physical technology often involves socially complex phenomena, for example, social relations and/or a culture, that is imperfectly imitable. Hence the exploitation of physical technology can often sustain a competitive advantage. Barney (1991) concludes by introducing a social welfare issue:

> The resource-based model developed here suggests that, in fact, strategic management research can be perfectly consistent with traditional social welfare concerns of economists. Beginning with the assumptions that firm resources are heterogeneous and immobile, it follows that a firm that exploits its resource advantages is simply behaving in an efficient and effective manner. . . . To fail to exploit these resource advantages is inefficient and does not maximize social welfare. (p. 116)

Conner (1991) reviews resource-based theory and, after comparing it with five alternative theories of the firm, concludes: "the resource-based approach is reaching for a theory of the firm . . . [because it] both incorporates and rejects at least one central feature of each" (p. 143). Comparing resource-based theory with neoclassical theory, she finds resource-based theory to be similar in that it views firms as combiners of resources. It differs, however, from neoclassical theory in that many critical resources are viewed to be heterogeneous and imperfectly mobile. Furthermore, there is no "given" production algorithm. Rather, production technologies, which resource-based theory views as another kind of *resource,* must be discovered and/or created in the face of imperfect information.

For Conner (1991), compared with "Bain-type" IO, resource-based theory is similar in that both view persistent, above-normal returns to be possible. Resource-based theory differs, however, in that (1) restraints on output through monopolistic or collusive action or artificial entry barriers are not primary sources of superior performance, (2) the firm (not the industry) is the appropriate unit of analysis for understanding superior performance, and (3) industry structure does not *determine* firm behavior. Compared with Schumpeter (1950), resource-based theory is similar in that (1) superior performance can result from new ways of competing, (2) entrepreneurship is important, and (3) potential imitators always exist. Resource-based theory differs, however, in that (1) imitators are constrained by difficult-to-copy resources, and (2) superior performance can result from less than "revolutionary" innovations.

In comparing resource-based theory with "Chicago" theory, similarities are that both view firms as efficiency seekers and the size and scope of firms reflect the results of efficiency differences. In contrast, however, efficiency seeking in resource-based theory goes beyond current products to new products and technologies, that is, firms are also *effectiveness* seekers. Compared with the Coase/Williamson transaction cost approach, both view asset specificity and small numbers as important. Resource-based theory differs, however, in that it focuses on the acquisition, development, and deployment of firm-specific resources rather than on the avoidance of opportunism.[6]

As to why market economies have heterogeneous firms, Conner (1991) concludes: "In this view, multiple, heterogeneous firms can continue to exist because the assets with which they will come to be mated are themselves heterogeneous, each making a better fit with (more specific to) some firms than with others" (p. 139). As to the future of resource-based theory, she believes: "The contributions that resource-based theory and empirics ultimately will make depend to great measure on how the approach is operationalized" (p. 145).

4.1.4 Competence-Based Theory

A second "internal factors" theory of business strategy is competence-based theory. The term "distinctive competence" traces to Selznick (1957) and was used by Andrews (1971) and his colleagues in the SWOT model to refer to what an organization could do particularly well, relative to its competitors. However, with the emphasis on formal strategic planning and portfolio analysis in the 1960s and 1970s and on external (industry) factors in the 1980s, attention to what individual firms could do particularly well—or even acceptably—languished. (Notable exceptions include Hofer and Schendel's [1978] discussion of competences as patterns of resource and skill deployment and the empirical works of Snow and Hrebiniak [1980] and Hitt and Ireland [1985, 1986] on activities within functional areas as sources of competence.)

Stimulating the development of competence-based theory in the early 1990s were the works of Chandler (1990); Hamel and Prahalad (1989, 1994a,b); Prahalad and Hamel (1990, 1993); Reed and DeFillippi (1990); Lado, Boyd, and Wright (1992); and Teece and Pisano (1994). Numerous theoretical and empirical articles have been developing competence-based theory in a systematic manner (Aaker 1995; Bharadwaj, Varadarajan, and Fahy 1993; Day and Nedungadi 1994; Hamel and Heene 1994; Heene and Sanchez 1996; Kay 1995; Sanchez and Heene 1997; Sanchez, Heene, and Thomas 1996).[7]

Chandler (1990) traces the historical development of the modern industrial enterprise by contrasting the development of what he labels *competitive managerial capitalism* in the United States with *personal capitalism* in Great Britain and *cooperative managerial capitalism* in Germany. He points out that for the period of 1880 to 1948, industries that were perfectly competitive were not the ones that prompted economic growth. Rather, "the industries spearheading American economic growth were those dominated by a small number of managerial enterprises" (p. 226). The key to understanding the large, managerial enterprise, he argues, is the concept of "organizational capabilities," which encompasses "the physical facilities in each of the many operating units—the factories offices, laboratories—and the skills of the employees working in such units" (p. 595). It is organizational capabilities that make the whole firm more productive than the sum of its operating units (p. 15). These organizational capabilities, which had to be created and maintained, "provided the source—the dynamic—for the continuing growth of the enterprise" (p. 594). Indeed, the creation and maintenance of firm capabilities are key for understanding the wealth of both firms and nations: "Because of these capabilities, the basic goal of the modern industrial enterprise became long-term profits based on long-term growth—growth that increased the productivity, and so the competitive power, that drove the expansion of industrial capitalism" (p. 594).

Paralleling the work of Chandler (1990), Hamel and Prahalad (1989) take a retrospective look at the field of business strategy and find that theories of strategy based on static assumptions, existing resources, industry and portfolio analyses, and formal planning have ill-served strategic management. Indeed, "the application of concepts such as 'strategic fit' (between resources and opportunities), 'generic strategies' (low cost vs. differentiation vs. focus), and the 'strategy hierarchy' (goals, strategies, and tactics) have often abetted the process of competitive decline" (p. 63). Business schools have also contributed to corporate decline "because they have perpetuated the notion that a manager with net present value calculations in one hand and portfolio planning in the other can manage any business anywhere" (p. 74). For Hamel and Prahalad, the "essence of strategy lies in creating tomorrow's competitive advantages faster than competitors mimic the ones you possess today," which implies investing in core competences because "an organization's capacity to improve existing skills and learn new ones is the most defensible competitive advantage of all." (p. 69).

Prahalad and Hamel (1990) argue that "the firm" should be viewed as both a collection of products or SBUs and a collection of competences because "in the long run, competitiveness derives from an ability to build, at lower cost and more speedily than competitors, the core competencies that spawn unanticipated products" (p. 81). For a competence to be *core,* they argue, it should (1) provide access to a wide variety of markets, (2) make a significant contribution to customers' perceptions of benefits, and (3) be difficult for rivals to imitate. It is from core competences that both core products and ultimate, end products emerge. Because core competences, unlike physical assets, do not deteriorate with use but are enhanced as they are applied and shared, top management should foster strategic innovations and growth by sending a message to middle managers: "the people critical to core competencies are corporate assets to be deployed by corporate management" (p. 90).

Reed and DeFillippi (1990) draw on Lippman and Rumelt's (1982) uncertain imitability approach to connect competences with sustained competitive advantage. Firm competences that result in competitive advantage, they argue, are often sustainable because they are kinds of "routines" (Nelson and Winter 1982) that are causally ambiguous. The causal ambiguity of competences stems from their tacitness, complexity, and specificity. Competences are tacit to the extent that they are uncodified and involve learning by doing that is accumulated by experience (Polanyi 1966). Indeed, some competences may "in-

volve so much idiosyncratic and 'impacted' tacit knowledge that even successful replication is problematic, let alone imitated from a distance" (Nelson and
Winter 1982, p. 124). Competences are complex when they involve a large
number of different technologies, skills, and routines. They are specific when
they are "durable investments that are undertaken in support of particular
transactions" (Williamson 1985, p. 55). Therefore, firms that have a competitive advantage resulting from tacit, complex, asset-specific, causally ambiguous competences should reinvest in them to protect their sustainability.

Lado, Boyd, and Wright (1992) build on Reed and DeFillippi (1990) by
pointing out that competence-based theory is a logical extension of resource-
based theory.[8] Managerial competences and strategic focus, they argue, lead to
the development of resource-based, output-based, and transformation-based
competences. These competences "do not merely 'accrue' to the firm (from a
good 'fit' with industry/environmental requirements), but may consciously
and systematically be developed by the willful choices and actions of the firm's
strategic leaders" (p. 78). Therefore, "achieving and sustaining a competitive advantage position requires that managers focus on developing and nurturing their
firms' idiosyncratic competencies that inhibit imitability" (p. 88).

Teece and Pisano (1994) further identify the specific kinds of competences
that create competitive advantage. Viewing competition in Schumpeterian
terms, they note that the accelerated pace of innovation and other environmental change requires firms to respond rapidly to its environment and also to
shape the direction of environmental change. Therefore, they stress the importance of "dynamic capabilities," which they define as "the subset of the compe-
tences/capabilities which allow the firm to create new products and processes,
and respond to changing market circumstances." They argue that a firm should
develop its strategy by taking into close account its "managerial and organizational processes, its present position, and the paths available to it" (p. 541). By
"position," they refer to the firm's "current endowment of technology and intellectual property, as well as its customer base and upstream relations with
suppliers . . . [and] its strategic alliances with competitors" (p. 541). For them,
"the competitive advantage of firms stems from dynamic capabilities rooted in
high performance routines operating inside the firm, embedded in the firm's
processes, and conditioned by its history" (p. 537).

Hamel and Prahalad (1994a,b) further develop and integrate their previous
works on competence-based theory by stressing its dynamic aspects and the
importance of industry foresight and resource leveraging. By the early 1990s,
most theorists in business strategy were acknowledging that resource-based
theory and competence-based theory were complementary. Indeed, as one of
their "starting premises," Hamel and Prahalad (1994a) state:

> The first premise is that the firm can be conceived of as a portfolio of resources (technical, financial, human, and so forth), as well as a portfolio of products or market-focused business units. A growing body of academic research and writing takes such a "resource-based view of the firm." (p. 157)

For Hamel and Prahalad (1994a), business strategy is not about finding a good fit between existing resources (competences) and existing opportunities; it focuses on industry foresight and competence leveraging. *Foresight* involves anticipating the future by asking what new types of benefits firms should provide their customers in the next five to fifteen years and what new competences should be acquired or built to offer such benefits. *Resource leveraging* focuses on the numerator in the productivity equation. Specifically, they argue that too much attention in analyses of firm productivity has been devoted to resource efficiency—the denominator—and too little on resource effectiveness—the numerator. For them, productivity gains and competitive advantage come through the resource leveraging that results from "more effectively concentrating resources on key strategic goals, . . . more efficiently accumulating resources, . . . complementing resources of one type with those of another to create higher-order value, . . . conserving resources wherever possible, and . . . rapidly recovering resources by minimizing the time between expenditure and payback" (p. 160).

The works of Hamel and Heene (1994), Sanchez, Heene, and Thomas (1996), and Heene and Sanchez (1996) further develop the formal requirements of competence-based theory. My review focuses on their explications of (1) terminological issues, (2) firms as goal-seeking, open systems, and (3) competitive dynamics.

As to terminology, competence-based theory has begun the important task of developing a conceptionally adequate, internally consistent language for discussing strategy, the firm, and competition. It defines (1) assets as anything tangible or intangible the firm can use in its processes for creating, producing, and/or offering its products (goods or services) to a market; (2) capabilities as repeatable patterns of action in the use of assets to create, produce, and/or offer products to a market; (3) resources as assets that are available and useful in detecting and responding to market opportunities or threats; (4) a competence as an ability to sustain the coordinated deployment of assets in a way that helps a firm achieve its goals; (5) competence building as any process by which a firm achieves qualitative changes to its existing stocks of assets and capabilities, including new abilities to coordinate and deploy new or existing assets and capabilities in ways that help the firm achieve its goals; and (6) competence leveraging as a firm applying its existing competences to current or new market opportunities in ways that do not require qualitative changes in the firm's assets or capabilities (Sanchez, Heene, and Thomas 1996, pp. 7-8).

Heene and Sanchez (1996) caution that "a firm must manage its competence(s) as a system and avoid excessive focusing of managerial attention on developing and managing a 'single competence' judged by some criteria to be 'core' " (p. 11). Furthermore, even though competence-based theory recognizes that "strictly speaking, capabilities are included in the term assets, it speaks of 'assets and capabilities' because capabilities are such an important category of assets" (Sanchez, Heene, and Thomas 1996, p. 7).

As to the firm's goals, competence-based theory views firms as having complex sets of strategic goals that must be managed holistically (Heene and Sanchez 1996). As such, the firm is a goal-seeking, open system of interrelated tangible and intangible assets guided by a strategic logic. A firm's strategic logic "refers to the rationale(s) employed (explicitly or implicitly) by decision makers in the firm as to how specific deployments of resources are expected to result in an acceptable level of attainment of the firm's goals" (Sanchez, Heene, and Thomas 1996, p. 10). Management processes, therefore, include all the activities designed to carry out the strategic logic. For competence-based theory, a key management task is "maintaining the effectiveness of the firm's competence building and leveraging processes by achieving consistency of strategic logic throughout the firm" (p. 10).

As to competitive dynamics, competence-based theory acknowledges that firms may at times find themselves in a steady-state environment. More typical, however, is the dynamic state where "managers in at least one firm change their assessments of the gap between the perceived and desired states of one or more system elements, modify the firm's goals, and begin to take gap-closing actions" (Sanchez, Heene, and Thomas 1996, p. 13). At such times of dynamic competition, "the interactions of firms that create dynamic competitive environments as they seek goal attainment through leveraging and building competences may therefore be likened to a state of perpetual corporate entrepreneurialism in which continuous learning about how to build new competences and leverage existing competences more effectively becomes a new dominant logic" (p. 14).

4.1.5 Business Strategy and R-A Theory

Resource-advantage theory draws extensively on and shares many affinities with the business strategy literature. First, R-A theory shares with industry-based theory the view that the firm's objective is superior financial performance and that the proximate cause of superior financial performance is market-place position. For R-A theory (see Figures 6.1 and 6.2), superior (parity, inferior) financial performance results from marketplace positions of competitive advantage (parity, disadvantage).

Second, R-A theory agrees that a "stress on resources must complement, not substitute for, stress on market positions" (Porter 1991, p. 108). Indeed, R-A theory integrates the marketplace position view with the resource view by positing that it is a comparative advantage (disadvantage) in resources that results in marketplace positions of competitive advantage (disadvantage) and superior (inferior) financial performance. Therefore, R-A theory provides an explanation for Porter's (1991) claim that some firms are superior to others in performing value-chain activities: such superior-performing firms have a comparative advantage in resources, for example, specific competences related to specific value-producing activities.

Third, R-A theory agrees that competitors, suppliers, and customers influence the process of competition and firm performance (see Figure 6.1). However, it disagrees with "Bain-type" IO that industry structure *entirely* determines performance. Indeed, it further disagrees with industry-based strategy that "industry" is the *major* determinant of performance. As discussed in Section 6.3, the empirical evidence is clear: Idiosyncratic firm factors, not industry factors, explain most of the variance in firm performance. Industry is the "tail" of competition; the firm is the "dog."

Resource-Based Theory. As to affinities between R-A theory and resource-based theory, R-A theory specifically adopts a resource-based view of the firm.[9] Defining resources as the tangible and intangible entities available to the firm that enable it to produce efficiently and/or effectively a market offering that has value for some market segment(s), R-A theory views firms as combiners of heterogeneous, imperfectly mobile resources that are historically situated in space and time. The premise that firms combine heterogeneous resources contributes to R-A theory's ability to explain firm diversity in size, scope, and financial performance (see Section 6.3). The premise that many firm resources are imperfectly mobile (i.e., not readily available for acquisition in the factor markets) contributes to R-A theory's ability to explain how some firms can have sustained, superior financial performance despite the efforts of rivals. Specifically, rivals will fail (or take a long time to succeed) to acquire, imitate, or find substitutes for a competitor's advantage-producing resource when either it is protected by such societal institutions as patents or it is causally ambiguous, socially complex, highly interconnected or tacit or has time compression diseconomies or mass efficiencies.

As a second affinity, both resource-based theory and R-A theory draw on the historical tradition (Chandler 1990) and view firms and their resources as historically situated entities. Indeed, historical "accidents" and luck can contribute to explaining firm performance. For example, a retailer's location may become valuable because, long after the site is chosen, a freeway is built adjacent to it. Therefore, "the firm" in R-A theory is not a mathematical abstraction to which the mathematics of calculus can be applied. Nonetheless, R-A theory is argued to be a general theory of competition that incorporates the production function, mathematical abstraction of the firm in neoclassical theory as a special case. Therefore, R-A theory shows when the production-function view of the firm will predict well (see Section 10.1).

However, as extensively discussed by Schulze (1994), many resource-based theorists view competition as an equilibrium-seeking process. Indeed, firms are often described as seeking "abnormal profits" or "economic rents," which in the neoclassical tradition imply "profits different from that of a firm in an industry characterized by perfect competition" and "profits in excess of the minimum necessary to keep a firm in business in long-run competitive equilibrium." Thus, because perfect competition is posited as ideal, that is, it is *perfect,* viewing competition as equilibrium seeking and the goal of the firm as *abnormal* profits or *rents* implies that the achievement of sustained, superior financial performance by firms is detrimental to social welfare.

In contrast, R-A theory denies that competition is equilibrium seeking and that perfect competition is an ideal form. Competition, for R-A theory, is the disequilibrating, ongoing process that consists of the constant struggle among firms for a comparative advantage in resources that will yield marketplace positions of competitive advantage and, thereby, superior financial performance. The achievement of superior financial performance—both temporary and sustained—is pro-competitive when it is consistent with and furthers the disequilibrating, ongoing process that consists of the constant struggle among firms for comparative advantages in resources that will yield marketplace positions of competitive advantage and, thereby, superior financial performance. It is anticompetitive when it is inconsistent with and thwarts this process. Therefore, R-A theory maintains that when superior financial performance results from pro-competitive ("pro" in the sense of R-A theory) factors, it contributes to social welfare because the dynamic process of R-A competition furthers productivity and economic growth through both the efficient allocation of scarce tangible resources and, more important, the creation of new tangible and intangible resources.

Specifically, the ongoing quest for superior financial performance, coupled with the fact that all firms cannot be simultaneously superior, implies not only that the process of R-A competition will allocate resources in an efficient manner but also that there will be (as discussed later in this section) both proactive and reactive innovations developed that will contribute to further increases in efficiency and effectiveness. Indeed, it is the process of R-A competition that provides an important mechanism for firms to learn how efficient-effective, inefficient-ineffective, they are (see Section 6.1.4). Similarly, it is the quest for superior performance by firms that results in the proactive and reactive innovations that, in turn, promote the very increases in firm productivity that constitute the technological progress that results in economic growth. Both empirical works on economic growth and works on endogenous growth models support the view that it is technological progress, not changes in the capital/labor ratio, that accounts for most economic growth (see Chapter 8). Therefore, "pure competition may no longer be regarded as in any sense 'ideal' for purposed of welfare economics" (Chamberlin 1933/1962, p. 214).

Competence-Based Theory. First, R-A theory agrees with competence-based theory that competition is fundamentally dynamic, that is, disequilibrium-provoking. For R-A theory, the quest for *superior* financial performance (i.e., *more* than, *better* than) is the major driver of dynamism in R-A competition. Because all rivals cannot be simultaneously superior, competition stimulates the proactive and reactive innovations that ensure dynamism. Proactive innovation is innovation by firms that, though motivated by the expectation of superior financial performance, is not prompted by specific pressures from specific competitors. As such, it is genuinely entrepreneurial in the classic sense of "entrepreneur," that is, in the sense of spotting new opportunities and subsequently developing market offerings (Kirzner 1979).

Central to proactive innovation in R-A theory is the role of *renewal* competences, such as those described by Teece and Pisano (1994) and Teece, Pisano, and Shuen (1997) as "dynamic capabilities," by Dickson (1996) as "learning how to learn," and by Hamel and Prahalad (1994a) as "industry foresight." Renewal competences prompt proactive innovation by enabling firms to (1) anticipate potential market segments (unmet; changing; and/or new needs, wants, and desires); (2) envision market offerings that might be attractive to such segments; and (3) foresee the need to acquire, develop, or create the required resources, including competences, to produce the envisioned market offerings. Therefore, firms are not viewed by R-A theory as just passively responding to a changing environment or looking for the best "fit" between existing resources and market "niches." Rather, firms are often proactive toward their environment.

Contrasted with proactive innovation, reactive innovation is directly prompted by the learning process of firms competing for the patronage of specific market segment(s). Firms learn through competing as a result of the feedback from relative financial performance signaling relative marketplace position, which in turn signals relative resources (see Figure 6.1). When firms competing for a market segment learn from their inferior financial performance that they occupy positions of competitive disadvantage (cells 4, 7, and 8 in Figure 6.2), the goal of superior performance motivates them to attempt to neutralize and/or leapfrog the advantaged firm (or firms) by acquiring the resource and/or reactive innovation.

Reactive innovation includes imitating the resource, finding (creating) an equivalent resource, or finding (creating) a superior resource. Resource-based theory has tended to focus on resource imitation and substitution. Although imitation and substitution are important forms of competitive actions, R-A theory recognizes that reactive innovation can also prompt disequilibrium-provoking behaviors. That is, reactive innovation in the form of finding (creating) a superior resource results in the innovating firm's new resource assortment enabling it to surpass the previously advantaged competitor in relative efficiency, relative value, or both. By leapfrogging competitors, firms realize their objective of superior returns, make competition dynamic, and shape their environments.

Second, R-A theory agrees with competence-based theory that firms learn. For competence-based theory, because organizational knowledge is fundamental to organizational competence, a key question is *how* organizations learn (Sanchez and Heene 1997). Defining organizational knowledge as "the shared set of beliefs about causal relationships held by individuals within a group," competence-based theory views organizational learning as the "flows that lead to a change in the stocks of beliefs within the organization" (p. 6). Therefore, "strategically important organizational learning consists both of the process for creating new knowledge within individuals and groups within a firm . . . and processes to leverage knowledge effectively within and across organizations" (p. 8).

Similarly, R-A theory recognizes that firms learn in many ways, for example, by conducting formal marketing research, dissecting competitors' products, "benchmarking," competitive intelligence, and test marketing. What R-A theory emphasizes is how the process of competition itself contributes to organizational learning: firms learn by competing as a result of feedback from relative financial performance signaling relative marketplace position, which in turn signals relative resources (see Figure 6.1). Through competition, firms come to *know* (or believe that they know) their relative resources and marketplace positions. Although firms can investigate their relative marketplace positions and resources through specific research projects, because neither the construct "relative market position" nor "relative resources" is directly observable, each must be inferred from other indicators (e.g., from the relative prices that a particular marketing offering commands and from estimates of relative costs).

Third, competence-based theory notes that much of strategy research is reductionist in nature, that is, it attempts to "explain firm performance in terms of the constituent parts of the firm (e.g., its resource endowments)" (Sanchez, Heene, and Thomas 1996, p. 32). But economic actors, their firms and economic systems, as Granovetter (1985) has argued, are embedded in a larger complex of social relations and societal structures. Therefore, competence theorists advocate a "macro organizational systems" approach that would seek "to explain firms and firm behaviors in terms of the larger system context which firms inhabit and which shape firm composition and actions" (Sanchez, Heene, and Thomas 1996, p. 32).

Similarly, R-A theory rejects both the atomized, undersocialized conception of human action in neoclassical economics and the *over* socialized view found in many sociological works. Instead, R-A theory is a moderately socialized, embedded, or *socio*economic theory of competition. That is, R-A theory takes seriously the view that societal resources, societal institutions, competitors, suppliers, consumers, and public policy shape—but do not *determine*—firms and firm actions and, thereby, influence how well the process of competition works. The issue of embeddedness is discussed in more detail in Section 4.2.3.

4.2 INSTITUTIONAL THEORY

As Powell and DiMaggio (1991) point out, the "study of institutions is experiencing a renaissance throughout the social sciences" (p. 2). In economics, organization theory, political science, history, and sociology, scholars are arguing that institutional arrangements, social structure, and social processes matter. Although the term "institution" is variously defined across (and within) disciplines, and it is often used loosely as synonymous with "convention," Powell and DiMaggio argue that only patterns of interaction that have *rulelike* status should be called *institutions*.

For example, Nobel laureate Douglass North (1990) defines institutions as "the humanly devised constraints that shape human interaction" (p. 3). He distinguishes formal institutions (constitutional law, statutory law, and common law) from informal institutions (cultural constraints, such as customs, traditions, and codes of conduct), and he distinguishes institutions (the rules of the game) from organizations (major players of the game). As a second example, Scott (1995) defines institutions as the "cognitive, normative, and regulative structures and activities that provide stability and meaning to social behavior" (p. 33). He argues that cognitive institutions (e.g., the generalized belief that conglomerates represent efficient organizational forms) are legitimated by culture; normative institutions (e.g., the generalized belief that one should consider the interests of multiple stakeholders in decision making) are legitimated by moral codes; and regulative institutions (e.g., the generalized belief that one should not collude to fix prices) are legitimated by law.

As a third example, Schotter (1981) defines a social "institution as a regularity in social behavior that is agreed to by all members of society, specifies behavior in specific recurrent situations, and is either self-policed or policed by some external authority" (p. 11). He argues that game theory can explain the rise of many social institutions. As a fourth example, Neale (1987) develops what he argues to be an "operational" definition:

> An *institution* is identified by three characteristics. First, there are a number of *people doing.* Second, there are *rules* giving the activities repetition, stability, predictable order. Third, there are *folkviews* . . . explaining or justifying the activities and the rules. (p. 1182)

Note that, even though the various definitions differ, they share the "rulelike" commonality. My review of approaches to the study of these rulelike entities will focus on three traditions: institutional economics, transaction cost economics, and economic sociology. Again, I review only those aspects that are relevant to R-A theory and point readers toward more comprehensive reviews.

4.2.1 Institutional Economics

Institutional economics traces to the turn-of-the-century scholars John R. Commons (1862-1949) and Thorstein Veblen (1857-1929).[10] Both Commons (1924, 1934) and Veblen (1899, 1904, 1914, 1919) opposed not only the mathematization of economics but also the developing neoclassical view that (1) human behavior is utility maximizing, (2) individuals are the only appropriate unit of analysis for economics, and (3) competition is equilibrating. For example, Veblen (1919) caricatured the neoclassical *homo economicus:*

> The hedonistic conception of man is that of a lightning calculator of pleasures and pains, who oscillates like a homogeneous globule of desire of happiness under the impulse of stimuli that shift him about the area, but leave him intact. He has neither antecedent nor consequent. He is an isolated, definitive human datum, in stable equilibrium except for the buffets of the impinging forces that displace him in one direction or another. Self-imposed in elemental space, he spins symmetrically about his own spiritual axis until the parallelogram of forces bears down upon him, whereupon he follows the line of the resultant. When the force of the impact is spent, he comes to rest, a self-contained globule of desire as before. Spiritually, the hedonistic man is not a prime mover. (p. 73)

Of course, as the "hard core" of mainstream economics solidified around the mathematics of static equilibrium, the twentieth century saw—as it did the "Austrian" school—the marginalization of the school of thought that came to be associated with Commons and Veblen. When institutionalist works were no longer acceptable in mainstream economics journals, economists in the tradition of Commons and Veblen formed their own association, the Association for Evolutionary Economics, and their own journal, the *Journal of Economic Issues* (Hodgson 1994). Many economists "gravitated to the institutionalist camp," chronicles Hodgson, because of "the mistaken and far too unqualified ideological association of mainstream economics with free-market policies" (p. 59).[11]

For institutional economists, an institution is "a way of thought or action of some prevalence and permanence, which is embedded in the habits of a group or the customs of a people. . . . Institutions fix the confines of and impose form upon the activities of human beings" (Hamilton 1932, p. 84). As Commons (1934) succinctly put it, "we may define an institution as Collective Action in Control of Individual Action" (p. 69). Therefore, institutions both constrain and license behavior by indicating what "individuals *must* or *must not* do (compulsion or duty), what they may do without interference from other individuals (permission or liberty), what they *can* do with the aid of collective power (capacity or right) and what they *cannot* expect the collective power to do in their behalf (incapacity or exposure)" (Commons 1924/1968, p. 6; italics in original).

Institutions are external to individuals, shape or guide their behavior, and have some permanence. But institutions, for institutional economics, are neither immutable nor always "instrumental" or functional. Because institutions evolve through time—hence, the Association for *Evolutionary* Economics—some previously instrumental institutions become "archaic" or largely "ceremonial" (Mayhew 1987). Furthermore, institutionalists adopt an "open systems" view (Kapp 1976) and subscribe to the instrumental theory of valuing: "valuing emerges [not in unanalyzable tastes but] in the process of trying to solve problems" (Neale 1987, p. 1197). Institutionalists have developed distinctive approaches to evolutionary theory, economic systems, the nature of capital, the nature of resources, and the value of interdisciplinary research.

As to evolutionary theory, institutional economists have followed Veblen in viewing (1) institutions, (2) certain positive human instincts (e.g., parental bent, idle curiosity, and workmanship), and (3) certain negative instincts (e.g., predation and the propensity for emulation) as analogous to genes in biology. As such, they are posited to explain certain economic behaviors. For example, the instinct of idle curiosity and the playful inventiveness it fosters are posited to contribute to producing the innovations that constitute technological change (Hodgson 1994).

As to economic systems, static equilibrium plays no significant role in institutional economics. For Veblen (1919), the economic system is not a "self-balancing mechanism" but a "cumulatively unfolding process." For him, "the economic life history of individuals is a cumulative process of adaptation of means to ends that cumulatively change as the process goes on, both the agent and his environment being at any point the outcome of the last process" (pp. 74-75). Indeed, he forecasted optimistically (at least for economics) that "modern science is becoming substantially a theory of the process of consecutive change, realized to be self-continuing or self-propagating and to have no final term" (p. 37).

As to the nature of capital, institutionalists decry the tendency of neoclassical theory to equate "capital" with, and *only* with, tangible, physical resources. Tracing his views to Veblen's (1919) argument that physical resources have no "autonomous productive potency," Ranson (1987) argues that "the productivity of capital goods (Veblen's 'material equipment of industry') depends crucially on the level of technology (Veblen's 'immaterial equipment of industry, especially as embodied in skilled workers')" (pp. 1267-68). Therefore, "the institutionalist theory of capital formation asserts that a community accumulates the agents possessing productive potency by all activities that raise its level of technology and its effectiveness in coordinating behaviors that apply technology" (p. 1271).

As to the nature of resources, DeGregori's (1987) institutionalist theory of resources maintains: "Resources are not things or stuff or materials; they are a set of capabilities. These capabilities use the stuff of the material and the non-material universe in a life-sustaining manner" (p. 1243). He argues against the view that resources are "natural" and "given"; rather, they are created by humans. Indeed, "the term 'resources' essentially has no meaning apart from a relationship to human beings" (p. 1242). Because resources are not fixed or finite, DeGregori argues that historical concerns about resource depletion are misguided. Contrasting the institutional approach with "the idea of scarcity, which some conceive to be fundamental organizing principle economics" (p. 1259), he concludes: "The liberating idea of technology and resource creation is the human potential that is there, if we are aware of it and if we frame our policies accordingly" (p. 1260). (Note how similar the institutionalist view of resources is to that of Hayek and the "Austrians"—see Section 2.2.4.)

As to ideas from other disciplines, institutional economists view their research tradition as more open than mainstream economics. Indeed, they encourage an interdisciplinary approach to theory development. For example, Adams (1992) describes himself as a "paleoinstitutionalist" and discusses the remarkable similarity between certain views of the institutionalist Karl Polanyi and the neoclassicist Ronald Coase. He concludes his analysis with:

> When the corporation is construed as a complex, multimodal nonmarket exchange system, combining workers, technicians, and managers in a common enterprise, then there is a large research agenda ahead for paleoinstitutionalists. My guess is that as it matures, there will be considerable overlap with work being done on the frontiers of industrial economics and organizational theory. (p. 405)

As R-A theory attests, Adams was correct in his forecast.

4.2.2 Transaction Cost Economics

Williamson (1975, 1981a,b, 1983, 1985, 1989, 1994, 1996), with whom transaction cost economics is most closely associated, uses "new" institutional economics as a label to distinguish his work from the "old" institutional approach that he associates with Commons and Veblen.[12] Transaction cost economics, one of the major, social science success stories in the last three decades, is proof-positive that an interdisciplinary research program can succeed. It draws on, shares affinities with, economics, law, and organization theory. However, "economics is first among equals" (Williamson 1996, p. 3).[13]

Transaction cost economics traces to the famous article of Nobel laureate Coase (1937), in which he pointed out that firms can avoid both search and contract negotiation costs by producing some of their own production inputs. Therefore, he maintained, each firm expands its operations until the marginal cost of producing an input in-house equals the market price of that input. Indeed, his extension of perfect competition explains not only the existence of large firms on the basis of minimizing the costs associated with market exchange but the existence of small firms as well. That is, individuals band together under the direction of an entrepreneur to purchase inputs and jointly produce an output because, compared with each individual acting alone, "certain marketing costs are saved" (Coase 1937/1952, p. 338).

Extending Coase's ideas, Williamson (1981b) believes that "the modern corporation is mainly to be understood as the product of a series of organizational innovations that have the purpose and effect of economizing on transaction costs" (p. 1537). That is, the "main case" of transaction cost economics is that "economizing on transaction costs is mainly responsible for the choice of one form of capitalist organization over another" (1996, p. 233). Such costs include all the "negotiation, monitoring, and enforcement costs necessary to assure that contracted goods and services between and within firms are forthcoming" (Alston and Gillespie 1989, p. 193). A key task, therefore, of transaction cost economics is to identify circumstances where a firm's avoidance of marketplace transaction costs are absolutely essential.

For transaction cost economics, a transaction occurs when a good or service crosses a technologically separable interface. Thus, there are three primary institutions or "governance mechanisms" through which transactions take place: markets, hierarchies, and hybrids. All three modes have transaction costs, that is, the "*ex ante* costs of drafting, negotiating, and *safeguarding* an agreement [to transact] and, more especially, the *ex post* costs of maladaptation and adjustment that arise when contract execution is misaligned as a result of gaps, errors, omissions, and unanticipated disturbances" (Williamson 1994, p. 103; italics in original). When transaction costs are high, hierarchies and hybrids become efficient. When such costs are low, autonomous, arms-length, market governance predominates.

Hierarchies, that is, *firms,* are characterized by "unified ownership (buyer and supplier are within the same enterprise) and subject to administrative controls (an authority relation, to include fiat)" (Williamson 1994, p. 102). Hybrids are "long-term contractual relations that preserve autonomy but provide added transaction-specific *safeguards* as compared with the *market*" (p. 102; italics in original). Both firms and hybrids emerge because of the high costs resulting from transaction-specific assets and opportunism. Asset specificity is a "characteristic of a specialized investment, whereby it cannot be redeployed to alternative uses or by alternative users except at a loss of productive value"

(p. 101). Opportunism is "self-interest seeking with guile, to include calculated efforts to mislead, deceive, obfuscate, and otherwise confuse" (p. 102).

Although Williamson acknowledges that not all economic agents behave opportunistically, he argues for assuming universal opportunism because it is "ubiquitous" (1981b, p. 1550) and opportunistic "types cannot be distinguished ex ante from sincere types" (1975, p. 27) or, at the very least, "it is very costly to distinguish opportunistic from nonopportunistic types ex ante" (1981b, p. 1545). The assumption of opportunism is so important to transaction cost economics that, in its absence, "the study of economic organization is pointless" (1981b, p. 1545). Similarly, "the interesting problems of comparative economic organization vanish if either hyperrationality or faithful stewardship is ascribed to economic actors" (1996, p. 365).

Although transaction cost economics assumes Simon's (1959) "bounded rationality," instead of his "satisficing" it accepts the neoclassical maximizing tradition: "Neoclassical economics maintains a maximizing orientation. This is unobjectionable, if all the relevant costs [i.e., the transaction costs] are included" (Williamson 1985, p. 45). Indeed, even "at the expense of realism of assumptions, maximization gets the job done" (1996, p. 231). Therefore, transaction cost economics explains vertically integrated firms on the basis that transaction-specific assets, when combined with the inevitable opportunism of customers and suppliers, make such governance mechanisms efficient outcomes of cost-economizing firms.

In contrast, bilateral dependency, that is, when a buyer and seller make specialized investments that support each other, results in a hybrid governance mechanism being efficient only when there are "hostages" or "credible commitments" as contractual safeguards. Credible commitments exist in a contract when "a promise is reliably compensated should the promisor prematurely terminate or otherwise alter the agreement" (Williamson 1994, p. 102).

Concluding our review, Williamson (1996) believes that the research program studying the economics of organization is a "huge success" and that "the prospects for a science of organization are excellent" (p. 374). He notes that societies have suffered because of neoclassical theory's preoccupation with price:

> If we only had a better theory of organization and institutions, the agonies—false starts, mistakes, conundrums—of economic reform in Eastern Europe and the former Soviet Union would be much relieved. Indeed, it is my belief that prices will largely take care of themselves once the reformers focus on and get the institutions right. (The tendency to neglect institutions in favor of the pricing instruments that economists know best is understandable, but that was more excusable for Oskar Lange [1938] than it is today). (1996, p. 375)

4.2.3 Economic Sociology

Smelser and Swedberg (1994) define economic sociology as "the application of the frames of reference, variables, and explanatory models of sociology
to that complex of activities concerned with the production, distribution, exchange, and consumption of scarce goods and services" (p. 3). Economic sociology traces to the turn-of-the-century works of Max Weber (1864-1920) and
Emile Durkheim (1858-1917). Thereafter, it has been strongly influenced by
Joseph Schumpeter (1883-1950), Karl Polanyi (1886-1964), Talcott Parsons
(1902-1979), and Neil J. Smelser (1930-).[14]

In the middle of the twentieth century, the gulf between economics and sociology was wide. Indeed, "few persons competent in sociological theory,"
wrote Parsons and Smelser (1956), "have any working knowledge of economics, and conversely . . . few economists have much knowledge of society"
(p. xviii). As noted by Smelser and Swedberg (1994), however, the sharp
boundary between economics and sociology has weakened in recent years. Sociologists (e.g., Coleman 1990; Etzioni 1988; Hechter 1987) now address
"hard core" economics issues; economists (e.g., Arrow 1974; Becker 1976;
Hirschman 1970; Solow 1990) now incorporate a social perspective. Indeed,
the advent of the "new" institutional economics prompted Granovetter's
(1985) seminal "embeddedness" article and spurred the development of the
"new economic sociology" (Smelser and Swedberg 1994). Reviewing Granovetter's (1985) critique of transaction cost economics provides a good frame
for understanding the importance of embeddedness in sociology, as well as its
relevance to R-A theory.

Granovetter (1985) decries the atomized, undersocialized conception of
human action in neoclassical economics because it either "disallow[s] by hypothesis any impact of social structure and social relations on production, distribution, or consumption" or "the fact that actors may have social relations
with one another has been treated . . . as a frictional drag that impedes competitive markets" (pp. 483-84). He notes that the boundedly rational conception of
action in the "new" institutional economics continues the undersocialized tradition by restricting institutions to the role of *dependent* variables. That is,
transaction cost economics does not approach societal institutions as independent variables that can cause changes in economic outcomes. Rather, it "mainly
takes the institutional environment as given" or views societal institutions as
"shift parameters" (Williamson 1996, pp. 5, 230) in comparative statics.

Granovetter (1985) argues that when transaction cost analyses posit that extant institutions (hierarchies, markets, and hybrids) result inexorably from efficiently solving certain problems, such analyses "fail the elementary tests of a

sound functional explanation laid down by Robert Merton in 1949" (p. 488). He further argues that the Darwinian selection processes posited to result in efficient solutions are "neither an object of study nor even a falsifiable proposition but rather an article of faith" (p. 503). Moreover, he argues that the undersocialized conception guarantees that it cannot account for the widespread existence of trust in economic affairs, let alone its importance. Indeed, the elaborate institutional arrangements that transaction cost economics argues for "do not produce trust but instead are a functional substitute for it" (p. 489).

Being evenhanded, Granovetter (1985) also chastises sociological works that adopt an *over*socialized conception of human action. Citing Duesenberry's (1960) quip that the "economics is all about how people make choices; sociology is all about how they don't have any choices to make" (p. 233), he argues that solving the problem of undersocialized accounts of human action in economic theories does not imply ignoring the importance of the rational pursuit of self-interest in for-profit organizations. Indeed, "the assumption of rational action . . . is a good working hypothesis that should not easily be abandoned" (p. 506). Instead, he advocates an embedded, moderately socialized view of economic and social relations:

> A fruitful analysis of human action requires us to avoid the atomization implicit in the theoretical extremes of under- and oversocialized conceptions. Actors do not behave or decide as atoms outside a social context, nor do they adhere slavishly to scripts written for them by the particular intersection of social categories that they happen to occupy. Their attempts at purposive action are instead embedded in concrete, ongoing systems of social relations. (p. 487)

Granovetter's (1985) "embeddedness" argument has prompted an institutional stream of research that focuses on the role of networks in the economy and the rise of network competition (Baker 1990; Davis, Diekmann, and Tinsley 1994; Lincoln, Gerlach, and Ahmadjian 1996; Podolny, Stuart, and Hannan 1996). As Powell and Smith-Doerr's (1994) review points out: "Competition no longer occurs on the basis of firm-to-firm combat, but among rival shifting alliances competing against one another on a project-by-project basis" (p. 384). Noting that network competition involves trust-based governance, but not "blind loyalty" (p. 385), they locate trust-based governance in four types of network-based collaboration: (1) industrial districts, that is, networks of place (Herrigel 1990; Sabel 1989; Saxenian 1994; Scott 1990), (2) R&D networks (Hagedoorn and Schakenraad 1990a,b; Powell 1993), (3) business groups (Dore 1987; Gerlach 1992a,b; Granovetter 1994), and (4) strategic alliances (Kanter and Myers 1991; Sabel, Kern, and Herrigel 1991; Sydow 1991).

Powell and Smith-Doerr (1994) emphasize that network relationships do not imply a lessening of competition. Rather, the relationships among autonomous firms in strategic networks that allow for trust-based governance also "allow them to be more competitive in comparison to nonaffiliated outsiders" (p. 390). The theme of Powell and Smith-Doerr that social structures can sometimes be competition enhancing has become common in economic sociology.

For example, Uzzi (1996) explores how embeddedness, network structure, and trust-based governance affect economic actions among "better" dress firms in the New York apparel economy. He finds that those organized into networks usually, but not always, had higher survival chances than firms maintaining arms-length market relationships. The survivability of embedded firms improves because: "As such issues of self-interest maximization, generalized reputation, and repeated-gaming fade into the background, issues of how social relations promote thick information exchange, rapid and heuristic decision-making, and the search for positive-sum outcomes take the fore" (p. 693). Indeed, "embeddedness increases economic effectiveness along a number of dimensions that are crucial to competitiveness in a global economy—organizational learning, risk-sharing, and speed-to-market" (p. 694). Nonetheless, he finds: "The outcomes of embeddedness are not unconditionally beneficial, . . . since embeddedness can paradoxically reduce adaptive capacity" (p. 694). In short, for Uzzi, social structures are *contingently* competition enhancing.

The import of some social structures being competition enhancing is that social structure can contribute to what Coleman (1988) calls "social capital." Coleman lauds the addition of human capital, that is, education and skills, by Schultz (1961) and Becker (1964) to the customary categories of financial and physical capital. Just as human capital comes from changes in skills and capabilities that enable people to act in new ways, argues Coleman (1988), "social capital . . . comes about through changes in the relations among persons that facilitate action." (p. S100). Therefore, viewing "social capital as a resource is one way of introducing social structure into the rational action paradigm" (p. S95). For example, Coleman likens the obligations and expectations among persons in social relations where there is mutual trust to "credit slips" of obligations and, hence, a form of social capital that people can draw on.

Other relational forms of social capital include relations that provide information efficiently and social norms, such as "the norm that one should forgo self-interest and act in the interests of the collectivity" (Coleman 1988, p. S104). A concern of Coleman is that though (1) the property rights inherent in physical and human capital imply that incentives for investment are clear (i.e., persons who invest in machinery and education reap significant personal benefits), and (2) the benefits of *some* forms of social capital are captured by those who invest them, (3) the fact that most forms of social capital are created or destroyed as by-products of other activities imparts a public goods quality to social capital. Hence, he fears society's underinvestment in social capital.

Returning to the requirement of embeddedness in theory construction, Granovetter (1985) delineates no specific set of requisites that a theory of competition would have to satisfy to qualify as moderately socialized, embedded, or socioeconomic. Nonetheless, his original analysis (1985) and his subsequent explication (1990), when combined with the works of Donaldson (1990), Etzioni (1988), Fligstein (1996), Uzzi (1996), Zald (1987), and Zukin and DiMaggio (1990), suggest a minimum of five. First, though the pursuit of financial performance by for-profit organizations should be prominent, the all-seeing, all-knowing hyperrationality of neoclassical theory should be rejected. As Zald (1987) puts it: "To deny profit maximization and hyperrationality is one thing; to deny . . . that a search for profits and efficient modes of production drives much of organizational choice is quite another" (pp. 705-6).

Second, opportunistic behavior by economic actors should be assumed to be neither universal nor nonexistent. As Etzioni (1988) and Donaldson (1990) argue, the universal opportunism assumption is not only empirically false but may be viewed as "guilt by axiom." Third, the outcomes of economic behaviors, both efficient and inefficient, should result from dynamic processes that an embedded theory explicates, not from the cavalier invocation of Darwinian "as if" metaphors. As Fligstein (1996) observes, works in economic sociology "have challenged the neoclassical economists' view that markets select efficient forms which, over time, converge to a single form" (p. 657).

Fourth, as per Uzzi (1996), the concrete social relations of economic actors should have the capacity to either inhibit or enhance the likelihood of attaining desirable economic outcomes, rather than be ignored or viewed exclusively as "friction." Fifth, as even Williamson (1994, p. 85) acknowledges (but holds as not providing any "deeper insights"), the trust resulting from concrete personal relations should be viewed as substitutes for the institutions invoked by transaction cost economics.

Concluding our review, Smelser and Swedberg (1994) survey the field of economic sociology and point out how counterproductive has been the "imperialistic mode" in both economics and sociology. Therefore, they argue for pluralism. Nonetheless, they lament the lack of theoretical syntheses:

> While the current pluralistic approach moves along the right lines, the bolder efforts of the classics in the area of theoretical synthesis are notably missing. Without the complementary line of theorizing, the field of economic sociology—like

any other area of inquiry that specializes and subspecializes—tends to sprawl. Continuing efforts to sharpen the theoretical focus of economic sociology and to work toward synthetic interpretations of its findings are essential. (p. 20)

R-A theory, I shall argue, is a synthesis theory.

4.2.4 Institutional Theory and R-A Theory

Resource-advantage theory shares many affinities with all forms of institutional theory. As to institutional economics, both view competition as dynamic and disequilibrating. Nonetheless, whereas static equilibrium plays no significant role in institutional economics, the situation is different for R-A theory. Because R-A theory is a general theory of competition, it incorporates neoclassical theory as a special case and explains when static equilibrium models will predict well (see Section 10.1).

Second, both institutional economics and R-A theory agree that neoclassical theory has been misled by the tendency to equate "capital" with tangible, physical resources. Furthermore, both agree that adding "human capital" to physical capital, though a step in the right direction, is still insufficiently expansive. Other forms of intangibles contribute to a society's wealth-producing capability. What R-A theory highlights in addition to social capital (Coleman 1988) is that, following Chandler (1990), the specific competences of specific firms in a society should be considered as *organizational* capital for that society (see Section 8.2).

Third, both institutional economics and R-A theory agree on the "capabilities" view of the nature of resources. That is, both agree that the term "resources" has no meaning apart from a relationship to human beings. Indeed, rather than resource allocation, R-A theory emphasizes the importance of resource *creation* in economic growth (see Chapter 9).

Resource-advantage theory also shares affinities with transaction cost economics. First, both are interdisciplinary research programs. Indeed, this chapter and its predecessor show how a research program need not be restricted to a disciplinary "silo." Second, both agree that many resources are firm-specific and that such firm-specific resources are important for explaining economic phenomena. Whereas transaction cost economics focuses on the importance of firm-specific assets for explaining governance mechanisms, R-A theory focuses on the importance of firm-specific (i.e., heterogeneous and imperfectly mobile) assets in competition.

Third, both transaction cost economics and R-A theory agree that opportunism occurs. However, R-A theory does not assume *universal* opportunism

(Donaldson 1989). Indeed, R-A theory maintains that trust-based governance is an alternative to the institutional arrangements (e.g., "hostage taking") posited by transaction cost economics. Thus, R-A theory contributes to understanding how trust plays a role in wealth creation (see Section 9.3.3). Fourth, while both agree that efficiency considerations (economizing on transaction costs) are important, R-A theory rejects the maximizing orientation. Among other things (see Section 5.4), imperfect information implies that firms cannot *maximize* anything. Instead, R-A theory argues that the primary objective of firms is to seek superior financial performance. It is the quest for superior performance, that is, *more* than, *better* than, that ensures that R-A competition is dynamic.

Finally, differing from transaction cost economics, R-A theory recognizes both efficiency differentials among firms and *effectiveness* differentials. Coase (1988) criticizes transaction cost economics because it has "tended to neglect the main activity of a firm, running a business" (p. 38). To be sure, "running a business" involves being alert to the dangers of opportunism. But is it central? For example, if the major reason that firms exist is that they have successfully overcome the dangers of opportunism that result from transaction-specific assets, is it also the major cause of the disappearance of existing firms? Do bankruptcies result primarily from firms falling victim to the opportunism, the guile, of their customers and suppliers? A major shortcoming of transaction cost economics is that it does not contribute to explaining why some firms are simply better than others at "running a business," that is, better at producing particular goods and services for particular markets. For R-A theory, the posit of heterogeneous resources (absent opportunism) accomplishes this objective. That is, successful firms have comparative advantages in resources that enable them to occupy marketplace positions of competitive advantage (see Figures 6.1 and 6.2).

Resource-advantage theory also shares many affinities with economic sociology. First, R-A theory specifically recognizes that institutions can be independent variables in analyses of competition. That is, societal institutions influence the process of competition (see Figure 6.1). Therefore, R-A theory can explain how societal institutions that promote trust contribute to wealth creation (see Section 9.3.3).

Second, both economic sociology and R-A theory agree that embedded social relations constitute a resource only contingently. Indeed, for R-A theory, *all* entities constitute resources only contingently. Again, recall that R-A theory views resources as the tangible and intangible entities available to the firm that enable it to produce efficiently and/or effectively a market offering that has value to some market segment(s). Thus, for example, a strategic alliance between two firms can be a resource for both, yet it is *owned* by neither. If, as in the case of Uzzi (1996), financial performance in an economic arena depends crucially on adaptive capacity, which in turn is negatively affected by a particular set of concrete social relations, then such a network of social relations would not contribute, *on net,* to the firm's ability to efficiently and/or effectively produce market offerings. In such circumstances, the network (e.g., a strategic alliance) would be categorized as a "contra-resource" (Hunt and Morgan 1995).

Third, R-A theory is moderately socialized because, referring to the five criteria previously discussed, (1) though the self-interest of individuals and the financial performance of firms are prominent in R-A theory, the maximization of self-interest and financial performance is rejected; (2) though the opportunistic behavior of economic actors is acknowledged, it is not assumed to be universal but a behavior that, when it occurs, is to be explored and explained; (3) though R-A theory is evolutionary, the dynamics leading to (local) efficiency and effectiveness are *explicated,* rather than being assumed by the invocation of the Darwinian "as if" metaphors; (4) though conspiracies and other types of malfeasance are recognized, R-A theory views the concrete social relations of economic actors to have the capacity to *either* inhibit or enhance the likelihood of obtaining desirable outcomes for society; and (5) though such institutions as "hostage taking" are acknowledged as solutions to incomplete contracting problems, R-A theory views the trust resulting from concrete personal relations as potential substitutes for such institutional solutions.

In short, R-A theory is the kind of "synthesis theory" called for by Smelser and Swedberg (1994). Because R-A theory heeds Granovetter's (1985, 1990) five requirements, it is moderately socialized. Because it is moderately socialized, it can contribute to explicating the process by which (1) environments shape firms, (2) firms shape their environments, and—equally important—(3) firms, through their renewal competences, reshape themselves.

NOTES

1. The parallels between Clark's (1954, 1961) pursuit of *differential* advantage and the advocacy by strategy theorists of the pursuit of a sustainable *competitive* advantage are striking. Perhaps because differential advantage theory was not incorporated into mainstream economics, the parallels are usually unacknowledged in the business strategy literature. As noted in Chapter 1, a disadvantage of research traditions is the erection of "silos."

2. Ansoff (1965) and Steiner (1969) are the classic works on strategic planning. Mintzberg (1994) provides a good summary and a critical review. See also Goold and Luchs (1993) and Davis, Diekmann, and Tinsley (1994) on diversification and conglomerates.

3. See Aaker (1988, 1995), Abell and Hammond (1979), and Day (1977) for expositions of the portfolio planning approaches to strategy.

4. As Mintzberg (1994) points out, no one should have been surprised by the failure of large-scale, formal planning in corporate America. Planning on a grand scale failed in the command economies, just as it did here (see Section 7.2). Indeed:

> The experiences of the Communist states stand as dramatic examples of the suspension of individual freedoms for the sake of unimpeded planning, with its own biases so evident that today hardly anyone is seriously proposing extensive government planning of the economy. How ironic, then, that the large corporations of the West—the central institutions in the unplanned, so-called free market economy—should have been the very ones to lead Western efforts to institutionalize formal planning! What was so terribly bad for the state, because of its effects on participation, commitment, and flexibility, . . . [produced] for business . . . the very same effects. (Mintzberg 1994, p. 168)

5. See Conner (1991), Grant (1991), and Montgomery (1995) for reviews of resource-based theory.

6. See Conner (1991, Table 1) for additional similarities and differences between each of the five theories and resource-based theory. See Conner and Prahalad (1996) for more on how resource-based theory differs from the transaction cost view of the firm and their argument that resource-based theory shows why the existence of firms does not *require* the transaction cost presumption of opportunism.

7. Reviews of competence-based theory are in Hamel and Heene (1994), Sanchez, Heene, and Thomas (1996), Heene and Sanchez (1996), and Sanchez and Heene (1997). Unless it is a direct quote, I adopt what appears to be becoming the dominant convention in the literature that the plural of *competence* is *competences,* rather than *competencies.*

8. See also Lado, Boyd, and Hanlon (1997) and its discussion of collaborative advantage.

9. I say *a,* not *the,* because there is no monolithic theory consistent with all works in the resource-based tradition.

10. For a broad introduction to institutional economics, see Hodgson, Samuels, and Tool (1993). For reviews, see Hodgson (1994) and Kapp (1976).

11. "Mistaken" because, as Hodgson (1992) points out, the equations of neoclassical theory are equally compatible with command and market-based economies (see Section 7.2).

12. In his later works, Williamson (1994, p. 78 and footnote 4) acknowledges that transaction cost economics has affinities with the work of John R. Commons, in that

both take the transaction as a fundamental unit of analysis. (See also Hodgson [1994, pp. 69-70] for more on the alleged affinity.)

13. See Williamson's trilogy (1975, 1985, 1996) for detailed expositions of transaction cost economics and his 1994 work for a brief review. See Joskow (1988) for a sympathetic review of empirical works and Moran and Ghoshal (1996) for a critical review of such works. Other reviews may be found in Donaldson (1990), Ghoshal and Moran (1996), Granovetter (1985), North (1986), Perrow (1981, 1986), Rindfleisch and Heide (1997), and Zald (1987).

14. See Smelser and Swedberg (1994) for a review of economic sociology.

Chapter 5

Resource-Advantage Theory

Foundational Premises

A ll theories are derived from their foundational postulates. Table 5.1 displays the foundational premises underlying the standard treatment of perfect competition found in microeconomics texts (e.g., Gould & Lazear 1989) and compares them with those that are posited for resource-advantage theory. *Foundational,* as used here, implies not that the premises are the minimum set of axioms required for deriving theorems but that these premises are centrally important for understanding the two theories. Epistemologically, each premise in R-A theory—contrasted with perfect competition—is considered a candidate for empirical testing. Those found false should be replaced with ones more descriptively accurate.

Although R-A theory's epistemology differs from its neoclassical counterpart, perfect competition is not being criticized here for its "unrealistic" assumptions. Rather, R-A theory is argued for on the grounds that it has superior explanatory and predictive power (see Chapters 6, 7, 8, and 9). Furthermore, it is argued to be a general theory of competition for which perfect competition is a special case (see Chapter 10). Therefore, because R-A theory incorporates perfect competition as a special case, it subsumes the extant explanatory and

TABLE 5.1 Foundational Premises of Perfect Competition and
Resource-Advantage Theory

	Perfect Competition Theory	Resource-Advantage Theory
P1. Demand is:	Heterogeneous across industries, homogeneous within industries, and static.	Heterogeneous across industries, heterogeneous within industries, and dynamic.
P2. Consumer information is:	Perfect and costless.	Imperfect and costly.
P3. Human motivation is:	Self-interest maximization.	Constrained self-interest seeking.
P4. The firm's objective is:	Profit maximization.	Superior financial performance.
P5. The firm's information is:	Perfect and costless.	Imperfect and costly.
P6. The firm's resources are:	Capital, labor, and land.	Financial, physical, legal, human, organizational, informational, and relational.
P7. Resource characteristics are:	Homogeneous and perfectly mobile.	Heterogeneous and imperfectly mobile.
P8. The role of management is:	To determine quantity and implement production function.	To recognize, understand, create, select, implement, and modify strategies.
P9. Competitive dynamics are:	Equilibrium-seeking, with innovation exogenous.	Disequilibrium-provoking, with innovation endogenous.

SOURCE: From "Resource-Advantage Theory: A Snake Swallowing Its Tail or a General Theory of Competition?" by Shelby D. Hunt and Robert M. Morgan, 1997, *Journal of Marketing* 61 (Oct.), p. 76. Copyright © 1997 by American Marketing Association. Reprinted with permission.
NOTE: The foundational premises of R-A theory are to be interpreted as descriptively realistic of the general case. Specifically, P1, P2, P5, and P7 for R-A theory are *not* viewed as idealized states that anchor endpoints of continua. For example, P1 posits that intra-industry demand in most industries (i.e., the general case) is *substantially* heterogeneous, not perfectly heterogeneous. In contrast, P1 for perfect competition assumes the idealized state of perfect homogeneity.

predictive successes of neoclassical theory. In so doing, R-A theory preserves the cumulativity of economic science.

Some might question whether perfect competition theory in Table 5.1 is the appropriate alternative for comparison purposes. Indeed, some might consider perfect competition to be straw man because (1) many economists themselves now question its applicability to real economies and (2) most management, marketing, and sociological scholars have never held perfect competition in high regard. However, perfect competition should—indeed, must—be the point of departure for developing a new theory of competition. First, the foundational premises of perfect competition are well developed and well known. Therefore, contrasting R-A theory with perfect competition communicates efficiently and with great precision the foundations and nature of R-A theory.

Second, because neoclassical theory argues that perfect competition is *perfect,* it continues to serve as the ideal form of competition against which all others are compared (see Section 1.1). Even many of those who have come to question perfect competition's descriptive accuracy still hold it out as an ideal form of competition. Indeed, because perfect competition underlies much public policy, especially antitrust law, perfect competition should serve as the comparison standard.

Third, even though many economists question perfect competition theory on numerous grounds, it dominates economics textbooks. Therefore, it is the only theory of competition that most students ever see that is alleged to be socially beneficial. Such theories as oligopolistic and monopolistic competition are presented only as departures from the ideal of perfection. Therefore, because R-A theory argues that perfect competition is not *perfect,* perfect competition theory should serve as a comparison standard.

Finally, R-A theory is a work in progress. Contrasting R-A theory with perfect competition constitutes an invitation to other scholars to develop rivals to R-A theory. Specifically, I invite scholars (in economics, management, marketing, and economic sociology) to identify the foundational premises of rival theories of competition and explicitly contrast them with the nine premises of R-A theory in Table 5.1. By doing so, we can then evaluate how and why the theories are consistent or inconsistent, saying different things or saying the same things differently, genuinely rival or actually complementary.

This chapter follows the outline of the premises in Table 5.1. I begin with how both theories view demand.

5.1 DEMAND

For perfect competition theory, demand is (a) heterogeneous across industries, (b) homogeneous within industries, and (c) static—see Section 3.1. That is, at different configurations of price across generic product categories, for example, footwear, televisions, and automobiles, perfect competition theory allows consumers to prefer different quantities of each generic product. Within each generic product category or "industry," however, consumers' tastes and preferences are assumed to be identical and unchanging through time with respect to desired product features and characteristics. Thus, neoclassical works speak of the "demand for footwear," and the group of firms constituting the footwear "industry" are presumed to face, collectively, a downward-sloping demand curve. Each individual firm in the footwear industry, however, faces a horizontal demand curve because of the homogeneous, intra-industry demand assumption.

For perfect competition, the assumptions of homogeneity of demand and supply are necessary for drawing the industry demand and supply curves required for determining the market clearing, equilibrium price. Absent homogeneous demand, the concept of *an* industry demand curve and *the* market clearing price make no sense. Therefore (see Section 3.1), the existence of firms in an industry having downward-sloping demand curves results from the kind of product differentiation that, according to Chamberlin (1950), consists of "irrational" preferences. That is, downward-sloping demand curves for individual firms are associated with preferences based on either "ignorance" or the "imperfect knowledge" that results from "the reprehensible creation by businessmen of purely fictitious differences between products which are by nature fundamentally uniform" (pp. 87, 88).

5.1.1 Demand and R-A Theory

Consistent with neoclassical theory, R-A theory accepts the premise of heterogeneous interindustry demand. However, drawing on the quasi-Austrian Chamberlin (1933/1962) and market segmentation theory (see Section 3.1.2 and 3.1.4), intra-industry demand is posited to be both substantially heterogeneous and dynamic: consumers' tastes and preferences differ greatly within a generic product category and are always changing. Heterogeneous intra-industry demand is argued to be the descriptively realistic general case of demand. That is, R-A theory posits that there are far more industries that are radically or significantly heterogeneous, for example, motor vehicles (SIC #3711), women's footwear (#3144), and book publishing (#2731), than there are relatively homogeneous, commodity industries, for example, corn (SIC #0115), gold ores (#1041), and industrial sand (#1446).

The implication of heterogeneous, intra-industry demand is that few *industry* markets exist. As an example, consider footwear (SIC #314). R-A theory views consumers' tastes and preferences for footwear to be substantially heterogeneous and constantly changing. Furthermore, not only do consumers have imperfect information concerning footwear products that might match their tastes and preferences, but obtaining such information is often costly in terms of both time and money. There is no "market for footwear" (SIC #314) or even separate, 4-digit markets for women's footwear (#3144) and men's footwear (#3143). Although all consumers require footwear and one can readily identify a group of firms that manufacture shoes, there is no shoe industry *market.* That is, the group of firms that constitute the footwear industry do not collectively face a *single,* downward-sloping demand curve—for the existence of such an industry demand curve would imply homogeneous tastes and preferences.

R-A theory maintains that to the extent that demand curves exist at all, they exist at a level of (dis)aggregation that is too fine to be an "industry." For example, even if (for purposes of argument) one considers there to be a homogeneous, men's walking shoe market, one certainly would not speak of the men's walking shoe *industry.* Nor would one speak of the 19-inch color television or the minivan *industries.* Yet R-A theory maintains that such market segments as these—and smaller yet—are central for understanding competition.

The heterogeneous, intra-industry demand premise contributes to R-A theory's explanatory and predictive power. First, it implies that identifying those segments most suitable for developing market offerings should be viewed—consistent with Austrian economics—as an entrepreneurial capability that affects firm performance. Second, that intra-industry demand is substantially heterogeneous in *most* industries contributes to R-A theory's ability (and neoclassical theory's inability) to make the correct prediction as to the diversity in business-unit financial performance (see Section 6.3).

Third, recall that the quasi-Austrian Chamberlin (1933/1962) concluded that the "diversity between firms is recognized as so all-pervasive as to make the conception of demand and cost curves for an 'industry' or for any category larger than a firm, fantastic and impossible" (p. 303). In contrast, that intra-industry demand is relatively homogeneous ("close enough") in at least *some* commodity industries, for example, gold ores (SIC #1041), makes drawing industry demand curves for some industries neither fantastic nor impossible. Indeed, it contributes to R-A theory's ability to explain those special cases where perfect competition predicts well (see Section 10.1).

5.2 CONSUMER INFORMATION

Perfect competition theory assumes that consumers have perfect and costless information about the availability, characteristics, benefits, and prices of all products in the marketplace. In contrast, drawing on Austrian economics, Stigler (1961), and Nelson (1970), R-A theory posits that consumers within market segments have imperfect information about goods and services that might match their tastes and preferences. Furthermore, the costs to consumers in effort, time, and money of identifying satisfactory goods and services, that is, *search* costs, are often considerable. Consequently, if products are viewed as bundles of attributes (Lancaster 1966), one purpose served by the legal protection of trademarks, patents, and licenses is the reduction of consumer search costs. Specifically, trademarks, licenses, and patents are societal institutions that reduce search costs by signaling the attributes of market offerings.

Consider, for example, the issue of trademarks and their relationship to competition. Specifically, are trademarks pro- or anti-competitive? The neoclassical Chamberlin (1933/1962) derives the implications of perfect competition theory for trademarks in a straightforward manner. He points out that the legal protection of trademarks fosters product differentiation and, therefore, a situation in which prices are higher, quantities produced are lower, excess capacity is permanent, products produced are inferior, and all factors of production are exploited (see Section 3.1.1). Because, for him, "the protection of trademarks from infringement . . . is the protection of monopoly" (pp. 270), he seeks the grounds, if any, for maintaining that "monopolies protected by the law of unfair competition and of trademarks may be justified" (p. 271).

As to the rights of producers in their own names, Chamberlin (1933/1962) first defines a trademark as "any sign, mark, symbol, word or words which indicate the origin or ownership of an article as distinguished from its quality," and he asks: "where does identification leave off and differentiation begin?" (p. 272). His analysis suggests that trademarks in fact not just stand as devices for "mere identification" but also signal levels of quality as well. Therefore, as to whether producers have intellectual property rights in their names:

> There seem to be no grounds upon which he [the producer] may justly claim such protection. Given that the consumer is equally satisfied with the goods of two sellers, the entrance of the second into the field [with the first seller's name] must be regarded as the natural flow of capital under competition to check the profits of the first and to adjust the supply of the commodity to the demand for it at cost. (p. 272)

As to the interests of consumers, Chamberlin (1933/1962) evaluates three arguments that seem to imply that consumers benefit from affording legal protection to trademarks: (1) trademarks stimulate variety, (2) trademarks protect consumers from deception and fraud, and (3) trademarks encourage producers to maintain the quality of their goods. As to the first, given the trade-off between more variety and the efficiency of more competition, he argues against trademark protection because "less monopoly would be created" and "useless differentiation would be discouraged" (p. 273). As to the second and third arguments, he maintains that "equally effective" as trademark protection "would be a policy of permitting imitation [of a trademark] only if it were perfect, or of defining standards of quality by law" (p. 273). Whereas he believes the former is "condemned by its impracticality," the latter solution "has large possibilities, especially in the case of staples" (p. 273).

Chamberlin (1933/1962) concludes his evaluation of the monopoly problem of trademarks by recommending that if legal protection is to be provided at all, it should be limited to five years. Such protection, he argues, would sufficiently prompt innovation and:

> The wastes of advertising . . . would be reduced, for no one could afford to build up goodwill by this means, only to see it vanish through the unimpeded entrance of competitors. There would be more nearly equal returns to all producers and the elimination of sustained monopoly profits. All in all, there would be a closer approach to those beneficent results ordinarily pictured as working themselves out under "free competition." (p. 274)

Chamberlin's (1933/1962) analysis of trademarks graphically illustrates the power of a research tradition to frame both what phenomena are problems and what factors get considered.[1] That consumers use trademarks as heuristics indicating quality is a problem to be solved because of neoclassical theory's exclusive focus on static equilibrium efficiency. That is, trademarks are a *problem* because they contribute to product differentiation, which is itself a *problem* because of its inconsistency with perfect competition and the welfare implications of static equilibrium. In contrast, because property rights are outside the scope of equilibrium analysis, the moral implications of transgressing the rights that producers have in their names is outside the scope of the analysis and not even considered. Similarly, "trademarks stimulate of variety" can be dismissed with a wave of the hand because the variety so stimulated is probably *useless* differentiation.[2] Furthermore, the goal of government is not to protect property rights. Rather, it is to increase static efficiency by encouraging the imitation of successful innovators through the use of the coercive power of the state to enforce common quality standards. Such coercion, Chamberlin assures us, will be "equally effective" as the use of trademarks in consumers' search for information. The foundational premises underlying a research tradition count.

5.2.1 Consumer Information and R-A Theory

In contrast, the fact that consumers have imperfect information and often use trademarks as heuristics of quality is not a *problem* for R-A theory. First, because heterogeneous, intra-industry demand and supply are viewed as natural by R-A theory, it is only natural that, facing imperfect information, consumers will often use trademarks as indicators of quality. Second, because a trademark is viewed as intellectual property and fully worthy of legal protection, R-A theory views firms' protecting the equity—see Aaker (1991) and K. L. Keller (1993, 1998)—in their trademarks as providing not only (1) a valuable source of information to consumers but also (2) a powerful incentive for producers to maintain quality market offerings and (3) a means by which manufacturers of shoddy or even defective and dangerous products can be held accountable. Third, because R-A theory rejects static equilibrium efficiency as the appropriate welfare ideal, the heterogeneity of demand and supply poses not a problem to be solved but a state of nature—and a desirable one at that. Indeed, R-A theory proposes that the best way to view the role of trademarks in market-based economies is that they are quality control and quality-enhancing institutions. Consider, for example, the case of trademarks in the Soviet Union.

As Goldman (1960) recounts, the Soviet Union in its first few decades treated advertising and trademarks as capitalist institutions that, consistent with neoclassical theory, promoted inefficiency. As one might expect, with Soviet production goals set in quantitative terms, shoddy products proliferated, despite the huge inspection costs brought about by an army of inspectors. By the 1950s, Goldman points out, not only was the Soviet Union finding that advertising was an efficient means to inform consumers about products, but Soviet planners, in a desperate attempt to improve quality, made it obligatory that every plant in the Soviet Union place a "production mark" *(proizvodstennaia marka)* on all output. Goldman quotes a Soviet planner as justifying making trademarks obligatory for all plants:

> This makes it easy to establish the actual producer of the product in case it is necessary to call him to account for the poor quality of his goods. For this reason, it is one of the *most effective weapons* in the battle for the quality of products. (p. 348; italics added)

But Goldman (1960) observes that holding Soviet producers accountable for shoddy quality was not the only benefit of obligatory trademarks. He also notes that a more elaborate and attractive form of mark, a *tovarnyi znak,* while sometimes optional, is obligatory for 170 groups of goods and for all exports.

Again, Goldman quotes a Soviet planner as to the quality-enhancing benefits of the "competition" resulting from mandating the use of trademarks:

> Due to its originality, the trade mark makes it possible for the consumer to select the good which he likes. . . . [T]his forces other firms to undertake measures to improve the quality of their own product in harmony with the demands of the consumer. Thus the trademark promotes the drive for raising the quality of production. (p. 351)

Therefore, the experience of the Soviet Union supports R-A theory's view that consumers' use of trademarks as indicators of quality is not a problem to be solved. Instead, trademarks are institutions that serve as important quality control and quality-enhancing devices in real economies. How important? So important that command economies *mandated* that firms use trademarks, even in those situations where all plants were supposed to produce homogeneous commodities. In short, trademarks and product differentiation are not problems for society to solve; they are institutions that solve societal problems. Static equilibrium analysis was a "wrong turning" (Robinson 1951) for welfare economics.

5.3 HUMAN MOTIVATION

Perfect competition theory assumes human motivation to be self-interest, that is, *utility,* maximization. In contrast, R-A theory posits that people are motivated by constrained self-interest seeking. Specifically, R-A theory maintains that the self-interest seeking of individuals is constrained and/or restrained by personal moral codes. Personal moral codes, in turn, are shaped or influenced by, among other things, such institutions as societal, professional, and industry moral codes.

To understand the differences between self-interest maximizing and constrained, self-interest seeking, as well as the implications thereof, consider the ontology of *utility* and *utility maximization* in the neoclassical tradition. Concepts in science are substantive, to use Etzioni's (1988) terminology, when they have or are posited to have existence in the real world. For example, "money," "land," and "capital" are labels in English that identify concepts that refer to *money, land,* and *capital.* Because substantive concepts are posited to *refer,* they figure prominently in assertions that are true or false empirically. In contrast, purely formal concepts, for example, "or," "not," "6," and "B," are labels in English (and certain other languages) that have no empirical content.

Although assertions containing *only* formal concepts may be true or false logically, mathematically, or by linguistic convention, such assertions have no observational or empirical truth content. Is *utility* substantive or formal in neoclassical theory?[3]

As discussed in Section 2.2, the concept of marginal utility enabled Jevons and Walras to import differential calculus into economics. For them, utility was a continuous function, and marginal utility was its first derivative, that is, $MU_x = dU/dx$. But what is the entity being maximized when one sets the first derivative of the utility function to zero? To what, if anything, does utility *refer?* Jevons and Walras interpreted their equations as representing a "calculus of pleasure and pain," consistent with the English philosopher Jeremy Bentham's (1748-1831) "hedonic calculus." Bentham (1789) had proposed that utility was the property in any object that produced pleasure or happiness, rather than pain or unhappiness, and that legislation is moral if it produces the greatest happiness for the greatest number. Therefore, for Jevons, Walras, and Bentham, utility was a substantive concept that referred to one's self-interest in pleasure or happiness.

The self-interest, hedonic view of utility as a substantive concept accords well with Adam Smith's theory of how marketplace transactions result in good consequences, even without altruism on the part of participants. Thus, Smith's (1776/1937) famous lines state:

> It is not from the benevolence of the butcher, the brewer or the baker that we expect our dinner, but from their regard to their own interest. We address ourselves not to their humanity but to their self-love, and never talk to them of our own necessities but of their advantages. (p. 14)

The neoclassical tradition often defines utility as a substantive concept that is consistent with the self-interest, hedonic view of Bentham, as each of four examples illustrates: "The members of a household will seek to maximize their total utility. This is just another way of saying that the members of households try to make themselves as well off as they possibly can in the circumstances in which they find themselves" (Lipsey and Steiner 1975, p. 142). "People consume goods and services because their wants, or preferences, are served by doing so: they derive satisfaction from consumption. . . . *Utility* is simply a subjective measure of the usefulness, or want satisfaction, that results from consumption" (Browning and Browning 1983, p. 56; italics in original). "Utility . . . [is] the total satisfaction derived from the consumption of goods and services" (Samuelson and Nordhaus 1995, p. 764). "Utility . . . [is] a measure of happiness or satisfaction" (Mankiw 1998, p. 781).

Etzioni (1988) uses "P-utility" as a label for the self-interest, hedonic interpretation of utility. He then defends it as a substantive concept: "P-utility has
longstanding philosophical and psychological foundations, it provides a major
explanatory concept and generates testable hypotheses. . . . [T]o the extent that
it is hypothesized that the pursuit of P-utility is a major explanatory factor, the
hypothesis is clearly valid. . . . [T]o argue that people are pleasure-driven . . .
surely explains a good part of human behavior" (pp. 28, 34).

Interpreting utility in the self-interest, hedonic manner poses a serious
problem for the neoclassical tradition: self-interest *maximizing* is empirically
false. Indeed, Etzioni (1988, pp. 51-66) notes the scores of studies indicating
that many people do act unselfishly on many occasions. He also notes that empirical works on economic decisions related to public goods, free riders, the
cooperative behaviors in Prisoner's Dilemma experiments, and the voting behaviors of citizens also contradict the self-interest maximizing thesis. For example, he discusses the findings of Marwell and Ames (1981):

> A large number of experiments, under different conditions, most of them highly
> unfavorable to civility, show that people do not take free rides, but pay voluntar-
> ily as much as 40 percent to 60 percent of what economists figured is due to the
> public till if the person was not to free ride at all. The main reason: the subjects
> consider it the "right" or "fair" thing to do. (Etzioni 1988, p. 59)

The empirical falsity of the substantive interpretation of utility maximization that Etzioni (1988) documents has not gone unnoticed in the neoclassical
tradition. Three responses are common. First, some argue that utility and utility maximization are not substantive. Instead, utility is a formal concept, an
empty abstraction. As Samuelson (1947/1983) puts it, utility is an "empty convention" and "meaningless in any operational sense" (p. 9). Similarly, utility
"is now simply a name for the ranking of options in accord with any individual's preferences" (Alchian and Allen 1977, p. 40). Likewise, "what modern
economists call 'utility' is nothing more than the rank ordering of preference"
(Hirshleifer 1976, p. 85). Indeed, the concept of utility "need not refer to anything" (Little 1957, p. 20).

The advantages for the neoclassical tradition of the purely formal, empirically empty, "revealed preference" view are that (1) the maximization of equations—a central, if not *the* central, part of the neoclassical tradition—is re-
tained, and (2) only ordinal, instead of cardinal, measurement of preferences is
required. The disadvantage of "saving the equations" through the purely formal, revealed preference interpretation is that it leads to incoherence. That is, it
is inconsistent for a research tradition to defend utility maximization as an

empty abstraction and then proceed to use the substantive, self-interest interpretation of utility in such areas as agency theory, game theory, transaction cost
economics, and public choice economics. Research and policy recommendations in all these areas, among others in the neoclassical tradition, treat utility
maximization as a substantive thesis that implies self-interest maximization.
Incoherence in a research tradition is not a technical nicety; it violates the
norms of science.

The second response to the empirical falsity of the substantive interpretation of utility maximization is to expand the concept of "self" in self-interest.
As Etzioni (1988) puts it, "when a person acts altruistically, this is explained by
the suggestion that the pleasure of the person who benefits from this act has become a source of the doer's pleasure, part of his or her utility." For example,
"those who give gifts are said to seek reciprocal gifts, reputation, status, ap-
proval, or some other goods the doer desires" (p. 25).

Numerous defenders of utility maximization expand the "self" in self-
interest.[4] For example, Boulding (1981) states: "All we have to suppose is that
the perception of one party, A, of the welfare of the other, B, is a variable in A's
utility function such that when A perceives that B is better off, A's utility rises"
(p. 6). Similarly, Margolis (1982) points out that it is now "fairly common" to
incorporate altruism into utility maximization because: "We have no more
need to distinguish between the bread Smith buys to give to the poor and that
which he buys for his own consumption, than to distinguish his neighbor's demand for sugar to make cookies from his demand for sugar to make gin in the
cellar" (p. 1). As a third example, Azzi and Ehrenberg (1975) attempt to incorporate religious activities into utility maximization through the concept of "af-
terlife consumption" and maintain that "this variable . . . [is] at least partially a
function of the household's investment of members' time in religious activities
during their lifetimes" (p. 28). As a fourth example, Lipsey and Steiner (1975)
defend the utility maximization assumption thus:

> The assumption is sometimes taken to mean that individuals are assumed to be
> narrowly selfish and devoid of any altruistic motives. This is not so. If, for exam-
> ple, the individual derives utility from giving his money away to others, this can
> be incorporated into the analysis, and the marginal utility that he gets from a dol-
> lar given away can be compared with marginal utility that he gets from a dollar
> spent on himself. (pp. 142-43)

As Stigler (1966) points out, expanding the "self" in self-interest to include
altruism is to "turn utility into a tautology" (p. 57). That is, expanding "self" to
incorporate, *post hoc,* all conceivable behaviors removes the empirical content

from both utility and its maximization. Tautologies are true by linguistic convention, not by empirical test. Therefore, as with the empty abstraction defense, it is incoherent to defend utility as a tautology and then proceed, as do the various research programs in the neoclassical tradition, to use the substantive, self-interest interpretation in research and public policy.

As a third response to the empirical falsity of the substantive interpretation of utility maximization, some writers return to Friedman's (1953) "close enough" argument. For example, recall from Section 4.2.2 that Williamson's (1975) transaction cost economics assumes that "economic man . . . is thus a more subtle and devious creature than the usual self-interest seeking assumption reveals" (p. 255). For transaction cost economics, *homo economicus* not only self-interest maximizes but does so with opportunistic "guile." Williamson argues for assuming universal opportunism because it is "ubiquitous" (1981b, p. 1550), "even among the less opportunistic types, most have their price" (1979, p. 234), and opportunistic "types cannot be distinguished ex ante from sincere types" (1975, p. 27) or, at the very least, "it is very costly to distinguish opportunistic from nonopportunistic types ex ante" (1981b, p. 1545). The assumption of opportunism is so important to transaction cost economics that in its absence, "the study of economic organization is pointless" (1981b, p. 1545). Indeed, "the interesting problems of comparative economic organization vanish if either hyperrationality or faithful stewardship is ascribed to economic actors" (1996, p. 365).

Clearly, transaction cost economics treats utility maximizing as neither an empty abstraction nor a tautology but a substantive concept that stresses self-interest. Equally clear is its acknowledgment of (1) the falsity of the view that all economic agents engage in malfeasance (see Williamson 1996, p. 48) and (2) the fact that "faithful stewardship" is separate and distinct from self-interest (see Williamson 1996, p. 365). That is, ethical behavior and faithful stewardship are neither assumed away nor tautologized as "warm glow," self-interest maximizing.

Why, then, for transaction cost economics, would assuming opportunism to be nonuniversal make the study of economic organization *pointless?* Why, then, would the *interesting* problems of economic organization *vanish?* Indeed, how does one justify universal opportunism in the face of its (acknowledged) empirical falsity? Answering these questions, I suggest, shows again the power of a research tradition. Because (1) universal self-interest maximization is central to the neoclassical tradition and (2) the tradition itself—not the characteristics of real-world economies—defines what constitutes "interesting" problems and when such problems "vanish," then (3) the absence of the assumption of universal opportunism would make the study of the interesting problems of economic organization pointless *within the neoclassical tradition.*

However, scholars outside any research tradition (from Galileo on) never accord legitimacy to the "not in my research tradition" argument. Such scholars require an alternative justification. For them, transaction cost economics defends universal opportunism on the grounds that it is "ubiquitous," opportunistic "types cannot be distinguished," or "it is very costly to distinguish opportunistic" types, and "most [people] have their price." In short, for outsiders, transaction cost economics defends universal opportunism because it is "close enough" (Friedman 1953).

In summary, the neoclassical research tradition assumes that human motivation is self-interest, that is, utility, maximization. However, the substantive interpretation of utility maximization is empirically false. Attempts to justify utility maximization in the face of its falsity turn the thesis into a tautology or an empty abstraction. However, self-interest seeking is a powerful, substantive concept that explains much behavior. Furthermore, the various research programs within the neoclassical tradition treat utility as a substantive concept that refers to self-interest. It is incoherent for a research tradition to defend a concept as empirically empty and then use it substantively in its research programs. Self-interest maximization is then defended as being so ubiquitous that it is "close enough."

Critics outside the neoclassical tradition maintain that the assumptions of transaction cost economics, including universal opportunism, are *not* close enough. To such critics, Williamson (1994) asks: "What are the deeper insights? What are the added implications?" (p. 85). Fair enough. The answer to Williamson's queries, for R-A theory, as discussed in Section 9.3.3, is that abandoning the assumption of universal opportunism contributes to our understanding the wealth of nations. To set the stage for that argument, however, we need to explicate R-A theory's view of human motivation.

5.3.1 Human Motivation and R-A Theory

R-A theory posits that human motivation is best viewed as constrained, self-interest seeking. That is, the self-interest seeking of individuals is constrained or restrained by personal moral codes, which are in turn shaped or influenced by, for example, societal, professional, industry, and organizational moral codes. North (1986) refers to personal moral codes as *ideology:*

Ideology consists of the set of individual beliefs and values that modifies behavior. It is frequently defined as altruism, and in the sense that any act that is not self-interested is altruistic, it is; yet the word is misleading. It is true that sometimes an act is deliberately altruistic, in that it takes into account other individuals' utility functions; but ideology is as often adhering to codes of conduct that are not deliberately concerned with the welfare of others but rather with self-imposed ethical or moral standards. . . . [I]t is the value of honesty, integrity, or political conviction not in the abstract, but as the premium we are willing to incur in specific institutional contexts. (pp. 234-35)

Like North (1986), the concept of personal moral codes in R-A theory draws on the normative theories of ethics in moral philosophy. In general, the moral codes that guide behavior follow one of the two major traditions in moral philosophy: deontology and teleology (Beauchamp and Bowie 1988). Because deontological codes focus on specific actions or behaviors and teleological codes focus on consequences, the former stress the inherent rightness-wrongness of a behavior and the latter emphasize the amount of good or bad embodied in a behavior's consequences.

Deontologists believe that "certain features of the act itself other than the value it brings into existence" make an action or rule right or wrong (Frankena 1963, p. 14). Moral codes based on deontology will emphasize the extent to which a behavior is consistent or inconsistent with such deontological norms as those proscribing lying, cheating, deceiving, or stealing and those prescribing honesty, fairness, justice, or fidelity. Accordingly, deontology emphasizes duties, obligations, and responsibilities to others. Teleologists, on the other hand, "believe that there is one and only one basic or ultimate right-making characteristic, namely, the comparative value (nonmoral) of what is, probably will be, or is intended to be brought into being" (p. 14).

Whereas deontological moral codes must address the difficult issue of conflicting norms, those emphasizing teleological factors must grapple with which stakeholders are to be valued. Those moral codes adopting *utilitarianism* hold that an act is right only if it produces for all people a greater balance of good over bad consequences than other alternatives (i.e., "the greatest good for the greatest number"). Although it focuses on consequences, because utilitarianism demands that decision makers consider an act's consequences on all stakeholders, it shares at least some common ground with deontology's emphasis on duties and responsibilities to *others*. In stark contrast, codes adopting ethical egoism—that is, those who adopt the substantive interpretation of utility maximizing—hold that an act is right only if the consequences of the act are

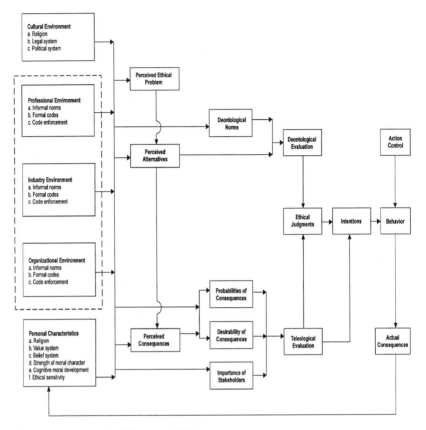

Figure 5.1. Hunt-Vitell Theory of Ethics

SOURCE: Hunt and Vitell (1986, 1993). Copyright © 1991 by Shelby D. Hunt and Scott J. Vitell.
NOTE: The portion of the model outside the dashed lines constitutes the general theory. The portion inside the dashed lines individuates the general model for professional and managerial contexts.

most favorable for the individual decision maker. The self-interest, utility-maximizing view of ethical egoism is directly opposed by deontological ethics.

Figure 5.1 shows a model developed by Hunt and Vitell (1986, 1993) that explicates the nature of personal moral codes and shows how such codes are influenced by deontological, teleological, and environmental factors.[5] The Hunt-Vitell (H-V) theory of ethics draws on deontological and teleological moral philosophy to explain (1) why people have such radically different views on the ethicality of alternative actions, and (2) why people engage in ethical/unethical behaviors. Briefly, the "triggering mechanism" of the model is the individual's perception that an activity or situation involves an ethical issue, which is followed by the perception of various alternatives or actions one might take to resolve the ethical problem. These alternatives are then evaluated both deontologically and teleologically in the "core" of the model.

For each alternative, the core of the H-V model assumes that the decision maker has access to a set of deontological norms that can be applied. The deontological evaluation process, therefore, consists of applying the norms to each alternative, checking for consistency (inconsistency), and resolving the conflicts that result when not all deontological norms can be satisfied simultaneously. Each alternative is also evaluated in the core by a teleological process that combines (1) the forecasting of each behavior's consequences for various stakeholder groups, with (2) estimating the probabilities of the consequences, (3) evaluating the consequences' desirability or undesirability, and (4) assessing the importance of each stakeholder group.

For the H-V model, the ethicality of an alternative, that is, *Ethical Judgments,* results from combining the deontological and teleological evaluations. For example, a strict deontologist would ignore totally the results of the teleological evaluation. In contrast, a strict utilitarian would (1) ignore the deontological evaluation, (2) assign equal weights to all individual stakeholders, and (3) maximize the ratio of good consequences over the bad. Like a strict utilitarian, a strict ethical egoist would ignore the deontological evaluation. However, a strict ethical egoist would also assign zero weights to all stakeholders other than the self and maximize the ratio of good consequences over the bad for oneself. The H-V theory does not suggest that individuals are (or ought to be) utilitarians, ethical egoists, or deontologists. Rather, it posits that most people in most situations evaluate the ethicality of an act on the basis of a *combination* of deontological and teleological considerations.

As to the nature of the personal moral codes that R-A theory posits to constrain or restrain self-interest seeking, the H-V model of ethics suggests that they consist of (1) the deontological norms an individual applies to decision situations, (2) the rules for resolving conflicts among norms, (3) the importance weights assigned to different stakeholders, and (4) the combinatory rules for merging the deontological and teleological evaluation processes. R-A theory draws on the H-V model and maintains that individuals differ greatly in their personal moral codes. Furthermore, the variance in moral codes is not a "black box" for the purpose of theory development and empirical research. Indeed, personal moral codes are shaped, but not determined, by experience and environment.

As to experience, note that Ethical Judgments in the H-V model drives Intentions and Behavior. That is, in most situations, ethical judgments, intentions, and behavior are congruent. (*Guilt* occurs when teleological evaluations drive intentions and behavior in a manner inconsistent with ethical evaluation.)

The H-V model shows a feedback loop from behavior through actual consequences to personal characteristics. Thus, individuals learn the appropriateness of the moral codes they apply through experiencing positive and negative consequences. This learning-by-experience shapes personal moral codes.

Personal moral codes are also shaped by lifelong, vicarious learning in different environments. First, different societies have different cultures that communicate and "pass on" different moral codes. Second, within societies, different groups, for example, professional associations, industries, and organizations, communicate different moral codes to their members. Third, different families have different moral codes. The H-V model views all these environmental factors as shaping—but not determining, for choices are still made as to which code to adopt—an individual's personal moral code.

Returning to the posit that human motivation is best described as self-interest seeking constrained by a personal moral code, R-A theory can account for the economic value to firms and societies of having individuals who are motivated by moral codes that emphasize deontological ethics, rather than ethical egoism.[6] In particular, when people share a moral code based primarily on deontological ethics, trust can exist and, therefore, the costs that firms and societies have that are associated with shirking, cheating, stealing, monitoring, free riding, "hostage-taking," and opportunism in general are avoided (see Section 9.3.3). Thus, R-A theory can provide the kinds of "deeper insights" asked for by Williamson (1994, p. 85) because, not being bound to the neoclassical tradition, it can abandon the assumption of universal opportunism.

5.4 FIRM'S OBJECTIVE AND INFORMATION

Consistent with its assumption that humans are self-interest maximizers, perfect competition theory assumes that owner-managed firms profit maximize. (Profits are the self-interest of owners.) Furthermore, maximizing occurs under conditions of perfect and costless information about product markets, production techniques, and resource markets. To incorporate time and risk, the neoclassical tradition posits wealth maximization as the firm's long-term objective. That is, owner-managed firms maximize the net present value of future profits using a discount rate that accounts for the time value of money and the risk associated with an expected stream of profits.

Of course, many modern corporations, including most large firms, are not owner managed. The separation of ownership from control and management (Berle and Means 1932) results in situations where the self-interests of owners, that is, shareholders, in maximizing their wealth may conflict with managers' own personal interests. This "principal-agent" problem is addressed in the neoclassical tradition by agency theory and its "nexus of contracts" view of the firm (Fama 1980; Fama and Jensen 1983; Jensen and Meckling 1976).[7] As with transaction cost economics, agency theory assumes universal opportunism by managers (see Section 2.1.2). Thus, measures must be taken to prevent managers from pursuing their self-interests at the expense of shareholders. Measures commonly recommended include developing financial incentives to align managers' interests with shareholder wealth maximization, instituting tight monitoring and control systems, maintaining a high proportion of independent, outside directors on boards of directors, and avoiding "CEO duality," that is, avoiding having the same person as both chief executive officer and chairperson of the board of directors.

5.4.1 Firm's Objective, Information, and R-A Theory

For R-A theory, the firm's primary objective is superior financial performance, which it pursues under conditions of imperfect and often costly to obtain information about extant and potential market segments, competitors, suppliers, shareholders, and production technologies.

As discussed in Section 5.3.1, R-A theory posits human motivation to be constrained, self-interest seeking. Consistent with self-interest seeking, superior financial performance is argued to be the firm's primary objective because superior rewards flow to the owners, managers, and employees of firms that produce superior financial results. These rewards include not only such financial rewards as stock dividends, capital appreciation, salaries, wages, and bonuses but also such nonfinancial rewards as promotions, expanded career opportunities, prestige, and feelings of accomplishment. Because it *enables* the firm to pursue other objectives, such as contributing to social causes or being a good citizen in the communities in which it operates, financial performance is viewed as primary. For-profit organizations differ from their not-for-profit cousins in that the former, but not the latter, are *for* profit. Indeed, prolonged inferior performance threatens the firm's survival and prevents the accomplishment of secondary objectives.

The "superior" in superior financial performance equates with both *more than* and *better than*. It implies that firms seek a level of financial performance exceeding that of some referent. For example, the indicators of financial performance can be such measures as accounting profits, earnings per share, return on assets, and return on equity. The referent against which the firm's performance is compared can be the firm's own performance in a previous time period, the performance of rival firms, an industry average, or a stock market average, among others. Both the specific measures of financial performance and the specific referents used for comparison purposes will vary somewhat from time to time, firm to firm, industry to industry, and culture to culture. That is, for R-A theory, both measures and referents are independent variables. Therefore, the theory provides a framework for investigating the role of different understandings of financial performance on firms, industries, productivity, economic growth, and social welfare.

Consider, for example, the issue of "short termism," that is, the claim that U.S. firms have short time horizons (compared with Japan, for example), which results in firms pursuing short-term profits instead of (presumably) more desirable, long-term investments. Many writers claim that short termism is a serious problem in the United States and locate the cause of the problem in the institutions that influence the financial indicators used by American managers to gauge performance. For example, both Jacobs (1991) and Porter (1990, 1992a,b) claim that fluid and impatient capital markets in the United States raise the cost of capital for U.S. firms by overemphasizing short-term performance. In contrast, in Germany and Japan, where banks and other large shareholders rarely trade their shares, long-term capital appreciation is more highly (and, for Porter and Jacobs, more correctly) valued.

The point to be emphasized here is not whether short termism exists in the United States or whether it is a major problem or whether impatient capital is its major cause. Rather, the point to be emphasized is that R-A theory acknowledges that different firms (and industries) in different societies may employ different indicators and referents of financial performance. Therefore, R-A theory provides a framework in which the questions "which indicators?" and "which referents?" make sense.[8]

Superior financial performance does not equate with the neoclassical concepts of "abnormal profits" or "rents" (i.e., profits differing from the average firm in a purely competitive industry in long-run equilibrium) because R-A theory views industry long-run equilibrium as a theoretical abstraction and such a rare phenomenon that the concept of "normal" profits in the neoclassical tradition cannot be an empirical referent for comparison purposes. Furthermore, the actions of firms that collectively constitute competition do not force groups of rivals to "tend toward" equilibrium. Instead, the pursuit of *superior* performance implies that the actions of competing firms are disequilibrating, not equilibrating. Indeed, consistent with Austrian economics, markets seldom if ever are in long-run equilibrium, and activities that produce turmoil in markets are societally beneficial because they are the engine of economic growth: "Capitalism, then, is by nature a form or method of economic change and not only never is but never can be stationary" (Schumpeter 1950, p. 82).

Positing that the firm's goal is superior financial performance ensures that R-A theory is dynamic, which accords well with the extant dynamism of competition in market-based economies. It is no accident that theories that are static equilibrium in nature assume profit or wealth maximization. But "saving the equations" through profit maximization has a price. If a firm is already making the maximum profit, why should it—absent environmental shocks—ever change its actions? For example, if a firm is maximizing profits producing a product at a certain quality level, why should it ever attempt to improve quality? If, however, firms are posited to (1) always seek *more* profits, *higher* earnings per share, and *greater* return on investment, and (2) they believe that there are always actions that can be taken to accomplish these goals, then (3) competition will be dynamic.

Nelson and Winter (1982) maintain that "firms in our evolutionary theory . . . [are] motivated by profit and . . . search for ways to improve profits," which differs from "profit maximizing over well defined and exogenously given choice sets" (p. 4). Likewise, Langlois (1986) points out that though economic "agent[s] prefer more to less all things considered," this "differs from maximizing in any strong sense" (p. 252). Similarly, though R-A theory posits that firms seek superior financial performance, the general case of competition is that they do not "strong sense" maximize because managers lack the capability and information to maximize (Simon 1979).[9] That is, though firms prefer more profits to less profits, a higher return on investment to a lower return, a higher stock price to a lower stock price, more shareholder wealth to less wealth, imperfect information implies that none of these financial indicators equates with profit or wealth *maximization.*

Real firms in real economies are not presented a menu of well-defined sets of alternatives for which *the* problem is to choose the profit- or wealth-maximizing option. Firms do indeed take actions; they do indeed take note of financial indicators; and they do indeed make causal attributions between actions and indicators. But even if—and this is a big if—managers have good reasons to claim to know that actions previously taken have led (or will lead) to increases in financial performance, they cannot know (or warrantedly claim to know) that some alternative action or set of actions (identified or not identified) would not have produced (or will not produce) even higher returns. Therefore *superior* financial performance, not maximum performance, better describes the firm's primary objective.

In addition to informational problems, firms do not "strong sense" maximize because of the personal moral codes of owners, managers, and subordinate employees. Recall that agency theory and transaction cost economics assume self-interest maximization and universal opportunism. In terms of ethical theory, all economic agents are ethical egoists: they ignore deontological considerations, assign zero weights to all stakeholders other than self, and maximize the ratio of good consequences over bad.

In contrast, R-A theory posits that personal moral codes are independent variables that vary across people (and peoples). Moral codes entail (1) the deontological norms an individual applies to decision situations, (2) the rules for resolving conflicts among norms, (3) the importance weights assigned to different stakeholders, and (4) the combinatory rules for merging the deontological and teleological evaluation processes. Thus, R-A theory acknowledges that nonowner managers guided by ethical egoism might not profit maximize when it conflicts with their self-interests. However, by treating personal codes as independent variables, R-A theory expands the kinds of situations beyond those that can be addressed by agency theory.

Consider, for example, the case of distributors of bottled water who could easily charge double the customary price when a natural disaster shuts down a community's water supply. Some firms, guided by ethical egoism, that is, self-interest maximization, might choose to double the price. Other firms, guided by "enlightened" self-interest seeking, might choose not to double the price because they believe the long-term, net present value of doubling is less than the "goodwill value" of nondoubling. However, the personal codes of the managers of still other firms might result in their resisting the doubling of prices even though they believe the long-term, net present value of doubling is greater than the goodwill value of nondoubling. In particular, firms guided by deontological ethics might resist doubling because they believe that it would constitute exploiting their customers and, hence, be deontologically *wrong*. In general (and inconsistent with agency theory and transaction cost economics), some firms do not profit or wealth maximize in particular decision situations because such maximizing behaviors would violate (either owner or nonowner) managers' sense of rightness and wrongness. This sense of rightness and wrongness results from managers' beliefs concerning their duties and responsibilities to nonowner stakeholders, that is, it stems from their personal moral codes based on deontological ethics.

Finally, efforts to profit maximize may also be thwarted by ethical code mismatches between managers and their subordinate employees. Suppose most of a firm's employees have moral codes stressing deontological ethics and, thus, they avoid shirking, cheating, stealing, and other opportunistic behaviors. In such a firm, the costs associated with monitoring and strong controls would be pure economic waste. If, however, the owner-manager is an ethical egoist and assumes that the employees are also ethical egoists (doesn't everyone utility maximize?), then expensive and unnecessary controls will be instituted.[10] Ironically, then, the assumption of utility maximization by managers can thwart efforts at profit maximization. Etzioni (1988) puts it this way: "The more people accept the [P-utility maximization part of the] neoclassical paradigm as a guide for their behavior, the more their ability to sustain a market economy is undermined" (p. 257).

In summary, superior financial performance is argued to be the best descriptor of the firm's primary objective because (1) superior rewards flow to owners, managers, and employees of firms that produce superior rewards, and (2) the pursuit of superior financial performance ensures that R-A theory is dynamic, which makes it consistent with the observed dynamism of market-based economies. Although firms do seek superior financial performance, they are argued to not maximize profit or wealth because (1) imperfect information makes maximization impossible, (2) agency problems associated with ethical egoism thwart maximization, (3) firms guided by deontological ethics may, at times, choose not to maximize, and (4) ethical code mismatches between (and among) owners, managers, and subordinate employees may result in nonmaximizing behaviors.

5.5 RESOURCES

For perfect competition theory, firm resources are factors of production. Two aspects of "resources are factors" are noteworthy. First, because neoclassical theory is completely mathematized, no entity can be a factor of production unless it can be represented in an equation that can be differentiated. Therefore, the customary factors are land, labor, and capital. Intangible entities, such as entrepreneurship, as Kirzner (1979, p. 187) points out, have no marginal product and cannot be a factor of production. It makes no sense to talk about the extra units of a commodity that can be produced for each additional *unit* of entrepreneurship.

Second, all resources are perfectly homogeneous and mobile. That is, each unit of labor and capital is identical with other units, and all units—being for sale in the factor markets—can move without restrictions among firms within and across industries. Again, labor and capital must be homogeneous to ensure that equations will be differentiable.

In addition to resources, all firms have access to a *production function,* that is, a technology that enables them to combine the factors of production to produce a product. Because of the assumption of perfect information, the production function for each firm within an industry is identical—no firm has access to a technology, capability, competence, or organizational form that is superior to those available to other firms. Because all innovation is exogenous (premise P9, Table 5.1), new technologies are given to firms by outside sources, for example, by government.

5.5.1 Resources and R-A Theory

Contrasted with "resources are factors," R-A theory adopts a resource-based view of firm (see Sections 4.1.3 and 4.1.5). Specifically, R-A theory defines resources as the tangible and intangible entities available to the firm that enable it to produce efficiently and/or effectively a market offering that has value for some market segment(s). Resources are categorized as financial (e.g., cash reserves and access to financial markets), physical (e.g., plant, raw materials, and equipment), legal (e.g., trademarks and licenses), human (e.g., the skills and knowledge of individual employees, including, importantly, their entrepreneurial skills), organizational (e.g., controls, routines, cultures, and competences—including, importantly, a competence for entrepreneurship), informational (e.g., knowledge about market segments, competitors, and technology), and relational (e.g., relationships with competitors, suppliers, and customers). Each entity is a resource to the firm if, and only if, it contributes to enabling it to produce efficiently and/or effectively a market offering that has value for some market segment(s).

R-A theory posits that resources are both significantly heterogeneous across firms and imperfectly mobile. Resource heterogeneity implies that each and every firm has an assortment of resources that is at least in some ways unique. Imperfectly mobile implies that firm resources, to varying degrees, are not commonly, easily, or readily bought or sold in the marketplace (the neoclassical factor markets). Because of resource immobility, resource heterogeneity can persist through time despite attempts by firms to acquire the same resources of particularly successful competitors.

Note that resources need not be owned by the firm, but just be available to it. For example, the relationships involved in relational resources are never *owned* by firms, but only available to them for the purpose of producing value for some market segment(s). Indeed, just as there is no neoclassical market—no demand or supply curve—for "reputations," there is no *market* for relationships with suppliers, customers, employees, and competitors. Nonetheless, relational resources have value.

The relationships that a firm has access to become a part of what R-A theory views as organizational capital, Falkenberg (1996) calls "behavioral assets," and Gummesson (1995) refers to as "structural capital." For example, Gummesson (1995) defines structural capital as "those resources built into the organization such as systems, procedures, contracts, and brands which are not dependent on single individuals" (p. 17). As he points out, there is a strong shift toward recognizing that the total value of a firm is primarily determined by what he calls "soft" assets, not inventory and equipment. Thus, the value of many organizations "cannot be correctly assessed from traditional information in the balance sheet and the cost and revenue statements of the annual report" (p. 18). Although accounting procedures for valuing these soft assets are in their infancy, firms are beginning to recognize "the fact that the customer base and customer relationships are . . . assets, even the most important assets" (p. 18).

The recent work of Falkenberg (1996) provides data on just how important organizational capital or soft assets are in determining the value of a firm. Falkenberg divides a firm's resources into (1) physical assets, (2) valuable paper (e.g., cash), and (3) "behavioral assets," which he defines as the "routines and competencies of the people involved . . . which are located not only inside, but outside the firm" (p. 4). As support for his thesis that it is behavioral assets that are the main source of wealth creation, he calculates the market price to book value ratio for numerous firms in different industries in different years. Because book value reflects only the (depreciated) value of physical assets and valuable paper, the difference is an (albeit crude) estimate of the value of a firm's behavioral assets.

Falkenberg's (1996) study finds substantial across-industry variation. For example, whereas the behavioral assets of Home Depot, Inc., are valued at 6.6 times its book value, Texaco's behavioral assets are only 2.0 times its book value. Furthermore, he finds substantial within-industry variation. For example, not only did his sample of consumer goods companies range from 0.8 (RJR Nabisco) to 15.0 (Coca Cola), but even within the petroleum industry the ratios ranged from 2.0 (Texaco) to 3.2 (Phillips Petroleum). Moreover, even across only two years' time (1993-1995), the ratio for individual firms changed dramatically, both up and down. For example, whereas Apple Computer went from 3.1 in 1993 to 2.1 in 1995, IBM went from 1.1 to 2.4 during the same time period.

In short, Falkenberg's (1996) work strongly supports the view that it is organizational capital—including a firm's relational resources—that is viewed by investors as the principal determinant of its wealth-creating capacity. Furthermore, it strongly supports R-A theory's contention that important firm resources are intangible, significantly heterogeneous, and immobile. In contrast, because neoclassical theory customarily admits only capital, labor, and land to qualify as firm resources (where capital is generally construed to be such tangible assets as machinery, inventory, and buildings), such intangibles as relationships are outside the scope of the concept "resources" and are not considered as having value in the production process.

At first glance, one might believe that neoclassical theory could accommodate the concept of organizational capital by the simple expedient of permitting such intangibles as relationships to be resources. But this is problematic in the extreme. The commitment of neoclassical theory to the derivation of demand and supply curves requires that all resources be homogeneous and mobile. That is, it is only by neoclassical theory viewing each unit of each factor of production as being obtainable in the marketplace (and identical with other units) that it can derive demand and supply curves for each factor. Why, then, couldn't neoclassical theory simply discard the necessity of having demand and supply curves for each factor of production? Because demand and supply curves are necessary for determining prices in static equilibrium—which is part of the neoclassical research program's "hard core" (Lakatos 1978). That is, the import of discarding the requirement that all factors of production have demand and supply curves would be that neoclassical theory would no longer be *neoclassical.*

5.6 ROLE OF MANAGEMENT

For perfect competition theory, the role of management is limited, to say the least. Because firms are price-takers and quantity-makers, the short-term role of management is to determine the quantity of the firm's single product to produce and to implement its standardized production function. Because all firms are profit maximizers, all firms in an industry will inexorably produce at an output rate where marginal cost equals marginal revenue (the product's market price). Therefore, because such resources as plant and equipment are relatively fixed in the short run, each firm will incur profits (or losses) depending on whether price exceeds (or is less than) the average total cost of producing the profit-maximizing quantity.

5.6.1 Management and R-A Theory

R-A theory, in contrast, views the role of management in the firm in a business strategy manner (see Section 4.1). Specifically, the role of management (both owner and nonowner managers) is to recognize and understand current strategies, create new strategies, select preferred strategies, implement the strategies selected, and modify strategies through time. "Implementation," of course, encompasses the thousands of day-to-day decisions that must be made and activities that must be undertaken to manage a modern firm (of any significant size). "Recognize and understand" acknowledges that firms sometimes (often?) fail to recognize accurately their respective marketplace positions and/or fail to understand the nature of the resources that led to such positions (McGrath, MacMillan, and Venkataramen 1995; Schoemaker and Amit 1994). Indeed, many strategies emerge through time and, thus, may be implicit (Mintzberg 1987). "Create" and "select" emphasize the cognitive and innovative dimensions of firms. Therefore, the strategic choices that managers make influence performance. "Modify" emphasizes that managers learn through the process of competing and can make adjustments or abandon underperforming strategies.

All strategies (at the business-unit level) involve, at the minimum, the identification of (1) market segments, (2) appropriate market offerings, and (3) the resources required to produce the offerings. Strategies that yield positions of competitive advantage and superior financial performance will do so when they rely on those resources in which the firm has a comparative advantage over its rivals. *Sustained* superior financial performance occurs only when a firm's comparative advantage in resources continues to yield a position of competitive advantage despite the actions of competitors (see Chapter 6 for a detailed explication of this process).

5.7 COMPETITIVE DYNAMICS

For neoclassical theory, all resources are variable in the long run and each firm in each industry adjusts its resource mix (e.g., its capital/labor ratio) to minimize its cost of producing the profit-maximizing quantity. These adjustments inexorably lead to a long-run equilibrium position in which each firm produces the quantity for which market price equals long-run marginal cost, which itself equals the minimum, long-run average cost. The position of long-run equilibrium is thus a "no profit" situation—firms have neither a pure profit (or rent) nor a pure loss, only an accounting profit equal to the rate of return obtainable in other perfectly competitive industries.

Each industry stays in equilibrium until something changes in its environment. Thus, all forms of innovation are exogenous factors and represent "shocks" to which each industry responds. Therefore, rather than "strategic choices matter," the firm's environment strictly determines its performance (i.e., its profits). Pure profits or rents occur only temporarily—just long enough for equilibrium to be restored. Through time, the dynamics of market-based economies are represented as "moving" equilibria.

Because both product and factor markets are interdependent, the possibility of a general equilibrium for an entire economy arises. Walras (1874/1954) was the first to identify the system of equations that an economy would have to "solve" for general equilibrium to exist. Conceptualizing a fictitious, all-knowing "auctioneer" who "cries" prices (that is, "bids" for all products and resources), Walras theorized that an economy characterized by perfect competition "gropes" toward general equilibrium. Schumpeter (1954) calls the work of Walras the "Magna Carta of economic theory" (p. 242). Indeed, precisely specifying and successfully analyzing the "Walrasian equations" are considered to be the crowning achievement of twentieth-century economics—as Nobel prizes to Kenneth Arrow in 1972 and Gerald Debreu in 1983 attest.

The welfare economics literature investigates the conditions prevailing at the position of Walrasian general equilibrium. If—and only if—all industries in an economy are perfectly competitive, then at general equilibrium, every firm in every industry has the optimum-sized plant and operates it at the point of minimum cost. Furthermore, every resource or factor employed is allocated to its most productive use and receives the value of its marginal product. Moreover, the distribution of products produced is Pareto-optimal at general equilibrium because the price of each product (reflecting what consumers are *willing* to pay for an additional unit) and its marginal cost (the extra resource costs society *must* pay for an additional unit) will be exactly equal. Therefore, the adjective "perfect" is taken literally in neoclassical theory: perfect competition is perfect. It is the ideal form. All other forms of competition are departures from perfection, that is, "imperfect" (see Section 3.1).

5.7.1 Competitive Dynamics and R-A Theory

In contrast, for R-A theory, competition is an evolutionary process in which the actions of firms are disequilibrium provoking. In this process, innovation is endogenous. Instead of the firm's environment, particularly the structure of its industry, strictly determining its conduct (strategy) and its performance (profits), R-A theory maintains that environmental factors only influence conduct and performance. Relative resource heterogeneity and immobility imply that strategic choices must be made and that these choices influence performance. All firms in an industry will not adopt the same strategy—nor should they. Different resource assortments suggest targeting different market segments and/or competing against different competitors.

R-A competition is not an "imperfect" departure from perfect competition. Rather, the process of R-A competition allocates resources efficiently and, because it creates new resources, generates increases in productivity (see Chapter 7). Furthermore, R-A competition produces economic growth (see Chapter 8) and wealth (see Chapter 9). Moreover, rather than R-A competition being an imperfect departure from perfect competition, perfect competition is a special case of R-A competition (see Chapter 10). To set the stage for discussing the welfare implications of R-A competition, we need to articulate the precise nature of the process of R-A competition. This is the subject of Chapter 6.

NOTES

1. The "trademarks are monopolies" implication of neoclassical theory led to the (ultimately unsuccessful) argument that Borden's equity in its ReaLemon trademark was anti-competitive (*Wall Street Journal* 1978).

2. Recall that Cowling and Mueller (1978), in estimating the social costs of product differentiation, treated all advertising expenditures in a society as inherently wasteful because "the argument for advertising as a provider of information should not be taken seriously" (p. 734). (See Section 2.2.3.)

3. See Etzioni for a detailed discussion of the concepts of utility and utility maximization in the neoclassical tradition. Our discussion here draws heavily on his work.

4. These examples I owe to Etzioni (1988).

5. The original model is in Hunt and Vitell (1986). The version reproduced here is a revision from Hunt and Vitell (1993). Discussions and tests of the model may be found in Hunt (1990a), Hunt and Vasquez-Parraga (1993), Mayo and Marks (1990), Menguc (1997), Singhapakdi and Vitell (1990, 1991), Sparks and Hunt (1998), and Vitell and Hunt (1990).

6. Etzioni (1988) refers to this view as "moderate deontology." Specifically, he argues that, rather than abandon P-utility, socioeconomics should (1) draw on deontological ethics and (2) theorize that moral commitment is a separate source of valuation. Thus, he hypothesizes that behavior is codetermined by P-utility and a moral commitment based on deontological ethics. By moderating the P-utility thesis with deontological ethics, argues Etzioni (1988), socioeconomics can account for trust, which "is pivotal to the economy . . . as, without it, currency will not be used, saving makes no sense, and transaction costs rise precipitously" (pp. 7, 8).

7. See Perrow (1986); Eisenhardt (1989); Bergen, Dutta, and Walker (1992); and Davis, Schoorman, and Donaldson (1997) for reviews of agency theory.

8. Laverty (1996) reviews the concept of short termism, as well as both the empirical evidence and explanations for it. He documents the paucity of the evidence for it and the tautological nature of the reasoning in many of the analyses, concluding that "the debate is clearly in need of new perspectives and a reframing of the issues" (p. 839).

9. However, Simon's (1979) "satisficing" differs from R-A theory's concept of *superior* financial performance. As Dickson (1992) notes:

Note that this view [Dickson's view] of relentless cost management cannot be accommodated in the satisficing model by simply assuming that the firm keeps raising its efficiency aspiration levels. A firm is likely to change its aspiration levels, but they are still only minimum performance standards, often linked to management and worker reward systems. Once its aspirations levels (performance standard goals) are met, the firm that prefers more profits over less will not stop seeking ways of reducing costs. Such motivation and behavior are antithetic to satisficing because the reality is that the firm is never satisfied with its current performance. (p. 72)

10. Davis, Schoorman, and Donaldson (1997) discuss the differences between agency theory and stewardship theory prescriptions as to corporate governance. They develop a Prisoner's Dilemma scenario concerning the "principal's choice" of either (1) acting opportunistically or (2) acting as a steward. Similar choices are then developed for managers (see their Figure 1, p. 39). Among other things, they discuss the costs of what are here called ethical code mismatches.

Chapter

Resource-Advantage Theory

*An Evolutionary, Process Theory
of Competition*

Competition is the constant struggle among firms for comparative advantages in resources that will yield marketplace positions of competitive advantage for some market segment(s) and, thereby, superior financial performance. For resource-advantage theory, (1) competition is disequilibrium provoking, and (2) both innovation and organizational learning are endogenous. That is, the process of R-A competition is status quo disturbing and leads to both innovation and learning. The pursuit of superior financial performance, for example, more profits than last year, ensures that rivals will engage in actions, including innovations, that disrupt any stasis that might temporarily occur.

This chapter begins by explicating the process of R-A competition and showing how it leads to innovation and organizational learning. Next, I argue that the process of competition is evolutionary. Finally, I use R-A theory to explore the issue of firm diversity.

135

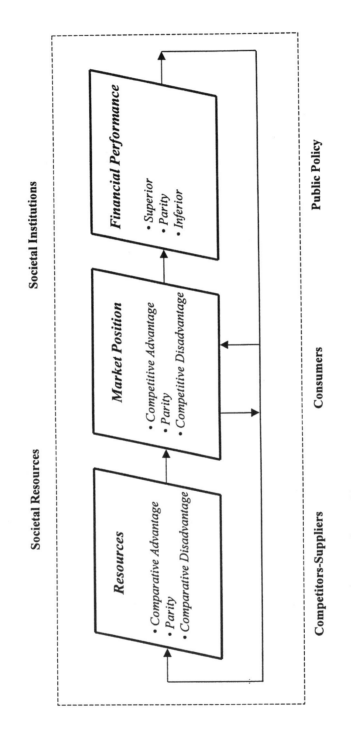

Figure 6.1. Resource-Advantage Competition

SOURCE: Adapted from "Resource-Advantage Theory: A Snake Swallowing Its Tail or a General Theory of Competition?" by Shelby D. Hunt and Robert M. Morgan, 1997, *Journal of Marketing* 61 (Oct.), p. 78. Copyright © 1997 by American Marketing Association. Reprinted with permission.
NOTE: Read: Competition is the disequilibrating, ongoing process that consists of the constant struggle among firms for a comparative advantage in resources that will yield a marketplace position of competitive advantage and, thereby, superior financial performance. Firms learn through competition as a result of feedback from relative financial performance "signaling" relative market position, which, in turn, signals relative resources.

Relative Resource-Produced Value

		Lower	Parity	Superior
Relative Resource Costs	Lower	1 Indeterminate Position	2 Competitive Advantage	3 Competitive Advantage
	Parity	4 Competitive Disadvantage	5 Parity Position	6 Competitive Advantage
	Higher	7 Competitive Disadvantage	8 Competitive Disadvantage	9 Indeterminate Position

Figure 6.2. Competitive Position Matrix[a]

SOURCE: From "Resource-Advantage Theory: A Snake Swallowing Its Tail or a General Theory of Competition?" by Shelby D. Hunt and Robert M. Morgan, 1997, *Journal of Marketing* 61 (Oct.), p. 78. Copyright © 1997 by American Marketing Association. Reprinted with permission.
[a]Read: The marketplace position of competitive advantage identified as Cell 3 results from the firm, relative to its competitors, having a resource assortment that enables it to produce an offering for some market segment(s) that (a) is perceived to be of superior value and (b) is produced at lower costs.

6.1 THE PROCESS OF R-A COMPETITION

Figures 6.1 and 6.2 provide schematics of the process of R-A competition. Because R-A theory draws heavily on Austrian economics and the Schumpeterian tradition in evolutionary economics, (a) innovation and organizational learning are endogenous to R-A competition, (b) firms and consumers have imperfect information, and (c) entrepreneurship and institutions affect economic performance. Because R-A theory incorporates marketing's heterogeneous demand theory, intra-industry demand is viewed as significantly heterogeneous as to consumers' tastes and preferences. Therefore, different market offerings are required for different market segments in the same industry. Because it adopts a resource-based view of the firm, firms are theorized to be combiners of heterogeneous, imperfectly mobile resources. Combining a resource-based view of the firm with heterogeneous demand and imperfect information results in diversity in the sizes, scopes, and levels of profitability of firms not only across industries, but also within the same industry. As Figures 6.1 and 6.2 show, R-A theory stresses the importance of market segments, a comparative advantage/disadvantage in resources, and marketplace positions of competitive advantage/disadvantage.

Market segments are defined as intra-industry groups of consumers whose tastes and preferences with regard to an industry's output are relatively homo-

geneous. Resources are defined as the tangible and intangible entities available
to the firm that enable it to produce efficiently and/or effectively a market offering that has value for some market segment(s). Just as international trade
theory recognizes that nations have heterogeneous, immobile resources—and
it focuses on the importance of a society's comparative advantage in resources
to explain the benefits of trade among *nations*—R-A theory recognizes that
many of the resources of firms within the same industry are significantly heterogeneous and relatively immobile. Therefore, it focuses on comparative advantages in resources among *firms*. That is, analogous to nations, some firms
will have resources resulting in a comparative advantage (and others a comparative disadvantage) in efficiently/effectively producing particular market
offerings that have value for particular market segments.

Specifically, when firms have a comparative advantage (or disadvantage) in
resources, they will occupy marketplace positions of competitive advantage
(or disadvantage), as shown in Figure 6.1 and explicated in Figure 6.2. Marketplace positions of competitive advantage (or disadvantage) then result in superior (or inferior) financial performance. Competition, therefore, is viewed as a
constant struggle among firms for comparative advantages in resources that
will yield marketplace positions of competitive advantage for some market
segment(s) and, thereby, superior financial performance. As Figure 6.1 shows,
how well competitive processes work to foster productivity and economic
growth is significantly influenced by five environmental factors: the societal
resources on which firms draw, the societal institutions that form the "rules of
the game" (North 1990), the actions of competitors and suppliers, the behaviors of consumers, and public policy decisions.

6.1.1 Positions of
Competitive Advantage

R-A theory posits that it is marketplace positions of competitive advantage
(or disadvantage) that result in superior (or inferior) financial performance. But the concept of positional advantage has a very precise meaning in R-A
theory. Specifically, it means occupying one of three cells (numbers 2, 3, or 6) in
Figure 6.2. The competitive position matrix, a key diagnostic contribution
unique to R-A theory, shows nine possible competitive positions for the various combinations of a firm's relative (to competitors) resource-produced value
for some segment and relative resource costs for producing such value. As discussed in Section 2.2.4, *value* refers to the sum total of all benefits that consumers perceive they will receive if they accept a particular firm's market of-

fering. Relative superior value, therefore, equates with perceived to be worth more.

Ideally, of course, a firm would prefer the competitive position of cell 3, where its comparative advantage in resources produces superior value at lower cost. The Japanese automobile companies, for example, had this position throughout the 1970s and into the 1980s in the United States. That is, their relatively more efficient and effective manufacturing processes were producing higher-quality products at lower costs. Firms in cell 2 have an efficiency advantage because their lower resource costs produce a market offering of parity value. Firms in cell 6 have an effectiveness advantage because their parity costs produce superior value. The efficiency-advantage position identified as cell 2, the effectiveness-advantage position of cell 6, and the "nirvana" position of cell 3 bring superior financial returns. In contrast, cell 5, the parity position, produces parity returns, and firms occupying cells 4, 7, and 8 have positions of competitive disadvantage and have inferior returns. However, firms occupying positions 1 and 9, though having a comparative advantage in either value or costs, may have superior, parity, or inferior returns.

In position 1, the advantage of lower relative resource costs is associated with (or results from) a sacrifice in relative value for consumers. Consequently, the offerings of firms in such a position will generally have lower prices than those, say, in cell 2. Hence, the position is indeterminate. Depending on the extent to which the price reductions are less than, equal to, or greater than their relative advantage in resource costs, cell 1 firms are at positions of competitive advantage, parity, or competitive disadvantage, respectively. For example, though American car companies in the 1970s and 1980s occupied position 7, in the 1990s they began to develop a relative cost advantage over imported Japanese makers (Lavin 1994). Nonetheless, because many consumers still perceived American cars to be somewhat lower in quality, they tended to move toward position 1, the indeterminate position (rather than into a position of competitive advantage).

Position 9, on the other hand, is equally indeterminate and describes the German car companies in the 1990s. Although the resources of BMW and Mercedes Benz (for cars produced in Germany) continued to produce products of superior perceived value in the luxury car segment, they did so at much higher resource costs (M. A. Keller 1993). Unlike the 1970s and 1980s, when the BMW and Mercedes Benz car companies occupied the competitive advantage of cell position 6, they shifted toward the indeterminate position of cell 9.

Cell 5, the parity position, is the marketplace situation addressed in part by perfect competition theory. If no firm can produce superior value for some particular market segment and no firm has a cost advantage, then all rivals competing for the segment have parity returns and an equilibrating model of competition might apply. Given that firms seek superior financial performance, however, R-A theory maintains that if *competition* exists, cell 5 is an inherently unstable marketplace position. Indeed, a *prima facie* case for market failure exists if all firms competing for the patronage of a market segment continue to occupy cell five in the long run. That is, why are there no innovators disrupting the status quo?

6.1.2 Comparative Resource Advantages

Are marketplace positions of competitive advantage short run or long run? As Figure 6.1 shows, it is comparative advantages in resources that result in marketplace positions of competitive advantage. Therefore, the life span of a particular marketplace position of competitive advantage is determined by the life span of its associated resource. For R-A theory, the life span of a particular comparative advantage in resources—its sustainability—is determined by factors both internal and external to the firm.

Internal Factors. A comparative advantage in resources can be dissipated, allowed to atrophy, or just plain squandered by several internal factors: (1) a firm's failure to reinvest, (2) the presence of causal ambiguity, and (3) a firm's failure to adapt. First, all resources require monitoring and maintenance expenditures (Dierickx and Cool 1989). For example, "a business with a reputation for superior quality could experience an erosion in quality as a source of SCA [sustainable competitive advantage] if it fails to continue investing for quality" (Bharadwaj, Varadarajan, and Fahy 1993, p. 87). Thus, failing to reinvest may shorten the life span of a position of competitive advantage.

Second, a firm may allow a comparative advantage in resources to dissipate because the relationship between its competitive advantage in the marketplace and its comparative advantage in resources is causally ambiguous (Lippman and Rumelt 1982). Is it, for example, product quality, superior service, an advantageous geographical location, or a unique set of product attributes that drives the observed superior performance? Sometimes, firms think wrongly on this question and allow an advantage to dissipate. That is, because of causal ambiguity, firms may fail to recognize or understand the sources of their superior financial performance.

Third, a firm may fail to modify, sell, relinquish, or abandon a resource or an assortment of resources in response to a changed environment. An asset that is a resource in one environment can become a nonresource in another if it no longer contributes toward the creation of value in the firm's market offerings. Even more seriously, something that was previously a resource can become a "contra-resource" and actually inhibit the creation of value in the firm's market offerings. As a case in point, consider the permanent employment issue.

Because "viewing employment as permanent creates the best incentive both for the company and its employees to invest in upgrading skills," Porter (1990) recommends that all companies "make the commitment to maintain permanent employment to the maximum extent possible" (p. 594). For Porter, the guarantee of permanent employment is a universal resource, that is, it contributes to the firm's ability to produce valued market offerings in all competitive environments. In contrast, as discussed in Section 4.2.4, R-A theory maintains that all entities constitute resources only contingently. Therefore, permanent employment, either as a formal policy or as an informal element of a firm's culture, is not necessarily a resource in all environments.

Consider IBM, an example used by Porter (1990) as evidence that permanent employment is a universal resource. It is true that IBM successfully resisted involuntary layoffs for 70 years and that this policy fostered worker loyalty and a low personnel turnover rate. By the 1990s, however, according to Hays (1994), the permanent employment aspect of IBM's culture had been transformed into a feeling by IBM employees that they were "entitled to their jobs," which then led to employee "lethargy." Thus, the resource of permanent employment became the contra-resource of job entitlement:

> Through the mid-1980s Big Blue enjoyed 40 percent of the industry's worldwide sales and 70 percent of all profits. The no-layoffs vow backfired badly when trouble hit in the late 1980s. From 1986-1993, IBM took $28 billion in charges, half of it for voluntary buy outs and cut the payroll by 37 percent. (Hays 1994, p. A5)

A policy of permanent employment may be a resource, nonresource, or contra-resource for a firm depending on its competitive position, its environment, and how it "fits in" with the firm's total assortment of resources. Entities constitute resources contingently.

External Factors. A firm's comparative advantage in resources can be fostered, neutralized, or destroyed by changes in societal resources and institutions and by the actions of consumers, government, suppliers, or competitors (see Figure 6.1 and Section 3.2). For example, changes in consumer tastes and preferences in a market segment can turn a resource into a nonresource or contra-resource. Thus, for example, a distribution system that emphasizes franchised dealers can shift from resource to nonresource if consumers decide that they desire to purchase the items in question from discount stores. In like manner, governmental actions can destroy the value-creating potential of a resource through laws and regulation. Changes in patent, trademark, franchising, and other laws can destroy a resource's comparative advantage. In this section, I focus on the actions of competitors that can affect a rival's resources.

Competitors' actions that can potentially neutralize a resource's comparative advantage include (1) purchasing the same resource as the advantaged competitor, (2) imitating the advantaged competitor's resource, (3) developing a strategically equivalent resource, and (4) developing a strategically superior resource (Barney 1991; Dierickx and Cool 1989; Lippman and Rumelt 1982; Peteraf 1993; Reed and DeFillippi 1990; Wernerfelt 1984). The effectiveness of these actions and the time it takes for them to neutralize a specific competitor's resource advantage successfully depend on certain characteristics of the marketplace offering and certain characteristics of the resources producing the offering.

As to the marketplace offering, the key characteristic is ambiguity. Although competitors may know that consumers in specific market segments strongly prefer their rival's offering, there may be great ambiguity as to precisely which attributes of the offering are making it perceived to be superior. Furthermore, there may be great ambiguity as to specifically which resources are being used and the precise nature of the resources that produce the highly valued attributes. These two sources of causal ambiguity (resource → offering; offering → consumer) can create great uncertainty and thus render ineffective attempts to neutralize a competitor's comparative advantage.

As to resources, the major characteristics affecting the life span of an advantage are mobility, complexity, interconnectedness, mass efficiencies, tacitness, and time compression diseconomies (see Sections 4.1.3 and 4.1.4). The advantage brought by mobile resources, those that are easily bought and sold in the marketplace (such as common kinds of machinery), can be neutralized effectively and quickly through resource acquisition. Intangible, higher-order resources, such as an organizational competence in new product testing, are relatively immobile and cannot be neutralized quickly through acquisition. In general, such resources as competences must be developed through time; they cannot acquired at a point in time. Similarly, socially complex resources, that is, those involving combinations of many resources, and interconnected resources, that is, those for which competitors may lack access to a critical component, make neutralization difficult and time-consuming. Mass efficiencies spring from the fact that some resources require a "critical mass" before they can be deployed effectively. Therefore, it may take time for competitors to develop the critical mass sufficient for neutralization. Tacit resources encompass skills that are noncodifiable and must be learned by doing and thus cannot be bought (Polanyi 1957); "learning by doing" takes time. Time compression diseconomies refers to the fact that some resources, such as a reputation for trustworthiness, by their very nature take time to acquire.

In summary, if a comparative advantage in resources stems from resources that are immobile, socially complex, interconnected, or tacit, or exhibit mass efficiencies or time compression diseconomies, then competitors will have difficulty acquiring, imitating, or developing a new resource that can neutralize a competitor's advantage-producing resource. These factors make a comparative advantage in such a resource, to varying degrees, *sustainable.*

6.1.3 Endogenous Innovation

Innovation is a natural outcome of, that is, it is endogenous to, the process of R-A competition (Figure 6.1). R-A theory distinguishes between *proactive* innovation (i.e., innovation by firms in the absence of their occupying positions of competitive disadvantage in Figure 6.2) and *reactive* innovation (i.e., innovation directly prompted by occupying positions of competitive disadvantage). Evolutionary and Austrian approaches to explaining the dynamism of market-based economies have placed great emphasis on the proactive, innovative activities of entrepreneurs in spotting opportunities and subsequently developing market offerings (see Sections 2.1 and 2.2). Likewise, R-A theory recognizes that people's entrepreneurial skills and organizations' entrepreneurial capabilities are organizational *resources.*

Proactive Innovation. What R-A theory contributes to extant work on proactive innovation is that it explicates the competitive process whereby such firm resources lead to economic change. Specifically, entrepreneurs and firms' entrepreneurial capabilities produce economic dynamism when they (1) produce proactive innovations that (2) contribute to efficiency and/or effectiveness in developing market offerings in such a way that the offerings (3) result in marketplace positions of competitive advantage and, thereby, (4) bring about superior financial performance.

As discussed in Sections 2.1.3 and 4.1.5, R-A theory incorporates both the competence-based approach to the firm and competence-based competition. R-A theory incorporates (by subsumption) the competence perspective by viewing competences as higher-order resources that are composed of distinct packages or bundles of basic resources. Competences are viewed as socially complex, interconnected, combinations of tangible basic resources (e.g., specific machinery) and intangible basic resources (e.g., specific organizational policies and procedures and the skills and knowledge of specific employees) that fit coherently together in a synergistic manner. Competences, then, play a major role in enabling firms to produce efficiently and/or effectively valued market offerings.

Competences are *distinct* resources because they are entities that contribute as distinct packages to the firm's ability to produce efficiently and/or effectively market offerings that have value for some market segment(s). That is, the whole (the competence) is more than the sum of its parts (the several basic resources). Because of the nature of competences, they are precisely the kinds of immobile resources for which a comparative advantage might have a long life span.

Consider, for example, the role of *renewal* competences, such as those described by Teece and Pisano (1994) and Teece, Pisano, and Shuen (1997) as "dynamic capabilities," by Dickson (1996) as "learning how to learn," and by Hamel and Prahalad (1994a) as "industry foresight." These authors echo the concerns expressed clearly and vividly by Gardner's (1965) call for a self-renewing society. A key factor for preventing societal stagnation he argued, is fostering, developing, and nurturing the capability of organizations to renew themselves:

> Perhaps the most distinctive thing about innovation today is that we are beginning to pursue it systematically. The large corporation does not set up a research laboratory to solve a specific problem but to engage in continuous innovation. That is good renewal doctrine. But such laboratories usually limit their innovative efforts to products and processes. What may be most in need of innovation is the corporation itself. Perhaps what every corporation (and every other organization) needs is a department of continuous renewal that would view the whole organization as a system in need of continuing innovation. (pp. 75-76)

How, then, do renewal competences, so necessary for societal renewal in Gardner's (1965) view, relate to competition? Renewal competences prompt proactive innovation by enabling firms to (1) anticipate potential market segments (unmet, changing, and/or new needs, wants, and desires); (2) envision market offerings that might be attractive to such segments; and (3) foresee the need to acquire, develop, or create the required resources, including competences, to produce the envisioned market offerings. Therefore, prompted by the quest for superior financial performance, renewal competences contribute to making R-A competition dynamic.

Reactive Innovation. However, R-A competition is dynamic even in the absence of the proactive innovations that spring from the renewal competences of entrepreneurially oriented firms. Recall that R-A theory proposes that at any point in time, competing firms are distributed throughout the nine cells in Figure 6.2 and that all firms seek the superior financial performance implied by cells 2, 3, and 6. Because all competitors cannot have superior performance simultaneously, firms occupying positions of competitive disadvantage (cells 4, 7, and 8) must attempt to neutralize and/or leapfrog the advantaged competitor through reactive innovation: by better managing existing resources, obtaining the same or equivalent value-producing resource, and/or seeking a new resource that is less costly or produces superior value. As previously discussed, the time required for reactive innovation to succeed depends on, among other things, the extent to which (1) an advantaged firm's resources are protected by such societal institutions as patents, (2) there is causal ambiguity, or (3) the resource is socially complex, interconnected, or tacit or has mass efficiencies or time compression diseconomies. Thus, R-A theory explicates the process by which endogenous competitive dynamism is ensured even in the *absence* of proactive innovation. Necessity, the mother of invention, ensures economic change in R-A competition.

Finally, note that reactive innovation includes imitating the resource, finding (creating) an equivalent resource, or finding (creating) a superior resource. Many authors have tended to focus on the equilibrating behavior of resource imitation and substitution. Although imitation and substitution are important forms of competitive actions, R-A theory recognizes that reactive innovation can also prompt disequilibrium-provoking behaviors. That is, reactive innovation in the form of finding (creating) a superior resource results in the innovating firm's new resource assortment enabling it to surpass the previously advantaged competitor in relative efficiency, relative value, or both. By leapfrogging competitors, firms realize their objective of *superior* returns, make competition dynamic, shape their environments, and renew society. In so doing, the process of reactive innovation stimulates the kinds of major innovations described as creative destruction by Schumpeter (1950). Imitation brings parity returns; parity returns are never enough.

6.1.4 Organizational Learning

Firms (attempt to) learn in many ways—by conducting formal marketing research, seeking out competitive intelligence, dissecting competitor's products, benchmarking, and test marketing. What R-A theory adds to extant work is how the process of competition itself contributes to organizational learning. As the feedback loops in Figure 6.1 show, firms learn by competing as a result of feedback from relative financial performance signaling relative market position, which in turn signals relative resources. Through competition, firms come to know (or believe they know) their relative resources and marketplace positions. Specifically, by occupying the marketplace positions identified as cells 2, 3, or 6 in Figure 6.2, firms learn that they are producing efficiently-effectively and by occupying cells 4, 7, or 8, they learn that they are producing inefficiently-ineffectively. That is, the process of competing provides an important mechanism for firms to learn how efficient-effective they are: competition, as Hayek (1945) stressed, is a *knowledge-discovery* process.

Our discussion of the roles of marketplace position, resource advantage, innovation, and competitive dynamics on organizational learning can be placed in graphic relief by returning to the automobile industry example. In the 1970s and early 1980s, American manufacturers occupied cell 7 in Figure 6.2, and Japanese car companies, which were producing superior value at lower costs, occupied the nirvana position of cell 3. Mercedes-Benz and BMW, producing superior value at parity costs relative to General Motors, Ford, and Chrysler, occupied cell 6. American car companies began losing market share. Indeed, the inferior financial performance of American companies, relative to the Japanese, prompted their attempts to learn the "secrets" of Japanese success.

Research pointed toward several factors that potentially contributed to the superior efficiency and effectiveness of Japanese car companies: corporate cultures promoting teamwork, just-in-time inventory systems, the treatment of suppliers as partners, and total quality management procedures. The American car companies began instituting changes (i.e., reactive innovations). Did they learn the right things? Were their reactive innovations the correct ones? R-A theory guarantees learning; it does not guarantee learning the *right* things.

Since the late 1980s, American car manufacturers have lowered their resource costs to below that of Japanese cars made in Japan (Lavin 1994; Suris 1996). Furthermore, BMW, Mercedes-Benz, and the Japanese car companies—for vehicles made in Germany and Japan, respectively—shifted to cell 9 as a result of their higher relative costs. But though American car companies continue to improve in overall reliability, none has yet learned how to match the reliability of Japanese nameplates—whether assembled in Japan or now the United States. In R-A theory terms, the resources that Japanese car companies rely on have not been successfully imitated, let alone surpassed or leapfrogged, by their American competitors. The automobile industry illustrates how causal ambiguity can make a comparative advantage in competences be sustainable.

To conclude this section, our discussion of organizational learning highlights the ability of R-A theory to frame important managerial and public policy issues facing market-based economies. For example, did American car companies learn the right things by imitating Japanese just-in-time inventory systems? Did German and Japanese car companies learn correctly that they should move some production facilities to the United States? Are firms paying attention to the financial indicators that result in an economic system that best contributes to long-term productivity and economic growth? Are firms learning the right things? Indeed, what are the things that we, as a society, want them to learn?

6.2 AN EVOLUTIONARY THEORY OF COMPETITION

All evolutionary theories are process theories, but not all process theories are evolutionary. Whether R-A theory is an evolutionary theory of competition can be determined only by comparing it with the characteristics that make a theory evolutionary. For Dosi and Nelson (1994), evolutionary theories in economics should explain the movement of economic variables through time by means of "both random elements which generate or renew some variation of the variables in question, and mechanisms that systematically winnow on extant variation" (p. 154). They identify (1) units of selection, (2) mechanisms that do the selecting, and (3) the criteria of selection, adaptation, and variation as the "building blocks" of evolutionary economic theories.

Hodgson (1993, pp. 39-51) provides a detailed analysis of the characteristics of the various kinds of evolutionary theories possible in economics. His taxonomy distinguishes developmental theories that focus on "stages" from genetic theories that concentrate on a "set of fairly durable human entities" and a "detailed causal explanation" of their interactions. Within genetic theories, he distinguishes ontogenetic theories that focus on "a set of given and unchanging" entities from phylogenetic theories that focus on the "complete and ongoing evolution of the population, including changes in its composition." He then distinguishes phylogenetic, consummatory theories that have end stages of "finality or consummation" from phylogenetic, nonconsummatory theories that permit never-ending evolution. Although not all phylogenetic theories sort through natural selection, the key requirements for those that do so, he maintains, are that they must have units of selection that are "fairly durable" and "heritable" and there must be a selection process that involves a "struggle for existence" that "encompasses a renewable source of variety and change," where the struggle results in the survival of the "fitter," not necessarily the "fittest."

The thesis defended here is that R-A theory, in Hodgson's terms, is a phylogenetic, nonconsummatory, evolutionary theory of competition. Both firms and resources are claimed to be the heritable, durable units of selection, and competition among firms is claimed to be the selection process that results in the survival of the "locally fitter," not "universally fittest."[1]

6.2.1 Units of Selection and Their Heritability

There are two units of selection in R-A theory: firms and resources. *Firms* are viewed as combiners of heterogeneous and imperfectly mobile resources, under conditions of imperfect and costly to obtain information, toward the primary objective of superior financial performance. *Resources* are the tangible and intangible entities available to the firm that enable it to produce efficiently and/or effectively a market offering that has value for some market segment(s). Note that both resources and firms satisfy the requirement of heritability, for the ownership of firms can be passed on to heirs, and resources constitute the entities being inherited. Because firms can acquire resources, using firms and resources as units of selection means that R-A theory is Lamarckian, which "differs from strict Darwinism mainly because it admits the possibility of the inheritance of acquired characters" (Hodgson 1993, p. 401).

6.2.2 Durability

For Hodgson (1993), as well as for Mirowski (1983), phylogenetic evolution involving natural selection must have units of selection that are relatively durable through time. Indeed, Mirowski (1983) stresses that evolutionary theories in economics must allow for "bankruptcy/death" because this is what "gives selection mechanisms their bite" (p. 764). For R-A theory, though many firms "die" each year, many others are extremely durable, with lives exceeding a century in some cases. Similarly, though some resources lose their efficiency/effectiveness potential, many resources are significantly durable.

As discussed in the preceding section, R-A theory stresses that a firm's comparative advantage in resources can "die" as a result of three factors internal to its own operation: (1) the failure to reinvest, (2) the failure to understand (causal ambiguity), and (3) the failure to respond to a changed environment. Furthermore, a comparative advantage in resources can "die" because of changes in (e.g., the depletion of) societal resources and societal institutions and as a result of the actions-behaviors of consumers, competitors, suppliers, and government. However, resource immobility implies that the life span of some resources can be relatively long.

6.2.3 Selection Process and Diversity

For Hodgson (1993), a phylogenetic evolutionary theory involving natural selection must contain a causal selection process that involves a struggle for existence. For R-A theory, it is *competition* that is the selection process. Specifically, firms and resources are selected as a result of the constant struggle among firms for comparative advantages in resources that will yield marketplace positions of competitive advantage for some market segment(s) and, thereby, superior financial performance. Through time, firms survive, prosper, and grow when they have resource assortments that enable them to occupy marketplace positions of competitive advantage. They suffer, shrink, and eventually die when they continually occupy positions of competitive disadvantage.

For Hodgson (1993), a phylogenetic, evolutionary theory involving natural selection should encompass a renewable source of diversity and change. For R-A theory, the impetus for change is the pursuit of superior financial performance through a comparative advantage in resources that leads to marketplace positions of competitive advantage. Because not all firms can have superior performance at the same time, the source of change is *renewable*—competition among diverse firms is an ongoing, never ending process. (I address the issue of firm diversity in greater detail in Section 6.3.)

6.2.4 Locally Fitter

For Hodgson (1993), there are powerful and persuasive arguments that economics, like biology, should reject the notion of "fittest" and focus instead on "fitter." First, he points out that Darwinian evolution emphasizes the importance of differential rates in *both* deaths and births. That is, Darwinian evolution "operates either because better-adapted organisms leave increased numbers of offspring, or because the variations of gene combinations that are preserved are those bestowing advantage in struggling to survive. . . . It is a matter of procreation as well as destruction" (p. 46). "Survival of the fittest," a phrase coined by Herbert Spencer, wrongly focuses only on differential rates of death. Second, fitness in biology is always relative to a given environment. Therefore, "fitter" is preferred because "the selection of some entities and the extinction of others does not necessarily imply that the favored entities are morally just, or that they are superior in an absolute sense" (Hodgson 1993, p. 49). Third, modern biology specifically acknowledges that initial starting conditions or "accidents" along the way may set in motion an evolutionary path that has no likelihood of reaching an optimal position. Therefore, path dependency implies, for Hodgson (1993), that there can be no guarantee that economic systems evolve toward some optimal state of efficiency, such as a long-term, Pareto-optimal equilibrium. For these reasons, Hodgson argues for "fitter," not "fittest."

For R-A theory, survival and success are specifically based on the "locally fitter." First, it is important to note that competition encourages firms to acquire, imitate, and "leapfrog" the resources of particular rivals who *currently* occupy marketplace positions of competitive advantage. It does not focus on rivals that are superior in some absolute sense. Second, R-A theory's selection mechanism, competition, brings about differential rates of both births and deaths—not just deaths. That is, the existence of firms enjoying superior financial performance as a result of having access to resources that place them in marketplace positions of competition advantage will encourage disadvantaged firms to give "birth" to new resources.

Third, R-A theory acknowledges competition's dependence on specific environments by focusing on rivals competing for particular market segments. That some firms are enjoying superior financial performance because they occupy marketplace positions of competitive advantage for a particular market segment does not imply that such firms would be equally advantaged (1) in other segments or (2) should the environment change. For example, should the tastes and preferences of the market segment change, there is no guarantee that previously advantaged firms will stay in the same marketplace positions. Therefore, not only does R-A theory specifically reject the notion of "absolute fittest," but it shows precisely why one would not expect competition to evolve toward any specific end point. In Hodgson's terms, an evolutionary theory that evolves toward a specific end point, for example, general equilibrium, is "consummatory." Thus, R-A theory is nonconsummatory.

Fourth, R-A theory specifically provides for path dependence effects. Suppose a rival has a resource that enables it to secure a position of competitive advantage. Suppose further that other rivals are successful in imitating the resource. Now suppose that a rival discovers a new resource that is marginally superior. If adopting a new resource requires it to abandon a resource in which it has much invested, then the innovative resource is unlikely to be adopted. In such circumstances, Schumpeter's "creative destruction" will occur only if a new rival, one who does not have heavy fixed investment at risk in the old resource, starts competing for the market segment. Therefore, R-A theory helps us understand why it is the case that creative destruction—in both industries and academic disciplines—often comes from the outside.

6.2.5 Path Dependence Effects

The subject of path dependence effects that was broached in the preceding section requires further elaboration. Since the works of David (1985) and Arthur (1989), path dependencies in economic systems have been much discussed. A path dependency occurs in an economic system when a "sequence of economic changes is one of which important influences upon the eventual outcome can be exerted by temporally remote events, including happenings dominated by chance elements rather than systematic forces" (David 1985, p. 332). The import of path dependencies is that history is important in the actual development of economies. Path-dependent processes occur because of the "network effect," that is, when the benefit of consuming a good or adopting a technology varies directly with the number of others who consume the good or adopt the technology (Katz and Shapiro 1985). Two common examples of alleged path dependencies resulting from network effects are the adoption of the VHS (over the Beta) format in VCRs and the continued use of the QWERTY over the DSK (Dvorak) keyboard.

It is undisputed that individual firms in market-based economies embark on paths wherein there are, as emphasized by Dickson (1996), "systemic negative or positive feedback effects" (p. 103). (Indeed, such path dependencies occur in both market-based and command economies, for in both there are positive and negative feedback effects.) What is greatly disputed is the effect of such path dependencies on the overall performance of economic systems.

The customary interpretation of path dependencies resulting from network effects is that they pose externalities that result in a technological "lock-in" of an inferior technology, which prevents market-based economies from evolving toward the *most* efficient technologies. Therefore, writers customarily argue that path dependence externalities prevent unregulated market-based economies from achieving optimal efficiency. Hence, government intervention is required "because there is no guarantee that efficient firms will actually be selected in a competitive, evolutionary process" (Hodgson 1993, p. 209).

The normal counterargument to the view that path dependencies thwart competition from reaching a maximally efficient state is that such situations are empirically rare. For example, Liebowitz and Margolis (1990, 1994, 1996) present strong, perhaps compelling, evidence that neither the QWERTY nor the VHS technologies were then (or now are) inferior to DSK and Beta, respectively: "The typewriter keyboard appears to be the best example where luck caused an inferior product to defeat a superior product. The story, though charming, is false" (1996, p. 31). Therefore, because the *best* examples of alleged path dependence externalities are empirically false "myths," they question whether path dependencies are a serious problem for market-based economies at all. Indeed, after distinguishing between harmless and harmful path dependencies, they (1995) provide a theoretical justification for the scarcity of real-world examples of the harmful variety.

How the literature on path dependencies will sort out is unknown. However, we can say that R-A theory permits path dependencies because, as an evolutionary, nonconsummatory theory of competition, it focuses on the "locally fitter," not the "maximally fittest." R-A competition promotes local efficiency and effectiveness; it does not guarantee maximal efficiency and effectiveness (but see Chapter 7 on productivity).

6.3 FIRM DIVERSITY

Firms differ. Indeed, the microphenomenon of the radical heterogeneity of firms is strikingly evident throughout the world's market-based economies. Across countries and within countries, and across industries and within industries, firms differ *radically* as to size, scope, methods of operations, and financial performance: (1) some firms are so large that their sales exceed the GDP of many countries; others sell flowers on a single street corner; (2) some produce hundreds of products; others sell only one; (3) some are vertically integrated "hierarchies" (Williamson 1975); others specialize in one activity; (4) some are highly profitable; others are unprofitable; and (5) some consistently maintain relatively high profits; others "fall back into the pack." As pointed out by Nelson (1991), explaining firm diversity should be a major goal of a satisfactory theory of competition.

Because perfect competition implies numerous small firms in every industry (with each firm producing a single product in the quantity dictated by its most efficient plant size), firm diversity poses an anomaly for neoclassical theory. In contrast, firm diversity is, as discussed in Section 6.2.3, is endogenous to R-A competition. First, recall that R-A theory rejects the neoclassical view that firms are mathematical abstractions. Indeed, following Chandler (1990), every firm is a unique entity in time and space. Therefore, as a result of their history in obtaining and deploying resources, firms will differ from their rivals. Second, different assortments of resources, owned or available to firms, may be equally efficient or effective in serving some market segments. For example, buying a component in the marketplace may be equally efficient and effective as producing it internally. These different assortments, therefore, lead to firms of varying sizes and scopes.

Third, heterogeneous demand implies that servicing different market segments in the same industry will lead to firms with different sizes and scopes. Some firms may be "niche" marketers, and others produce "a product for every purse." Fourth, diverging from transaction cost economics (Williamson 1993), firms tend to conduct activities in-house, rather than contract them out, when they constitute, or are part of an assortment of resources that constitutes, a competence. Indeed, "competence leveraging" (Sanchez, Heene, and Thomas 1996) is a key strategic objective. Therefore, because firms will be more hierarchical on those dimensions that constitute competences, differences in competences will promote diversity. Fifth, when firms servicing some market segment have a comparative advantage in resources that competitors cannot imitate, find substitutes for, or leapfrog with an entirely new resource, there will be firm diversity in the very important area of financial performance.

Firm diversity in financial performance provides an area for testing directly the relative merits of R-A versus neoclassical theory. If (1) firms are viewed as combiners of homogeneous, perfectly mobile resources by means of a standard production function and (2) intra-industry demand is viewed as homogeneous, then the variance in financial performance across firms and their business units must result from such industry factors as collusion. This, of course, is the standard view of the structure $\rightarrow$ conduct $\rightarrow$ performance model in industrial organization economics (Bain 1956). As Schmalensee (1985) observes, a "central hypothesis in virtually all [neo]classical work was that increases in seller concentration tend to raise industrywide profits by facilitating collusion" (p. 342). Empirically, therefore, neoclassical theory predicts that "industry effects" should explain most of the variance in firms' performance and "firm effects" should explain little, if any.

In contrast, if firms are viewed as combiners of heterogeneous, imperfectly mobile resources and intra-industry demand is viewed as heterogeneous, then "firm effects" should dominate "industry effects." Thus, on the issue of diversity of financial performance, R-A theory and neoclassical theory make empirically testable, opposite predictions.[2]

6.3.1 An Empirical Test

Schmalensee's (1985) study investigated the industry effects versus firm effects issue using variance components analysis. This analysis technique, unlike regression, allows one to assess the independent importance of nested business unit, corporate, and industry effects, where "the firm" in the neoclassical tradition is conceptually closest to the business unit. Using the Federal Trade Commission's line of business data and 1975 business unit return on assets as the measure of financial performance, Schmalensee (1985) finds industry effects to account for 19.5% of the variance of business unit return on assets and corporate effects to be not significant. He concludes: "[This] supports the classical focus on industry level analysis as against the revisionist tendency to downplay industry differences" (p. 349).

However, since Schmalensee's (1985) study, not only have studies using different samples and methodologies uniformly failed to corroborate the "industry is all that matters" conclusion (Cubbin and Geroski 1987; Hansen and Wernerfelt 1989), but so also have direct replications and extensions. Rumelt (1991) pointed out that Schmalensee's use of only one year's data not only confounded stable industry effects with transient annual fluctuations but also make it impossible to separate the effects of the overall corporation from those of the individual business unit. When Rumelt (1991) supplemented Schmalensee's 1975 data with the FTC data for 1974, 1976, and 1977, he found that whereas industry effects explained only 8% of the variance, corporate and business units effects explained 2% and 44%, respectively. Therefore, he finds "total firm" effects of 46% (2% + 44%) to be almost six times those of industry effects.

Supporting Rumelt's findings, Roquebert, Phillips, and Westfall (1996) find industry, corporate, and business unit effects to be 10%, 18%, and 37%, respectively (resulting in "total firm" effects of 18% + 37% = 55%). Notably, their database was much larger (more than 6,800 manufacturing corporations), was from a more recent time period (1985-1991), used a longer time period (7 years vs. 4), had a broader base (more than 940 SIC, 4-digit categories), and (unlike FTC data) included both small and large corporations. Similarly, McGahan and Porter (1997) find industry, corporate, and business unit effects for their sample of 7,003 corporations (for the time period 1982-1988) to be 19%, 4%, and 32%, respectively (resulting in "total firm" effects of 4% + 32% = 36%).[3] Likewise, Mauri and Michaels (1998) use a sample of 264 single-business companies from 69 4-digit SIC code industries, for the time period 1988-1992, and find industry and firm effects to be 5% and 30%, respectively. Similarly, for the time period 1978-1992, Mauri and Michaels find the comparable figures to be 4% and 19%.

In summary, depending on the database used, it appears that industry effects account for 4% to 19% of the variance in performance, as measured by return on assets, and firm effects account for 19% to 55%.[4] In short, industry is the "tail" of competition; the firm is the "dog."

The empirical studies on the diversity of financial performance indicate that R-A theory makes the correct prediction on the issue of financial performance diversity. Competition simply does not produce the requisite "as if" conditions and/or the competitive circumstances in the U.S. economy are not "close enough" to the assumptions of perfect competition to enable neoclassical theory to make the correct prediction. If predictive accuracy is the criterion for theory assessment (Friedman 1953), then the fact that "firm effects" account for two to six times the variance accounted for by "industry effects" implies that neoclassical theory fails the test of predictive accuracy. In contrast, because R-A theory proposes that firms are *best* construed as combiners of heterogeneous, imperfectly mobile resources and intra-industry demand is *best* construed as substantially heterogeneous, then the fact that "firm effects" dominate "industry effects" is precisely what one expects. That is, the descriptively more accurate premises of R-A theory enable it to make the correct prediction.

NOTES

1. The discussion here follows closely that in Hunt (1997c).

2. It is useful to consider the prediction that transaction cost economics would make with respect to financial performance diversity. As discussed in Section 4.2.2, transaction cost economics posits economizing on transaction costs as its "main case" explanation of firms (Williamson 1996, p. 233). Furthermore, it assumes universal opportunism and adopts the maximizing tradition: "Neoclassical economics maintains a maximizing orientation. This is unobjectionable, if all the relevant costs [i.e., the transaction costs] are included" (Williamson 1985, p. 45). Indeed, even "at the expense of realism of assumptions, maximization gets the job done (Williamson 1996, p. 231). However, if transaction cost minimizing is the *main case* and all firms in an industry engage in opportunism, then the maximizing tradition would seem to imply that all firms in an industry would ultimately wind up at precisely the same size, scope, and profitability—the one that minimizes total costs, including each firm's identical costs of opportunism. Therefore, transaction cost economics would seem to predict, like neoclassical theory, that "industry effects" should dominate "firm effects."

3. By the time of McGahan and Porter (1997), the entire nature of the debate over firm performance had changed dramatically. Originally, advocates of industry-based strategy (e.g., Montgomery and Porter 1991) were citing Schmalensee (1985) to justify their focusing on "choosing industry" as the key strategic decision. After Rumelt's (1991) replication and extension of Schmalensee found firm factors to account for almost six times the variance of industry factors (46% vs 8%), the debate shifted toward

whether industry choice matters at all. Thus, McGahan and Porter's (1997) study, which finds that firm effects dominate industry effects by *only* 36% to 19%, is interpreted by its authors as confronting the challenge from Rumelt and others that industry, far from being *key,* doesn't seem to matter at all. The point to be emphasized here is that no one now claims empirical support for the neoclassical position. That is, after Rumelt's (1991) and other studies, no one argues seriously the neoclassical position that either industry is everything or industry effects dominate firm effects. Stated differently, even though Schmalensee (1985) is still cited frequently, no one arguing the neoclassical position on firm performance can now be taken seriously.

4. For a comprehensive review of studies on firm performance diversity, see Bowman and Helfat (1998). For a discussion of whether findings of "more variance explained" should be equated with "more important," see Brush and Bromiley (1997).

Chapter 7

Productivity, Efficiency, and Effectiveness

For all economic entities, be they firms, industries, or entire economies, measures of productivity are ratios of outputs to inputs. For example, the productivity of automobile manufacturers is often measured as the number of labor-hours required to assemble a car. For economies as a whole, the key productivity ratios are those relating gross domestic product (GDP) to a factor of production, for example, labor or capital. Materially abundant economies are generally those that are high in total factor productivity, that is, GDP divided by the total labor and capital employed. As Coase (1998) points out: "The welfare of a human society depends on the flow of goods and services, and this in turn depends on the productivity of the economic system" (p. 73).

In the eighteenth century, the GDP per capita of the richest Western nation was approximately five times that of the poorest African country; by the end of the twentieth century, the gap was about 400 to 1 (Landes 1998, p. xx). The productivity of European nations, compared with the rest of the world, began to diverge in the 1700s with the industrial revolution and its substitution of (1) the factory system of production for the craft system and (2) water and steam power for human and animal power. From its beginning in Manchester, England, in the mid-1700s, industrialization spread to Belgium in the early 1800s, to France and the United States in the mid-1800s, and to Germany in the late 1800s. By the end of the nineteenth century, Great Britain's place as the world's leader in productivity was assumed by the United States (Baumol, Nelson, and Wolff 1994). In the twentieth century, the Soviet Union and other socialist countries claimed that planned economic systems would be much more efficient, much more productive, than market-based ones. Hence, "we will bury you." Many Western economists and political leaders agreed, right up to the collapse of the planned economies in the late 1980s and early 1990s (Yergin and Stanislaw 1998).

Undoubtedly, the single most important macroeconomic phenomenon of the twentieth century was the collapse of planned or "command" economies, which were premised on state-owned firms cooperating among each other under the direction of a central planning board, and the concomitant triumph of market-based economies, which are premised on competition among self-directed, privately owned firms. Adam Smith versus Karl Marx represents perhaps the greatest natural experiment in recorded history. The results of the experiment show that economies premised on privately owned, self-directed, *competing* firms are far superior to economies premised on state-owned, state-directed, cooperating firms in terms of both abundance, that is, productivity, and the overall quality of goods and services.

Both the quantitative lack of goods and services, that is, low GDP, and the fact that the goods that were produced were so shoddy plagued the East bloc countries: "The Stalinist model of Authoritarian centralized controls . . . produced low growth, shoddy products, ques, and shortages" (Maddison 1994, p. 57). Therefore, why economies *premised* on competition are superior to command economies in productivity and the quality of goods and services produced is a macrolevel question that should be addressed by any satisfactory *theory* of competition.

For more than half a century, the neoclassical tradition's definition of economics has focused on the allocation of scarce resources: "Economics is the science which studies human behaviour as a relationship between ends and scarce means which have alternative uses" (Robbins 1932/1984, p. 16).[1] Therefore, one might expect that neoclassical theory could contribute to explaining the superior productivity of market-based economies by pointing to the resource allocation efficiencies of perfect competition and then arguing that market-based economies are "close enough" (Friedman 1953) to perfect competition to benefit from such efficiencies. However, ever since what is labeled the "socialist calculation debate" that pitted the "Austrians" against the socialists in the 1920s, 1930s, and 1940s, neoclassicists have argued that perfect competition theory and general equilibrium analysis provide no theoretical grounds for favoring market-based economies (Hodgson 1992; Keizer 1989; Lavoie 1985).

For example, Nobel laureate Knight (1936), who Stigler (1957) credits with formalizing perfect competition theory, claims that "the problems of collectivism are not problems of economic theory . . . and the economic theorist, as such, has little or nothing to say about them" (p. 255). Because (a) Knight's conclusion of "little or nothing to say" is so counterintuitive, (b) R-A theory draws heavily on and has affinities with the "losing" side of the socialist calculation debate, that is, Austrian economics (see Section 2.2), and (c) there are valuable lessons to be learned from the debate as to how a theory of competition can differentiate economies premised on competition from command economies, our analysis of productivity requires that we understand the arguments in the debate.

This chapter and its two successors examine several aspects of the wealth of nations. The focus of this chapter is on the issue of productivity. Specifically, this chapter explores the nature of productivity and why economies premised on privately owned, self-directed firms competing among each other are more productive than those premised on state-owned, state-directed firms cooperating among each other.

First, I discuss the issue of the quality differentials between the goods of market-based and command economies and why such differentials are inconsistent with perfect competition. I then review the neoclassical approach to resource allocation efficiency. Next, I review the socialist calculation debate and explain how it came to be that mainstream economics concluded that neoclassical theory provided no theoretical grounds for predicting that socialist economies would be less efficient than their market-based counterparts. Finally, I discuss how R-A theory approaches productivity and show how it contributes to explaining the superior productivity of market-based economies.

7.1 NEOCLASSICAL THEORY, QUALITY, AND EFFICIENCY

As to quality differentials, perfect competition cannot contribute to explaining why market-based economies have higher-quality products than command economies. The assumptions of homogeneous consumer demand (premise P1, Table 5.1), perfect knowledge of production functions (P5), and homogeneous and perfectly mobile resources (P7) mean that (a) all consumers must desire precisely the same quality level within each product class, (b) all firms have equal access to all production technologies (i.e., firm-specific competences are disallowed), and (c) all firms have equal access to all resources. Therefore, there is no reason to believe that East-bloc firms in each and every industry could not (and would not) have (1) had access to the same production functions, (2) purchased the same, homogeneous factors of production, and (3) implemented in an equally competent manner the same standard production functions to (4) produce the same quality products as did their Western, market-based counterparts.

Unless consumers in East-bloc economies *desired* lower-quality products (an assumption refuted by the premium prices commanded by Western goods in such economies) or unless the resource endowment, for example, labor, was intrinsically inferior in command economies (also a tenuous assumption), perfect competition cannot contribute to explaining the historical shoddiness of East-bloc products. Perfect competition isn't "close enough" (Friedman 1953). (The issue of quality and R-A theory is deferred to Section 7.3.1.)

7.1.1 Perfect Competition and Efficiency

It would appear that perfect competition could potentially explain differences in productivity. As discussed in Sections 1.1 and 5.7, the neoclassical tradition regards perfect competition as *perfect* because every long-run, perfectly competitive, equilibrium set of prices yields a Pareto-optimal allocation of resources. Conversely, every Pareto-optimal allocation of resources implies a long-run, perfectly competitive, equilibrium set of prices.

That is, the Walrasian equations of general equilibrium imply a set of commodity prices that have the following characteristic: Given the utility functions (preferences) of all consumers and their respective incomes, no price change can increase the utility of one consumer except by decreasing the utility of another consumer. Likewise, the equations of general equilibrium imply a set of factor prices that allocates resources in such a manner that no reallocation of resources can produce more of any single commodity without producing less of another. Thus, perfect competition and general equilibrium theory, taken together, imply that the price of each commodity (reflecting what consumers are *willing* to pay for an additional unit) and its marginal cost (the extra resource costs society *must* pay for an additional unit) will be exactly equal. Perfect competition is Pareto-optimally *perfect*.

Mainstream economists readily admit that such productive and abundant economies as the United States are not characterized by perfect competition.

However, they claim that the U.S. economy is close enough to perfect competition to benefit from its efficiency-producing characteristics (e.g., Shepherd 1982; Stigler 1949). Therefore, a naive reading of neoclassical theory would be that it could potentially contribute to explaining the superior productivity of market-based economies on the grounds of their superior resource allocation efficiency. That is, lacking the equilibrium prices produced by self-directed, privately owned firms competing among each other, socialist planners would lack the "signals" as to where to deploy (and redeploy) resources efficiently. Therefore, the inability of socialist planners to allocate resources as efficiently as the marketplace would depress the overall productivity of command economies.

The reason that the argument in the preceding paragraph is a "naive reading" of neoclassical theory is that mainstream economists, economic historians, and neoclassical specialists in comparative economic systems, as a result of the "socialist calculation debate," agreed uniformly that perfect competition plus general equilibrium theory provide no theoretical grounds for predicting the superior productivity of market-based economies.[2] This surprising conclusion stems from neoclassicists' interpretation of the "socialist calculation debate" that pitted the "Austrians" (principally Hayek 1935a,b,c, 1937, 1940, 1945, 1948; Mises 1920, 1922, 1949; Robbins 1934) against advocates of socialism (principally Dickinson 1933; Lange and Taylor 1936, 1938; Lerner 1934, 1936, 1937, 1938; Taylor 1929). The debate's question was, "[Can] one central authority . . . solve the problem of distributing a limited amount of resources between a practically infinite number of competing purposes . . . with a degree of success equating or approaching the results of competitive capitalism?" (Hayek 1935a/1948, pp. 130-31). Austrian economists argued for the superior resource allocation efficiency of capitalism; socialists argued for central planning.

Not surprisingly, Hayek (1978) believed that "anybody studying these discussions" would surely conclude that any "attempt at centralized collectivist planning of a large economic system was . . . bound greatly to decrease productivity" (p. 235). Also unsurprisingly, socialist economists claimed that *they* clearly won the debate: "Lange thus not only refutes the antisocialist case of Mises and his followers but . . . [shows] that socialism possesses definite advantages where they [the "Austrians"] regard it as most vulnerable" (Sweezy 1949, p. 231). What might surprise noneconomists, however, is that the consensus among neoclassical economists, economic historians, and specialists in comparative economic systems is that the socialists had shown that perfect competition theory and general equilibrium provide no theoretical grounds for predicting that market-based economies would be more productive than command economies. Understanding how mainstream economics came to this counterintuitive conclusion is the task of the next section.

7.2 THE SOCIALIST CALCULATION DEBATE

Mises' (1920, 1922) original challenge was to Marxian socialism, which demanded, among other things, the abolition of *all* "bourgeois" economic institutions, for example, the private ownership of the means of production, the profit motive, money, and prices. Marx's objectivist theory of value maintained that the true value of a commodity was not its subjective, marketplace price in money terms but the socially necessary number of labor-hours to produce it. Mises quotes Engels's famous discussion of how socialist planners can make calculations that compare (a) the utility of various amounts of commodities produced against (b) their labor-hour production costs:

> As soon as society takes possession of the means of production and applies them to production in their directly socialised form, each individual's labour, however different its specific utility may be, becomes *a priori* and directly social labour. The amount of social labour invested in a product need not then be established indirectly; daily experience immediately tells us how much is necessary on an average. Society can simply calculate how many hours of labour are invested in a steam engine, a quarter of last harvest's wheat, and a 100 yards of linen of given quality.... To be sure, society will also have to know how much labour is needed to produce any consumption-good. It will have to arrange its production plan according to its means of production, to which labour especially belongs. The utility yielded by the various consumption-goods, weighted against each other and against the amount of labour required to produce them, will ultimately determine the plan. People will make everything simple without the mediation of notorious "value" [of marketplace-determined prices]. (Engels, as quoted in Mises 1920, p. 112)

The "simple" calculations that Engels alludes to proved much more complex in practice. Although the Soviet Union experimented with vouchers ("to each according to his need") and other alternatives to money and prices in the "War Communism" period (pre-1920), the result was economic chaos: "In 1920 production is said to have fallen to 13 percent of that of the pre-war period. The cause of this decline was not only the war, but also, to a large extent, the utterly defective distribution of the means of production under the system of natural [i.e. Marxian] socialism.... It almost never happened that production goods allotted to an undertaking by various Governing Boards were matched in quantity or quality" (Brutzkus 1922/1935, pp. 106-7).

As a consequence of the economic chaos, the Soviet Union abandoned vouchers and reinstated the institutions of money and prices. In so doing, the Soviet Union abandoned key aspects of Marxian socialism for the very reasons Mises argued. Reviewing Mises' arguments, therefore, is instructive for understanding key aspects of the debate.

Mises (1920) argued that the very capitalist institutions excoriated by Marx were essential for the rational economic calculation required for resource allocation efficiency. First, he argued, money is required to permit cardinal accounting procedures. (Although one can add the dollar value of labor, iron ore, and machinery and compare the sum to the dollar value of steel produced, one cannot add labor-hours, the number of machines, and tons of iron ore and compare the total to the utility of tons of steel—as Engels had naïvely maintained.) Second, prices (in money terms) of both commodities and resources are required. Third, because the prices must be those that result from privately owned firms engaged in entrepreneurial, rivalrous competition, the institution of private property is required for economic calculation and resource allocation efficiency. Therefore, argued Mises (1920), socialism is "quite impossible" because: "Where there is no free market, there is no pricing mechanism; without a pricing mechanism, there is no economic calculation. . . . [W]e have the spectacle of a socialist economic order floundering in the ocean of possible and conceivable economic combinations without the compass of economic calculation. . . . Socialism is the abolition of rational economy" (pp. 110-111).

Socialist economists countered Mises in two ways. First, directly contradicting Marx's explicit writings and ignoring the actual experiences of the Soviet Union in the War Communism period, they claimed that Marxian socialism did not imply the abolition of money and prices. Thus, they claimed, Mises' argument was a "straw-dragon" (Sweezy 1936, p. 423). Second, and much more important, they (wrongly) interpreted Mises' use of "competition" as meaning "perfection competition" (instead of Austrian, rivalrous competition), and they interpreted "economic calculation" and "rational economy" as meaning (again wrongly) "solving the Walrasian equations." With such a (mis)interpretation of Mises, they argued that Mises' position had already been refuted.

Barone (1908), socialist economists argued, had already demonstrated that a Pareto-optimum solution for a socialist economy would involve solving the same kind of Walrasian equations as for a capitalist economy. One simply substitutes the real, live, central planning board for the fictitious Walrasian "auctioneer." Indeed, instead of the wasteful "groping" for Pareto optimality under capitalism, the planning board would solve the n equations with n unknowns directly. Solving the equations directly would enable the central planning board to determine prices that cleared all markets, while at the same time planners could redistribute income to promote equality. Because the neoclassical tradition was rapidly being mathematized and was coming to equate "efficiency" with "Walrasian equation solving," neoclassicists—without exception—found the socialists' counter to be theoretically correct and a proper response to Mises' challenge (Lavoie 1985).[3]

7.2.1 Robbins and Hayek

Robbins (1934) entered the debate by addressing a version of the "democratic" or "market" socialism that was being advanced as an alternative to Marxian socialism. Under market socialism, consumers are given sums of money (instead of vouchers), and they bid for the various commodities available. Guided by these market-revealed preferences, the central planning board "would seek so to distribute its productive resources so that the demand for all commodities was satisfied to the same level of urgency" (p. 150).

Although a plan for distributing the resources among rival uses is technologically feasible, Robbins (1934) argued, there is no way to determine the plan's *economic* efficiency, that is, the value of the opportunities foregone by the plan chosen. Although the Walrasian equations may offer a solution "on paper," in practice there is "no hope . . . of discovering the relative sacrifices of alternative kinds of investment" (p. 151).

What private property in capitalist economies provides, and what socialist economies do not have, Robbins (1934) argued, is a market for capital in which prices contain information about the scarcity of resources in terms of opportunity costs. Indeed, "the prices of the various factors of production, which are the resultant of the competitive bidding of the different *entrepreneurs,* tend to reflect the value of their contribution to the production of different products. . . . Computations of costs and prices under competitive conditions are, as it were, a short cut to the solution of the millions of equations" (p. 152; italics in original). (Readers should note carefully the allusion of Robbins to "millions of equations.")

Hayek (1935a,b,c, 1937, 1940, 1945, 1948) entered the debate next. He argued that Mises had been fully aware of Barone's work on static equilibrium under socialism but believed it was irrelevant to the economic problem of efficiency because markets in real (contrasted with theoretical) economies are always in a disequilibrium state. Indeed, as Mises (1922/1951) put it, "under stationary conditions there no longer exists a problem for economic calculation to solve. . . . [T]he problem of economic calculation is of economic dynamics: it is no problem of economic statics" (p. 139). Thus, argued Hayek, when socialist economists couch the debate in neoclassical, Walrasian, general equilibrium terms, they miss a crucial point in Mises' critique, which makes their arguments not relevant to the debate.

Hayek acknowledged that socialist planners could set prices for capital goods that cleared markets. Such prices, however, would not fulfill the role of marketplace prices in capitalism. Marketplace prices determined by rivalrous competition convey information about the relative scarcities of resources, such information being widely dispensed among individuals:

> The economic problem of scarcity is thus not merely a problem of how to allocate "given" resources—if "given" is taken to mean given to a single mind which deliberately solves the problem set by these "data." It is rather a problem of how to secure the best use of resources known to any of the members of society, for ends whose relative importance only these individuals know. Or, to put it briefly, it is a problem of the utilization of knowledge which is not given to anyone in its totality. (Hayek 1945/1948, pp. 77-78)

Although Hayek believed general equilibrium theory to be an impressive analytical achievement, he viewed competition as a process, not a theoretical state. It is through the process of competitive rivalry that firms in market economies gain the knowledge of what works, what doesn't, what is efficient, and what is not. Competition is a process of knowledge-discovery. Therefore, argued Hayek, as a practical matter, central planning boards would lack the knowledge required for efficient resource allocation.

7.2.2. The Socialist Response

Socialist economists interpreted Robbins's and Hayek's arguments as a retreat from, as they saw it, the Mises position that socialist equilibrium is "theoretically impossible" to the new view that it was "possible, but impracticable" (Lavoie 1985). That is, it is impractical to solve the "millions of equations" alluded to by Robbins. They then argued for the practicality of socialist equilibria.

Lange showed that socialist and capitalist equilibria were *equally* practicable by relying, in part, on the fact that Walrasian equilibrium uses the "as if" procedure. That is, since the Walrasian "auctioneer" is a fictitious entity with limited information, equilibrium is reached (if reached at all) through a series of successive trials or *tatonnements,* that is, as if it were "groping" (Lange and Taylor 1936). Similarly, argued Lange, equilibrium in market socialism could just as easily be reached by Taylor's (1929) "trial and error" method. Starting from an initial guess as to equilibrium prices, product surpluses (or shortages) would indicate to the central planning board that prices are too high (or too low) and prices adjusted accordingly.

As to factors of production, Lange argued that production would be just as efficient as in capitalism because plant managers would be *instructed* (a) to combine factors of production so that the average cost is minimized and (b) to produce at the quantity where marginal cost equals marginal revenue (Lange and Taylor 1936). Therefore, as Taylor (1929) had argued:

> [I]f economic authorities of a socialist state would recognize equality between cost of production on the one hand and the demand price of the buyer on the other as being the adequate and the only adequate proof that the commodity in question ought to be produced, they could, under all ordinary conditions, perform their duties, as the persons who were immediately responsible for the guidance of production, with well-founded confidence that they would *never* make any other than the right use of the economic resources placed at their disposal. (p. 8; italics added)

After establishing the *equivalence* between socialism and capitalism on efficiency grounds, Lange argued for socialism's *superiority* on other grounds. Specifically, he claimed that the state could ensure income equality and solve the problem of externalities. Furthermore, because the state can eliminate monopolies, it could reduce prices, increase the rate of innovation, and eliminate business cycles (Lange and Taylor 1936). Lange viewed "the real danger of socialism" to be that of the "bureaucratization of economic life." Nonetheless, he argued, "[socialists] do not see how the same, or even greater, danger can be averted under monopolistic capitalism. Officials subject to democratic [socialist] control seem preferable to private corporation executives who practically *are responsible to nobody*" (Lange and Taylor 1938, p. 110; italics in original). After Lange's articulation of what the economic historian Kuhn (1970) refers to as a "closely reasoned theory of socialism" (p. 455), socialists claimed victory. Mainstream economists agreed.[4]

Thereafter, a wide body of literature developed, called "planometrics," that attempted to systematize the "trial and error" planning process. It was believed that the advent of linear, nonlinear, and integer programming, with the aid of computers, would enable planners to efficiently allocate resources. Such sophisticated techniques, it was alleged, further demonstrated just how wrong

Mises and Hayek were (Lavoie 1985). As Lange (1967), writing retrospectively, put it:

> Were I to rewrite my essay today, my task would be much simpler. My answer to Hayek and Robbins would be: so what's the trouble? Let us put the simultaneous equations on an electronic computer and we shall obtain the solution in less than a second. The market process with its cumbersome tatonnements appears old fashioned. Indeed, it may be considered as a computing device on the pre-electronic age. (p. 58)

Similarly, as Cave (1980) put it:

> The potential impact of computers on economic planning is enormous. To appreciate this one only has to recall one of the arguments made in the debate in the 1930s on the feasibility of central planning. It was asserted then that an efficient allocation of resources in a centrally planned economy was inconceivable because such an allocation would require the solution of "millions of equations." At the time, of course, no electronic computers were available. Today the situation is quite different and the computational objection would have much less force. (p. vii)

The consensus among neoclassicists is that the arguments of socialist economists, as depicted in Table 7.1, provided "an answer acceptable to economists" when they "decided to meet von Mises on his own terms" (Goldman 1971, p. 10). (Note the "his own terms.") Indeed, concludes Little (1950), "Thus, and with some irony, the static welfare-theory armament [i.e., the use of perfect competition and general equilibrium] of the supporters of *laissez-faire* was seized by their opponents, and effectively used against them" (p. 254).

Therefore, Lekachman (1959) concludes that socialist economists have used the equations of neoclassical theory and "proved that a Central Planning Board could impose rules upon socialist managers which allocated resources and set prices as efficiently as a capitalist society of the purest stripe and more efficiently than the capitalist communities of experience" (pp. 396-97). Similarly, Landauer (1947) concludes that socialist economists did "an excellent job" of interpreting neoclassical theory and make "it impossible to question the practicality of advance calculation of values by a planning board" (p. 51). Likewise, Balassa (1974) finds that "the workings of a purely competitive system" and those of the "market solution for socialism," as well as "the results they lead to," are "essentially the same" (p. 5).

Even Schumpeter (1950)—often considered an ally of Austrian economists—found the "trial and error" solution to be "eminently operational"

TABLE 7.1   The Socialist Calculation Debate: Economic Efficiency and
                 Productive Economies

	Perfect Competition	*Socialism*
1. Goal	Pareto optimal allocation of resources	Pareto optimal allocation of resources
2. Quantity of each good	MC = MR	MC = MR (instructed by planners)
3. Plant size	Point of minimum average cost	Point of minimum average cost (instructed by planners)
4. Economic efficiency	Solving Walrasian equations for general equilibrium	Solving Walrasian equations for general equilibrium
5. Method for Walrasian equation solving	Walrasian "auctioneer" and bidding ("as if")	Central planning board (and computers)
6. Price setting in practice	"Groping"	"Trial and error" by central planning board (and computers)
7. Conclusion	Perfect competition leads to the efficient allocation of resources and, therefore, a productive economy	Socialism leads to an even more efficient allocation of resources and a more productive economy

(p. 186). For him, "there is a strong case for believing in its [i.e., socialism's] superior economic efficiency" (p. 188). Indeed, the conclusion that neoclassical theory implies that socialism, at least theoretically, is equally efficient as capitalism became orthodoxy in microeconomic theory textbooks and enshrined as the "Lange-Lerner rule" (e.g., Ferguson 1966, p. 377).

7.2.3 Implications of the Debate

The task now, of course, is not to predict whether command economies will be as productive as market-based economies—for the twentieth century showed that they are not. Furthermore, the purpose of reviewing the debate is not to criticize mainstream economics for having made the wrong prediction, for all scholars in all disciplines err, and many economists have changed their minds on the virtues of socialism. For example, whereas Heilbroner (1970) argued in the 1970s that socialist planners "would receive exactly the same information from a socialized economic system as did entrepreneurs under a market system" (p. 88), two decades later he states: "it was felt that Lange had decisively won the argument for socialist planning. . . . It turns out, of course, that Mises was right" (Heilbroner 1990, p. 92).

The task now is to use the resource-advantage theory of competition to explain why market-based economies are more productive than their socialist counterparts. Not only does the socialist calculation debate help us understand why neoclassical theory, as interpreted by mainstream economists, cannot contribute to explaining such productivity differences, but the debate can guide theory development. There are lessons to be learned—five, I suggest—from the socialist calculation debate about the minimum desiderata for a satisfactory theory of competition.

The first lesson is that the dynamics of competition in real economies cannot be approximated by a series of moving equilibria. Rather, an evolutionary, process theory is required. Second, the efficiency problems of real economies cannot be approximated by a series of differential equations. Instead, a process theory is required that will have key relationships among constructs that cannot be expressed as differential equations. That is, the complete mathematization of neoclassical theory was a "wrong turning" (Robinson 1951). Third, the institutions of capitalism, particularly private property, cannot be superfluous to understanding competition. Rather, institutions must be able to contribute essentially to the efficiency-producing characteristics of the process of competition. Fourth, production technologies cannot be assumed to be "given." Instead, organizational learning must be endogenous in a theory of competition and the process of learning must be explicated. Fifth, innovation cannot be exogenous to competition. Rather, innovation must be endogenous to the evolutionary process of competing.

R-A theory can contribute to explaining the productivity difference between market-based and command economies. It does so, I argue, because it heeds the lessons of the socialist calculation debate.

7.3 PRODUCTIVITY AND R-A THEORY

Because productivity is a ratio of outputs to inputs, R-A theory highlights the fact that increases in productivity can result from increases in either efficiency or effectiveness, that is, from (a) *more* efficiently creating value or (b) efficiently creating *more* value. Efficiency is increased, for example, when a firm produces a market offering at reduced resource costs that is perceived by consumers in a market segment as equivalent to the firm's previous offering. In contrast, effectiveness is increased when a firm, at the same resource costs, produces a market offering with attributes that consumers perceive to be worth more than a previous offering. In the efficiency example, the cost reductions might come from a variety of sources, including (1) substituting lower cost resources for those of higher cost, (2) developing a new organizational competence (e.g., "just-in-time inventory"), or (3) improving an existing competence (e.g., making "just-in-time inventory" procedures work *better*). Similarly, in the effectiveness example, the value enhancement might come from such sources as (1) being able to substitute a higher-quality resource for one of lower quality, (2) outsourcing a key component to a supplier who has superior competence in producing it, or (3) improving an existing, in-house competence for making a key component.

In short, in reference to Figure 6.2, firms become more efficient when they move vertically in the competitive position matrix (from bottom to top) and more effective when they move horizontally (from left to right). A contribution of R-A theory to the productivity debate, therefore, is to provide a theory of competition that can expand the discussion beyond the efficiency-enhancing (read: resource cost-reducing) dimension of productivity. Using the expanded conceptualization of the relationships among productivity, efficiency, and effectiveness, R-A theory contributes to explaining the superior productivity of market-based economies on four grounds: the motivations for innovation, the ability to make economic calculations that result in productivity, the ability to learn to be productive, and the ability to create resources.

7.3.1 The Motivations for Innovation

First, recall that R-A theory is an evolutionary, process theory of competition. Specifically, competition is the disequilibrating, evolutionary process that consists of the constant struggle among firms for comparative advantages in resources that will yield marketplace positions of competitive advantage and, thereby, superior financial performance. Therefore, the motivations that R-A theory posits as driving competition contribute to its ability to explain the superior productivity of market-based economies.

The process of R-A competition is motivated by the expectation that superior rewards will flow to those owners, managers, and employees whose firms achieve superior financial performance, that is, more than, better than. Therefore, the pursuit of superior financial performance motivates firms to develop, acquire, discover, or create particular kinds of resource assortments. These specific assortments are those that enable firms to produce market offerings of value to particular market segments with such efficiency and/or effectiveness that they will move upward and to the right in Figure 6.2 and occupy the marketplace positions identified as cells 2, 3, or 6.

The process of competing, then, motivates the constant drive toward efficiency-enhancing and effectiveness-enhancing innovation (see Section 6.1.3). Command economies, to their detriment, lack the mechanisms to motivate this ongoing *process.* Neoclassical theory, to its detriment, attempted to approximate the process with a series of moving equilibria in which all productivity-enhancing innovation was exogenous. Equilibrium analysis was indeed a "wrong turning" (Robinson 1951).

The preceding argument that the objective of superior financial performance—more than, better than—motivates the process of R-A competition that results in productivity-enhancing innovation shows why the empirical findings on financial performance diversity discussed in Section 3.1 are so important. As will be recalled, firm factors explain more of the variance in financial performance of business units than do industry factors. The implication, of course, is that superior firm performance is possible *without* such anticompetitive, antisocial practices as colluding with one's competitors to fix prices. Therefore, it is rational for firms to seek superior performance through pro-social, productivity-enhancing innovations.

Consider the issue of quality. As discussed in Section 7.1, neoclassical theory cannot explain the superior quality of products in market-based economies. In contrast, superior quality is a natural outcome of the process of R-A competition. Although definitions differ as to what "quality" means in various contexts, note that when superior quality is perceived by consumers in a market segment to add value, producing superior quality market offerings can enable firms to occupy marketplace positions of competitive advantage (cells 3 and 6 in Figure 6.2). Note also, however, if superior relative quality results from or is concurrent with higher relative costs, the firm occupies the indeterminate position of cell 9 in Figure 6.2. Thus, producing the highest-quality products that consumers in a market segment are willing to pay for is a natural consequence of R-A competition. In contrast, planned economies have no natural mechanisms for rewarding firms that produce higher-quality goods and services. As a result, quality suffers.

Now return to the issue of quality and neoclassical theory. Note perfect competition's assumptions of the homogeneity of intra-industry demand (premise P1, Table 5.1), perfect knowledge of production functions (premise P5), homogeneous and perfectly mobile resources (premise P7), and all innovation being exogenous (premise P9). As a consequence, neoclassical theory could accommodate firms' efforts to produce superior quality market offerings only through the "market imperfection" of the (allegedly) anti-competitive, productivity-depressing activity of product differentiation (see Section 3.1). For neoclassical theory, the premises of intra-industry, homogeneous demand; perfect knowledge; homogeneous, mobile resources; and exogenous innovation were a wrong turning.

7.3.2 Economic Calculation and Productivity

As a second way that R-A theory contributes to explaining the superior productivity of market-based economies, recall that R-A theory is an evolutionary, process theory in which (1) firms are entities that are historically situated in space and time; (2) firms and resources are the heritable, durable units of evolutionary selection; and (3) competition for a comparative advantage in resources constitutes the selection process (see Section 6.2). Therefore, rather than being mathematical abstractions (as in neoclassical theory), *firms* and *competition* in R-A theory are constructs that refer to real, property-owning entities in real, competitive processes. Because R-A theory incorporates the institution of private property, I argue, economic calculation in the Austrian sense results from R-A competition.

For example, consider an entrepreneur in R-A competition who spots an unserved market segment. Should the entrepreneur plan to invest in the resources necessary to produce and sell the product associated with the segment?[5] Answering this question requires estimating the stream of (potential) future profits of the opportunity and comparing the result with the (much more certain) costs of the present investment. For the entrepreneur, the investment makes economic sense only if the expected value of the stream of future profits is greater than the costs of the present investment. From society's perspective, argue the Austrians, the entrepreneur's plan to invest makes sense, that is, it is productivity enhancing, only if the prices of the tangible, scarce, resources allocated to the investment by the entrepreneur tend to represent their scarcity value, that is, their value in current uses.

For the Austrians, economic calculation in the sense of our example is impossible in socialism because, even though the central planning board in a socialist economy can set resource prices, only the bidding of privately owned firms in the capital markets can set prices that contain information about the opportunity costs, as seen by the bidders, of the alternative uses of resources. The central planning board does not have, cannot acquire, the information to set prices that reflect opportunity costs. No input-output analyses, no artificial game playing, no simulations can take the place of real capital markets, with real entrepreneurs putting their money at risk.[6]

Therefore, Austrian economics contributes to explaining the superior productivity of market-based economies on the basis that the economic calculations of privately owned firms competing among each other result in prices that reflect opportunity costs. Thus, in the aggregate, firms can allocate scarce, tangible resources efficiently by setting prices through competitive bidding. Because R-A theory is an evolutionary theory whose constructs of "the firm" and "competition" incorporate the institution of private property and the real process of firms competing for resources by bidding for them, it incorporates the Austrian, economic calculation argument as to why market-based economies have superior productivity.

7.3.3 Learning to Be Productive

As a third ground, recall that firms seek to occupy marketplace positions identified as cells 2, 3, or 6 in Figure 6.2 because these positions of competitive advantage yield superior financial performance and, thereby, superior rewards. Note that firms in cell 2 have a comparative advantage in resources such that they can more efficiently produce a valued market offering. In contrast, firms in cell 6 are more effective because they can efficiently produce a market offering that is more valuable (e.g., having higher quality). Finally, those fortunate firms in cell 3 can produce *both* more efficiently and more effectively. The point to stress is that it is by occupying competitive positions in the marketplace that firms come to know whether they are producing efficiently and/or effectively. This knowledge comes after competing, not before. By competing, firms learn.

When firms occupy the positions of competitive disadvantage identified as cells 4, 7, or 8, they *learn* that they must (a) use existing resources more efficiently and more effectively or (b) seek other resources. Therefore, they will be motivated to neutralize and/or leapfrog advantaged competitors by better managing existing resources and/or acquisition, imitation, substitution, or major innovation. Should these efforts at reactive innovation (see Section 6.1.3) succeed, then all firms serving a market segment become more efficient and/or effective. Should these efforts fail, firms seek market segments for which their resource assortments might provide a comparative advantage—thus, redeploying these resources will promote efficiency/effectiveness in other segments. Should these efforts also fail and financial performance fall below minimum acceptable standards, firms or parts of firms are dissolved or sold and their salvageable resources redeployed by other firms. This redeployment, again, promotes efficiency/effectiveness elsewhere.

Because perfect competition theory assumes perfect knowledge of all possible production functions and all possible resource assortments for producing all products (premise P5, Table 5.1), it deprives itself of a powerful means for differentiating market-based from command economies, that is, organizations learn from the process of competing. Because command economies lack the process of competition, their firms lack a powerful means (i.e., actual financial performance stemming marketplace positions) for determining how efficient and effective they are. Indeed, it may be argued, it was the premium prices of Western imports that communicated to socialist planners just how *ineffective* socialist firms were.

7.3.4 Creating Productivity-Enhancing Resources

As a fourth ground, note from Table 5.1 that R-A theory expands the concept of resources (from land, labor, and capital) to include such resources as organizational culture, trademarks, knowledge, competences, and strategic alliances. For R-A theory, such intangibles as these are resources when (and only when) they contribute to the firm's ability to efficiently and/or effectively produce a market offering that has value for a market segment(s).

Two points are evident from R-A theory's viewing intangibles as potential resources. First, because neoclassical theory is completely mathematized, such intangibles as organizational culture and competence cannot be a resource, that is, they cannot be a factor of production. For, example, it makes no sense to talk about the "marginal product of culture." Because one cannot take the first derivative of any equation in which culture is a construct, "the rate of change in output to additional units of culture" is gibberish. Therefore, because R-A theory is not a series of differential equations, it—but not neoclassical theory—can accommodate intangibles as resources.

The second point evident from acknowledging intangibles as potential resources is that not all resources are scarce. That is, though such resources as organizational culture, competence, and knowledge (e.g., knowledge of consumers' tastes and preferences in a market segment) may be asymmetrically distributed among rivals, such resources are replicable, not *scarce*. For example, when a firm successfully imitates or replicates the competence of another, the imitated firm's (absolute) competence doesn't decrease, as would a scarce resource.

In R-A theory, a comparative advantage in intangible resources, for example, a new organizational form, process, "routine" (Nelson and Winter 1982), or competence created by the firm, can yield a marketplace position of competitive advantage. Thus, rewards flow to those that successfully create new resources, which provides firms with a powerful motivation to engage in both major and incremental innovation. Indeed, the new resources created by innovating firms may result in the industry upheavals envisioned by Schumpeter's (1950) creative destruction, or they may form the basis for the countless, small improvements in efficiency and effectiveness that constantly improve the productivity of market-based economies.

Therefore, the process of R-A competition results in both the efficient and effective allocation of scarce, tangible resources and the creation of new resources. These new resources may be tangible (e.g., new machines), intangible (e.g., a new organizational form), or ones that are complex or "higher order" (e.g., a new competence; see Section 4.1.5).

7.3.5 Summary

In summary, R-A theory contributes to explaining the superior productivity of market-based economies on four grounds. First, the evolutionary process of R-A competition motivates efficiency-enhancing and effectiveness-enhancing innovation. Command economies, in contrast, lacked this process. Second, because R-A theory is an evolutionary, process theory in which the constructs of "firm" and "competition" incorporate the institution of private property, the process of R-A competition results in prices of capital goods that tend to reflect opportunity costs and, hence, make economic calculation (in the Austrian sense) efficient in allocating scarce, tangible resources. Command economies, in contrast, by lacking the institutions of capitalism, lacked the marketplace-determined prices required for the efficient allocation of scarce, tangible resources.

Third, it is through observing actual financial performance (superior, parity, inferior) and then inferring marketplace positions (competitive advantage, parity, disadvantage) that the process of R-A competition results in firms in market-based economies coming to learn how efficient and effective they are. Command economies, in contrast, by lacking financial performance indicators, marketplace positions, the motivation of superior financial performance, and the process of competition, lack equivalent means for learning or discovering (a) the relative efficiency and effectiveness of extant resource assortments, (b) when to manage existing resources more efficiently and effectively,

(c) when to seek alternative resource assortments, and (d) when to redeploy existing resources.

Fourth, because rewards flow to firms that successfully create new resources, R-A competition motivates the creation of productivity-enhancing, tangible, intangible, and complex or "higher order" resources. In contrast, command economies lacked the process of R-A competition and, as a consequence, lacked the process that results in both efficient-effective resource allocation and creation. Therefore, on these four grounds, R-A theory contributes to explaining why command economies have proved less productive than market-based economies.

Lest there be any misunderstanding, it is important to keep in mind what is being argued here. It is not being argued that R-A theory, by itself, can explain the collapse of the command economies, because that resulted from a constellation of social, political, and economic factors. What is being argued here is that R-A theory is a theory of competition that can *contribute* to explaining and, therefore, understanding the factors that depressed the productivity of the command economies, when compared with their market-based counterparts. On this issue, perfect competition theory has "little or nothing to say" (Knight 1936, p. 255).

NOTES

1. Alternatives to the "science of resource-allocation" view of economics are those of Rosenberg (1992), who finds economics to be a branch of applied mathematics, and Becker (1976), who views economics as not a science but a *method:* "The combined assumptions of maximizing behavior, market equilibrium, and stable preferences, used relentlessly and unflinchingly, form the heart of the economics approach as I see it" (p. 5). Criticizing the "economics is a method of analysis" view, Coase (1998) traces it to John Maynard Keynes and Joan Robinson and states: "I think economists do have a subject matter: the economic system, a system in which we earn and spend our incomes" (p. 73).

2. The most detailed and complete history of the socialist calculation debate—on which the analysis here draws extensively—is that of Lavoie (1985). Hodgson (1992), Keizer (1989), and Klein (1996) provide brief reviews. See Bergson (1948, 1967) for the socialist account of the debate. See also Kirzner (1988) for a discussion of how the Austrians actually learned from the debate just how much their process view of competition differed from the evolving neoclassical tradition. He points out that, at least as late as 1932, Mises thought that the Austrian and "Anglo-American" [read: neoclassical] schools of thought "differ only in their mode of expressing the same fundamental idea and that they are divided more by their terminology . . . than by the substance of their teachings" (p. 9). Kirzner (1988) goes on to state:

Clearly, the major opponents of Austrian economic theory were, in 1932, perceived by Mises not as being the followers of Walras or of Marshall, but as being the historical and institutionalist writers (as well as a sprinkling of economic theorists) who rejected marginal utility theory. . . . Certainly, the mathematicization of mainstream microeconomics that was occurring (as Walrasian ideas became merged with the Marshallian tradition) during this period helped crystallize the equilibrium emphasis that came to characterize mainstream theory. What helped crystallize the process emphasis of the Austrians was the dramatic use made by the socialist economists of mainstream price theory to refute the Misesian challenge—a challenge that Mises had believed to be based solidly on that very mainstream theory of price. (pp. 9-10)

3. Readers who are aware of exceptions are urged to advise me of such for future editions.

4. See Lavoie (1985) for extensive and meticulous documentation that mainstream economists agreed with socialist economists.

5. Mises and Hayek, of course, were not arguing against planning, *per se*. Both recognized that, for example, families and firms plan. Indeed:

Every human action means planning. What those calling themselves planners advocate is not the substitution of planned action for letting things go. It is the substitution of the planner's own plan for the plans of his fellow men. (Mises 1947, p. 493)

Therefore, as Klein (1996) discusses in detail, both Mises and Hayek were arguing that there are definite limits to planning. For example, Rothbard (1976) discusses the Austrian view of the limits to vertical integration and firm size. For him, Austrian economics:

serves to extend the notable analysis of Professor Coase on the market determinants of the size of the firm, or the relative extent of corporate planning within the firm as against the use of the exchange and the price mechanism. Coase pointed out that there are diminishing benefits and increasing costs to each of these two alternatives, resulting, as he put it, in an " 'optimum' amount of planning" in the free market system. Our thesis adds that the costs of internal corporate planning become prohibitive as soon as markets for capital goods begin to disappear, so that the free-market optimum will always stop well short not only of One Big Firm throughout the world market but also of *any* disappearance of specific markets and hence the economic calculation in that product or resource. (p. 76)

6. Mises argues that the existence of marketplace-determined prices for capital goods in the West explains the limited success that socialist economies actually achieved in allocating resources. With reference to those "mathematical economists" who pointed to the alleged productivity of the Soviet Union and Nazi Germany as evidence of the superior efficiency of socialism, he states:

People did not recognize that these were not isolated socialist systems. They were operating in an environment in which the price system still worked. They could resort to economic calculation on the ground of the prices established abroad. Without the aid of these prices their actions would have been aimless and planless. Only because they were able to refer to these foreign prices were they able to calculate, to keep books, and to prepare their much talked about plans. (1949, p. 698)

Endogenous
Economic Growth

E conomic growth is highly valued; understanding why is easy. Consider two economies, *A* and *B,* that each have a starting GDP per capita of $1,000. If *A* grows at 1% per year and *B* at 3% per year, *B*'s standard of living after ten years is 21.6% higher; after fifteen years, it is 34.2% higher; and after 20 years, it is 48% higher. That is, "only" a 2% difference in growth rates over twenty years results in an almost 50% differential in the two nations' standard of living. As a concrete example, both Pakistan and Taiwan had GDPs per capita of less than $450 (in 1980 dollars) in 1900; both were desperately poor. Yet, because Taiwan grew at 2.8% per year and Pakistan grew at 0.9%, the Taiwanese by 1987 were moderately affluent (GDP per capita of $4,744), while the Pakistanis were still relatively poor (GDP per capita of $885) (Maddison 1989). Theorizing as to why economies grow, then, has occupied economists since the "birth" of modern economics in the latter half of the eighteenth century.

Adam Smith (1776/1937) was an optimist with respect to a rising standard of living. Smith believed that population growth expands markets, which in turn increases the gains achievable through the "division of labor." Increases in productivity result from each worker specializing in ever-more-narrowly defined jobs. As per capita income rises, the population grows and a further division of labor is possible. Thus, for Smith, per capita income growth is a self-perpetuating, ongoing process.

In contrast, Smith's successors, Robert Malthus and David Ricardo, painted a gloomy prospect for per capita economic growth (Kuhn 1970). For Malthus, because population grows geometrically and food supply grows arithmetically, stagnation at subsistence levels is inevitable. For Ricardo, landowners will not invest their "rents" in real capital formation because, as a class, they prefer ostentatious consumption. Therefore, as progressively less fertile land is cultivated to feed a growing population, food prices rise and stagnation at subsistence levels occurs. The pessimistic theories of Malthus and Ricardo earned economics its appellation of "dismal science."

But economic output, contra Malthus and Ricardo, has outpaced population growth since the industrial revolution. Indeed, Maddison (1991) provides estimates of the real, per capita growth rates for 14 advanced economies from 1820 to 1989. He finds that compared with the 1820-1870 time period, growth rates from 1870 to 1989 actually accelerated.[1] If worldwide stagnation at subsistence levels of income is inevitable, why isn't the world making "progress" toward the inevitable?

Starting with works of Domar (1947) and Harrod (1948), models of economic growth in the neoclassical tradition have focused on the role of increases in net investment driving an economy's growth. The major difference between the Harrod-Domar models and present-day, neoclassical growth theory is that in the former, but not the latter, "there is no possibility of substituting labor for capital in production" (Solow 1956, p. 65).

This chapter contrasts neoclassical theory's focus on investment with R-A theory's focus on the innovations prompted by the process of competition. Economic growth, for R-A theory, is endogenous to, that is, it is produced by, the process of competition. Specifically, the process of competition prompts the productivity-enhancing, proactive, and reactive innovations of firms that, in the aggregate, produce new resources, increases in capital, technological progress, and economic growth.

Our discussion of economic growth is organized as follows. First, I provide a brief review of neoclassical growth theory and develop five predictions or theses from it: (1) the capital/labor ratio dominates technological progress in fostering economic growth, (2) investment *causes* economic growth, (3) technological progress is exogenous to competition, (4) growth is economic system-neutral, and (5) growth is institutions-neutral. I then develop R-A theory's view that economic growth is endogenous to the process of competition and show how it makes five predictions that are opposite to those of neoclassical growth theory. The remainder of the chapter explores the empirical evidence regarding the first four of the five theses. Discussion of the fifth is deferred to Chapter 9.

8.1 NEOCLASSICAL GROWTH THEORY

The neoclassical model of economic growth stems from the works of Solow (1956, 1957), Swan (1956), Cass (1965), and Koopmans (1965). Robert Solow's seminal efforts earned him the Nobel prize in 1987. Hence, the model is often referred to as the "Solow Model." Using the notation of Romer (1994), a simple version of the neoclassical model starts with an aggregate production function of the Cobb-Douglass form.[2]

(8.1) $$Y = A(t)K^{1-\beta}L^{\beta}$$

In equation 8.1, Y is net national product, A is the level of technology, K is the stock of capital, L is the stock of labor, and β denotes the share of output attributable to labor. Because neoclassical theory assumes perfect competition, β is also the share of total income *paid* to labor (see Sections 1.1 and 5.7). $A(t)$ signals the standard assumption in neoclassical theory that though technology is changing through time, it is changing for reasons outside the model. Specifically, technology is an exogenously provided public good that changes not through the efforts (purposive or otherwise) of competitors but from the "basic science" efforts of such entities as government or universities.

Economic growth, for neoclassical growth theory, can result from increases in labor (L), capital (K), the capital/labor ratio (K/L), and from the productivity increases resulting from changes in $A(t)$. Increases in the K/L ratio are referred to as "capital deepening" and increases in $A(t)$ are referred to as "technological progress." Therefore, economic growth can come from movements along the existing, aggregate production function (by increases in L, K, and the K/L ratio) or from a shift to a new production function (by increases in technological progress).

Because the growth rates of L and $A(t)$ are both exogenous in neoclassical growth theory, it focuses on K and K/L. In a closed economy, if s is the fraction of total output saved by consumers each year, then s is also the ratio of net new investment to net national product. Therefore, sY is the rate of growth of capital stock K. If $y = Y/L$ signifies output per worker, $k = K/L$ denotes the available capital per worker, and a "∧" over a variable signifies its exponential rate of growth, then the growth in income per worker in an economy can be stated as:

$$(8.2) \qquad \hat{y} = (1-\beta)\,\hat{k} + \hat{A}$$

If n is the exogenous growth rate of the labor force, then substituting in equation 8.2 an expression for $\hat{k}$ in terms of s, n, $A(t)$, and y yields:

$$(8.3) \qquad \hat{y} = (1-\beta)\left[sA(t)^{1/(1-\beta)}\, y^{(-\beta)/(1-\beta)} - n \right] + \hat{A}$$

Equations 8.2 and 8.3 imply both a theory of economic growth and a procedure for partitioning the overall growth of income per worker into its components. The neoclassical theory of economic growth implied by equations 8.2 and 8.3 maintains that economies with a low K/L ratio will have a high marginal product of capital. Therefore, if, for example, a constant fraction s of the income generated by new investment is saved, then the gross investment in new capital goods may not only offset depreciation but also exceed the amount necessary to equip new entrants to the workforce. The increase in the K/L ratio results in increases in income per worker, or what is referred to as *extensive growth*. In short, economic growth is a resource reallocation problem: reallocating resources from consumer goods to capital goods results in extensive growth.

For neoclassical growth theory, as K/L rises through time the marginal product of new capital decreases, that is, there are decreasing returns to capital as a result of *capital deepening*. Eventually, the savings accruing to new additions to capital decrease to the point where they are just sufficient to cover depreciation and equip new entrants to the workforce (e.g., adding one tractor to a field increases labor productivity greatly; the second tractor increases it less, etc.). At this point, the economy is at long-run equilibrium and—like the gloomy predictions of Malthus and Ricardo—the standard of living stagnates.[3]

8.1.1 Neoclassical Growth Theory: Assumptions, Implications, Predictions

Neoclassical growth theory is, of course, *neoclassical*. If capital and labor are "close enough" (Friedman 1953) to being homogeneous and mobile for firms and industries and if technology is "close enough" to a public good available to all competitors (see Table 5.1), then, argue neoclassicists, (1) an aggregate production function and its associated level of technology may be assumed to be available to economies as a whole, and (2) economies may be viewed as producing national income by combining homogeneous capital and labor. Also like the neoclassical treatment of firms and industries, neoclassical growth theory (1) is mathematized and (2) predicts that economies—absent exogenous technological progress—will stagnate at the long-run equilibrium position. However, the "economies are aggregated, production-function firms" assumption is not our focus here. Rather, five specific assumptions of neoclassical growth theory and their associated implications and predictions need to be highlighted.[4]

First, equation 8.2 implies that increases in the capital/labor ratio, which result in capital deepening, are key for explaining economic growth. Capital deepening is the *main* cause of growth. Increases in technological progress, in contrast, are subsidiary. Therefore, the prediction of neoclassical growth theory is that most of the variance in per capita economic growth across nations should be accounted for by differences in the *K/L* ratio and little variance accounted for by technological progress.

Second, the policy implication of neoclassical growth theory is that low-growth nations should save more to fund additional investment. The increased investment will, in turn, increase the capital/labor ratio and stimulate economic growth. That is, the assumption of neoclassical growth theory is that increases in savings and investment *cause* economic growth; it is not just that investment and growth are correlated. In time series analyses, therefore, the prediction is that increases in investment should precede increases in economic growth.

Third, neoclassical growth theory assumes that technological progress is exogenous and not a result of the profit-driven actions of firms competing with each other. Indeed, because the theory assumes perfect competition, which is a zero economic profit (but not a zero *accounting* profit) situation, firms cannot have any profits to invest in output-augmenting research and development. Therefore, the prediction is that most of the technological progress that influences economic growth stems from the "basic science" conducted by such institutions as government and universities; little or no technological progress stems from the actions of profit-driven firms.

Fourth, neoclassical growth theory, being a system of equations, is economic system-neutral. Just as in the socialist calculation debate over productivity (see Section 7.2), equation 8.2 does not refer, necessarily, to a market-based economy. That is, equation 8.2 states that economic growth results from net investment plus technological progress; it does not state that such investment and technological progress occur in a market-based economy. Therefore, the prediction of neoclassical growth theory is that both command and market-based economies will, with increases in their capital/labor ratios, experience capital deepening and cease to grow.

Fifth, neoclassical growth theory is institutions-neutral. As in neoclassical theory in general (see Section 4.2), there is no provision in equation 8.2 for different societal institutions to affect economic growth. The prediction, therefore, is that, if increases in investment are controlled for, societal institutions will explain only small amounts, if any, of the variance across nations in economic growth per capita.

The preceding five predictions or theses of neoclassical growth theory we may refer to as (1) the *K/L* ratio dominates technological progress, (2) investment causes economic growth, (3) technological progress is exogenous, (4) growth is economic system-neutral, and (5) growth is institutions-neutral. Later in the chapter, we shall examine the empirical evidence for the first four of the five theses. Before doing so, however, we need to explicate R-A theory's approach to explaining economic growth.

8.2 ECONOMIC GROWTH AND R-A THEORY

Resource-advantage theory maintains that economic growth is endogenous to, that is, it is produced by, the *process* of competition. Recall that competition is the disequilibrating, ongoing process that consists of the constant struggle among firms for comparative advantages in resources that will yield marketplace positions of competitive advantage for some market segment(s) and, thereby, superior financial performance. R-A theory views economic growth, that is, increases in per capita income, as the normal, natural outcome of vigorous, R-A competition. The constant struggle for comparative advantages in resources leads not only to increases in the efficient allocation of scarce, tangible resources but also—and more important—to innovations that result in the creation of new tangible, intangible, and "higher order" resources that drive economic growth.

Because of its premise that firms seek superior financial performance (e.g., the drive for more profits than last year, the drive for a higher rate of return than one's competitors), the status quo is always unsatisfactory in R-A competition, and the economic stagnation implied by general equilibrium is not inevitable. In terms of Figure 6.2, there is a constant drive to move upward and to the right, to become more efficient and more effective. Recall that R-A competition prompts efficiency-enhancing and effectiveness-enhancing innovations (see

Sections 6.1.3 and 7.3.1). In the aggregate, it is the productivity-enhancing, proactive, and reactive innovations that are prompted by the process of competition that produce new resources, increases in capital, technological progress, and economic growth. "Capital," however, is a much richer concept in R-A theory than the physical capital in neoclassical theory.

Recall that R-A theory (1) defines resources as the tangible and intangible entities that enable a firm to efficiently and/or effectively produce market offerings that have value for some market segment(s) and (2) views firms as combiners of heterogeneous and imperfectly mobile resources (see Sections 4.1.5 and 5.5.1). Therefore, the relationship between a firm's output and its resources may be expressed as:

(8.4) $Output = f(FR, PR, LeR, HR, IR, RR, OR)$

In equation 8.4, "Output" refers to the quantity and attributes of the firm's market offerings, "*FR*" stands for financial resources (e.g., cash reserves and access to financial markets), "*PR*" for physical resources (e.g., buildings and machinery), "*LeR*" for legal resources (e.g., trademarks and licenses),[5] "*HR*" for human resources (e.g., the skills and knowledge of individual employees), "*IR*" for informational resources (e.g., the stock of knowledge resulting from technical research and consumer and competitor intelligence), "*RR*" for relational resources, (e.g., the firm's relationships with suppliers and customers), and "*OR*" for organizational resources (e.g., the firm's competences, policies, controls, "routines" [Nelson and Winter 1982], and culture).

Total firm revenues derive from the prices that the attributes of the firm's offerings command in the marketplace and the quantity of the offerings produced and sold. Total firm costs derive from the costs of the seven forms of resources that, collectively, produce the firm's output. Firm growth, that is, increases in profits, therefore, can result from numerous kinds of efficiency-enhancing and effectiveness-enhancing innovations.[6]

For example, extant firms can grow and/or new firms can be formed by (1) increasing the perceived value of the attributes of the firm's offerings by the better use of extant resources, (2) increasing the perceived value of the firm's offerings through adding to the quantity or quality of extant resources, (3) decreasing the cost of the firm's market offerings through the better use of extant resources, (4) decreasing the cost of the firm's market offerings through adding to the quantity and quality of extant resources, (5) identifying through entrepreneurship new market opportunities for the firm's extant resources, (6) identifying through entrepreneurship unserved market opportunities that require additions to or improvements in the quantity and quality of the firm's stock of resources, (7) identifying through entrepreneurship market opportunities unserved by extant firms and then forming new firms by acquiring and/or developing the resources to produce new market offerings, (8) increasing the quantity of the firm's offerings by the better management of extant resources, and (9) increasing the quantity of the firm's extant offerings by adding to the quantity or quality of the firm's extant resources.

In R-A theory, because of its premises of heterogeneous products, imperfect information, and heterogeneous resources (see Table 5.1), any or all of the preceding nine forms of innovation (which are not meant to be exhaustive) can (1) result from the quest for superior financial performance, (2) produce growth in output of extant firms, and (3) produce growth in output by adding new firms. In contrast, because neoclassical growth theory adopts perfect competition and its assumptions of homogeneous products, perfect information, and homogeneous resources (see Table 5.1), it restricts itself to the "innovation" of adding to the quantity of resources, which is identified as a portion of the ninth form of innovation (improving the quality of resources is an innovation not available to the neoclassical firm because of perfect information). Specifically, because neoclassical theory limits itself to those resources that have a marginal product, neoclassical growth theory limits itself to the "innovation" of increasing the quantity of homogeneous physical resources and homogeneous labor.

The concept of an economy's private sector "capital," therefore, in neoclassical growth theory refers to the aggregate of the homogeneous physical resources of the firms in an economy, sometimes augmented by "human capital," as measured by, for example, the percentage of the secondary school-age population enrolled in secondary school (e.g., see Mankiw, Romer, and Weil 1992). In contrast, R-A theory expands the concept of private sector capital to refer to the aggregate of the financial, physical, legal, human, informational, relational, and organizational resources of the firms in an economy.

8.2.1 Expanding the Concept of Capital

R-A theory can adopt an expanded, richer view of capital because it is not committed to neoclassical theory's position that a zero economic profit for firms is optimal and all resources must have a marginal product. The premise of R-A theory that firms seek superior financial performance, plus its acknowledgment that superior financial performance is possible, when combined with its position that entities need not be capable of being in a differential equation to qualify as a resource, enable it to accommodate an important fact: Firms, through the process of competition, accumulate, develop, and create the various kinds of tangible, intangible, and "higher order" resources that collectively constitute an economy's private sector capital. Consider, for example, the nature of human, informational, relational, and organizational capital.

Human Capital. The stock of human resources of a firm, its human capital, consists of the skills and knowledge of its individual employees. Some aspects of the skills and knowledge of employees are codifiable; others are "tacit" (Polanyi 1957, 1966) and involve or imply "learning by doing" (Arrow 1962). To the extent that a firm expects that increased investment in, for example, employee training programs will increase its ability to efficiently and/or effectively produce market offerings that have value to a market segment(s) and, thereby, achieve superior financial performance (i.e., to the extent that it expects that such increases will add to its *competitiveness*), a firm will invest in human capital.

Because of (1) differences among employees as firms hire them (e.g., differences in formal education), (2) differences in policies and procedures regarding human capital development among firms, and (3) differences in the histories of firms, human capital across firms in the same industry at any point in time is significantly heterogeneous and asymmetrically distributed. In the aggregate, therefore, human capital across nations is also significantly heterogeneous and asymmetrically distributed. Furthermore, because of the heterogeneous nature of an economy's human capital, such measures as the extent of secondary school education of the workforce are likely to capture only a small part of the differences across nations in human capital.

In short, increases in human capital are the natural outcome of competition in an economy when such increases are viewed by firms as contributing to their competitiveness (as "competitiveness" is defined by R-A theory). Hence, R-A competition promotes firm investments that lead to human capital formation and economic growth.

Informational Capital. The stock of informational resources of a firm, its informational or *knowledge* capital, includes its stock of knowledge concerning, at the minimum, (1) its products, production processes, customers, and resources and (2) its competitors' products, production processes, customers, and resources. Increases in a firm's knowledge capital result from expenditures on technical research and development, marketing research, and competitive intelligence. Such expenditures will be undertaken by firms when they expect that they will contribute to their competitiveness (as R-A theory defines competition). Because of differences in the histories of firms with respect to investments in informational capital, the knowledge capital of firms in the same industry will be heterogeneous and asymmetrically distributed. In the aggregate, therefore, the informational or knowledge capital across nations is heterogeneous and asymmetrically distributed.

Because perfect competition is a zero economic profit condition, there are no profits available to firms for the purpose of any kind of informational capital investment. Therefore, because the neoclassical research tradition is committed to the perfection of perfect competition, neoclassical theory cannot accommodate the growth-enhancing potential of private sector investment in knowledge capital. Because R-A theory denies the perfection of perfect competition and views information as a resource, it acknowledges the growth-enhancing potential of the accumulation of private sector, knowledge capital. Therefore, increases in informational capital are the natural outcome of competition in an economy when such increases are viewed by firms as contributing to their competitiveness. Hence, R-A competition promotes firm investments in informational capital that lead to the innovations that promote economic growth.

Relational Capital. The stock of relational resources of a firm, its relational capital, includes its stock of relationships with such entities as customers, suppliers, competitors, governmental agencies, and unions (Berry 1995; Berry and Parasuramen 1991; Dwyer, Schurr, and Oh 1987; Gronroos 1996; Morgan and Hunt 1994; Parvatiyar, Sheth, and Whittington 1992; Sheth and Parvatiyar 1995a,b; Thorelli 1995; Varadarajan and Cunningham 1995; Young and Wilkinson 1989). (Each relationship constitutes a resource, it must be remembered, when and only when it contributes to the firm's ability to efficiently and/or effectively produce a market offering that has value to some market segment(s). A price conspiracy, for example, is not a resource.) Such relational resources as strategic alliances and cooperative relationships with unions are radically heterogeneous and immobile. There is no—can be no—central marketplace where such entities as strategic alliances and union relationships are traded.

In the aggregate, the relational resources of firms form an economy's private sector, relational capital. In turn, private sector, relational capital constitutes part of what Coleman (1988) calls "social capital" (see Section 4.2.3). As discussed in Chapter 9, social capital contributes to the wealth of nations. Because neoclassical growth theory is undersocialized (see Section 4.2.3), it cannot accommodate the growth-enhancing aspects of relational capital. Because R-A theory is moderately socialized (see Sections 4.2.4 and 9.3.3), it can. Therefore, increases in relational capital, for example, adding new strategic alliances, are the natural outcome of competition in an economy when such increases are viewed by firms as contributing to their competitiveness. Hence, R-A competition promotes firm investments that lead to relational capital formation and economic growth.

Organizational Capital. The stock of organizational resources of a firm, its organizational capital, includes the firm's policies, culture "routines" (Nelson and Winter 1982), and competences. In one sense, of course, all of a firm's resources are *organizational* because they are either owned by or otherwise available to the firm. But "organizational," as used here, implies more than just that the entity is owned by or available to the firm; it implies that the entity could not exist independent of or separate from the firm.

For example, as discussed in Sections 2.1.3 and 4.1.5, R-A theory incorporates both competence-based theory from business strategy and the competence view of the firm in evolutionary economics. Competences, for R-A theory, are viewed as socially complex, interconnected, combinations of tangible basic resources (e.g., basic machinery) and intangible basic resources (e.g., specific organizational policies and procedures and the skills and knowledge of specific employees) that fit coherently together in a synergistic manner.

Differences in specific competences explain why some firms are simply better than others at *doing* things (Hamel and Heene 1994; Heene and Sanchez 1996; Langlois and Robertson 1995; Sanchez and Heene 1997; Sanchez, Heene, and Thomas 1996). Firms can have superior entrepreneurial competences (Foss 1993), dynamic capabilities (Teece and Pisano 1994; Teece, Pisano, and Shuen 1997), learning capabilities (Dickson 1996; Sanchez and Heene 1997), industry foresight capabilities (Hamel and Prahalad 1994a), research and development competences (Roehl 1996), specific production technologies (Prahalad and Hamel 1990), customer and competitor intelligence (Glazer 1991; Jaworski and Kohli 1993; Kohli and Jaworski 1990; Narver and Slater 1990; Slater and Narver 1994, 1995), marketing (Conant, Mokwa, and Varadarajan 1990; Day 1992), and competitive agility (Nayyan and Bantel 1994).

Competences are distinct resources because they exist as distinct packages of basic resources. Because competences are causally ambiguous, tacit, complex, and highly interconnected, they are likely to be significantly heterogeneous and asymmetrically distributed across firms in the same industry. In the aggregate, therefore, organizational capital, of which competences are a key component, is heterogeneous and asymmetrically distributed across nations. Investments in organizational capital are the natural outcome of competition when such investments are viewed by firms as contributing to their competitiveness. Hence, R-A competition promotes the investments in organizational capital that promote economic growth.

8.2.2 R-A Theory's Five Predictions

We now return to the five predictions or theses of neoclassical growth theory. In each case, R-A theory makes the opposite prediction.

Technological Progress versus K/L Ratio. First, recall that neoclassical theory predicts that most of the variance in per capita economic growth across nations should be accounted for by differences in the K/L ratio (where "K" is restricted to physical capital) and little variance accounted for by technological progress. In contrast, because (1) it focuses on the role of proactive and reactive innovations in promoting increases in productivity, and (2) it expands the concept of capital to include not only physical capital but also human, informational, relational, and organizational capital, R-A theory predicts that what is labeled "technological progress"—the residual in cross-country regressions—will account for most of the variance in per capita economic growth. Much less variance will be accounted for by differences in the K/L ratio.

Investment. Second, recall that neoclassical growth theory posits that increases in investment in physical capital causes economic growth. Neoclassical theory's focus is on the growth of firm output that results from a portion of number nine in our list in Section 8.2, that is, it focuses on increasing the quantity of the firm's extant offerings by increasing the quantity of the firm's extant, homogeneous, physical resources and labor. Therefore, in time series analyses, increases in investment should precede increases in economic growth. In contrast, R-A theory acknowledges that all nine of the efficiency-enhancing and effectiveness-enhancing forms of innovation can result in firm growth or new firms and, hence, can contribute to economic growth. Furthermore, though some forms of innovations result in increases in physical capital investment that, in turn, increase output, most do not. Indeed, in most cases, increases in output result in increases in physical capital investment. Therefore, for R-A theory, though some increases in physical capital may precede or be concomitant with economic growth, the main case in time series analyses should be that economic growth precedes increases in physical capital investment.

Endogenous Technological Progress. Third, recall that neoclassical growth theory predicts that most of the technological progress that influences economic growth stems from the "basic science" conducted by such institutions as government and universities; little or no technological progress stems from the actions of profit-driven firms. In contrast, because of its focus on the proactive and reactive innovations prompted by the process of competition, R-A theory predicts that most of the technological progress that drives economic growth stems from the actions of profit-driven firms.

System-Neutral. Fourth, recall that neoclassical growth theory is economic system-neutral. Therefore, it predicts that both command and market-based economies will, with increases in their capital/labor ratios, experience capital deepening and cease to grow. In contrast, R-A theory presupposes a market-based economy and predicts that as long as there is vigorous R-A competition, there should be innovations that prevent the economic stagnation that results from capital deepening. In short, R-A theory implies that neoclassical theory is not "close enough" (Friedman 1953) to a market-based economy to predict well its growth path. Before proceeding, however, we must address whether neoclassical growth theory is "close enough" to a command economy to result in it predicting well the growth path of a socialist economy.

As discussed in Section 7.2, recall that socialist economists used neoclassical theory to argue—to the satisfaction of mainstream economists—that command economies should be just as efficient as market-based economies. That is, mainstream economists agreed with socialist economists that neoclassical theory is "close enough" to accurately depict the efficiency characteristics of command economies. Critics of neoclassical theory now agree. For example, Coricelli and Dosi (1988) examine the Walrasian foundations of neoclassical theory and conclude: "It is not far from the truth to say that the current neoclassical approach to the microfoundations of macroeconomics is based on the representation of the economy as a *centralized* system" (p. 130; italics in original). Similarly, Hodgson (1992) concludes that:

> in the fantasy world of Walrasian theory, the auctioneer knows all, and what he or she does not know is eliminated from the model. Consequently, the Walrasian model of neoclassical theory does not correspond to a real market system where much information and knowledge is decentralized. It corresponds more closely to a mythical, centralized, nonmarket economy where the central authorities know everything, and all other knowledge that cannot be fitted into the plans and conceptions of the center is systematically disregarded, destroyed, or rendered

useless. To drive the point home, we may suggest that the Walrasian market model conjures up the idea of a totalitarian police state rather than a liberal market system, despite common rhetoric to the contrary. (p. 754)

On the basis of the preceding, it would appear that neoclassical theory in general may indeed be "close enough" to a command economy for neoclassical *growth* theory to predict well. Therefore, neoclassical growth theory predicts that both market-based and command economies should experience capital deepening and stagnate thereafter. In contrast, R-A theory predicts that (1) as long as there is vigorous R-A competition in a market based-economy, there should be innovations that prevent the economic stagnation that results from capital deepening, and (2) lacking the productivity-enhancing process of competition, command economies should suffer economic stagnation from capital deepening.

Institutions-Neutral. Fifth, recall that neoclassical growth theory is institutions-neutral. Indeed, as discussed in Section 4.2, neoclassical theory—a system of equations—does not assume even the institution of private property. Therefore, neoclassical growth theory predicts that, if increases in investment are accounted for, societal institutions will explain little, if any, of the variance across nations in economic growth per capita.

In contrast, R-A theory is, most assuredly, not institutions-neutral. For example, adopting the historical tradition's view (Chandler 1990) that firms are historically situated in space and time, R-A theory incorporates the institution of private property. Furthermore, note that R-A theory, as depicted in Figure 6.1, posits that the process of competition is significantly influenced by six environment factors: societal resources (e.g., "infrastructure" capital and labor force skills), societal institutions (e.g., culture, the "rule of law," and moral codes), the characteristics of competitors (e.g., their innovativeness and competences), the characteristics of suppliers (e.g., their dependability and competences), consumers (e.g., their tastes and preferences), and public policy (e.g., patent, trademark, and antitrust policies). For R-A theory, these environmental factors influence the process of competition and how well the process *works*. Therefore, R-A theory predicts that, after increases in investment are accounted for, differences in societal institutions across nations will explain significant variance in economic growth per capita.

To conclude this section, neoclassical growth theory and R-A theory make empirically testable (or at least empirically addressable) opposite predictions on five key issues concerning economic growth. The rest of this chapter will focus on the first four of these five theses. Discussion of thesis five will be deferred to Chapter 9.

8.3 DOES THE *K/L* RATIO DOMINATE TECHNOLOGICAL PROGRESS?

The first major test of neoclassical growth theory was by Robert Solow, himself. He (1957) develops (a version of) equation 8.2 and seeks to apply it to the growth of the U.S. economy from 1909 to 1949. In this period of time, he notes, gross output per work-hour doubled (from $.623 to $1.275). What is needed, he notes, is a "growth accounting" procedure. That is, one needs to partition the $.65 increase into the factors accounting for it. Specifically, for *A(t)*, what is required "to disentangle the technical change index *A(t)* are series for output per man hour, capital per man hour, and the share of capital" (p. 313). Solow (1957) obtains estimates of these variables from the best sources available at the time and calculates the technical change index for each year from 1909 to 1949. He concludes that "8 cents of the 65 cent increase [from 1909 to 1949] can be imputed to increased capital intensity [increases in the *K/L* ratio], and the remainder to increased productivity" (p. 316). In percentage terms, "$87\frac{1}{2}$ per cent of the increase [is] attributable to technical change and the remaining $12\frac{1}{2}$ per cent to increased use of capital" (p. 320).

Solow (1957) cautions the reader that his findings do not imply that increases in *K/L* are *completely* unimportant. Instead, he avers: "Obviously much, perhaps nearly all, innovation must be embodied in new plant and equipment to be realized at all" (p. 320). As to when the U.S. economy will stagnate, he forecasts: "Capital-saturation would occur whenever the gross marginal product of capital falls to .03-.05, . . . [which] would happen at *K/L* ratios of around 5 or higher, still well above anything ever observed" (p. 320).

Since Solow's (1957) original estimate that technological progress accounts for $87\frac{1}{2}\%$ of economic growth and the *K/L* ratio only $12\frac{1}{2}\%$, numerous studies have documented that technological progress dominates the *K/L* ratio (e.g., see Denison 1985). Because "technological progress" is a catchall residual in empirical studies, efforts have focused on identifying variables that reduce the size of the residual. Many of the growth accounting empirical works now attempt to explain differences in average, cross-country growth rates and use a version of the "Penn World Table" data set developed by Summers and Heston (1991).[7] The set includes 27 variables for approximately 138 economies for 1950 to 1988.

Levine and Renelt (1991) review 41 growth accounting studies that attempt to explain average annual growth rate per capita (GYP) and reduce the "Solow residual." Thirty-three studies include the investment share of gross domestic product (INV), 29 include population growth (GPO), 13 include a human capital measure (SEC), and 18 include a measure of initial income (RGDPG60). For example, for the time period 1960-1989 and a sample of 101 economies, Levine and Renelt (1992) estimate the following equation (with SEC measured as initial secondary-school enrollment rate):

(8.5) GYP = -0.83 -0.35 RGDP60 -0.38 GPO + 3.17 SEC + 17.5 INV
           (0.85)   (0.14)   (0.22)   (1.29)   (2.68)

The equation, with standard errors in parentheses, indicates that economic growth per capita across the 101 economies appears to be related to initial income (negatively), population growth (negatively), human capital (positively), and investment (positively).[8] Important for our purposes in this section, even when measures of human capital, population growth, and initial income are added to investment, the resulting R^2 is only .46. That is, "technological progress," the label given to the residual, still accounts for more than half the variance in growth rates in GDP per capita across economies.

In conclusion, as to the first thesis, the empirical evidence indicates that technological progress dominates the K/L ratio in economic growth. Neoclassical growth theory is not "close enough" for it to make the correct prediction. In contrast, R-A theory predicts correctly.

8.4 DOES INVESTMENT CAUSE ECONOMIC GROWTH?

The policy implication of neoclassical growth theory is that low-growth nations should save more to fund additional investment because increases in savings and investment *cause* economic growth. In time series analyses, therefore, the prediction is that increases in investment should precede increases in economic growth. In contrast, for R-A theory, though some forms of innovations result in increases in physical capital investment that, in turn, increase output, in most cases just the reverse is true: Increases in output result in increases in physical capital investment. Therefore, for R-A theory, though some increases in physical capital may precede or be concomitant with economic growth, the main case in time series analyses should be that economic growth precedes increases in physical capital investment.

8.4.1 The Case for Investment Causing Growth

The works of De Long and Summers (1991, 1993) provide the strongest empirical case for neoclassical theory's emphasis on investment. De Long and Summers (1991) point out that "work in the aggregated growth accounting tradition ... has typically concluded that capital accumulation accounts for only a relatively small fraction of productivity growth in individual countries, or of differences across countries" (p. 445). Indeed, these studies indicate that "even a doubling of the U.S. net private investment would ... raise the growth rate of real income by less than half a percentage point per year" (p. 446). They argue that neoclassical theory's disappointing results may be due to an inappropriate level of aggregation. Specifically, they argue that it is investment in machinery and equipment that drives economic growth, not total investment (which includes, for example, investment in structures).

De Long and Summers (1991) investigate the machinery-drives-growth thesis using 1960-1985 data from the United Nations International Comparison Project (see Kravis, Heston, and Summers 1982 and United Nations 1985) and Summers and Heston (1991). They focus on those twenty-five "high productivity" countries with GDP per capita greater than 25% of that of the United States in 1960. For these countries in this time period, equipment investment averages 28% of total investment.

Using labor force growth rates, the level of GDP per worker, and the nonequipment investment-to-GDP ratio as control variables, De Long and Summers (1991) regress GDP per worker growth rate on the equipment-to-GDP ratio. Their resulting equation, with an R^2 of .662, shows GDP per worker growth rates to be negatively related to labor force growth rate, positively related to the "gap" between each country's level of GDP and that of the United States, negatively related to nonequipment investment, and—as a test of their thesis—positively related to equipment investment. Indeed, their regression equation "implies that an increase of three percentage points (one standard deviation) in the share of GDP devoted to equipment investment leads to an increase in the growth of GDP per worker of 1.02 percent per year, which cumulates to a 29 percent difference over the 25 years of the sample" (pp. 445-46).

De Long and Summers (1991) investigate whether the relationship between equipment investment and growth is causal and argue on four grounds that it is. First, they argue for causality because they "find a much closer relationship between productivity growth and equipment investment than between productivity growth and labor force growth" (p. 470). Second, they enter 1960-1975 growth rates to equations estimating 1975-1985 growth as a "plausible proxy" for unobserved third variables that might be causing both economic growth and equipment investment. When they do, "the inclusion of past growth does not add much explanatory power" (p. 474). Third, they investigate the joint behavior of prices and quantities of equipment and find that "fast growth goes with high quantities and low prices of equipment and this is not easy to reconcile with the belief that the high quantity of equipment investment is due to some other factor" (p. 470). Fourth, they "instrument equipment investment with a number of alternative variables and check whether its estimated impact changes" (p. 477). When they include estimates for equipment prices, rates of national saving, and measures of trade liberalization, five of six of their regressions produce "no material difference" for the effect of equipment investment.

Therefore, De Long and Summers (1991) conclude that higher equipment growth causes economic growth. Indeed, their results suggest "that the private return to equipment investment is below the social return, and that the social return to equipment investment is very high" (p. 482). Furthermore, their results call "into question views that overemphasize human capital accumulation through formal education" (p. 486).[9]

Unfortunately, the kind of cross-sectional analyses conducted by De Long and Summers for a single time period (1960-1985) cannot disentangle cause from effect. What is needed (at the minimum) to assert confidently that either investment causes growth or growth causes investment are analyses of these variables through time. Lipsey and Kravis (1987) and Blomström, Lipsey, and Zejan (1996) provide such analyses.

8.4.2 The Case for Growth Causing Investment

Blomström, Lipsey, and Zejan (1996) point out that a previous study by Lipsey and Kravis (1987) had shown that the rate of economic growth per capita was more closely related to capital formation rates in succeeding periods than to contemporary or preceding periods. The question they address now is whether such a finding would be replicated using the same data set as that used by De Long and Summers (1991). First, they divide the 1960 to 1985 time period into five equal time periods (1960-1965; 1965-1970, etc.). They then conduct seven different analyses to explore for causality. Each has a common interpretation: increases in economic growth appear to cause increases in investment.

For example, Blomström, Lipsey, and Zejan (1996) regress real growth in GDP per capita (RGDPC) in each five-year time period on the ratio of fixed capital formation to GDP (INV) for the preceding, current, and following time periods. The resulting beta coefficients, t-statistics, and R^2 for INV are .30 (t = 3.42, R^2 = .03) for the preceding period, 0.60 (t = 5.71, R^2 = .07) for the current period, and 0.80 (t = 8.94, R^2 = .16) for the following period. That is, the pattern of increasing betas and R^2 shows that "the case for effects running from growth rates to subsequent capital formation is stronger than that for the effects running from capital formation to subsequent growth" (p. 270).

Blomström, Lipsey, and Zejan (1996) point out that a potential problem in pooling time series and cross-section data is that the cross-sectional data reflect permanent features of the countries that influence both investment and growth. Using country dummies, they note, addresses such biases. When country dummies are entered into the regressions, the results for INV are -1.00 (t = 3.95, R^2 = .16), -0.01 (t = 0.004, R^2 = .12), and 1.65 (t = 6.78, R^2 = .23) for the preceding period, current period, and following period, respectively. Again, the results show the same pattern: growth appears to precede, not follow, investment.

Blomström, Lipsey, and Zejan (1996) also conduct multiple regressions with RGDPC in each time period as the dependent variable and five independent variables often used in growth accounting studies: initial (1960) per capita income level, the proportion of the relevant age group enrolled in secondary school, income changes due to world price structure, changes in labor force participation rate, and inflows of direct foreign investment to GDP. When INV is added as a sixth variable to the equations, the betas, t-statistics, and R^2 for INV are 0.25 (t = 1.94, R^2 = .12), 0.62 (t = 4.56, R^2 = .16), and 1.04 (t = 8.85, R^2 = .27), for the preceding period, current period, and following period, respectively. When the regression includes country dummies, the results for INV are -0.63 (t = 2.43, R^2 = .42), 0.31 (t = 1.26, R^2 = .41), and 1.27 (t = 4.88, R^2 = .46). Again, the patterns of beta coefficients and R^2 show that growth appears to precede, not follow, investment.

Blomström, Lipsey, and Zejan (1996) point out that using the machinery and equipment variable of De Long and Summers (1991), instead of total fixed capital investment, does not change the results. When they add the machinery and equipment to GDP ratio to the five control variables in their regressions, the beta coefficients, t-statistics, and R^2 for equipment investment are -1.10 (t = 1.03, R^2 = .50), 1.60 (t = 1.49, R^2 = .51), and 5.00 (t = 4.00, R^2 = .54). Once again, the pattern shows us that growth precedes investment, not the reverse. Contra De Long and Summers (1991, 1993), the empirical failure of neoclassical theory's focus on investment appears not to result from the problem of "level of aggregation."[10] Blomström, Lipsey, and Zejan (1996) conclude:

> Thus, we find no evidence that fixed investment (or equipment investment) is the key to economic growth. This conclusion is in line with the last 25 years of research in development economics, which shows that the path to growth and development is much more than simply raising saving and investment rates from 5 to 15 percent, as Arthur Lewis, Walter Rostow, and others suggested in the 1950s. Institutions, economic and political climate, and economic policies that encourage education, inflows of direct investment, lower population growth, and the efficient use of investment seem to be the chief foundations for economic growth. (p. 276)

The findings of Blomström, Lipsey, and Zejan (1996) support (1) the findings of Baumol, Blackman, and Wolff (1989) that domestic savings in modern, open economies matter little in determining productivity performance and (2) some of the insights of Schumpeter on economic development. Schumpeter (1934/1983) maintained that the major portion of the funds for investment come not from "savings . . . [or] thrift in the strict sense, that is, from abstaining from the consumption of part of one's regular income, but it consists of funds which are themselves, the result of successful innovation and in which we shall later recognize entrepreneurial profit" (p. 72). That is, Schumpeter is claiming that it is entrepreneurial innovations that produce economic growth, which results in entrepreneurial profits that, in turn, fund new investment in physical resources.

The findings of Blomström, Lipsey, and Zejan (1996) have been replicated by Barro (1997). He uses three-stage, least squares estimation techniques on panel data for roughly one hundred countries over three time periods: 1965-1975, 1975-1985, and 1985-1990. When the period-average investment ratio for the *preceding* five years is entered into multiple regressions with eleven control variables (and real, per capita GDP growth rates are used as the dependent variable), the beta coefficient for investment is not statistically significant. However, when *contemporaneous* investment is entered, its coefficient is positive and significant. Barro (1997) concludes: "These findings suggest that much of the positive estimated effect of the investment ratio on growth in typical cross-country regressions reflects the reverse relation between growth prospects and investment" (p. 33).

In conclusion, as to the second thesis, the empirical evidence indicates that the main case is that increases in economic growth cause increases in investment in physical capital. Neoclassical theory is not "close enough" to make the correct prediction. In contrast, R-A theory predicts correctly.

8.5 IS TECHNOLOGICAL PROGRESS EXOGENOUS?

Neoclassical growth theory assumes or predicts that most of the technological progress that influences economic growth stems directly from the basic science conducted by such institutions as government and universities; little or no technological progress stems from the innovations of profit-driven firms. In contrast, because of its focus on the proactive and reactive innovations prompted by the process of competition, R-A theory predicts that most of the technological progress that drives economic growth stems from the actions of profit-driven firms.

The ideal procedure for this section would be—as in Section 8.4—to first present the best or strongest case for the neoclassical view. However, no contemporary scholar of innovation now argues that the basic science conducted by government and universities drives technological progress. Schumpeter (1950) was prescient:

> What we have got to accept is that it [the imperfect competition of large corporations] has come to be the most powerful engine of that progress and in particular of the long-run expansion of total output. . . . In this respect, perfect competition is not only impossible but inferior, and has not title to being set up as a model of regulation of industry on the principle that big business should be made to work as the respective industry would work in perfect competition. . . . [Is] not the observed [high growth] performance due to that stream of inventions that revolutionized the technique of production rather than to the businessman's hunt for profits? The answer is in the negative. The carrying into effect of those technological novelties was of the essence of that hunt. And even the inventing itself . . . was a function of the capitalist process. . . . It is therefore quite wrong—and also quite un-Marxian—to say, as so many economists do, that capitalist enterprise was one, and technological progress a second, distinct factor in the observed development of output; they were essentially one and the same thing or, as we may also put it, the former was the *propelling force* of the latter. (pp. 106, 110; italics added)

Since the time of Schumpeter (1950), studies of innovation routinely stress the role of profit-oriented firms. For example, Schmookler's (1966) historical analysis concludes:

Despite the popularity of the idea that scientific discoveries and major inventions typically provide the stimulus for inventions, the historical record of important inventions in petroleum refining, paper making, railroading, and farming revealed not a single, unambiguous instance in which either discoveries or inventions played the role hypothesized. Instead, in hundreds of cases, the stimulus was the recognition of a costly problem to be solved or a potentially profitable opportunity to be seized; in short, a technical problem or opportunity evaluated in economic terms. (p. 199)

Studies of innovations in such industries as machine tools (Rosenberg 1963), aircraft (Constant 1980), synthetic chemicals (Freeman 1982), metallurgy (Mowery and Rosenberg 1989), and semiconductors (Dosi 1984) all support the view that the profit motive stimulated innovations. For the few recalcitrants who continue to view innovations and technological progress as exogenous to competition, Grossman and Helpman (1994) ask them to ponder: "What would the last century's growth performance have been like without the invention and refinement of methods for generating electricity and using radio waves to transmit sound, without Bessemer's discovery of a new technique for refining iron, and without the design and development of products like the automobile, the airplane, the transistor, the integrated circuit, and the computer?" (p. 32). No "*t* tests" are necessary to answer their query.

In conclusion, as to the third thesis, the innovations that constitute technological progress and drive economic growth are endogenous to the process of competition.[11] Neoclassical theory is not "close enough" to make the correct prediction. In contrast, R-A theory predicts correctly.

8.6   IS GROWTH ECONOMIC SYSTEM-NEUTRAL?

Neoclassical growth theory is economic system-neutral. Therefore, it predicts that both command and market-based economies will, with increases in their capital/labor ratios, experience capital deepening and cease to grow. In contrast, R-A theory predicts that (1) as long as there is vigorous R-A competition in a market based-economy, there should be innovations that prevent the economic stagnation that results from capital deepening, and (2) lacking the productivity-enhancing process of competition, command economies should suffer economic stagnation from capital deepening.

Of course, the U.S. economy and those in Western Europe and elsewhere continue to grow. If capital deepening is to doom such market economies as these to stagnation, the time has not yet come. On the other hand, it is well known that the command economies stagnated after about 1960. Explaining their poor performance has been a subject of much debate. Because it was the largest command economy and the geopolitical center of the communist movement, studies of the economic implosion of the Soviet Union have been prominent (e.g., Banerjee and Spagat 1991; Bergson 1987a,b; Desai 1987; Easterly and Fischer 1994, 1995; Ofer 1987; Weitzman 1990).

Easterly and Fischer (1994, 1995) apply standard, growth accounting methods on post-collapse economic data to attempt to explain the pattern of historical growth of the Soviet Union. Reviewing their comprehensive econometric study sheds light on whether neoclassical growth theory, particularly the capital deepening prediction, applies to command economies.

8.6.1 The Economic Growth of the Soviet Union

Any study of the growth of the Soviet economy faces the daunting problem of the unreliability of Soviet official data. For example, Easterly and Fischer (1995)—hereafter, EF—report that the "official" Soviet estimate of the increase in per capita net material product for 1928 to 1987 was 6% per year. It was Soviet estimates of this kind of rapid growth that led neoclassical historians, in reviewing the socialist calculation debate (see Section 7.2), to claim that socialist economists have "proved that a Central Planning Board could impose rules upon socialist managers which allocated resources and set prices as efficiently as a capitalist society of the purest stripe and more efficiently than the capitalist communities of experience" (Lekachman 1959, pp. 396-97). Such growth estimates also fostered the textbook conventional wisdom that central planning was a tremendous engine of economic growth. For example, as late as 1989, textbooks were claiming:

> But it would be a mistake to dwell on the shortcomings. Every economy has its contradictions and difficulties. . . . What counts is results, and there can be no doubt that the Soviet planning system has been a powerful engine for economic growth. (Samuelson and Nordhaus 1989, pp. 840, 842)

Easterly and Fischer (1995) point out that the 6% per year figure is highly inflated when compared with the post-collapse estimate of 3% per year estimate of GNP per capita growth by Gomulka and Schaffer (1991) for the same 1928-1987 time period. Even though not spectacular, a 3% per year growth rate is certainly respectable.[12] However, EF note that almost all the growth took place before 1960. When they insert the Soviet Union into the Levine and Renelt (see Section 8.3) growth equation for 1960 to 1989, they find that "the

Soviet economic performance conditional on investment and human capital accumulation was the worst in the world from 1960 to 1989" (p. 346). Explaining why the Soviet economy grew respectably until about 1960 and then took a nosedive thereafter is the subject of EF's inquiry.

As to why the Soviet economy grew until about 1960, EF find that the growth resulted almost exclusively from extensive growth, that is, from the large increases in capital investment per worker commanded by central planning. Indeed, between 1950 and 1986, the capital-output ratio for the Soviet economy rose from 2.0 to 5.0. However, numerous market-based economies had rising capital-ratios in this time period (see EF's Appendix 1). Ask EF (1995): "why did the extensive growth strategy lead to [capital deepening and then to] eventual stagnation in U.S.S.R., whereas the same strategy sustained growth in Japan and Korea?" (p. 351). Why was there a decline in Soviet total factor productivity growth every decade from the 1950s to the 1980s? Why did total factor productivity "growth" actually become negative (-0.2% per year) for 1980 to 1987?[13] These questions cannot be answered by the "excess defense spending" hypothesis because EF find that the effect of defense spending was "not very quantitatively important" (p. 361). Similarly, the "lack of R&D spending" hypothesis fails because Soviet R&D spending actually *rose* (from less than 1.5% of GDP in 1950 to more than 3.0% in 1986).

Why, then, did the Soviet economy stagnate? EF (1995) find that "diminishing returns to extensive growth were much sharper in the U.S.S.R. than in market economies because the substitutability of capital for labor was abnormally low" (pp. 360-61). As to why the substitutability was so low, EF suggest that command economies lack what R-A theory refers to as the competences that make up organizational capital (see Section 8.2.1). In EF's words, command economies lack "such market-oriented types of physical and human capital as entrepreneurial skills, marketing and distributional skills, and information-intensive physical and human capital" (p. 363). Indeed, EF's penultimate conclusion speaks directly to whether growth is economic system-neutral:

> Our results with the U.S.S.R. in the international cross-sectional growth and productivity regressions suggest that the planned economic system itself was disastrous for long-run economic growth in the U.S.S.R. Although this point may now seem obvious, it was not so apparent in the halcyon days of the 1950s, when the Soviet example was often cited as support for the neoclassical model's prediction that distortions do not have steady-state growth effects. Economic systems with low substitutability may deceptively generate rapid growth with high investment, only to stagnate after some time. (p. 363)

In conclusion, as to the fourth thesis, economic growth is not economic system-neutral: neoclassical growth theory predicts (1) incorrectly for market-based economies (for capital deepening does *not* cause them to cease growing) and (2) correctly for command economies (for capital deepening does cause them to stagnate). That is, neoclassical growth theory is "close enough" to predict well for command economies, but not close enough to predict well for market-based economies. Indeed, declares Weitzman (1990), "the history of the Soviet economic growth . . . is to my mind as neat and relevant an application of the Solow growth model to economic history as has ever been made" (p. 339).

In contrast, R-A theory makes the correct predictions: (1) as long as there is vigorous R-A competition in a market based-economy, there should be innovations that prevent the economic stagnation that results from capital deepening, and (2) lacking the productivity-enhancing process of competition, command economies should suffer economic stagnation from capital deepening. Neoclassical growth theory was a "wrong turning."

NOTES

1. The countries are Australia, Austria, Belgium, Denmark, Finland, France, Germany, Italy, Japan, Netherlands, Norway, Sweden, United Kingdom, and the United States. The average annual growth rate of per capita GDP was 0.9% (1820-1870), 1.67% (1870-1950), 3.9% (1950-1973), and 2.2% (1973-1989).

2. The version of the neoclassical model discussed here draws on that in Romer (1994). The Cobb-Douglass production function stems from Cobb and Douglass (1928).

3. See Cass (1965) for a version of the model that shows that even with a more complex theory of savings, there will inevitably be economic stagnation under the neoclassical theory of economic growth.

4. Readers will note that the "convergence" dispute is not listed as one of the five assumptions, implications, and predictions highlighted. Many economists maintain that "capital deepening" implies that poor nations should grow faster than rich nations. Others maintain that neoclassical growth theory simply implies that each economy should converge to its steady-state position. See Romer (1994) for a review of the convergence debate and his argument that the entire convergence controversy has been misguided. See Grossman and Helpman (1994, pp. 27-32) for a rebuttal to the conclusion of Mankiw, Romer, and Weil (1992) that the Solow model can be salvaged.

5. "*Le*" is used instead of "*L*" to prevent confusing it with the neoclassical "labor."

6. These eight kinds of innovations parallel the five forms of entrepreneurial "carrying out new combinations" identified by Schumpeter (1934) as driving economic growth:

(1) The introduction of a new good . . . or of a new quality of good. (2) The introduction of a new method of production. . . . (3) The opening of a new market . . . whether or not this market has existed before. (4) The conquest of a new source of supply of raw materials or half-manufactured goods, again irrespective of whether this source already exists. . . . (5) The carrying out of the new organization of any industry. (p. 66)

7. The first version was published in 1980.

8. Levine and Renelt's (1992) extreme bounds analysis indicates that the negative association between GYP and population growth is not robust to other variables. A discussion of other findings by Levine and Renelt (1992) is deferred to the next chapter.

9. De Long and Summers (1993) extend their 1991 article by improving their database and focusing on developing countries. They conclude that "there is a very strong growth-equipment investment association even when rich industrialized countries are not considered" (p. 395).

10. Blomström, Lipsey, and Zejan (1996) also draw on the works of Granger (1969) and Sims (1972) to determine whether economic growth "Granger-causes" investment. They find in the affirmative. Similarly, Lach and Schankerman (1989) find, in a study of 191 U.S. manufacturing firms, that R&D expenditures "Granger-cause" capital investment, but capital investment does not Granger-cause R&D.

11. The acknowledgment that technological progress is endogenous to competition has spurred the development of formal models of endogenous growth. A discussion of these models is deferred to Chapter 9.

12. Easterly and Fisher (1995) point out (see their Table 1) that other post-collapse estimates of Soviet growth are much lower than that of Gomulka and Schaffer (1991).

13. Easterly and Fisher report two different sets of estimates for Soviet total factor productivity growth rates. In Table 4 of EF (1994), they report -1.2% per year for 1928-1940, -0.2 for 1940-1950, 1.3 for 1950-1960, -0.1 for 1960-1970, -0.8 for 1970-1980, and -1.2 for 1980-1987. In Table 4 of EF (1995), estimates for the same time periods are 0.6, 2.8, 0.8, 0.1, and -0.2, respectively.

Chapter

9

The Wealth of Nations

Chapter 7 focused on the nature of productivity and its impact on the wealth of nations. It asked: why are economies premised on privately owned, self-directed firms, competing among each other more productive than those premised on state-owned, state-directed firms cooperating among each other? Resource-advantage theory contributes to explaining the superior productivity of market-based economies over command economies on four grounds: (1) The evolutionary process of R-A competition motivates productivity-enhancing innovation. (2) The process of R-A competition results in prices of capital goods that tend to reflect opportunity costs and, therefore, make economic calculation efficient in allocating scarce, tangible resources. (3) The process of R-A competition results in firms in market-based economies coming to learn how efficient and effective they are. (4) The process of R-A competition motivates the creation of productivity-enhancing, tangible, intangible, and complex or "higher order" resources.

Chapter 8 focused on endogenous economic growth and its impact on the wealth of nations. It argued that economic growth is endogenous to the competitive *process*. This process consists of firms struggling for comparative advantages in resources that yield marketplace positions of competitive advantage for some market segment(s) and, thereby, superior financial performance. The constant struggle for comparative advantages in resources leads not only to increases in the efficient allocation of scarce, tangible resources but also to innovations that result in the creation of new tangible, intangible, and "higher order" resources that drive economic growth. Thus, increases in per capita income are the normal, natural outcome of vigorous R-A competition.

Continuing our discussion of the issues in Chapters 7 and 8, this chapter focuses on two questions related to the wealth of nations. First, if, as discussed in Chapter 8, the neoclassical growth model does a poor job of representing the growth patterns of extant economies because it views the innovations that constitute technological progress as *exogenous,* is it possible to develop formal, that is, mathematical, models of economic growth in which innovations are *endogenous?* Second, if the central economic lessons of the twentieth century are that (1) market-based economies are more productive than command economies (Chapter 7), and (2) market-based economies can sustain economic growth (Chapter 8), why aren't all market-based economies wealthy?

As to the first question, this chapter provides a brief overview of a class of formal models, known as "endogenous growth models," that make endogenous the innovations that constitute technological progress. I then show why such models of growth are inconsistent with perfect competition theory and develop the minimum set of characteristics, five in number, that a theory of competition must have to provide a theoretical foundation for them. I then discuss how R-A theory has the requisite characteristics and, thus, can provide a theoretical foundation for endogenous growth models.

As to the second question, recall from Chapter 8 that the fifth thesis or implication of the equations that constitute neoclassical growth theory is that growth is institutions-neutral. The empirical prediction, therefore, is that, if increases in investment are controlled for, differences in societal institutions will explain only small amounts, if any, of the variance across nations in economic growth per capita.

In contrast, as to the second question and thesis five, R-A theory maintains that wealth creation, that is, increases in productivity and sustained economic growth, stem from vigorous R-A competition. The vigorous R-A competition necessary for wealth creation, in turn, requires a favorable institutional environment (see Figure 6.1). Therefore, R-A theory predicts that, if increases in investment are accounted for, differences in societal institutions across nations will explain significant variance in economic growth per capita. That is, because R-A theory is a substantive theory, not a series of equations, it is not institutions-neutral.

Specifically, as depicted in Figure 6.1, R-A theory posits that the process of competition is significantly influenced by six environment factors: societal resources (e.g., "infrastructure" capital, "natural" resources, formal education, and labor force skills), societal institutions (e.g., culture, the "rule of law," and moral codes), the characteristics of suppliers (e.g., their dependability and competences), consumers (e.g., their tastes and preferences), and public policy (e.g., patent, trademark, and antitrust policies). For R-A theory, these environmental factors, of which societal institutions and public policy are prominent, influence the process of competition and how well the process *works*. In so doing, they determine the extent to which competition is *vigorous*. Which institutions, however, promote R-A competition and economic growth?

This chapter has three major sections. The first discusses endogenous growth models. The second focuses on the institutions that promote vigorous, R-A competition and, consequently, influence wealth creation by promoting economic growth. The third and concluding section focuses on institutions of a distinctly cultural nature. Specifically, it addresses a question that has prompted much discussion: why is it that social trust seems closely related to the wealth of nations? The section shows that R-A theory can contribute to explaining how trust-producing societal institutions can be productivity enhancing and how the absence of such institutions can depress economic growth.

9.1 ENDOGENOUS GROWTH MODELS

Since the works of Romer (1986) and Lucas (1988), most formal models of economic growth have abandoned the view that the capital/labor ratio should be the key endogenous variable (e.g., Aghion and Howitt 1991; Barro and Sala-i-Martin 1997; Grossman and Helpman 1991, 1994; King and Levine 1993; Lucas 1988, 1993; Romer 1986, 1987a,b, 1990, 1993a,b, 1994; Stokey 1991; Young 1991, 1993). Romer (1994) states the consensus:

> Everyone agrees that a conventional neoclassical model with an exponent of about one-third on capital and about two-thirds on labor cannot fit the cross-country or cross-state data. Everyone agrees that the marginal product of investment cannot be orders of magnitude smaller in rich countries than in poor countries. (p. 10)

Because technological progress accounts for most economic growth, theorists argue that technological change can no longer be considered exogenous in growth models. However, if technological change is endogenous to competition, then perfect competition cannot provide the underlying theoretical foundation for growth models.

Several of the early models of endogenous growth, by "sleight of hand" (Romer 1994, p. 15), were able to retain perfect competition. As Romer (1987a) discusses, an early model of his assumed that each unit of capital investment not only increases the stock of physical capital but also increases the level of technology for all firms in the economy through knowledge "spillovers." Romer (1994) states: "If you want to run regressions, investment in human capital is a variable that you can use, so use it I did" (p. 20). He states that he is "now critical of this work," referring to it as his "greatest regret," and points out that it was motivated "partly in an attempt to conform to the norms of what constituted convincing empirical work in macroeconomics" (p. 20).

In reviewing the history of the shift toward endogenous growth models, Romer (1994) characterizes it as "the passing of perfect competition" and notes that "it is obvious in retrospect that endogenous growth theory would have to introduce imperfect competition" (pp. 11, 14). He argues:

> The economics profession is undergoing a substantial change in how we think about international trade, development, economic growth and economic geography. In each of these areas, we have gone through a progression that starts with models based on perfect competition, moves to price-taking with external increasing returns, and finishes with explicit models of imperfect competition. It is likely that this pattern will repeat itself in other areas like the theory of macroeconomic fluctuations. The effects of this general trend may be far-reaching. Ultimately, it may force economists to reconsider some of the most basic propositions in economics. (p. 19)

Similarly, Solow's (1994) review of endogenous growth models points out that "no one could ever have intended to deny that technological progress is at least partially endogenous to the economy." Indeed, he believes that making technological progress endogenous is "probably the most promising aspect of the current third wave of growth theory" and that "the incorporation of monopolistic competition into growth theory is an *unambiguously* good thing" (pp. 48-49; italics added). Grossman and Helpman (1991) concur:

> Technological progress often has been treated as an exogenous process in long-run economic analysis. This treatment would be appropriate for studying the growth of modern industrial economies if advances in industrial know-how followed automatically from fundamental scientific discoveries and if basic research was guided mostly by nonmarket forces. . . . But neither of these descrip-

tions of the learning process seems in accordance with the available evidence. Scientific advances no doubt facilitate invention. But substantial investments are needed to transform abstract ideas into commercially viable products. . . . We take the view that technological progress results from the intentional actions of economic agents responding to perceived profit opportunities. Firms and entrepreneurs devote resources to R&D when they see prospects for reaping returns on their investments. Returns come most often in the form of economic rents in imperfectly competitive product markets. Thus monopoly profits provide the impetus for growth, just as in the Schumpeterian process of "creative destruction." (pp. 334-35)

The impetus for endogenous growth models stems from four economic facts about growth that are now widely acknowledged. First, economic output has outpaced population growth since the industrial revolution. The pessimism, therefore, of Malthus and Ricardo was unwarranted. Second, the growth paths of different countries are not converging to a common level of per capita income, as it was argued would be expected if the capital/labor ratio were the key endogenous variable explaining growth.[1] Third, technological progress is the main driver of economic growth. And fourth, the innovative ideas that collectively constitute technological progress have most often involved, either at their conception or commercial exploitation (or both), the profit-driven actions of firms (Grossman and Helpman 1994; Romer 1993b, 1994; Solow 1994). As Lucas (1993) points out, the innovations that drive endogenous economic growth require us to reconceptualize "human capital":[2]

The main engine of growth is the accumulation of human capital—of knowledge—and the main source of differences in living standards among nations is differences in human capital. Physical capital accumulation plays an essential but decidedly subsidiary role. Human capital accumulation takes place in schools, in research organizations, and in the course of producing goods and engaging in trade. Little is known about the relative importance of these different modes of accumulation, but for understanding periods of very rapid growth in a single economy, learning on the job seems to be by far the most central. (p. 270)

9.1.1 Three Examples of Endogenous Growth Models

Contrasted with the Solow (1956) model's assumption that technological knowledge is an exogenously provided public good, endogenous growth models make technology grow as a result of the specific, profit-driven actions of firms. Three examples serve to illustrate the implications of making technology endogenous.

First, Romer's work (1990, 1993a,b, 1994) highlights the fact that technological knowledge, like labor and capital, is a *resource* used in the production process. However, technological knowledge and other innovative ideas differ from labor and capital in that they are nonrival goods (i.e., their use by one firm doesn't preclude their use by others) that are at least partially excludable (i.e., firms possessing knowledge and/or creating ideas can inhibit—but not necessarily stop—others from using them). Therefore, the problem confronting the economics of technological knowledge involves not how such knowledge is allocated (the focus of neoclassical theory) but how knowledge is created and disseminated.

Romer (1994) starts with the aggregate production function that we designated in Chapter 8 as equation 8.1:

$$(8.1) \qquad Y = A(t)K^{1-\beta}L^{\beta}$$

He (1994) notes that, if "A" stands for the aggregate amount of an economy's technology at a point in time, "All models of growth need at least one equation which describes the evolution of something like $A(t)$" (p. 17). For example, his 1990 model makes A evolve in proportion to the total human capital that firms devote to R&D. This implies that an economy with a larger stock of human capital will not just have greater output but will also experience faster growth. Furthermore, "a subsidy to physical capital accumulation may be a very poor substitute for direct subsidies that increase the incentive to undertake research" (p. 99). Romer (1993b) stresses that the motivation for investing in R&D must be the expectation of rents, which can only result from the existence of market power, which in turn implies abandoning the assumption of marginal cost pricing and perfect competition. Therefore, the goal of a long-run, Pareto-optimal, general equilibrium must also be abandoned because "there is no hope that a decentralized equilibrium in which new ideas are discovered will be first-best Pareto optimal" (p. 76).

As a second example, Stokey's (1991) model recognizes that increased productivity can result from firms being either more efficient or more effective. Her model has individuals make investments in education in the expectation of higher wages balancing the opportunity cost of a later entry to the workforce. In the aggregate, these investments increase the social stock of knowledge, which increases firms' effectiveness in producing higher-quality goods (where quality has Lancasterian [1966] characteristics). Therefore, her model implies that "as aggregate human capital grows, output growth consists of dropping lower-quality goods from production and adding higher quality goods" (p. 588). That is, growth occurs not from additional physical capital enabling firms to produce homogeneous commodities more *efficiently* (moving vertically in Figure 6.2) but from human capital enabling firms to produce heterogeneous goods more *effectively* (moving horizontally to the right in Figure 6.2).

As a third example, Young (1993) develops a hybrid model that integrates models focusing on the inventions resulting from R&D (e.g., Grossman and Helpman 1991; Romer 1990; Segerstrom, Anant, and Dinopoulous 1990) with models of "learning by doing" (e.g., Arrow 1962; Lucas 1988). It also highlights the role of societal institutions. Specifically, Young's model assumes that (1) developing inventions requires firms to shift resources from current production to R&D, (2) innovators receive infinite-lived patents, (3) production experience generates productivity-enhancing knowledge, but such "learning by doing" is bounded, and (4) productivity-enhancing knowledge spills over into other sectors. The model implies that, rather than reducing growth rates, "rent seeking . . . might, in fact, encourage growth by allowing innovators to reap rewards greater than those that could be achieved under a free-market system" (p. 464).[3]

9.1.2 Grounding Endogenous Growth Models

Essentially, formal *models* of endogenous economic growth imply the following, endogenous technological progress, *theory* of economic growth: (1) Certain aspects of the process of monopolistic competition, including the rational expectation of rents, engender innovative ideas at the firm level. (2) These competition-induced innovations, through time, result in both firm- and industry-level technological changes. (3) These technological changes, cumulatively, result in increases in total factor productivity for the economy, that is, technological progress. (4) Thus, competition-induced technological progress, through time, results in economic growth. However, when Romer, Solow, and others advocate incorporating "imperfect competition" or "monopolistic competition" into growth models, they are using these terms generically. That is, they are not urging the adoption of either Robinson's (1933) specific theory of imperfect competition or Chamberlin's (1933) specific theory of monopolistic competition as a theoretical foundation for endogenous growth models. Indeed, they *cannot* so argue: neither of these theories views competition as a process wherein innovations result in technological progress.

A theory of competition that could ground endogenous growth models would be, at the minimum, a process-oriented theory with five requisites. First, technology cannot be assumed to be freely available to all firms, but must be a resource in the production process that is a nonrival, partially excludable good. Second, innovation must not be exogenous, but must be an outcome of the process of competition. Third, the innovations that result in economic growth cannot be exclusively of the Schumpeterian "creative destructive" kind:

> To understand growth we need to understand not only how big [Schumpeterian] ideas, such as high-temperature super conductors, are discovered and put to use but also how millions of little ideas such as better ways to assemble shirts, are discovered and put to use. To understand development, we need to understand how both kinds of ideas, but especially the millions of small ones, can be used and produced in a developing country. (Romer 1993b, pp. 69-70)

Fourth, firms cannot not be price-takers, but must have the rational expectation that rents will be earned from innovations that contribute to their efficiency and/or effectiveness. And fifth, societal institutions, such as the patent system, should be viewed as potentially facilitating or inhibiting competition-induced economic growth.

9.1.3 Endogenous Growth Models and R-A Theory

A theory of competition having the five requisites necessary for grounding formal models of endogenous growth would depart not only from perfect competition but also from all extant theories of monopolistic competition in the neoclassical tradition. Indeed, because it could not focus exclusively on major innovations, it would also depart from "Schumpeterian" competition.[4] The thesis defended here is that R-A theory has the five requisites and, therefore, can theoretically ground endogenous growth models.

Technology as a Resource. As to requisite one, because it defines resources as the tangible and intangible entities available to the firm that enable it to produce efficiently/effectively a market offering that has value for some market segment(s), R-A theory provides grounds for the view that technologies are nonrival, partially excludable resources. First, if technologies are viewed as distinctive ways for firms to produce value, then a specific technology is a distinctive pattern or "routine" (Nelson and Winter 1982) that describes the firm's process for combining inputs to produce valued outputs. In R-A terminology, for a firm to possess a specific technology is equivalent to its having a specific organizational competence. Because R-A theory recognizes that technologies or competences can be replicated by other firms, it acknowledges that they are nonrival goods.

Second, R-A theory provides a rationale for why technologies or competences are partially excludable. Note that it proposes that a comparative advantage in resources, of which technologies, that is, competences, are prominent, is the manner by which firms achieve marketplace positions of competitive advantage and, thereby, superior financial performance. Therefore, how technologies become partially excludable is simply part of the following, more fundamental question: what determines the life span of the comparative advantage of *any* advantage-producing resource? That is, why are some resources less easily replicable, more easily excludable, than others? Simple resources, such as standard pieces of machinery, can customarily be purchased in the factor markets and, by themselves, are unlikely to produce a comparative advantage with anything beyond a very short life span. R-A theory maintains that the long life spans of some advantage-producing resources result from the protection afforded by such societal institutions as patents, as Young's (1993) model assumes, or their long life spans result from resources that are causally ambiguous, socially complex, or tacit or have time compression diseconomies (see Sections 4.1.5, 5.5.1, and 8.2.1 for explications of these concepts).

Endogenous Innovation: Major and Incremental. The second and third requisites are that innovations, both major and incremental, should be an outcome of competition. R-A theory identifies two different kinds of innovative activities: proactive and reactive (see Section 6.1.3). The former occurs when, for example, a firm's market research department identifies a previously unserved market segment and tailors a market offering for it. (Note that the effectiveness of a firm's marketing research department contributes to its entrepreneurial competence.) A firm is also being proactive when its R&D department develops a market offering and the firm then finds a market segment for it. Finally, a firm is being proactive when it engages in continuous process improvements, as in total quality management (TQM) programs. When proactive, innovative activities successfully produce innovations that contribute to efficiency/effectiveness, firms will be rewarded by marketplace positions of competitive advantage and, thus, accomplish their goal of superior financial performance. The innovations, it must be stressed, may be major or incremental. Indeed, numerous incremental innovations—as in TQM programs—may cumulatively have a *major* impact on the performance of the individual firm, industry, and overall economy.

Reactive innovative activities occur when inferior financial performance signals firms that their comparative disadvantage in resources has resulted in their occupying marketplace positions of competitive disadvantage. Upon so learning, firms react by attempting to acquire their rivals' advantage-producing resource, by imitating it, by finding an equivalent resource for it, or by finding (creating, developing, assembling) a superior resource. Firms having a comparative disadvantage in resources are motivated to innovate by their desire for superior financial performance; necessity is, indeed, the mother of invention (see also Section 7.3.1.).

Rents. The fourth requisite is that firms must have the rational expectation of rents to be earned from innovations that contribute to their efficiency and/or effectiveness. Although the label "rents" is not used, R-A theory maintains that firms can expect superior financial performance when they have a comparative advantage in resources that leads to marketplace positions of competitive advantage. That is, as shown in Figures 6.1 and 6.2, firms can have superior financial performance when their resources, relative to their rivals, enable them to produce market offerings that are perceived by some market segment(s) as (1) having superior value, while produced at parity costs; (2) having superior value, while produced at lower costs; or (3) having parity value, while produced at lower costs. In cases one and two, firms are able to charge higher than parity prices. In case three, they can achieve superior performance at parity prices because of lower costs. Important for R-A theory, the expectation of superior financial performance is rational because (as discussed in Section 6.3) empirical works reveal large, within-industry variance in financial performance.

Institutions. The fifth requisite is that such societal institutions as the patent system should contribute to facilitating or inhibiting competition-induced economic growth. Because a discussion of institutions that promote vigorous R-A competition is the subject of the rest of this chapter, here I simply make two points. First, the institution of a patent system fosters efficiency/effectiveness by extending the life span of the advantage produced by an innovation. Absent an effective patent system, the financial rewards for inventions would often be insufficient for promoting the investment in R&D required for their discovery.

Second, note that trademarks are considered to be resources in Table 5.1. Therefore, the legal protection of trademarks, by protecting the investment that firms have in them, encourages firms to safeguard this resource by maintaining high-quality market offerings. Because, as shown in Table 5.1, R-A theory maintains that consumers have imperfect information and that gathering information is costly, trademarks not only help reduce consumer search costs but also serve as quality control mechanisms for society (see Section 5.2.1).

To conclude this section, endogenous growth models have abandoned neoclassical growth theory by making technological progress endogenous to the process of competition. In so doing, however, neoclassical perfect competition theory must also be abandoned: perfect competition isn't *perfect*. A theory of competition that could ground endogenous growth models would have five characteristics. R-A theory—alone among extant theories of competition—has all five of the requisites.

9.2 INSTITUTIONS AND ECONOMIC GROWTH

If vigorous, R-A competition produces the innovations that drive economic growth and institutions influence the vigor of competition, which institutions promote economic growth? Recall that R-A theory posits that (1) the firm's primary objective is superior financial performance, which it pursues under conditions of imperfect and often costly to obtain information about extant and potential market segments, competitors, suppliers, shareholders, and production technologies, and (2) human motivation is constrained, self-interest seeking. Consistent with self-interest seeking, superior financial performance is argued to be the firm's primary objective because superior rewards flow to the owners, managers, and employees of firms that produce superior financial results. These rewards include not only such financial rewards as stock dividends, capital appreciation, salaries, wages, and bonuses, but also such nonfinancial rewards as promotions, expanded career opportunities, prestige, and feelings of accomplishment (see Sections 5.3.1 and 5.4.1). Therefore, certain institutions that promote the firm's primary objective will promote R-A competition and the innovations that drive economic growth. These institutions are those that promote the achievement of superior financial performance as a result of firms occupying marketplace positions of competitive advantage stemming from a comparative advantage in resources.[5]

Although numerous institutions can promote or depress R-A competition, as an evolutionary, process theory of competition, the *sine qua nons* of institutions that promote competition and economic growth are those that protect the rights of individuals and firms in their property. Property rights are the rights that individuals and firms appropriate over their labor and output, respectively, as well as over the goods and services they possess. "Appropriation is a function of legal rules, organizational forms, enforcement, and norms of behavior—that is, the institutional framework" (North 1990, p. 33).

Because R-A theory stresses the importance of proactive and reactive innovations in driving economic growth, it emphasizes the importance of protecting the property rights of individuals and firms in innovations. As Poirot (1993) puts it, "in order for an existing institutional structure to direct economic activity along a path that is conducive to economic growth, individuals must be able to reap the gains from innovation" (p. 892). Because R-A theory stresses the role of intangible resources in competition, it emphasizes the importance of protecting intellectual property rights, for example, the protection of trademarks (see Section 5.2.1). Because R-A theory views firms as combiners of heterogeneous, imperfectly mobile resources, reaping the gains from innovation becomes theoretically *possible*. Because R-A theory recognizes the importance of institutions protecting property rights, reaping the gains of innovation becomes empirically *likely*.

Romer (1994) argues that the concept of *evidence* should be expanded in economic science:

> In evaluating different models of growth, I have found that Lucas's (1988) observation, that people with human capital migrate from places where it is scarce to places where it is abundant, is as powerful a piece of evidence as all the cross-country growth regressions combined. But this kind of fact, like the fact about intra-industry trade or the fact that people make discoveries, does not come with an attached t-statistic. As a result, these kinds of facts tend to be neglected in discussions that focus too narrowly on testing and rejecting models. (p. 19)

Following Romer's suggestion, I argue that R-A theory's claim that societal institutions protecting property rights are key for competition and growth (1) is consistent with historical evidence on the sources of the wealth of nations and (2) is supported by empirical evidence of the "t-test" variety. Specifically, as to historical evidence, North's (1990, 1991) work supports R-A theory's claim. As to "t-test" evidence, empirical tests show that differences in societal institutions that protect property rights will explain significant variance in economic growth per capita across nations. I begin with the work of North (1990).

9.2.1 Historical Evidence

What explains the tremendous disparity in GDP per capita among nations? Why are Third World countries so poor, relative to the Western nations and Japan? North's (1990) historical analysis concludes:

> Third World countries are poor because the institutional constraints define a set of payoffs to political/economic activity that do not encourage productive activity. Socialist economies are just beginning to appreciate that the underlying institutional framework is the source of their current poor performance and are at-

tempting to grapple with ways to restructure the institutional framework to redirect incentives that in turn will direct organizations along productivity-increasing paths. (p. 110)

North's argument is richly detailed and difficult to reduce to a few paragraphs. Stated briefly, North (1990) defines institutions as "the humanly devised constraints that shape human interaction" (p. 3), and he distinguishes formal institutions (constitutional law, statutory law, and common law) from informal institutions (cultural constraints, such as customs, traditions, conventions, and codes of conduct). He also distinguishes institutions (the rules of the game) from organizations (major players of the game). Organizations influence a society's institutional framework, and, conversely, institutions influence organizational activities and performance.

Important for understanding economic growth, a society's institutional framework determines its property rights, that is, "the rights individuals appropriate over their own labor and the goods and services they possess" (North 1990, p. 33). Property rights, in turn, influence a society's productivity and economic growth. Although Alchian's (1950) evolutionary hypothesis would suggest that vigorous competition would weed out inferior institutions, North argues that evolutionary change does not guarantee efficient, that is, productivity-enhancing, institutions. Indeed, throughout history, "rulers devised property rights in their own interest and transaction costs resulted in typically inefficient property rights prevailing" (p. 7).

For example, both "England and Spain faced crises in the seventeenth century, but the contrasting paths that they took appear to have reflected deep underlying institutional characteristics of the societies" (North 1990, p. 116). In England, the triumph of Parliament over the Crown laid the groundwork for the development of a private capital market, more secure property rights, changes in patent laws, and the decline of mercantilist restrictions. These institutional changes, taken in combination, provided expanded opportunities for English firms in both domestic and international markets. The "English path" of secure property rights and economic growth was then transported to its colonies in North America:

U.S. economic history has been characterized by a federal political system, checks and balances, and a basic structure of property rights that have encouraged the long-term contracting essential to the creation of capital markets and economic growth. Even one of the most costly civil wars in all of history failed to alter the basic institutional matrix. (p. 116)

In contrast, North (1990) argues, in Spain the Crown triumphed over the Cortes (the Spanish parliament), and the monarchy instituted a large, centralized bureaucracy that suppressed property rights through confiscation, price controls, and rent controls: "Every detail of the economy as well as the polity was structured with the objective of furthering the interests of the crown in the creation of the most powerful empire since Rome" (p. 114). The centralized, bureaucratic control over the economy, with its suppression of property rights, was then transported to Latin America. The transported institutional framework was disastrous to both Spain and its colonies: "In a century—the seventeenth—Spain declined from the most powerful nation in the Western world since the Roman empire to a second-rate power" (p. 115).

North (1990) explains the persistence of inefficient institutions in Spain and its colonies by adopting the evolutionary, path-dependence, "lock-in" view of David (1985). That is, "the resultant path of institutional change is shaped by (1) the lock-in that comes from the symbiotic relationship between institutions and the organizations that have evolved as a consequence of the incentive structure provided by those institutions and (2) the feedback process by which human beings perceive and react to changes in the opportunity set" (p. 7). This feedback can result in "either efficient or *persistently* inefficient paths" (p. 8). Indeed, the positive feedback in Spain's locked-in path resulted in an "inability of the crown and its bureaucracy to alter the direction of the Spanish path in spite of their awareness of the decay and decline overcoming the country" (p. 115).

For North (1990), then, societies that have become wealthy through time have become so "because the underlying institutional framework persistently reinforced incentives for organizations to engage in productive activity" (p. 9). In contrast, "in many Third World countries today as well as those that have characterized much of the world's economic history, [t]he opportunities for political and economic entrepreneurs are still a mixed bag, but they overwhelmingly favor activities that promote redistributive rather than productive activity, that create monopolies rather than competitive conditions, and that restrict opportunities rather than expand them" (p. 9).

If wealthy nations are wealthy because they have evolved sets of institutions that protect property rights and hence are efficient in creating economic growth, how do poor societies, often with political "lock-ins," go about creating institutions that encourage productivity? North (1990) admits that he has no ready answer. Nonetheless, he identifies the goal that policymakers should adopt: "One gets *efficient* institutions by a polity that has built-in incentives to create and enforce efficient property rights" (p. 140). He notes, however, that the serious study of institutions that can further this goal has been long ne-

glected in economics. Furthermore, he laments, the dominant, neoclassical research tradition represents a serious, perhaps insurmountable, obstacle for
anyone attempting to understand how societies can create efficient institutions
because the tradition is "locked-in": "But it is hard—maybe impossible—to
model such a polity with wealth-maximizing actors unconstrained by other
considerations" (p. 140).

To conclude this section, North's (1990) work provides historical evidence
supporting R-A theory's emphasis on the importance of institutions that protect property rights for the goal of furthering competition and economic
growth. Furthermore, note that North's historical analysis emphasizes that understanding economic growth requires (1) abandoning the premise that economic and political actors are wealth maximizers, (2) adopting the view that
competition is a historical process and, (3) recognizing that the evolutionary
development of polities and economies can result in path dependencies. In like
manner, for R-A theory, (1) human behavior is posited to be constrained, self-
interest seeking, (2) firms, following Chandler (1990), are posited as entities in
space and time, not mathematical abstractions, and (3) the evolutionary process of R-A competition, because it results in the survival of the "locally fitter,"
not the "maximally fittest," can produce path dependencies (see Table 5.1 and
Sections 2.1.3, 6.2.5, 6.2.4, and 6.3).

Therefore, North's work and R-A theory reinforce each other. Indeed, R-A
theory—alone among extant theories of competition—provides a theoretical
foundation for North's work.

9.2.2 Empirical Evidence

Growth accounting studies have long been plagued by both data unavail-
ability and the poor quality of data that *have* been available. The situation began to change with the publication of the Penn World Table data set assembled
painstakingly by Kravis, Heston, and Summers (1982), which used data from
the United Nations Comparison Project. The most recent (as of this writing) it-
eration of the data set provides data on 27 economic variables (including real
GDP per capita income data in purchasing-power parity 1985 dollars) for 139
economies for the years 1950 to 1990 (Summers and Heston 1991, 1993). Because of its acknowledged high quality, most cross-country regression analyses of economic growth use the Summers and Heston data set, sometimes augmented by other data sources. One immediately apparent consequence of
using the Summers and Heston data set is that any study using it to investigate
economic growth can go back no further than 1950. Whether this is a problem,

of course, depends on whether the sources of economic growth in recent history, that is, since 1950, will hold in the future—and no one knows, or can know, whether this assumption is justified.

In addition to the potential "recent history" bias in growth accounting regressions, there are several other problems for cross-country, empirical works on growth. First, because neoclassical theory is institutions-neutral, there has been no theoretical framework to guide such empirical analyses. As Levine and Renelt (1992) observe, "there does not exist a consensus theoretical framework to guide empirical work on growth" (p. 943). Therefore, empirical works tend to be highly exploratory in nature.

Abramowitz (1989), one of the founders of modern, growth accounting, points out that a second problem is that for an institution to influence growth, there often must be one or more other institutions present:

> Growth accounting holds that the sources it measures act independently of one another so that each makes its own contribution. There are good reasons, however, to question that claim. The growth sources feed from one another. The most important interactions are those between technological progress and the accumulation of tangible capital and between technological progress and the build-up of human capital through education and training. (p. 23)

In other words, just as there are distinctive patterns or packages of interconnected resources that make up an organization's competences and impact a *firm's* growth (see Sections 2.1.2, 4.1.4, and 8.2.1), there are distinctive packages of interconnected institutions that (1) impact an economy's productive capabilities in the aggregate and (2) drive an *economy's* growth.

Indeed, Levine and Renelt (1992) find that the correlations between economic growth and many fiscal expenditure variables, monetary policy indicators, and political stability indices become nonsignificant ("nonrobust") when additional variables are added to the regressions: "This implies that there is not a reliable, independent statistical relationship between a wide variety of macroeconomic indicators and growth" (p. 943). Just as R-A theory recommends that firms and their growth be viewed in terms of their competences, that is, their packages of resources, Levine and Renelt recommend: "National policies appear to be a complex *package,* and future researchers may wish to focus on macroeconomic policy *regimes* and interactions among policies as opposed to the independent influence of any particular policy" (p. 960; italics added).

Maddison (1994) identifies yet a third problem. He divides the sources of economic growth into "ultimate" causes and "proximate" causes. For him, proximate causes include such standard economic variables as investment per capita, labor hours, and education. Ultimate causes include institutions, ideologies, historical accidents, and national economic policy. As to ultimate causes, Maddison (1994) notes:

> They are virtually impossible to quantify, and thus there will always be legitimate scope for disagreement on what is important. However, it is a mistake to ignore causality at this level. . . . The serious problems that the Soviet Union and Eastern Europe have had in switching to capitalism have made it abundantly clear that the capitalist model is not simply a reliance on market forces but has a complex institutional underpinning. (p. 32)

The preceding, well-known, problems with growth accounting regressions—recent history bias, lack of theory, interconnectedness of causes, and focus on proximate causes—serve as a caveat for anyone seeking definitive, empirical results. With this caveat in mind, four studies seem particularly relevant to R-A theory and the issue of the relationship between property rights and economic growth: Knack and Keefer (1995); Barro (1997); Johnson, Holmes, and Kirkpatrick (1998); and Gwartney, Lawson, and Block (1996). I review each, in turn.

Knack and Keefer. The work of Knack and Keefer (1995) focuses specifically on the influence on economic growth of institutions that protect property rights. Previous research, they point out, has relied on democracy indices, such as the ones by Gastil (1991), to measure the extent to which a nation protects property rights. However, the Gastil democracy indices, which measure revolutions, coups, and assassinations, are poor proxies for the protection of property rights because the mere absence of political violence does not signify well the protection of private property. Indeed, "dictators who are most effective in repression of dissent may be the most successful in avoiding coups, revolutions, and assassinations, but offer the worst protection for property rights" (p. 209).

As better measures of the extent to which nations protect property rights, Knack and Keefer (1995) argue for two indices provided by private international investment risk services: International Country Risk Guide (ICRG) and Business Environmental Risk Intelligence (BERI). The ICRG index is a composite of five separate indices, each of which impacts on property rights: (1) quality of bureaucracy, for example, autonomy from political pressure; (2) corruption in government, for example, bribes and other illegal payments; (3) the rule of law, for example, an independent judiciary; (4) expropriation risk, for example, risk of confiscation and forced nationalization; and (5) repudiation of contracts by government, for example, risk of modification of contracts by a new government. Similarly, the BERI index is a composite of four indices: (1) nationalization potential, for example, preferential treatment for national firms; (2) contract enforceability, for example, degree to which contracts are honored; (3) bureaucratic delays, for example, efficiency of civil service; and (4) infrastructure quality, for example, quality of transportation and communications.[6] Knack and Keefer note that the ICRG and BERI indices are highly correlated with each other, but neither is highly correlated with the Gastil democracy indices.

To explore the relationship between the protection of property rights and economic growth, Knack and Keefer (1995) use data from Levine and Renelt (1992) for 1974 to 1989 and run several regressions. Important for our purposes, when they use average GDP per capita growth as the dependent variable (and, as control variables, initial GDP per capita, secondary education, primary education, average private investment, and percentage of government consumption in GDP), the beta coefficients for both ICRG and BERI in the regression are positive and significant.[7] Likewise, when average private investment for the time period is the dependent variable (and the same control variables are used), ICRG and BERI are, again, positive and significant.[8] The finding on investment implies that "one way that insecure property rights hinder growth is by deterring investment, an effect that is captured by investment itself when it enters the regression" (p. 219). Knack and Keefer conclude: "institutions that protect property rights are crucial to economic growth and investment" (p. 223).

In conclusion, the work of Knack and Keefer (1995) provides empirical evidence supporting R-A theory's emphasis on institutions in general and property rights in particular. Institutions are important determinants of the vigor of R-A competition and how well such competition produces the innovations that promote economic growth. Institutions that protect property rights are particularly important, because even when investment is controlled for, property rights explain significant variance in economic growth. However, one should note that Knack and Keefer (1995) use *concurrent* investment (average investment 1974-1989) in their regressions, not investment in some preceding time period. Thus, the issue of causality is raised again (see Sections 8.4.1 and 8.4.2). The work of Barro (1997) corrects this deficiency.

Barro. Barro (1997) provides one of the most extensive analyses yet of the empirics of economic growth. He augments the Summers and Heston (1991,

1993) data set with the other sources of data (including World Bank data) and uses three-stage, least squares estimation techniques for a panel of approximately 100 countries for three time periods: 1965 to 1975, 1975 to 1985, and 1985 to 1995. His methodology, therefore, enables him to explore for both cross-sectional (between-country) and time series (within-country) effects.

Barro's (1997) work takes seriously the admonition of Blomström, Lipsey, and Zejan (1994, 1996) that growth accounting studies should consider the issue of causality. Thus, a key issue is whether measures of independent variables should precede economic growth or be concurrent with it. His final regressions (see his Table 1.1, p. 13), which focus on explaining economic growth in terms of real GDP per capita growth rates for the three time periods, contain nine independent variables that are measured *concurrently* with the time period of growth: (1) male secondary and higher schooling, (2) log (life expectancy), (3) log (GDP × male schooling), (4) ICRG rule of law index, (5) terms of trade change, (6) inflation rate, (7) sub-Sahara Africa dummy, (8) Latin America dummy, and (9) East Asia dummy.

Barro (1997) argues that, in contrast, causality implies that six variables should be measured in time periods that *precede* the growth period to be explained: (1) log GDP, (2) log (fertility rate), (3) government consumption rate, (4) Gastil democracy index, (5) Gastil democracy index squared, and (6) investment.[9] That is, for each of these six variables, he inputs measures for 1960-1964 to explain 1965-1975 growth, 1970-1974 to explain 1975-1985 growth, and 1980-1984 to explain 1985-1995 growth.

Barro's (1997) final equation for GDP per capita growth in the three time periods explains 60%, 52%, and 47%, respectively, of the variance. Important for our purposes, though preceding time period investment is not significant in the final equation, the three measures that specifically relate to the protection of property rights are. The ICRG rule of law index is positive and significant; the democracy index is positive and significant; and the democracy index squared is negative and significant.[10] Barro (1997) speculates as to why there is a positive linear effect of democracy on economic growth but a negative quadratic effect:

> The pattern of results—a positive coefficient on the linear term and a negative coefficient on the square—means that growth is increasing in democracy at low levels of democracy, but the relation turns negative once a moderate amount of political freedom has been attained. . . . One way to interpret the results is that in the worst dictatorships, an increase in political rights tends to increase growth and investment because the benefit from limitations on governmental power is

the key matter. But in places that have already achieved a moderate amount of democracy, a further increase in political rights impairs growth and investment because the dominant effect comes from the intensified concern with income redistribution. (pp. 58-59)

In conclusion, Barro's (1997) exploratory work—keeping in mind the caveat at the beginning of this section—provides empirical evidence supporting R-A theory's emphasis on institutions in general and property rights in particular. Institutions that promote the rule of law and democracy, by protecting property rights, promote competition and economic growth. However, as North (1990) envisioned, Barro (1997) provides evidence that when the feedback effects of increases in democracy have the *primary* consequence of promoting income redistribution, rather than protecting the rights of individuals and firms in their output, then increases in democracy decrease the effectiveness of competition in promoting economic growth.

Thus, Barro's (1997) work and R-A theory reinforce each other. Indeed, R-A theory—alone among theories of competition—can explain the findings of Knack and Keefer (1995) and Barro (1997).

Johnson, Holmes, and Kirkpatrick. Under the auspices of the Heritage Foundation and the *Wall Street Journal,* Johnson, Holmes, and Kirkpatrick (1998) accept the suggestion of Levine and Renelt (1992) that researchers explore the role of packages of institutions in promoting economic growth. Each year, since 1995, they publish their *Index of Economic Freedom* for 154 countries. The *Index* is a package of ten institutional factors: (1) trade policy, for example, average tariff rate; (2) taxation, for example, top individual and corporate tax rates; (3) government intervention in the economy, for example, government consumption as a percentage of GDP; (4) monetary policy, for example, average inflation rate; (5) capital flows and foreign investment, for example, restrictions on repatriation of earnings; (6) banking, for example, government ownership of banks; (7) wage and price controls, for example, minimum wage laws; (8) property rights, for example, government expropriation of property; (9) regulation, for example, licensing requirements; and (10) black market, for example, piracy of intellectual property.

Each factor is equally weighted in the *Index* and given a score of 1 to 5, where low numbers equate with more economic freedom. Countries whose average overall score is less than 2.00 are classified as *free;* those whose score is 2.00 to 2.99 are *mostly free;* 3.00 to 3.99 are *mostly unfree;* and 4.00 to 5.00 are *repressed.* The factors in the *Index* are all governmental policies that represent inputs to overall economic freedom. As such, in the terms of North (1990) and R-A theory, they would be considered "formal" institutions.

In 1997, nine countries (Hong Kong, Singapore, Bahrain, New Zealand, Switzerland, the United States, Luxembourg, Taiwan, and the United Kingdom) were rated as economically free. Sixty-four countries were mostly free; 58 were mostly unfree; and 25 were repressed. Important for our purposes, the nine countries classified as economically free in 1997 had an average annual real per capita growth rate (1980-1993) of 2.88%. In contrast, the average growth rates for the 64 mostly free, 58 mostly unfree, and 25 repressed countries for the same time period were 0.97%, -0.32%, and -1.44%, respectively (Johnson, Holmes, and Kirkpatrick 1998, p. 7). When the goal is promoting economic growth, the message of the *Index* is clear: formal institutions that promote economic freedom *work*.

In conclusion, the work of Johnson, Holmes, and Kirkpatrick (1998) supports R-A theory's emphasis on packages of institutions for promoting vigorous competition and economic growth. Specifically, the separate institutions that promote economic freedom interact with each other as a package to provide an environment that promotes R-A competition and the innovations that produce economic growth.

Gwartney, Lawson, and Block. Under the auspices of the Fraser Institute, Gwartney, Lawson, and Block (1996) and Gwartney and Lawson (1997) also explore the role of packages of institutions in promoting economic growth. Their *Index of Economic Freedom* focuses on property rights, personal choices, and voluntary transactions: "Individuals have economic freedom when (a) property they acquire without the use of force, fraud, or theft is protected from physical invasions by others and (b) they are free to use, exchange, or give their property to another as long as their actions do not violate the identical rights of others" (1996, p. 12). The *Index* is a package of seventeen components that fall into four major groupings: (1) money and inflation (i.e., four components measuring the protection of money as a store of value and medium of exchange), (2) government operations and regulations (i.e., six items indicating the freedom of individuals to decide what is produced and consumed), (3) takings and discriminatory taxation (i.e., three items indicating the freedom to keep what one earns), and (4) restraints on international exchange (i.e., four items indicating one's freedom to exchange with foreign nationals).[11]

Although Gwartney, Lawson, and Block (1996) experimented with several different schemes for weighting the seventeen components (including weighting each equally), they argue that weights based on the opinions of experts provide "the most reliable indicator of differences in economic freedom across a wide range of countries" (p. xxi). With a constraint that the weights must sum to 100 points, their survey results provided weights for each of the seventeen components in the four major groupings as follows: (1a) money expansion, weighted 4.7; (1b) inflation variability, 5.3; (1c) foreign currency accounts, 3.0; (1d) deposits abroad, 2.7; (2a) government consumption, 6.2; (2b) government enterprises, 6.5; (2c) price controls, 7.1; (2d) entry into business, 6.7; (2e) equality under the law, 4.7; credit market, 3.4; (3a) transfers and subsidies, 10.9; (3b) marginal tax rates, 12.7; (3c) conscription, 3.6; (4a) trade taxes 6.7; (4b) exchange rate controls, 6.2; (4c) size of trade sector, 3.7; (4d) capital mobility constraints, 5.9 (see their Exhibit 1-2, p. 38). Thus, the highest weighted component (marginal tax rates) receives 4.7 times the weight of the lowest component (deposits abroad).

Gwartney, Lawson, and Block (1996) and Gwartney and Lawson (1997) provide mean *Index of Economic Freedom* ratings (on a scale of 0 to 10) for approximately 100 countries for 1995, 1990, 1985, 1980, and 1975. For 1995, the *Index* showed the five freest nations to be Hong Kong (9.3), Singapore (8.2), New Zealand (8.0), the United States (7.9), and Mauritius (7.6), and the five least free nations to be Haiti (2.9), Burundi (2.7), Syria (2.7), Croatia (2.4), and Algeria (1.9) (1997, p. 27). Although the average country freedom rating increased only slightly from 1975 (mean = 4.2) to 1985 (mean = 4.3), it rose significantly in 1990 (mean = 4.6) and 1995 (mean = 5.2) (1996, p. xxx).

The increase in economic freedom in the late 1980s and early 1990s is even more dramatic when one considers that all communist economies are excluded from the 1975 ratings and it wasn't until the revision by Gwartney and Lawson (1997) that most of the former communist economies were included, retrospectively, in the 1995 *Index*. Furthermore, each of the former communist economies, with the exceptions of Estonia and Lithuania, had *Index* scores in 1995—as reported in Gwartney and Lawson (1997)—below the overall mean of 5.2! One can argue that the collapse of communism *caused* many nations to "free-up" their economies. That is, the failure of the command economies was a learning experience for other nations. But one cannot argue that the change in the *Index* from 1975 to 1990-1995 simply reflects changes in the command economies themselves.

Important for our purposes are the relationships Gwartney, Lawson, and Block (1996) find between the *Index* and both wealth and economic growth. When they grade nations A, B, C, D, F, and F- on the basis of 1995 level of economic freedom, the average 1994 GDP per capita for each group (in 1985 dollars) was $15,800, $13,700, $7,900, $3,800, $3,100, and $1,700, respectively (p. xxii). That is, economically free nations have much more productive economies. When they compute the average growth rate of GDP per capita (1980-

1994) for the same groupings, the percentages are 3.3, 2.0, 1.5, 1.3, 0.8, and -1.3, respectively (p. xxii). That is, the more economically free a nation is, the faster the economy grows. When they compare the average growth rates (1980-1994) of the ten countries with the largest *increases* in economic freedom to the ten with the largest *decreases,* the averages were 2.7% and -1%. That is, increasing economic freedom produces increased growth; decreasing economic freedom depresses growth (p. xxvii). These striking results do not appear to be an artifact of how the *Index* is constructed. Indeed, it is:

> essential that the measure of economic freedom not beg any questions by depending on outcomes; it was essential that it depend only on objective characteristics of an economy. This may seem obvious but I assure you that it is not. After all, the rate of economic growth or the level of living may be an excellent proxy for economic freedom, just as an auto's maximum speed may be an excellent proxy for the power of its motor. But any such connections must be demonstrated not assumed or taken for granted. There is nothing in the way the indexes are calculated that would prevent them from having no correlation whatsoever with such completely independent numbers as per capita GDP and the rate of growth of GDP. (Friedman 1996, p. viii)

Why the strong relationships between economic freedom, productivity, and economic growth? Gwartney, Lawson, and Block (1996) cite the works of Kirzner (1973)—see Section 2.2—and North (1990)—see Sections 4.2 and 9.2.1—and argue:

> There are essentially four sources of increases in productivity and income: (1) improvements in the skills of workers, (2) investment and capital formation, (3) advancements in technology, and (4) better economic organization. These four factors are interrelated and, in varying degrees, are all influenced by economic freedom. If people are not permitted to keep what they produce and earn, they will have little incentive to either upgrade their skills or invest in structures and machines designed to enhance future productivity. Additionally, if individuals are not allowed to try new ways of doing things, innovation and improvements in technology will be stifled. Most importantly, economic freedom is reflective of institutional arrangements. If an economy's institutions are consistent with economic freedom, it will be easier for people to cooperate with each other, specialize in areas where they have a comparative advantage, and realize gains from trade and entrepreneurship. Correspondingly, institutional arrangements that restrain trade, increase transaction costs, weaken property rights, and create uncertainty will reduce the realization of gains from trade and also the incentive of individuals to engage in productive activities. (Gwartney, Lawson, and Block 1996, pp. 89-90)

In conclusion, the works of Gwartney, Lawson, and Block (1996) and Gwartney and Lawson (1997) on economic freedom support R-A theory's emphasis on packages of institutions for promoting vigorous competition and economic growth. Indeed, R-A theory—alone among extant theories of competition—can explain their findings: formal institutions promoting economic freedom promote R-A competition, which, in turn, promotes efficiency, effectiveness, and the innovations that drive economic growth.

9.3 CULTURE AND ECONOMIC GROWTH

Max Weber (1864-1920), a German historian and sociologist, theorized at the turn of the century that the work ethic associated with Protestantism was largely responsible for the differences in wealth between Northern and Southern Europe. Since then, numerous sociologists, historians, and institutional economists have explored the extent to which cultural differences among nations contribute to explaining differences in their productivity, economic growth, and wealth (e.g., Bethell 1998; Harrison 1992; Hofstede 1980; Landes 1998; McNeill 1963; Rosenberg and Birdzell 1986). In the terms of Maddison (1994), their efforts seek the "ultimate causes" of wealth, such causes often stoutly resistant to accurate measures that can be inserted into the regression equations of mainstream economics. Nonetheless, ultimate causes are important: "if we learn anything from the history of economic development, it is that culture makes all the difference" (Landes 1998, p. 517).

Cultural institutions, such as customs, traditions, conventions, and codes of conduct, differ from formal institutions, such as laws and governmental policies, in their *chosenness*. In principle at least, laws, regulations, and policies that stunt economic growth can be changed, modified, or totally reversed at will by individuals having political power. Thus, formal institutions are in this sense *chosen*. In contrast, institutions of a distinctly cultural nature may change or shift through time. Nonetheless, the cultural institutions of a people are not selected or chosen, they *evolve*.

A significant problem facing any scholar seeking to investigate the relationship between culture and productivity, economic growth, and wealth is the thorny issue of cultural relativism. Because "criticisms of culture cut close to the ego, injure identity and self-esteem" (Landes 1988, pp. 516-17), any scholar arguing that differences in cultural institutions contribute to explaining wealth runs the risk of being labeled an "ethnocentrist" or "Eurocentrist" or "racist" and then being censured (or worse) by advocates of multiculturalism and diversity.

Because cultural relativism is a serious impediment to scholarship and a form of philosophical relativism, a brief discussion of *relativism* is in order. Therefore, this section begins with a discussion of relativism. It then examines the role that one cultural institution—trust—has to play in promoting economic growth and wealth. Finally, it explores the relationships among trust, R-A theory, and the wealth of nations.

9.3.1 On Relativism

"Relativism" is a term of art from philosophy.[12] All genuine forms of relativism have two theses: (1) the relativity thesis that something is relative to something else and (2) the nonevaluation thesis that there are no objective standards for evaluating *across* the variance kinds of "something else" (Siegel 1987). Five forms of relativism are especially significant:

1. *Cultural relativism* holds that (a) the elements embodied in a culture are relative to the norms of that culture, and (b) there are no objective, neutral, or nonarbitrary criteria to evaluate cultural elements across different cultures.

2. *Ethical relativism* holds that (a) what is ethical can be evaluated only relative to some moral code held by an individual group, society, or culture, and (b) there are no objective, impartial , or nonarbitrary standards for evaluating different moral codes across individuals, groups, societies, or cultures.

3. *Rationality relativism* holds that (a) the canons of correct or rational reasoning are relative to individual cultures, and (b) there are no objective, neutral, or nonarbitrary criteria to evaluate what is called "rational" across different cultures.

4. *Conceptual framework relativism* holds that (a) knowledge claims are relative to conceptual frameworks (theories, paradigms, worldviews, or *Weltanschauungen*), and (b) knowledge claims cannot be evaluated objectively, impartially, or nonarbitrarily across competing conceptual frameworks.

5. *Constructionism* (alternatively spelled "constructivism") is the same thing as *reality relativism,* which holds that (a) what comes to be known as "reality" in science is constructed by individuals relative to their language (or group, social class, theory, paradigm, culture, worldview, or *Weltanschauungen*), and (b) what comes to count as "reality" cannot be evaluated objectively, impartially, or nonarbitrarily across different lan-

guages (or groups, etc.). Closely related to relativism, *subjectivism* is the thesis that there is something basic to the human condition—usually something about human perception and/or language—that categorically prevents objective knowledge about the world.

Although philosophy of science flirted with relativism, constructionism, and subjectivism in the 1960s, by the 1970s most philosophers of science had adopted some version of scientific realism (Suppe 1977), even though, as Leplin (1984) puts it, "Scientific realism is a majority position whose advocates are so divided as to appear in a minority" (p. 1).

To understand why relativism, constructionism, and subjectivism are minority views within the philosophy of science, consider how these "isms" would respond to the following questions: "Does the sun revolve around the earth, or does the earth revolve around the sun?" The relativism of Kuhn (1962) answers: "First I must know whether you subscribe to the paradigm of Copernicus or Ptolemy, for these paradigms—like all paradigms—are incommensurable, and, therefore, there is no *truth* to the matter independent of the paradigm you hold." And subjectivism, with great exasperation, responds: "Because scientists see what their theories and paradigms tell them is there, the theory-ladenness of observation tells us that an *objective* answer to your query is impossible."

Question two: "Was Great Britain morally *right* in leading the drive in the nineteenth century to abolish slavery in cultures throughout the world?" Relativism responds: "Since slavery is a cultural element that cannot be evaluated independently of the norms of the culture within which it exists, no judgment on this matter can be made—to apply one's own norms elsewhere is simply cultural ethnocentrism." Question three: "Should Great Britain work toward the abolition of the few remaining states, for example, Mauritania (Masland et al. 1992), where slavery continues to exist?" Answer: "See response to previous question." Question four: "Did the Holocaust occur?" Answer: "Since the Holocaust is a 'constructed' reality (Lincoln and Guba 1985, p. 84), just one of many 'multiple realities,' the Holocaust's occurrence or nonoccurrence cannot be objectively appraised independent of the worldview of a particular social grouping or culture."

Question five: "Is a culture that is tolerant of individuals from other cultures preferable to a culture that oppresses everyone outside the dominant culture?" Answer: "Although the predisposition toward tolerance is a cultural element that varies widely across different cultures, no judgment can be made across cultures as to the moral superiority of tolerant versus intolerant cultures." Question six: "Should an academic discipline be open to the views of those outside the discipline?" Answer: "Although it is true that different academic disciplines differ in their relative openness to the views of outsiders, no judgment can be made across disciplines as to the relative desirability of such openness."

It should be easy now to understand why relativism, constructionism, and subjectivism are minority views in the philosophy of science. Relativism does not imply a constructively critical stance toward knowledge claims, nor does it imply acknowledging that the knowledge claims of science are fallible. Relativism implies nihilism—the belief that we can never have genuine knowledge about anything. Relativists, incoherently, *know* that no one else can ever know anything. Furthermore, relativism doesn't imply a tolerant stance toward outside ideas and other cultures; it implies *indifference* to the norm of tolerance. Moreover, relativism does not imply ethical sensitivity; it implies ethical impotence. Finally, subjectivism does not caution science to work at minimizing bias; it maintains that the human condition makes the very ideas of objectivity to be a chimera. Therefore—like truth—it should be abandoned.

In contrast, most scientists and philosophers of science not only adopt fallibilism and realism but hold the ideals of truth and objectivity in high regard. Modern philosophy of science recognizes that there is nothing in the nature of human perception, nothing in the nature of human language, nothing in the nature of "paradigms" that makes true theories and objective knowledge to be—in principle—impossible. (Indeed, the fact that each and every one of our theories *may* be wrong does not imply that they necessarily *must* be wrong.)[13]

Although cultural relativism, like other forms of relativism, is a misguided philosophy and can provide no foundation for individual action or public policy, scholars of the cultural dimensions of economic growth acknowledge that reasoned arguments provide scant protection from academic pogroms by advocates of multiculturalism and diversity. For example, Landes (1998) asks: "Why did Europe ("the West") take the lead in changing the world?" (p. xxi). He accuses those whose cultural relativism implies that it is immoral to even address such a question of succumbing to "goodthink":

As the historical record shows, for the last thousand years, Europe (the West) has been the prime mover of development and modernity. . . . Some would say that Eurocentrism is bad for us, indeed bad for the world, hence to be avoided. Those people should avoid it. As for me, I prefer truth to goodthink. I feel surer of my ground. (p. xxi)

9.3.2 Trust and the Wealth of Nations

Which dimensions of culture promote economic growth? Which "informal institutions" (North 1990) positively affect the wealth of nations? Many scholars, across numerous disciplines, focus on the importance of institutions that promote *social trust* (e.g., Fukuyama 1995; Gambetta 1988; Harrison 1992; Loasby 1991a; Phelps 1975). In economics, for example, Arrow (1972) hypothesized more than two decades ago that because "[v]irtually every commercial transaction has within itself an element of trust, . . . [it] can be plausibly argued that much of the economic backwardness in the world can be explained by the lack of mutual confidence" (p. 357). He refers to trust as one of society's "invisible institutions." As such, trust stems from "principles of ethics and morality" and promotes economic growth because it is an "important lubricant of the social system" (1974, pp. 23, 26).

As a second example of the importance of institutions promoting trust, Harrison (1992) starts from the perspective of being in the "trenches" in the U.S. Agency for International Development. He asks: "Why do some nations and ethnic groups do better than others?" And he answers: "The overriding significance of culture is the paramount lesson I have learned in my thirty years of work on political, economic, and social development" (p. 1). As a self-declared, "lifelong Democrat" (p. 221), Harrison knows the danger of contradicting the orthodoxy of cultural relativism, "which asserts that all cultures are essentially equal and eschews comparative value judgments" (p. 16). Nonetheless, he maintains that "cultural relativism flies in the face of reality" because "some cultures are progress-prone, while others are not" (p. 16). Thus, he seeks to explain not only why some nations are more prosperous than others, but also why some ethnic groups (he identifies Jews, Chinese, Japanese, and Koreans as prototypical examples) seem to prosper even in societies that, overall, are relatively poor.

What, then, are the characteristics of a culture that will engender prosperity, one that is progress-prone? This is Harrison's (1992) answer:

> There are, in my view, four fundamental factors: (1) the degree of identification with others in a society—the radius of trust, or the sense of community; (2) the rigor of the ethical system; (3) the way authority is exercised within the society; and (4) attitudes about work, innovation, saving, and profit. (p. 16)

The radius of trust, for Harrison, is the extent to which individuals identify with, or have a sense of community with, others in a society. The smallest radius of trust is a society in which individuals trust only themselves. Next would be those in which the radius extends only to members of the immediate family and other kin. Because of the narrow radius of trust in "familistic" societies: "Commercial and industrial enterprises . . . are usually weighted down by centralization, including a variety of checking mechanisms and procedures designed, ostensibly, to assure conformity and to control dishonesty" (p. 11). In contrast, the economies of such high-trust countries as Japan have proved to be relatively productive, in large part, because "successful enterprise usually depends on effective organization and cooperation, which in turn depend on trust" (p. 11).

Whereas Harrison focuses on trust as one of four cultural factors that promote prosperity, Fukuyama (1995), a social policy analyst motivated by what he sees as the "crisis of trust" (p. 267) in American society, maintains that trust is the *sine qua non* of societal productivity and economic growth.[14] Defining trust as "the expectation . . . of regular, honest, and cooperative behavior, based on commonly shared norms" (p. 26), he maintains that a community's set of shared ethical values contributes to its capacity for *spontaneous sociability*, which "refers to the wide range of intermediate communities, distinct from the family or those deliberately established by governments" (p. 27). Indeed, where sociability and trust are low, governments often have to step in to promote community.

Fukuyama (1995) argues that spontaneous sociability contributes to the social capital (see Sections 4.2.3, 4.2.4, and 8.2.1) of high-trust societies and to their ability to innovate organizationally: "Hence highly sociable Americans pioneered the development of the modern corporation in the nineteenth and twentieth centuries, just as the Japanese have explored the possibilities of network organizations in the twentieth" (p. 27). In contrast, in low-trust societies, where the radius of trust extends only to kin, the cooperation necessary for large corporations can be obtained only "under a system of formal rules and regulations, which have to be negotiated, agreed to, litigated, and enforced, sometimes by coercive means" (p. 27). This legal and regulatory apparatus, which is unnecessary in a high-trust society, serves as a substitute for trust and imposes a high burden of transaction costs on low-trust societies: "Widespread distrust in a society, in other words, imposes a kind of tax on all forms of economic activity, a tax that high-trust societies do not have to pay" (pp. 27-28).

In summary, a provocative, heterodoxical view is emerging among scholars across disciplines as to why only *some* market-based economies have evolved into wealthy societies. This view is that it is differences in the informal institutions that constitute culture that distinguish wealthy from nonwealthy societies. Some informal institutions are productivity enhancing; others are not. Some foster economic growth; others do not. Because they reduce transaction costs, institutionalized moral codes that promote social trust are thought to be particularly important. But I argue, not all moral codes will be equally trust inducing.

Consider the ethical code implied by the neoclassical tradition. As discussed in Section 5.3, the only substantive interpretation of utility maximization is the self-interest maximizing, hedonic view, that is, ethical egoism in philosophical terms. For example, recall from Section 4.2.2 that Williamson's (1975) version of transaction cost economics assumes that "economic man . . . is thus a more subtle and devious creature than the usual self-interest seeking assumption reveals" (p. 255). For transaction cost economics, *homo economicus* not only self-interest maximizes but does so with opportunistic "guile." Williamson argues for assuming universal opportunism because it is "ubiquitous" (1981b, p. 1550), "even among the less opportunistic types, most have their price" (1979, p. 234), and opportunistic "types cannot be distinguished ex ante from sincere types" (1975, p. 27) or, at the very least, "it is very costly to distinguish opportunistic from nonopportunistic types ex ante" (1981b, p. 1545). Even though, as Williamson (1994) acknowledges, "to craft credible commitments . . . is to create functional substitutes for trust" (p. 97), he maintains that "the study of economic organization is better served by treating economic organization without reference to trust" (1993, p. 99).

Therefore, not only are all moral codes unequally trust inducing, but if a society's dominant culture actually embraces the ethical egoism of neoclassical theory, social trust *cannot* exist: the universal opportunism of ethical egoism implies that one must always presume nontrustworthy behavior by others. As a consequence, Etzioni (1988) points out: "The more people accept the [utility maximization part of the] neoclassical paradigm as a guide for their behavior, the more their ability to sustain a market economy is undermined" (p. 257).

Etzioni (1988) cites empirical studies suggesting that neoclassical theory, as interpreted by students, licenses opportunism. For students, "is" becomes "ought." For example, the studies of Marwell and Ames (1981) find a positive correlation between formal training in economics and the frequency of free riding. If everyone free rides, students apparently conclude, they might as well free ride also. As a second example, Frank, Gilovich, and Regan (1993) distributed questionnaires to students concerning their likelihood of engaging in dishonest behavior at the beginning and end of three classes: (1) an economics class in which both the book and the instructor stressed neoclassical theory, (2) an economics class in which the book stressed neoclassical theory but the instructor did not, and (3) an astronomy class as a control. Students in all three classes were more dishonest at the end of the semester than at the beginning.

However, the shift toward dishonesty by students in the two economics classes was greater than that of those in the control group. Furthermore, the shift toward dishonesty was greater in the economics class where the professor emphasized and supported neoclassical theory than in the class where only the textbook did so. Students, as Etzioni (1988) points out, are indeed "learning" the lesson of neoclassical theory: opportunism is universal, why fight it?

In contrast, Etzioni (1988) argues for deontological ethics because a society whose dominant culture embraces deontological ethics (see Section 5.3.1) can sustain social trust and enjoy its wealth-creating attributes. That is, when the people of a society share a moral code based primarily on deontological ethics, trust can exist. When trust exists, the costs that firms and societies have that are associated with opportunism, that is, shirking, cheating, stealing, dishonesty, monitoring, free riding, and "hostage-taking," are avoided. Consequently, argues Etzioni, a culture emphasizing deontological ethics should contribute to a society's productivity.

If (at the microlevel) the primary objective of firms is superior financial performance, but (at the macrolevel) a key factor distinguishing wealthy from nonwealthy societies is trust-promoting institutions, the challenge for any theory of competition is to explicate the process by which such macrolevel, trust-promoting institutions as moral codes can contribute to (or detract from) firm-level, superior financial performance. A detailed example shows how R-A theory explicates this process.

9.3.3 Trust, R-A Theory, and the Wealth of Nations

Recalling the role of relative, resource costs and resource-produced value in R-A theory (see Figure 6.2), consider two organizations, A and B, that are competing for the same market segment. Assume that A is located in an area populated primarily by ethical egoists and B is in an area of deontologists (or, alternatively, B's hiring procedures screen out egoists). Because most of A's employees will be guided by egoism (self-interest or utility maximization) and *B's by a code stressing deontological ethics,* A will have transformational costs (e.g., costs associated with shirking, cheating, monitoring, and free riding) that B avoids. In R-A theory's terms, the fact that B's employees are guided by deontological ethics and, hence, are trustworthy results in an intangible, comparative advantage-producing *resource* for B, when competing with A. *Ceteris paribus,* B will then occupy a marketplace position of competitive advantage in Figure 6.2 *vis-à-vis* A and enjoy superior financial performance—its primary objective.

Now recall that heterogeneous organizational competences are foundational in R-A theory (see Section 4.1.5) and assume that both A and B seek a strategic alliance with C, who has a particular competence that both A and B lack. For example, perhaps C can produce a key component of A's and B's products that is of particularly high quality—a quality that neither A nor B can match. Further assume that, because of their employees' different moral codes, B has a reputation for integrity and A for opportunism. Because C would fear A's *opportunism*, C would either (1) decline the alliance or (2) insist that A absorb the high monitoring and other costs resulting from A's moral code. In contrast, B is an attractive partner for C because C recognizes that B's moral code lessens the likelihood of B's engaging in opportunistic behavior. Thus, B will be able to align itself with C, and A will have to do without C's competence. B's strategic alliance with C will then become what R-A theory calls a "relational resource" (see Section 5.5.1) that makes B more *effective* in competing with A. That is, B is now more likely to achieve marketplace positions identified as cells 2 and 3 in Figure 6.2 and, thus, enjoy superior financial performance.

Now assume that A and B are nation-states, instead of organizations, where A's dominant culture has a moral code tending toward ethical egoism and B's toward deontological ethics. *Ceteris paribus, A* will be less productive than B for three reasons. First, the firms in A must absorb transaction and transformational costs that the firms in B avoid. Therefore, B is more *efficient* than A in producing valued market offerings. Second, recalling again that organizational competences are heterogeneous, firms in A will be less successful in forming cooperative alliances or networks. Therefore, the alliances and networks in B will make it more *effective* than A in producing valued market offerings for both domestic and global markets. B's greater efficiency and effectiveness, therefore, increases its productivity relative to A. Third, assume that firms in A are competing with those in B for the business of firms in nation C. *Ceteris paribus, B*'s firms will be in an advantageous position over those in A because B's firms will be both more efficient and more effective in producing valued market offerings. Therefore, nation B is better able than A to reap the gains from trade with C, resulting in further increases in B's productivity and growth, relative to A.

Recall that a resource is any entity, tangible or intangible, that is available to (not necessarily *owned by*) the firm that enables it to produce valued market offerings (Section 5.5.1). The preceding analysis implies that just as employees having a moral code stressing deontological ethics constitute a *firm* resource, a society having a dominant culture with a moral code stressing deontological ethics has a *societal* resource upon which firms can draw. Thus, R-A theory—alone among theories of competition—can explain how such macrolevel, informal institutions as moral codes can contribute to (or detract from) firm-level, superior financial performance. In so doing, it contributes to explaining how societal institutions that promote social trust also promote the wealth of nations.

NOTES

1. This fact led to the "convergence debate" that Romer (1994) shows—from a theoretical view—to be so misguided. See also endnote 4 in Chapter 8 and Baumol, Nelson, and Wolff (1994).

2. Note that the definition of "human capital" that Lucas (1993) uses is a far cry from something like the percentage of the population of the appropriate age groups that is enrolled in secondary school.

3. Even many endogenous growth modelers who recognize that economic growth is fostered by "imperfect competition" still embrace the neoclassical tradition and its language. Thus, note that Young (1993) equates "perfect competition" with a "free market system." R-A theory, of course, denies the synonymity.

4. As Rothbard (1987) discusses in detail, Schumpeter's starting point for analyzing business cycles is Walrasian general equilibrium. Economies "escape" from equilibrium in the "boom" phase of the business cycles by major innovations that come in clusters and are financed by inflationary bank credit. However, as Rothbard (1987) points out, there is no evidence of the process of innovations coming in clusters or their causing booms. For Schumpeter, starting from equilibrium economics was a "wrong turning" (Robinson 1951).

5. Note that institutions promoting price conspiracies would be inconsistent with R-A theory. Although a price conspiracy might contribute to superior financial performance, it is not a resource because it does not contribute to the firm's ability to efficiently and/or effectively produce a market offering of value to some market segment(s).

6. Knack and Keefer (1995) justify the inclusion of infrastructure quality on the grounds that it "allows some approximation to be made to the efficiency with which governments allocate public goods" (p. 212).

7. Because ICRG and BERI are highly correlated, they are entered in separate equations. See column 3 in their Tables 2 and 3. The discussion of adding investment as a control variable is on their page 219.

8. See their Table 5, columns 2 and 5.

9. Barro's (1997) exploratory work included a host of other variables. The ones listed here include only those found significant and which appear in his Table 1.1, column 2, plus investment, which was found to be nonsignificant and discussed on his pages 32-34. See also Barro and Sala-i-Martin (1995).

10. Barro's other statistically significant findings are that male schooling, life expectancy, terms of trade, and East Asia dummy are related to growth positively. Initial GDP, GDP × male schooling, fertility rate, government consumption, sub-Sahara dummy, and Latin America dummy are related to growth negatively. Many, if not most, of these variables may be viewed as institutional in nature or proxies for institutions.

11. There are numerous differences between the economic freedom indexes of Johnson, Holmes, and Kirkpatrick (1998) and Gwartney, Lawson, and Block (1996).

Nonetheless, the respective 1995 ratings correlate .75 for the 87 countries that are common to the two studies.

12. See Krausz and Meiland (1982) for a good introduction to philosophical relativism. Siegel (1987) provides, in my judgment, a definitive refutation. Hunt (1991a, pp. 305-45) provides summaries of Siegel's arguments and chronicles the rise and fall of relativism in philosophy of science.

13. See Boyd (1984), Harré (1986), and Hunt (1990b) for a discussion and defense of truth in theory and research and a discussion of critical realism. See Hunt (1993, 1994) for a resolution of the theory ladenness/objectivity debate that has plagued philosophy of science.

14. As Putnam (1995) points out, the percentage of Americans agreeing with "most people can be trusted" fell from 58% in 1960 to 37% in 1993.

Chapter
10

Conclusion

W hat is the relationship between resource-advantage theory and neoclassical, perfect competition theory? Are they mutually exclusive
rivals, complementary, or something else? If they were rivals, then one being
true would imply that the other must be false. If they were complementary, then
each would focus on explaining and predicting different phenomena. Rather
than their being rivals or complements, this chapter argues for the "something
else" option. Specifically, it argues that R-A theory is a general theory of competition that incorporates perfect competition theory as a special case. As such,
R-A theory preserves the cumulativity of economic science.

If R-A theory is a general theory of competition, what are its public policy
implications? With respect to antitrust legislation, does R-A theory imply *lais-
sez faire?* This chapter argues that the debate between the advocates of the
"wealth transfer" view of antitrust and the "efficiency" view has been misguided by the neoclassical tradition. Furthermore, it argues that to the extent
that productivity, economic growth, and wealth creation are valued, formal institutions promoting vigorous R-A competition should be the objective of public policy.

Therefore, this chapter begins with the argument that R-A theory is a general theory of competition that incorporates perfect competition as a special case. Next it begins a, very preliminary, discussion of the public policy implications of R-A theory. The chapter concludes by noting that R-A theory is a work in progress and suggesting directions for future research.

10.1   A GENERAL THEORY OF COMPETITION

R-A theory is an evolutionary, process theory of competition. How, then, do evolutionary economists view the relationship between evolutionary, process theories in general and neoclassical theory? Unfortunately, no consensus has emerged on the issue of how neoclassical, static-equilibrium theories relate (or should relate) to evolutionary, process theories. Several alternatives have been offered. For example, Dosi (1991) suggests that on many issues separating the evolutionary and orthodox approaches, "there is no clear discontinuity, . . . but some fuzzy continuum" (p. 5). Consistent with Dosi's continuum view, Nelson (1995) argues that evolutionary theories should incorporate the empirical truth-content of their neoclassical counterparts. For example, in reviewing evolutionary growth theory, he cautions that "for evolutionary theory to have credibility these predictions had better be similar [to neoclassical theory], because any broad growth theory needs to be consistent with the basic empirically documented broad features of economic growth as we have experienced it" (p. 71).

On the other hand, Hodgson (1992) seems closer to viewing evolutionary and neoclassical theory as being mutually exclusive. He argues that even though evolutionary theory is not a "panacea," it does "offer a metaphor for economics that is superior to the mechanistic model" because, among other things, it can "incorporate the temporal as well as the moral aspects of all economic activity" (p. 760). Nonetheless, he asks: "assuming it is possible to build a superior economic framework for economic theory, would it subsume neoclassical theory within itself as a special or limiting case?" (p. 749). After reviewing the deficiencies of neoclassical theory, he concludes: "It is argued here that the reform of economics is not a question of adding additional dimensions to neoclassical economic theory. A theoretical revolution is required at the core of economics itself" (p. 760).

In contrast, Foss (1994b) advances the "speculative conjecture" that evolutionary and neoclassical economics will eventually have a "kind of consistency relation . . . in which a more encompassing theory is constructed that can incorporate previously unrelated theories as special cases" (p. 36). What would it mean for a theory to "incorporate" other theories, as Foss argues? Meritorious, I suggest, is the answer to this question from the philosophy of science approach of Sellars (1963) and Levy (1996). They argue that science progresses *best* when a new theory can satisfactorily explain the explanatory and predictive successes of its predecessor. When a new theory incorporates its predecessor in this manner, the new theory has the highly desirable benefit of preserving the cumulativity of a discipline.

The classic example of incorporation, of course, is that Newtonian theory (which maintains that the acceleration of two masses increases as they approach each other) incorporates Galileo's Law of Descent (which assumes that acceleration is constant between two bodies) and thereby explains all the predictive successes of Galileo's Law. Simply put, if d is the distance of a body from the surface of the earth and D is the radius of the earth, Galileo's Law predicts well for most falling objects because the ratio d/D is—as argued in economics by Friedman (1953)—"close enough" to zero that assuming g to be constant in $S = \frac{1}{2} g t^2$ is nonproblematic. Therefore, the foundations of Newtonian theory are such that they incorporate Galileo's Law as a special case, thereby preserving the cumulativity of physics.

The thesis defended here is that (1) R-A theory and its foundations (Table 5.1) represent the general case of competition and (2) perfect competition and its foundations are a special case. Therefore, (3) R-A theory incorporates perfect competition, (4) explains the explanatory and predictive successes of perfect competition, and (5) preserves the cumulativity of economic science. Empirical evidence provides a *prima facie* case for this thesis.

As discussed in Section 6.3.1, the massive studies on the diversity of financial performance, depending on the database used, come to the following conclusion: industry effects account for 4% to 19% of the variance in performance, as measured by return on assets, and firm effects account for 19% to 55%. The finding that firm effects dominate industry effects supports viewing the *process* identified by R-A theory (Figures 6.1 and 6.2) as the general case of the *process* of competition. Therefore, because a theory is derived from its assumptions, the evidence supports viewing each of R-A theory's foundational premises (Table 5.1) to be either descriptively realistic or, at least, "close enough" (Friedman 1953). I now argue that the foundational premises of perfect competition are, indeed, special cases of R-A theory and, consequently, R-A theory incorporates perfect competition. I do so by showing when the latter's foundations are "close enough" to predict.

10.1.1 Demand, Information, and Resource Characteristics

How should foundational premises P1, P2, P5, and P7 in Table 5.1, concerning demand, information, and resource characteristics, be interpreted? Note that each assumption could be viewed as an idealized state that anchors an endpoint on a continuum. That is, demand (P1) can be conceptualized as a continuum with perfect homogeneity and perfect heterogeneity as idealized anchor points. Similar continua could be conceptualized for information and its cost (P2 and P5) and for the homogeneity-heterogeneity and mobility-immobility of resources (P7).

However, whereas perfect competition is customarily interpreted in the idealized, anchor-point manner, in no case is R-A theory to be interpreted as the anchor point *opposite* perfect competition. Rather, each foundational premise of R-A theory is proposed as the descriptively realistic general case. Therefore, intra-industry demand (P1) is to be interpreted for R-A theory as *substantially* heterogeneous. Similarly, information for both firms (P5) and consumers (P2) is substantially imperfect and costly. Likewise, many, but not all, resources (P6) are substantially heterogeneous and immobile.

Consider again the example used in Section 5.1.1, that is, footwear (SIC #314). R-A theory views consumers' tastes and preferences for footwear to be substantially heterogeneous and constantly changing. Furthermore, consumers have substantially imperfect information concerning footwear products that might match their tastes and preferences, and obtaining such information is often costly in terms of both time and money. The implication of heterogeneity is that few—if any—*industry* markets exists: there are only market segments *within* industries. There is no "market for shoes" (SIC #314), or even separate markets for women's shoes (SIC #3144) and men's shoes (SIC #3143). Although all consumers require footwear and one can readily identify a group of firms that manufacture shoes, there is no shoe industry *market.* That is, the group of firms that constitute the shoe industry do not collectively face a *single,* downward-sloping demand curve—for such an industry demand curve would imply homogeneous tastes and preferences.

For R-A theory, to the extent that demand curves exist at all, they exist at a level of (dis)aggregation that is too fine to be an "industry." For example, even if there were a men's walking shoe market, one certainly would not speak of the men's walking shoe *industry.* The fact that intra-industry demand is substantially heterogeneous in *most* industries (even at the 4-digit SIC level) contributes to R-A theory's ability (and neoclassical theory's inability) to make the correct prediction as to the diversity in business-unit financial performance.

Likewise, the fact that intra-industry demand is relatively homogeneous ("close enough") in at least *some* commodity industries, for example, gold ores (SIC #1041), contributes to explaining those special cases where perfect competition predicts well. Therefore, R-A theory's premises P1, P2, P5, and P7 are the general case; perfect competition's premises are special cases.

10.1.2 Human Motivation

Now consider how perfect competition and R-A theory treat human motivation (P3). As discussed in Section 5.3, whereas perfect competition assumes self-interest (utility) maximization, R-A theory proposes that such self-interest seeking is *constrained*. In particular, R-A theory maintains that an individual's self-interest seeking is constrained by a personal moral code. I argue that R-A theory incorporates perfect competition on the grounds that, whereas the descriptively realistic R-A theory allows for different people (and different *peoples*) to have different moral codes, perfect competition, at least when it treats utility substantively, restricts itself to the special case in which everyone has one particular moral code—ethical egoism.

Because R-A theory posits that human behavior is motivated by constrained self-interest seeking, consumers, owners, and managers are constrained in their self-interest seeking by their personal moral codes, that is, by considerations of what is right, proper, ethical, moral, or just plain appropriate. In turn, recall that individuals' moral codes are shaped, but not determined, by societal institutions (see Figure 6.1). Because codes of behavior are shaped by institutions, R-A theory is embedded (Granovetter 1985). Because such codes are not *determined* by institutions, R-A theory adopts a moderately socialized view of human behavior. Consider the issue of opportunism. R-A theory does not deny that some individuals are ethical egoists and will act opportunistically. Rather, constrained self-interest seeking implies that opportunism is not assumed to be universal. That is, R-A theory maintains that the extent to which people behave opportunistically in various contexts is a research question to be explored and explained—not presumed *a priori*.

Therefore, because of R-A theory's posit that human behavior is best characterized as constrained, self-interest seeking, it can contribute to explaining the role of trust in the wealth of nations (see Section 9.3.3). Because R-A theory recognizes the existence of various personal moral codes, its premise P3 in Table 5.1 is the general case. Because perfect competition recognizes only one moral code, ethical egoism, its premise P3 is a special case.

10.1.3 Firm's Objective and Firm's Information

Now consider how perfect competition and R-A theory treat the firm's objective (P4) and information (P5) in Table 5.1. As discussed in Section 5.4, because it maximizes the self-interests of the owner, perfect competition assumes the special case that owner-managed firms profit maximize. Profit maximization (or wealth maximization, i.e., the maximization of the net present value of future profits) occurs under conditions of, again, the special case of perfect and costless information about product markets, production techniques, and resource markets. In contrast, R-A theory proposes that the firm's primary objective is superior financial performance, which it pursues under conditions of imperfect (and often costly to obtain) information about extant and potential market segments, competitors, suppliers, shareholders, and production technologies.

For R-A theory, superior financial performance is indicated by such measures as profits, earnings per share, return on investment, and capital appreciation. Here, "superior" equates with both "more than" and "better than." It implies that firms seek a level of financial performance exceeding that of some referent. For example, the referent can be the firm's own performance in a previous time period, the performance of rival firms, an industry average, or a stock market average, among others. Affecting the process of competition, both the specific measure and specific referent will vary somewhat from time to time, firm to firm, industry to industry, and culture to culture.

Firms are posited to pursue superior financial performance because superior rewards—both financial and nonfinancial—will then flow to owners, managers, and employees. Superior financial performance does not equate with "abnormal profits" or "rents" (i.e., profits differing from the average firm in a purely competitive industry in long-run equilibrium) because R-A theory views industry long-run equilibrium as such a rare phenomenon that "normal" profits cannot be an empirical referent for comparison purposes. Furthermore, the actions of firms that collectively constitute competition do not force groups of rivals to "tend toward" equilibrium. Instead, the pursuit of *superior* performance implies that actions of competing firms are disequilibrating, not equilibrating.

As argued in Section 5.4.1, superior financial performance describes the *general* case of the firm's primary objective because (1) superior rewards do indeed flow to owners, managers, and employees of firms that produce superior financial performance, (2) the pursuit of superior financial performance ensures that R-A theory is dynamic, and (3) the dynamism of R-A theory is consistent with the observed dynamism of market-based economies. In contrast, profit or wealth maximization is argued to be the special case because (1) imperfect information in most circumstances makes maximization impossible, (2) agency problems associated with ethical egoism in many cases thwart maximization, (3) firms guided by deontological ethics may, at times, choose not to maximize, and (4) ethical code mismatches between (and among) owners, managers, and subordinate employees may result in nonmaximizing behaviors.

R-A theory's premises that firms seek superior financial performance (P4) in the face of imperfect information (P5) are the general case. Perfect competition's premises P4 and P5, because they are infrequently encountered, are special cases.

10.1.4 Evolutionary Processes and Equilibrium

For all the first eight foundational premises shown in Table 5.1, I argue that R-A theory's foundations are descriptively realistic of the general case of competition and perfect competition's assumptions are special cases. However, P9, the issue of competitive dynamics, provides an opportunity to explicate the argument in detail. Under what set of circumstances will the process of R-A competition (which is disequilibrium provoking, with innovation endogenous) result in perfect competition (which is equilibrium seeking, with innovation exogenous)?

Consider the following scenario. First, assume that a set of firms producing an offering for a particular market segment within an industry has been competing according to R-A theory. Therefore, because of resource heterogeneity (say, different levels of a key competence), the firms are distributed throughout the nine marketplace positions in Figure 6.2. Some firms, because of their comparative advantage in resources, are enjoying superior returns; others, because of their comparative disadvantage in resources, have inferior returns; and still others, because of their parity resources, have parity returns (see Figure 6.1).

Next assume that, through time, both disadvantaged and parity firms (1) gradually learn how the advantaged firms are producing their offerings more efficiently and/or effectively and (2) successfully imitate the advantaged firms by acquiring or developing the requisite resources. For example, assume that they gradually develop competences equivalent to the advantaged firms. Then assume that, even though all firms seek *superior* financial performance, no firm finds it possible to acquire, develop, or create new resources (e.g., developing a new competence) that will enable it to produce a market offering more efficiently or effectively than any other firm. That is, for some reason or set of reasons, all competition-induced innovation stops, both proactive and reactive. Consequently, all competition-induced technological change stops. Under these economic conditions, then, the resources of all firms serving this market segment become relatively homogeneous and there will be parity resources producing parity offerings.

Next assume that the tastes and preferences of consumers in all other market segments served by the firms in this industry shift toward the original segment. Industry consumer demand will then become relatively homogeneous. Suppose further that consumers' tastes and preferences remain stable throughout a significant period of time and that consumers become very knowledgeable about the relative homogeneity of firms' offerings. There will then be parity resources producing parity offerings, which results in all firms having parity marketplace positions (cell 5 in Figure 6.2).

Next assume that firms have accurate information about competitive conditions and there are no institutional restraints preventing them from producing their market offerings in the profit-maximizing quantity. Under these economic circumstances, the industry experiences no endogenous technological change, firms become price-takers, and a static equilibrium theory of competition, such as perfect competition, applies. That is, there will be parity resources producing parity offerings, which results in parity marketplace positions and parity performance (see Figure 6.1). The industry has now become a candidate for "industry effects" to dominate "firm effects" in empirical studies, for collusion and barriers to entry to become viable explanations for any industrywide, superior financial performance, and, in general, for industry-level theoretical analyses to be appropriate.

Next assume that the preceding process occurs in every industry in an entire economy. Then, if this set of economic circumstances persists through time, all competition-induced technological change ceases, all endogenous technological progress stops, all endogenous growth ceases, and a long-run, general equilibrium theory applies (such as Walrasian general equilibrium). In such an economy, growth comes only from exogenous sources, including those sources (e.g., government R&D or a state planning board) that might develop innovations that result in exogenous technological progress, as in neoclassical growth theory (see Section 8.1).

Note that the preceding analysis began with the process of R-A competition for a market segment and sketches the special economic circumstances that must prevail for the competitive process to result in a static equilibrium situation in an industry. Among other conditions, it showed that a very important circumstance is that all endogenous innovation must stop (or be stopped). Such a stoppage might come as a result of collusion, complacency, institutional restrictions, governmental fiat, or lack of entrepreneurial competence. The analysis then sketched the special circumstances for a long-run general equilibrium to develop, and, again, it showed that all endogenous technological progress in all industries—hence, all endogenous economic growth—in an economy must cease.

Therefore, the statics of perfect competition, both partial equilibrium and general equilibrium, may be viewed as a special case of the dynamics of R-A theory. R-A theory relates to perfect competition in the same way that Newtonian mechanics relates to Galileo's Law: the former incorporates the latter. As such, R-A theory preserves the cumulativity of economic science by explaining when perfect competition will be "close enough" to explain and predict well.

10.2 PUBLIC POLICY AND ANTITRUST LEGISLATION

Since the passage of the Sherman Act in 1890 and the Clayton and Federal Trade Commission Acts in 1916, the official, "antitrust" policy of the United States government has been that competition is good, hence it is to be encouraged and protected. In contrast, monopoly is bad, hence it is to be discouraged and punished. For over a century, Congress and the states have passed (relatively) ambiguous laws designed to protect competition and punish monopolists, leaving it up to lawyers, economists, regulators, judges, and juries to work out the details. Debate has swirled around such contentious "details" as how competition and monopoly are to be conceptually defined and empirically identified. Debate has also been spirited as to the public policy goals of antitrust legislation, because the goals of such legislation reflect why it is believed that competition is good for society and monopoly is bad. Figure 10.1 can be used as a generic diagram to help understand major themes in the debate.[1]

Figure 10.1 shows a downward-sloping demand curve for some commodity and a flat average cost curve AC_c. Under perfect competition and an (implicit) supply curve S, then, the price P_c will equal AC_c and the quantity of the product produced and sold will be Q_c. Under a monopoly, the monopolist (or a cartel acting as a monopolist) will restrict output to Q_m, which it can then sell at P_m. If, however, the formation of monopoly (by, for example, a merger) allows the monopolist to take advantage of certain production efficiencies (resulting from, for example, economies of scale), then average cost drops from AC_c to AC_m.

The triangle **I** and the rectangles **R** and **E** figure prominently in the antitrust debates. The area of **I** is an estimate of the "deadweight" welfare-loss resulting

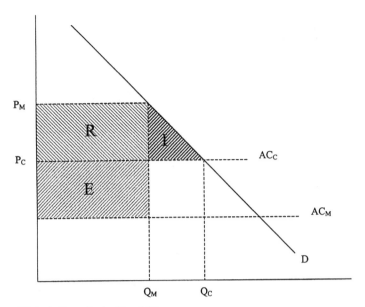

Figure 10.1 A Generic Antitrust Diagram

SOURCE: Versions of the diagram, with somewhat different notation, appear in Block (1994), Bork (1978), Lande (1988), Posner (1986), and Williamson (1968).

from the resource allocation inefficiency of monopoly. That is, under perfect competition the price system would have directed additional resources toward the commodity and consumers would have gotten Q_c at P_c, instead of only Q_m at P_m. Area **R** is an estimate of the rents or economic profits that accrue to the monopolist. At P_c, of course, no economic profits are earned, only an accounting profit sufficient to keep firms in business. Therefore, compared with perfect competition and P_c, area **R** represents a wealth transfer from buyers of the commodity to sellers of the commodity. Area **E** is an estimate of the resource cost savings as a result of the shift from perfect competition to monopoly. Compared with the deadweight inefficiency loss of triangle **I**, rectangle **E** is a societal efficiency gain. Net efficiency losses and gains depend on the size of rectangle **E** compared with triangle **I**. With the preceding description of Figure 10.1 in mind, we can discuss the major themes of the antitrust debate.

10.2.1 The Antitrust Debate

In terms of Figure 10.1, the arguments by proponents of the Sherman Act in the latter part of the nineteenth century focused on rectangle **R** (as well as several other issues, such as the importance of the dispersion of economic power, the desirability of the reduction of political influence of large firms, and the promotion of small business and entrepreneurial opportunity) (Fox 1981). As Lande (1988) documents, Senator Sherman referred to the prices resulting from monopolies as "extorted wealth," and other supporters used such terms as "robbery" to describe the actions of the trusts, because they "aggregate to themselves great enormous wealth by extortion which makes the people poor" (p. 449). In short, monopolies were argued to be bad because of their wealth-transfer effects. The major economic goal of the proponents of the Sherman Act was to prevent the wealth transfers resulting from monopoly (Lande 1982, 1988).

That proponents of the Sherman Act focused on rectangle **R**, not triangle **I**, to argue against monopoly is unsurprising. The first edition of Marshall's *Principles* appeared in 1890, the very year that the Act passed—and it was Marshall who conceived of triangle **I** as a graphical depiction of the deadweight loss resulting from inefficient resource allocation (Scherer 1977). Not only was the "Sherman Act . . . framed and debated in the pre-expert era, when economists as a professional group were not directly consulted by legislators" (Hofstadter 1965, p. 199), but: "A careful student of history of economics would have searched long and hard, on July 2, 1890, the day the Sherman Act was signed by President Harrison, for any economist who had ever recommended the policy of actively combating collusion or monopolization in the economy at large" (Stigler 1982, p. 3). Proponents of the Clayton and Federal Trade Commission Acts also focused on rectangle **R** (and dispersing economic and political power, etc.) (Lande 1982, 1988).

As to how "competition" and "monopoly" should be defined in antitrust legislation, though Marshall (1890) gave equal prominence to both evolutionary and mechanistic metaphors, between 1890 and 1950 the evolutionary metaphor was "suppressed" (Foss 1991) and the neoclassical research tradition "hardened" (Lakotos 1978) around static equilibrium, profit maximization, firms-are-cost-curves, perfect competition, and the language of mathematics (see Section 2.1). In mainstream economics, the term "competition" lost its Adam Smith roots concerning rivalry. Indeed, "competition" became so synonymous with *perfect* competition that "perfect" was dropped in most academic discourse as redundant. A similar metamorphosis occurred with *monopoly*. Whereas "monopoly" in classical economics denoted the control of the supply of a homogeneous commodity—and Chamberlin (1954, pp. 255-56) put up a valiant fight to retain this view—by the 1950s the term was being equated with simply any firm facing a downward-sloping demand curve. Hence, the term "monopoly" morphed into "monopoly power" and "market power."

As to how the Justice Department, Federal Trade Commission (FTC), and the courts in general should measure the *degree* of monopoly in an industry, the neoclassical tradition and industrial organization economics ("IO") provided regulators, lawyers, and the courts with the SCP model of Mason (1939) and Bain (1954, 1956, 1968) (see Section 4.1.2). Argued IO economists, a four-firm concentration ratio greater than 75% indicated a dangerously concentrated industry, one in which mergers should be prohibited and corporate dissolutions considered. In contrast, a four-firm concentration ratio of less than 50% implied that it was "close enough" (Friedman 1953) to be considered competitive and, thus, no cause for concern. A ratio between 50% and 75% was "worrisome" and firms in the industry should be watched carefully.

As to why firms with downward-sloping demand curves, that is "monopolies" in the neoclassical sense, are bad for society, the neoclassical tradition added the deadweight loss of triangle **I** in Figure 10.1 to rectangle **R**. That is, firms with market power not only transfer wealth from buyers to sellers, area **R**, but also inefficiently allocate resources, area **I**. What Lande (1988)—a forceful advocate of vigorous antitrust enforcement—calls the "big is bad; small is good" (p. 436) interpretation of antitrust dominated until the late 1970s and the rise of the "Chicago School," so called because of its association with such University of Chicago economists as Aaron Director, Milton Friedman, and George Stigler.[2]

The Chicago School of Antitrust. Posner (1979) points out that the Chicago School of Antitrust was the product of meticulous analyses of such specific issues as the historical context of antitrust law and the intent of legislators (Bork 1954, 1966), tying agreements (Bowman 1957), predatory pricing (McGee 1958), and "fair trade" laws (Telser 1960). Contrasted with the "big is bad; small is good" school, each was analyzed in strict accordance with neoclassical price theory. From these analyses, the Chicago School reached the general conclusion that antitrust policy had been woefully misguided. Defining "unilateral action" as "action that does not involve agreement with a competitor," the School concluded that:

> firms cannot in general obtain or enhance monopoly power by unilateral action—unless, of course, they are irrationally willing to trade profits for position. Consequently, the focus of antitrust laws should not be on unilateral action; it should instead be on: (1) cartels and (2) horizontal mergers large enough either to create monopoly directly, as in the classic trust cases, or to facilitate cartelization by drastically reducing the number of significant sellers in the market. Since unilateral action . . . [has] been the cutting edge of antitrust policy for a great many

years, to place it beyond the reach of antitrust law . . . implied a breathtaking contraction in the scope of antitrust policy. (Posner 1979, p. 928)

Landmark treatises on the Chicago approach to antitrust include Posner (1976, 1986), Bork (1978), and Brozen (1982). The Chicago approach came to be known as the *efficiency* approach to antitrust: "The whole task of antitrust can be summed up as the effort to improve allocative efficiency without impairing productive efficiency so greatly as to produce either no gain or a net loss in consumer welfare" (Bork 1978, p. 91).

The efficiency thesis can be explicated by returning to Figure 10.1. Except for the absence of area **R**, monopoly rents, Bork (1978, pp. 107-8) uses a diagram similar to our Figure 10.1 to argue the Chicago School's efficiency thesis.[3] Ignoring area **R** is justified by the Chicago School on the grounds that it represents only transfer payments from one group of consumers (the buyers of particular firms' products) to another group of consumers (the producers of the products).

Bork (1978) argues that when an industry's aggregate efficiency is maximized, it promotes the goal of the "maximization of wealth or consumer want satisfaction" (p. 91). Therefore, the proper administration of the antitrust laws entails *only* comparing area **I** with area **E**. If, in the case of a proposed merger, **E** exceeds **I**, then the merger is efficient and the merger should be allowed. Conversely, if **I** exceeds **E**, then the merger should be blocked:

> This diagram [Figure 10.1] can be used to illustrate all antitrust problems, since it shows the relationship of the only two factors involved, allocative inefficiency and productive efficiency. The existence of these two elements and their respective amounts are the real issues in every properly decided antitrust case. They are what we have to estimate—whether the cause is about the dissolution of a monopolistic firm, a conglomerate merger, a requirements contract, or a price fixing agreement . . .
>
> It must also be remembered that there need not always be a tradeoff [between **I** and **E**]. In most cases, in my opinion, economic analysis will show that one of the areas does not exist, and a decision of the case is therefore easy. Some phenomena involve only a dead-weight loss and no, or insignificant, cost savings. That is the case with the garden-variety price-fixing ring. Output is restricted so that $[Q_m]$ is to the left of $[Q_c]$, creating the area **[I]**, but there is no downward shift of costs, no line $[Ac_m]$, and hence no area **[E]**. (Bork 1978, p. 108; notation changed for consistency with Figure 10.1)

If it appears that Bork (1978) is arguing that the Justice Department and FTC should administer the antitrust laws by actually estimating the sizes of areas **I** and **E**, this would be incorrect. More than two decades earlier, Chamberlin (1954) had described attempting such estimates as "flights of fancy" (p. 257). Bork (1978) agrees: "Passably accurate measurement of the actual situation [i.e., areas **I** and **E**] is not even a theoretical possibility; much less is there any hope of arriving at a correct estimate of the hypothetical situation" (p. 125). Firms do not know and regulators cannot know the shape of the requisite demand and cost curves to estimate areas **I** and **E** because such curves "change continually" (p. 126). Therefore, because a case-by-case approach is impossible, administrative rules should be devised that presume that unilateral action is efficiency enhancing and pro-competitive. Antitrust should restrict itself to cartels and other instances of collusion because "most of the mergers the Supreme Court strikes down and the 'price discriminations' the Robinson-Patman Act is intended to stamp out . . . are examples . . . which involve only efficiency gain and no dead-weight loss" (pp. 108-9).

In the 1970s, the Supreme Court began to rely increasingly on efficiency-based antitrust reasoning (e.g., *Continental T.V. Inc. v. GTE Sylvania*, 433 U.S. 36, 1977). In the 1980s, under the Reagan administration, the Justice Department and FTC began to embrace efficiency reasoning and, accordingly, modified its merger guidelines (Taylor 1982a,b): "The only goal of antitrust is economic efficiency" (1982b, p. 28). Also in the 1980s, what Lande (1988) calls a "counterrevolution" (p. 447) began that emphasized the wealth-transfer effects of market power (e.g., Areeda 1983; Campbell 1983; Fox and Sullivan 1987; Hovenkamp 1985). In this ongoing, heated debate, Chicago School proponents are characterized as "efficiency extremists," whereas wealth-transfer (area **R**) advocates are described as "open-minded thinkers" (Lande 1988, p. 455).

In the early 1990s, efficiency-based reasoning was dealt a setback by the Supreme Court in *Eastman Kodak v. Image Technical Services* (Lande 1993). Also in the 1990s, under the Clinton administration, regulatory bodies began downplaying efficiency reasoning. And so the debate continues. What are competition and monopoly? How can they be empirically identified? What should be the goal (or goals?) of public policy concerning competition? Using R-A theory as a foundation, we next appraise the antitrust debate.

10.2.2 The Antitrust Debate: An R-A Theory Appraisal

The striking aspect of the antitrust debate is not the points of disagreement but the commonalities between advocates of the wealth-transfer and efficiency views. Both sides agree that partial equilibrium analysis (Figure 10.1) is the appropriate method of analysis; neither side argues from an evolutionary economics or Austrian economics perspective (Block 1994). Both sides agree that "competition" means *perfect* competition; neither side argues for an evolutionary, process view (High 1984-1985).[4] Both sides agree that "monopoly" means simply a downward-sloping demand curve; neither side argues that "monopoly" should be restricted to the control of the supply of some generic commodity. Both sides agree that market power (downward-sloping demand curves) results in a misallocation of resources and constitutes a major problem for society; neither side argues that downward-sloping demand curves are natural and contribute to the efficient allocation of resources. Both sides agree that firms are production functions that can be represented as a series of cost curves; neither side argues that cost curves are an inappropriate model for understanding the aspects of firms that are important for public policy. Both sides agree that firm efficiency (reducing costs, while providing equivalent value) is an important consideration; neither side argues that firm effectiveness (increasing value, while maintaining equivalent costs) should also be considered. Both sides agree that the goal of efficiency is important; neither side argues for the importance of both efficiency and economic growth as goals.

In summary, both sides agree that the neoclassical research tradition is the appropriate starting point for analysis. Points of disagreement center on the primary goal of antitrust, that is, is it to prevent wealth transfers or promote efficiency, and such "details" as the relative sizes of triangle **I** and rectangles **E** and **R** in Figure 10.1. As Block (1994) points out, it is not the case, for example, that Austrian arguments against antitrust are considered, then rejected. Rather, Austrian arguments aren't considered at all because they cannot be expressed in "blackboard economics." That is, Austrian arguments—for example, that the debate wrongly assumes that interpersonal comparisons of utility are possible—are not considered because they cannot be expressed in terms of shifts in demand and cost curves in static equilibrium.

The antitrust debate is another example of the power of a research tradition to frame all aspects of a debate. I argue that both good science and good public policy require moving the antitrust debate beyond the neoclassical tradition. Using R-A theory as a guide, the analysis shows that *both* the wealth-transfer and efficiency approaches to antitrust are misguided.

A Meaningless Debate. The key to understanding how misguided the antitrust debate has been is recognizing that Figure 10.1 is meaningless in most antitrust cases. The existence of P_c, *the* competitive price, and Q_c, *the* quantity produced under perfect competition, requires the intersection of *a* demand curve and *a* supply curve for *a* homogeneous commodity. But a homogeneous commodity requires the existence of both homogeneous industry demand and homogeneous industry supply. Homogeneous industry demand, in turn, requires homogeneous tastes and preferences. Likewise, homogeneous supply requires firms to be combiners of homogeneous and perfectly mobile resources using a standard production function. In most industries, however, demand is not homogeneous (see Sections 3.1 and 5.1.1). Similarly, the firms in most industries cannot be approximated by the cost curves associated with homogeneous and perfectly mobile resources and a standard technology (see Sections 4.1 and 5.5).

Therefore, in most of the antitrust cases actually prosecuted, the demand and (implicit) supply curves in Figure 10.1 do not exist and *cannot* exist. To use Chamberlin's (1933/1962, p. 9) famous example, it makes no sense to refer to *the* demand for automobiles. Because the existence of *the* competitive price P_c and *the* competitive quantity Q_c in Figure 10.1 requires industry demand and supply curves (with all firms expanding output to the quantity such that price equals marginal cost equals minimum average cost), P_c and Q_c are meaningless concepts in Figure 10.1. Therefore, because demand D, price P_c, and quantity Q_c are meaningless concepts in most antitrust cases, the deadweight loss **I**, monopoly rents **R**, and efficiency gain **E** are equally meaningless.

In short, Figure 10.1 (in all its various manifestations) is meaningless in most antitrust cases and cannot be used to provide a foundation for meaningful debate on antitrust policy and implementation. Hence, the antitrust debate framed by Figure 10.1, for advocates of both the wealth-transfer and efficiency approaches, has been misguided by the neoclassical tradition.

It is important to distinguish between the *meaningless* claim of R-A theory and the *measurability* claim of the Chicago School. Recall that Bork (1978), though claiming that Figure 10.1 applies to "all antitrust problems" (p. 108), argues that accurate measures of rectangle **E** and triangle **I** are impossible because the shapes of the requisite demand and supply curves "change continually" (p. 126). It is no doubt true that even in those few industries where demand and supply are "close enough" to being homogeneous, empirically estimating such curves for the purpose of antitrust is thwarted by (among other things) changing economic circumstances. However, the claim of R-A theory is much more radical than just pointing out a difficult problem of measurement. R-A theory implies that, in the overwhelming majority of actual antitrust cases, Figure 10.1 is totally meaningless—it makes no sense at all. It is not the case that demand and supply curves are difficult to measure; it is the case that demand and supply curves cannot exist and, hence, *cannot* be estimated. Making sense should be a minimum desideratum of any science—and Figure 10.1 fails the sense-making criterion of science.

One can potentially argue that some firm's prices and profits, on some particular criterion, are too high; one cannot, however, use Figure 10.1 to so argue. Furthermore, one can potentially argue, on some particular criterion, that wealth should be redistributed from producers or buyers of a product to other buyers or producers—but one cannot use Figure 10.1 to so argue. Likewise, one can potentially argue, on some particular criterion, that a merger between two firms promotes efficiency. However, one cannot use Figure 10.1 to so argue. Similarly, one can potentially argue, on some particular criterion, that "big is bad; small is good." Assuredly, however, one cannot use Figure 10.1 to so argue. In the new millennium, as in the old, the primary determinant of what is legal or illegal, rewarded by accolades or punished by fines (and jail sentences!), is not antitrust *law*. Rather, it is the ideology of elected presidents and appointed regulators and judges, in conjunction with the rhetorical skills of lawyers and expert witnesses. This should concern all who value civil liberties and the rule of law.

10.3 PUBLIC POLICY AND R-A THEORY

Recall that in the neoclassical tradition, "monopoly," "monopoly power," and "monopoly profits" morphed from the control of the supply of a generic commodity and the power and profits associated with such control to firms (a) having downward-sloping demand curves, (b) being price-setters and quantity-takers (rather than price-takers and quantity-setters), and (c) having the profits associated with price-setting. Thus, "monopoly profits" in the neoclassical tradition became not the profits of *monopoly* but the profits of any firm having pricing discretion.

Consider the "5% rule" in the merger guidelines adopted by the U.S. Department of Justice in 1982.[5] The guidelines state that the "unifying theme . . . is that mergers should not be permitted to create or enhance 'market power' or to facilitate its exercise . . . [because] the result is a transfer of wealth from buyers to sellers and a misallocation of resources" (pp. 2-3). As to whether "market power" exists, as a "first approximation the Department will hypothesize a price increase of five percent and ask how many sellers could sell the product to such customers within one year" (p. 13). Note that any firm is *automatically* suspected of antisocial, anti-competitive behavior when it has a competence that enables it to produce a market offering that is more reliable or has higher quality and, hence, is worth 5% more. Note also that the "5% rule" was promulgated by those labeled as free-market *extremists* by advocates of even more stringent antitrust enforcement (Lande 1988). Such is how neoclassical theory has misguided the debate.

Sensible debate on public policy requires reconceptualizing "competition" and "monopoly." For R-A theory, "competition" implies a particular kind of evolutionary process, not a particular kind of market structure. Likewise, for R-A theory, the term "monopoly" has its classical meaning, that is, a firm having control over the supply of a generic commodity. Furthermore, the existence of firms having downward-sloping demand curves signifies neither the absence of competition nor a problem for government to solve. Rather, such curves are the natural product of heterogeneous demand and signify the presence of the evolutionary process of competition. Moreover, because the general case of competition is that firm resources are heterogeneous and imperfectly mobile, then—contra the "5%" rule"—one expects competition to produce price differentials that are often long-lasting. It is the *process* of R-A competition, I argue, that public policy should encourage.

Sensible debate on public policy also requires revisiting the issue of "static efficiency" versus "dynamic efficiency." It is sometimes maintained that public policymakers face a trade-off between "static" and what is (misleadingly) referred to as "dynamic" efficiency. That is, policies that promote competition and the efficient allocation of scarce, tangible resources are often argued to be inconsistent with the goal of promoting the innovations that result in economic growth. However, the trade-off disappears once one moves beyond defining "competition" as *perfect* competition: vigorous *R-A* competition promotes (1) the efficient allocation of scarce tangible resources, (2) the proactive and reactive innovations that result in increases in effectiveness (see Section 7.3), and (3) the creation of the new tangible, intangible, and "higher order" resources that drive economic growth (see Section 8.2).

Therefore, to the extent that the goals of public policy are wealth creation, productivity (i.e., efficiency and effectiveness), and economic growth, then policymakers should promote formal and informal institutions that promote R-A competition. That is, public policy should promote the evolutionary process that consists of the constant struggle of firms for comparative advantages in resources that yield marketplace positions of competitive advantage and, therefore, superior financial performance. As discussed in Chapter 9, important formal institutions are those that protect property rights in particular and promote economic freedom in general. Important informal institutions include those that promote social trust (see Section 9.3.3). Consider, for example, the cases of marginal tax rates and intellectual property rights.

Recall that R-A theory posits that the primary objective of firms is superior financial performance because such performance leads to superior rewards flowing to owners, managers, and employees. Institutions that promote the *linkage* between performance and rewards, therefore, promote vigorous R-A competition. That is, individuals must perceive the link between superior firm performance and their own personal rewards. Consequently, low marginal tax rates for both firms and individuals promote the linkage between performance and rewards, which in turn promotes R-A competition and thus productivity and economic growth.

Now recall that R-A competition prompts the proactive and reactive innovations that create the new tangible, intangible, and "higher order" resources that ultimately result in productivity and economic growth. Vigorous competition, therefore, requires institutions that promote the *linkage* between resource creation and rewards. That is, vigorous competition requires institutions that protect the property rights that firms and individuals have in the innovations they create. With its focus on intangible and higher-order resources, R-A theory emphasizes the importance of protecting *intellectual* property rights, as stressed by Sherwood (1990).[6] That is, it is not just protecting tangible, physical property from expropriation or protecting inventions by a strong patent system that is important. Equally important is institutional protection for trade secrets, copyrights, trademarks, and "mask works."[7]

Analyses similar to the above can easily be made showing how other aspects of economic freedom, for example, low tariffs, low inflation, and the absence of quotas and licensing requirements, promote R-A competition. In short, formal institutions protecting property rights and promoting economic freedom promote R-A competition. In turn, R-A competition promotes productivity and economic growth. To the extent that the goals of public policy are wealth creation, productivity, and economic growth, therefore, policymakers should promote formal and informal institutions that promote R-A competition.

10.4 A WORK IN PROGRESS

Resource-advantage theory is an interdisciplinary theory of competition. I thank profoundly those scholars in marketing, management, economic sociology, neoclassical economics, institutional economics, socioeconomics, and evolutionary economics who have contributed and are continuing to contribute to its development.

Although it is still a relatively new theory, efforts to develop it to date show that R-A theory:

- contributes to explaining firm diversity (Section 6.3),

- makes the correct prediction concerning financial performance diversity (Section 6.3.1),

- contributes to explaining observed differences in quality, innovativeness, and productivity between market-based and command economies (Section 7.3),

- shows why competition in market-based economies is dynamic (Section 5.7.1),

- incorporates a resource-based view of the firm (Section 4.1.5),

- incorporates the competence view of the firm (Sections 2.1.3 and 4.1.5),

- has the requisites of a phylogenetic, nonconsummatory, disequilibrium-provoking, theory of competition (Section 2.1.3),

- explicates the view that competition is a process of knowledge-discovery (Sections 2.2.3 and 6.1.4),

- contributes to explaining why social relations constitute a resource only contingently (Section 4.2.4),

- has the requisites of a moderately socialized theory of competition (Section 4.2.4),

- shows how path-dependence effects can occur (Sections 6.2.4 and 6.2.5),

- expands the concept of *capital* (Section 8.2.1),

- predicts correctly that technological progress dominates the K/L ratio in economic growth (Section 8.3),

- predicts correctly that increases in economic growth cause increases in investment (Section 8.4),

- predicts correctly that most of the technological progress that drives economic growth stems from the actions of profit-driven firms (Section 8.5),

- predicts correctly that R-A competition can prevent the economic stagnation that results from capital deepening (Section 8.6),

- contributes to explaining the growth pattern of the (former) Soviet Union (Section 8.6.1),

- provides a theoretical foundation for why formal institutions promoting property rights and economic freedom also promote economic growth (Section 9.2),

- provides a theoretical foundation for why informal institutions promoting social trust also promote economic growth (Section 9.3.3),

- has the requisites of a general theory of competition that incorporates perfect competition as a limiting, special case, thereby incorporating the predictive successes of neoclassical theory and preserving the cumulativeness of economic science (Section 10.1),
- shows why the debate over antitrust legislation and implementation has been so misguided (Section 10.2.2), and
- provides some—preliminary, to be sure—recommendations for public policy (Section 10.3).

All in all, some positive steps have been made in developing R-A theory. Nonetheless, resource-advantage theory is, most assuredly, a work in progress. Much conceptual and empirical work must be done to test, explore, and further explicate the structure, foundations, and implications of the theory. Are there additional foundational premises that should be included? If so, which ones and why? Should any of the foundational premises be modified or deleted? If so, why? Are there other theories of competition that should be compared with R-A theory? If so, what are the foundational premises and structures of these theories? Specifically, how do the premises of each theory differ from those articulated in Table 5.1, and how does the structure of each theory differ from that articulated in Figures 6.1 and 6.2? Note that it is only by comparing rival structures and foundational premises that one can clearly evaluate how and why theories are consistent or inconsistent, saying different things or saying the same things differently, genuinely rival or actually complementary.

Finally, a great deal of work remains to be done on developing the public policy implications of resource-advantage theory. Recall that R-A theory implies that public policy should promote vigorous R-A competition to the extent that the goals of public policy are wealth creation, productivity, and economic growth. What if the goal of an equitable distribution of income is adopted? Are equity and economic growth via R-A competition in conflict? If so, what definition of "equitable distribution" is implied? These questions and many others remain unanswered to date. In short, there is still a lot of work to be done—*a lot of work.*

Notes

1. Diagrams similar to Figure 10.1 appear in many contemporary analyses of antitrust by disputants who come to very different conclusions (e.g., Block 1994; Bork 1978; Lande 1988; Posner 1986; Williamson 1968). Hence, I refer to Figure 10.1 as *generic.*

2. See Posner (1979) for a history of the Chicago School of antitrust. Posner uses the label "Harvard School" to designate the "big is bad; small is good" approach.

3. See Bork's (1978) Figure 1 on his page 107.

4. Indeed, High (1984-1985) argues that Bork's (1978) analysis is a paradoxical blend of static and dynamic theory.

5. See U.S. Department of Justice, Merger Guidelines, June 14, 1982.

6. Sherwood (1990) argues that the protection of intellectual property is—contrary to conventional wisdom—at least as important to developing countries as it is to developed countries for promoting economic growth.

7. A *mask work* is defined as "the expression of a design for elements of a semiconductor 'chip' which is exclusive to its creator; it falls between patent and copyright in concept" (Sherwood 1990, p. 12).

References

Aaker, David A. 1988. *Strategic Market Management.* New York: John Wiley.

———. 1991. *Managing Brand Equity.* New York: Free Press.

———. 1995. *Strategic Market Management.* 4th ed. New York: John Wiley.

Abell, Derek F., and J. S. Hammond. 1979. *Strategic Market Planning: Problems and Analytical Approaches.* Englewood Cliffs, NJ: Prentice Hall.

Abramowitz, M. 1989. *Thinking about Growth.* Cambridge, UK: Cambridge University Press.

Adams, J. 1992. "The Corporation Versus the Market." *Journal of Economic Issues* 26 (June): 397-405.

Addleson, Mark. 1994. "Competition." Pp. 96-102 in P. Boettke, ed., *The Elgar Companion to Austrian Economics.* Brookfield, VT: Edward Elgar.

Aghion, Philippe, and Peter Howitt. 1991. "A Model of Growth through Creative Destruction." *Econometrica* 60 (March): 322-52.

Alchian, Armen A. 1950. "Uncertainty, Evolution and Economic Theory." *Journal of Political Economy* 58: 211-21.

Alchian, Armen A., and William R. Allen. 1977/1983. *Exchange and Production: Competition, Coordination, and Control.* 2nd and 3rd eds. Belmont, CA: Wadsworth.

Alderson, Wroe. 1957. *Marketing Behavior and Executive Action.* Homewood, IL: Richard D. Irwin.

———. 1965. *Dynamic Marketing Behavior.* Homewood, IL: Richard D. Irwin.

Allenby, Arora, Greg M. Noeroj, and James L. Ginter. 1998. "On the Heterogeneity of Demand." *Journal of Marketing Research 35* (Aug.): 384-89.

Alston, Lee J., and William Gillespie. 1989. "Resource Coordination and Transaction Costs: A Framework for Analyzing the Firm/Market Boundary." *Journal of Economic Behavior and Organization* 11 (2): 191-212.

Andrews, Kenneth R. 1971/1980/1987. *The Concept of Corporate Strategy.* Homewood, IL: Richard D. Irwin.

Ansoff, H. I. 1965. *Corporate Strategy.* New York: McGraw-Hill.

Areeda, P. 1983. "Introduction to Antitrust Economics." *Antitrust Law Journal* 52: 523-36.

Arrow, Kenneth J. 1962. "The Economic Implications of Learning by Doing." *Review of Economic Studies* 29 (June): 155-73.

———. 1972. "Gifts and Exchanges." *Philosophy and Public Affairs* 1 (4): 343-61.

———. 1974. *The Limits of Organization.* New York: Norton

Arthur, W. Brian. 1989. "Competing Technologies, Increasing Returns, and Lock-in by Historical Events." *Economic Journal* 99 (1): 116-31.

Azzi, Corry, and Ronald Ehrenberg. 1975. "Household Allocation of Time and Church Attendance." *Journal of Political Economy* 38 (1): 27-56.

Baird, Charles W. 1994. "Profit and Loss." Pp. 143-50 in P. Boettke, ed., *The Elgar Companion to Austrian Economics.* Brookfield, VT: Edward Elgar.

Bain, Joe S. 1954. "Conditions of Entry and the Emergence of Monopoly." Pp. 215-44 in E. Chamberlin, ed., *Monopoly and Competition and Their Regulation.* London: Macmillan.

———. 1956. *Barriers to New Competition.* Cambridge, MA: Harvard University Press.

———. 1968. *Industrial Organization.* 2nd ed. New York: John Wiley.

Baker, Michael J., C. D. Black, and S. J. Hart. 1994. "Competitive Success in Sunrise and Sunset Industries." In J. Saunders, ed., *The Marketing Initiative.* London: Prentice Hall.

Baker, Wayne. 1990. "Market Networks and Corporate Behavior." *American Journal of Sociology* 89: 589-625.

Balassa, Bela A. 1974. "Success Criteria for Economic Systems." Pp. 2-18 in M. Bernstein, ed., *Comparative Economic Systems.* Homewood, IL: Richard D. Irwin.

Banerjee, Abhijit, and Michael Spagat. 1991. "Productivity Paralysis and the Complexity Problem: Why Do Centrally Planned Economies Become Prematurely Gray?" *Journal of Comparative Economics* 15 (Dec.): 646-60.

Barksdale, Hiram C., and Bill Darden. 1971. "Marketers Attitudes toward the Marketing Concept." *Journal of Marketing* 35 (Oct.): 29-36.

Barney, Jay. 1986. "Strategic Factor Markets: Expectations, Luck and Business Strategy." *Management Science* 32: 1231-41.

———. 1991. "Firm Resources and Sustained Competitive Advantage." *Journal of Management* 17 (1): 99-120.

———. 1992. "Integrating Organizational Behavior and Strategy Formulation Research: A Resource-based Analysis." Pp. 39-61 in P. Shrivastava, A. S. Hugg, and J. E. Dutton, eds., *Advances in Strategic Management.* Greenwich, CN: JAI Press.

———. 1995. "Looking Inside for Competitive Advantage." *Academy of Management Executive* 9: 49-61.

Barney, Jay, and M. H. Hansen. 1994. "Trustworthiness as a Source of Competitive Advantage." *Strategic Management Journal* 15: 175-90.

Barney, Jay B., and William G. Ouchi. 1986. *Organizational Economics.* San Francisco: Jossey-Bass.

Barone, E. 1908. "The Ministry of Production in the Collectivist State." F. A. Hayek, Trans. *Il ministro della produzione nello stato collectivista.* Pp. 245-90 in F. A. Hayek, ed., 1935, *Collectivist Economic Planning: Critical Studies on the Possibilities of Socialism.* London: Routledge.

Barro, Robert J. 1997. *Determinants of Economic Growth.* Cambridge: MIT Press.

Barro, Robert J., and Xavier Sala-i-Martin. 1995. *Economic Growth.* New York: McGraw-Hill.

——— and ———. 1997. "Technological Diffusion, Convergence, and Growth." *Journal of Economic Growth* 2 (1): 1-27.

Baumol, William, Sue Anne Batey Blackman, and Edward N. Wolff. 1989. *Productivity and American Leadership: The Long View.* Cambridge and London: MIT Press.

Baumol, William, Richard R. Nelson, and Edward N. Wolff, eds. 1994. *Convergence of Productivity.* New York: Oxford University Press.

Beauchamp, T. L., and N. E. Bowie. 1988. *Ethical Theory and Business.* 3rd ed. Englewood Cliffs, NJ: Prentice Hall.

Becker, Gary. 1964. *Human Captial.* New York: National Bureau of Economic Research.

———. 1976. "The Economic Approach to Human Behavior." In G. Becker, *The Economic Approach to Human Behavior.* Chicago: University of Chicago Press.

Bentham, Jeremy. 1789. *Introduction to the Principles of Morals and Legislation.* Oxford, UK: Oxford University Press.

Bergen, Mark, Shantanu Dutta, and Orville Walker. 1992. "Agency Relationships in Marketing: A Review." *Journal of Marketing* 56 (3): 1-24.

Bergson, Abram. 1948. "Socialist Economics." Pp. 412-48 in H. S. Ellis, ed., *A Survey of Contemporary Economics.* Homewood, IL: Richard D. Irwin.

———. 1967. "Market Socialism Revisited." *Journal of Political Economy* 75: 655-73.

———. 1973. "On Monopoly Welfare Losses." *American Economic Review* 63 (Dec.): 853-70.

———. 1987a. "Comparative Productivity: The U.S.S.R., Eastern Europe, and the West." *American Economic Review* 77 (3): 342-57.

———. 1987b. "On Soviet Real Investment Growth." *Soviet Studies* 39 (3, July): 406-24.

Berle, Adolph A., and G. C. Means. 1932. *The Modern Corporation and Private Property.* New York: Macmillan.

Berry, Leonard L. 1995. "Relationship Marketing of Services: Growing Interest, Emerging Perspectives." *Journal of the Academy of Marketing Science* 23 (4): 237-45.

Berry, Leonard L., and A. Parasuraman. 1991. *Marketing Services.* New York: Free Press.

Bethell, Tom. 1998. *The Noblest Triumph: Property and Prosperity through the Ages.* New York: St. Martin's Press.

Bharadwaj, Sundar, P. Rajan Varadarajan, and John Fahy. 1993. "Sustainable Competitive Advantage in Service Industries: A Conceptual Model and Research Propositions." *Journal of Marketing* 57 (4): 83-99.

Black, Janice A., and Kim B. Boal. 1994. "Strategic Resources: Traits, Configurations, and Paths to Sustainable Competitive Advantage." *Strategic Management Journal* 15: 131-48.

Black, Max. 1962. *Models and Metaphors: Studies in Language and Philosophy.* Ithaca, NY: Cornell University Press.

Blaug, Mark. 1980. *The Methodology of Economics.* Cambridge, UK: Cambridge University Press.

Block, Walter. 1980. "On Robert Nozick's 'On Austrian Methodology.' " *Inquiry* 23 (3): 299-330.

———. 1988. "On Yeager's 'Why Subjectivism?' " *Review of Austrian Economics* 1: 199-208.

———. 1994. "Total Repeal of Antitrust Legislation: A Critique of Bork, Posner, and Brozen." *Review of Austrian Economics* 8 (1): 35-70.

Blomström, Magnus, Robert E. Lipsey, and Mario Zejan. 1996. "Is Fixed Investment the Key to Economic Growth?" *Quarterly Journal of Economics* 3 (Feb.): 269-76.

———, ———, and ———. 1994. "What Explains the Growth of Developing Countries?" Pp. 243-59 in W. Baumol, R. Nelson, and E. Wolff, eds., *International Convergence of Productivity.* London: Oxford University Press.

Boettke, Peter. 1994a. "Alternative Paths Forward for Austrian Economics." Pp. 601-15 in P. Boettke, ed., *The Elgar Companion to Austrian Economics.* Brookfield, VT: Edward Elgar.

———, ed. 1994b. *The Elgar Companion to Austrian Economics.* Brookfield, VT: Edward Elgar.

Borden, Neil. 1964. "The Concept of the Marketing Mix." *Journal of Advertising Research* 4 (June): 2-7.

Bork, Robert H. 1954. "Vertical Integration and the Sherman Act: The Legal History of an Economic Misconception." *University of Chicago Law Review* 22: 157-201.

———. 1966. "Legislative Intent and the Policy of the Sherman Act." *Journal of Law and Economics* 9: 7-48.

———. 1978. *The Antitrust Paradox: A Policy at War with Itself.* New York: Basic Books.

Boulding, K. E. 1981. *Evolutionary Economics*. 2nd ed. Cambridge, MA: Harvard University Press.

Bowman, Edward H., and Constance Helfat. 1998. "Does Corporate Strategy Matter?" Wharton School Working Paper No. 98-01. Philadelphia: Wharton School.

Bowman, J. 1957. "Tying Arrangements and the Leverage Problem." *Yale Law Journal* 67: 19-47.

Boyd, R. N. 1984. "The Current Status of Scientific Realism." Pp. 41-82 in J. Leplin, ed. *Scientific Realism*. Berkeley: University of California Press.

Browning, Edgar K., and Jacqueline M. Browning. 1983. *Microeconomic Theory and Applications*. Boston: Little, Brown.

Brozen, Yale. 1982. *Concentration, Mergers, and Public Policy*. New York: Macmillan.

Brumagim, A. L. 1994. "A Hierarchy of Corporate Resources." Pp. 81-112 in P. Shrivastava, A. S. Huff, and J. E. Dutton, eds. *Advances in Strategic Management*. Greenwich, CN: JAI Press.

Brush, Thomas H., and Philip Bromiley. 1997. "What Does a Small Corporate Effect Mean?" *Strategic Management Journal* 18: 825-35.

Brutzkus, Boris. 1922. *Economic Planning in Soviet Russia*. 1935 ed. translated by Gilbert Gardner. London: Routledge and Sons.

Business Week. 1984. "The New Breed of Strategic Planner." (Sept. 17): 62-66, 68.

Buzzell, Robert D., Bradley T. Gale, and Ralph G. M. Sultan. 1975. "Market Share: A Key to Profitability." *Harvard Business Review* 53 (Jan.-Feb.): 97-106.

Campbell, R. 1983. "Has Economics Rationalized Antitrust?" *Antitrust Law Journal* 52: 607-17.

Carlsson, B., and G. Eliasson. 1991. "The Nature and Importance of Economic Competence." Working Paper No. 294. Stockholm: Industrial Institute for Economic and Social Research.

Cass, David. 1965. "Optimum Growth in an Aggregate Model of Capital Accumulation." *Review of Economic Studies* 32 (July): 233-40.

Cave, Martin. 1980. *Computers and Economic Planning: The Soviet Experience*. Cambridge, UK: Cambridge University Press.

Cecil, J., and M. Goldstein. 1990. "Sustaining Competitive Advantage from IT." *McKinsey Quarterly* 4: 74-89.

Chamberlin, Edward. 1933/1962. *The Theory of Monopolistic Competition*. Cambridge, MA: Harvard University Press.

———. 1950. "Product Heterogeneity and Public Policy." *American Economic Review, Papers and Proceedings* 40 (2): 85-92.

———. 1951. "Monopolistic Competition Revisited." *Economica* 18: 343-62.

———, ed. 1954. *Monopoly and Competition and Their Regulation*. London: Macmillan.

Chandler, Alfred D. 1990. *Scale and Scope: The Dynamics of Industrial Capitalism*. Cambridge, MA: Harvard University Press.

Chonko, Lawrence B., and Patrick M. Dunne. 1982. "Marketing Theory: A Status Report." Pp. 43-46 in R. F. Bush and S. D. Hunt, eds., *Marketing Theory: Philosophy of Science Perspectives*. Chicago: American Marketing Association.

Christensen, C. R., K. R. Andrews, J. L. Bower, G. Hamermesh, and M. E. Porter. 1982. *Business Policy: Text and Cases*. Homewood, IL: Richard D. Irwin.

Clark, John Maurice. 1940. "Toward a Concept of Workable Competition." *American Economic Review* 30 (June): 241-56.

Clark, John Maurice. 1954. "Competition and the Objectives of Government Policy." Pp. 317-37 in E. Chamberlin, ed., *Monopoly and Competition and Their Regulation*. London: Macmillan.

———. 1961. *Competition as a Dynamic Process*. Washington, DC: Brookings Institution.

Coase, Ronald H. 1937. "The Nature of the Firm." *Economica* 4: 386-405. Reprinted 1952, pp. 331-51 in G. T. Stigler and K. E. Boulding, eds., *Readings in Price Theory*. Chicago: Richard D. Irwin.

———. 1988. "The Nature of the Firm: Influence." *Journal of Law, Economics and Organizations* 4: 33-47.

———. 1998. "The New Institutional Economics." *AEA Papers and Proceedings* 88 (2): 72-74.

Cobb, Charles, and Paul H. Douglass. 1928. "A Theory of Production." *American Economic Review Supplement* 18 (March): 139-65.

Colander, D. 1995. "Marshallian General Equilibrium Analysis." *Eastern Economic Journal* (Summer): 281-93.

Coleman, Jones S. 1988. "Social Capital in the Creation of Human Capital." *American Journal of Sociology* 94 (Suppl.): S95-S112.

———. 1990. *Foundations of Social Theory.* Cambridge, MA: Harvard University Press.

Collis, David J. 1991. "A Resource Based Analysis of Global Competition." *Strategic Management Journal* 12 (1): 49-68.

———. 1994. "How Valuable Are Organizational Capabilities?" *Strategic Management Journal* 15: 143-52.

Collis, David J., and Cynthia Montgomery. 1995. "Competing on Resources: Strategy in the 1990s." *Harvard Business Review* (July-Aug.): 118-28.

Commons, John R. 1924/1968. *Legal Foundations of Capitalism.* New York: Macmillan. (1968 edition by the University of Wisconsin Press)

———. 1934. *Institutional Economics: Its Place in Political Economy.* New York: Macmillan. Reprinted 1990 with a new introduction by M. Rutherford, New Brunswick, NJ: Transaction Books.

Conant, Jeffrey S., Michael P. Mokwa, and P. Rajan Varadarajan. 1990. "Strategic Types, Distinctive Marketing Competencies, and Organizational Performance." *Strategic Management Journal* 11 (Sept.): 365-83.

Conner, Kathleen. 1991. "A Historical Comparison of Resource-Based Theory and Five Schools of Thought within Industrial-Organization Economics: Do We Have a New Theory of the Firm?" *Journal of Management* 17 (March): 121-54.

Conner, Kathleen, and C. K. Prahalad. 1996. "A Resource-Based Theory of the Firm: Knowledge Versus Opportunism." *Organization Science* 7 (5): 477-501.

Constant, Edward W. 1980. *The Origins of the Turbojet Revolution.* Baltimore: Johns Hopkins University Press.

Coricelli, F., and Dosi, G. 1988. "Coordination and Order in Economic Change and the Interpretive Power of Economic Theory." Pp. 123-47 in G. Dosi, C. Freeman, R. R. Nelson, G. Silverberg, and L. Soete, eds., *Technical Change and Economic Theory.* London: Pinter.

Cowling, K., and D. C. Mueller. 1978. "The Social Cost of Monopoly Power." *Economic Journal* 88 (Dec.): 727-48.

Coyne, K. P. 1985. "Sustainable Competitive Advantage: What It Is, What It Isn't." *Business Horizons* 29 (Jan.-Feb.): 54-61.

Cubbin, J., and P. Geroski. 1987. "The Convergence of Profits in the Long Run: Inter-firm and Inter-industry Comparisons." *Journal of Industrial Economics* 35: 427-42.

David, P. A. 1985. "Clio and the Economics QWERTY." *American Economic Review* 75: 332-37.

Davis, Gerald F., Kristina A. Diekmann, and Catherine A. Tinsley. 1994. "The Decline and Fall of the Conglomerate Firm in the 1980s: The Deinstitutionalization of an Organizational Form." *American Sociological Review* 59 (Aug.): 547-70.

Davis, James H., F. David Schoorman, and Lex Donaldson. 1997. "Toward a Stewardship Theory of Management." *Academy of Management Review* 22 (1): 20-47.

Day, George S. 1977. "Diagnosing the Product Portfolio." *Journal of Marketing* 41 (April): 29-38.

———. 1984. *Strategic Market Planning: The Pursuit of Competitive Advantage.* Minneapolis, MN: West.

———. 1992. "Marketing's Contribution to the Strategy Dialogue." *Journal of the Academy of Marketing Science* 20 (Fall): 323-30.

Day, George S., and Prakesh Nedungadi. 1994. "Managerial Representations of Competitive Advantage." *Journal of Marketing* 58 (April): 31-44.

Day, George S., and Robin Wensley. 1988. "Assessing Advantage: A Framework for Diagnosing Competitive Superiority." *Journal of Marketing* 52 (April): 1-20.

Day, R. H. 1984. "Disequilibrium Economic Dynamics: A Post-Schumpeterian Contribution." *Journal of Economic Behavior and Organization* 12: 57-76.

Debreu, Gerald. 1990. "The Mathematization of Economic Theory." *American Economic Review* 81 (1): 1-7.

DeGregori, T. R. 1987. "Resources Are Not: They Become: An Institutional Theory." *Journal of Economic Issues* 21 (Sept.): 1241-63.

De Long, J. Bradford, and Lawrence Summers. 1991. "Equipment Investment and Economic Growth." *Quarterly Journal of Economics* 106: 445-502.

———, and ———. 1993. "How Strongly Do Developing Countries Benefit from Equipment Investment?" *Journal of Monetary Economics* 32: 395-415.

Demsetz, H. 1988. "The Theory of the Firm Revisited." *Journal Law, Economics, and Organization* 4: 141-62.

Denison, Edward F. 1985. *Trends in American Economic Growth, 1929-1982.* Washington, DC: Brookings Institution.

Desai, Padma. 1987. *The Soviet Economy: Problems and Prospects.* Oxford, UK: Basil Blackwell.

Dickinson, H. D. 1933. "Price Formation in a Socialist Community." *Economic Journal* 43: 237-50.

Dickson, Peter Reid. 1992. "Toward a General Theory of Competitive Rationality." *Journal of Marketing* 56 (Jan.): 69-83.

———. 1996. "The Static and Dynamic Mechanics of Competitive Theory." *Journal of Marketing* 60 (Oct.): 102-6.

Dierickx, Ingemar, and Karel Cool. 1989. "Asset Stock Accumulation and Sustainability of Competitive Advantage." *Management Science* 35 (Dec.): 1504-11.

Dixit, Avinash K., and Joseph E. Stiglitz. 1977. "Monopolistic Competition and Optimum Product Diversity." *American Economic Review* 67 (June): 297-308.

Domar, E. 1947. "Expansion and Employment." *American Economic Review* 37 (March): 343-55.

Dopfer, Kurt. 1986. "Causality and Consciousness in Economics: Concepts of Change in Orthodox and Heterodox Economics." *Journal of Economic Issues* 20 (June): 509-23.

Donaldson, Lex. 1990. "The Ethereal Hand: Organization Economics and Management Theory." *Academy of Management Journal* 15 (3): 369-81.

Donaldson, Thomas. 1989. *The Ethics of International Business.* Oxford, UK: Oxford University Press.

Dore, Ronald. 1987. *Taking Japan Seriously.* Stanford, CA: Stanford University Press.

Dosi, Giovanni. 1984. *Technical Change and Industrial Transformation.* London: Macmillan.

———. 1991. "Some Thoughts on the Promises, Challenges, and Dangers of an 'Evolutionary Perspective' in Economics." *Journal of Evolutionary Economics* 1: 5-7.

Dosi, Giovanni, and Richard Nelson. 1994. "An Introduction to Evolutionary Economic Theories." *Journal of Evolutionary Economics* 4: 153-72.

Dosi, Giovanni, C. Freeman, R. Nelson, G. Silverberg, and L. Soite, eds. 1988. *Technical Change and Economic Theory.* London: Pinter.

Duesenberry, James. 1960. "Comment on an Economic Analysis of Fertility." In Universities—National Bureau Committee for Economic Research, ed., *Demographic and Economic Change in Developed Counties.* Princeton, NJ: Princeton University Press.

Dwyer, F. Robert, Paul H. Schurr, and Sejo Oh. 1987. "Developing Buyer-Seller Relationships." *Journal of Marketing* 51 (April): 11-27.

Easterly, W., and S. Fischer.1994. *The Soviet Economic Decline: Historical and Republican Data.* Working Paper No. 4735. Cambridge, MA: National Bureau of Economic Research.

———, and ———. 1995. "The Soviet Economic Decline." *World Bank Economic Review* 9 (3): 341-71.

Economist. 1991. "A Survey of International Finance: The Ebb Tide." (April 27, special section): 44.

Eisenhardt, Kathleen M. 1989. "Agency Theory: An Assessment and Review." *Academy of Management Review* 14 (Jan.): 57-74.

Eliasson, G. 1990a. "Business Competence, Organizational Learning and Economic Growth." Working Paper No. 264. Stockholm: Industrial Institute for Economic and Social Research.

———. 1990b. "The Firm as a Competent Team." *Journal of Economic Behavior and Organization* 13: 275-98.

Etzioni, Amitai. 1988. *The Moral Dimension: Toward a New Economics.* New York: Free Press.

Faber, M., and J. L. R. Proops. 1990. *Evolution, Time, Production, and the Environment.* Berlin, Germany: Springer.

Falkenberg, A. 1996. "Marketing and the Wealth of Firms." *Journal of Macromarketing* 16 (Spring): 4-24.

Fama, Eugene F. 1980. "Agency Problems and the Theory of the Firm." *Journal of Political Economy* 88 (April): 288-307.

Fama, Eugene F., and Michael C. Jensen. 1983. "Separation of Ownership and Control." *Journal of Law and Economics* 26 (June): 301-25.

Ferguson, C. E. 1966. *Microeconomic Theory.* Homewood, IL: Richard D. Irwin.

Fligstein, Neil. 1996. "Markets as Politics: A Political Cultural Approach to Market Institutions." *American Sociological Review* 61 (Aug.): 656-73.

Foss, Nicolai. 1991. "The Suppression of Evolutionary Approaches in Economies: The Case of Marshall and Monopolistic Competition." *Methodus* (Dec.): 65-72.

———. 1993. "Theories of the Firm: Contractual and Competence Perspectives." *Journal of Evolutionary Economics* 3: 127-44.

———. 1994a. "The Biological Analogy and the Theory of the Firm: Marshall and Monopolistic Competition." *Journal of Economic Issues* 28 (4): 1115-36.

———. 1994b. "Realism and Evolutionary Economics." *Journal of Social and Evolutionary Systems* 17 (1): 21-40.

———. 1994c. "The Theory of the Firm: The Austrians as Precursors and Critics of Contemporary Theory." *Review of Austrian Economics* 7 (1): 31-65.

———. 1997. "Ethics, Discovery, and Strategy." *Journal of Business Ethics* 16: 1131-42.

Foss, Nicolai, C. Knudsen, and C. A. Montgomery. 1995. "An Exploration of Common Ground: Integrating Evolutionary and Strategic Theories of the Firm." Pp. 1-18 in C. A. Montgomery, ed., *Resource-Based and Evolutionary Theories of the Firm: Towards a Synthesis.* Norwell, MA: Kluwer Academic Publishers.

Fox, Eleanor M. 1981. "Modernization of Antitrust: A New Equilibrium." *Cornell Law Review* 66: 1142-55.

Fox, Eleanor M., and Lawrence A. Sullivan. 1987. "Antitrust Retrospective and Perspective: Where Are We Coming From? Where Are We Going?" *New York University Law Review* 62 (Nov.): 936-88.

Frank, Robert H., Thomas Gilovich, and Dennis T. Regan. 1993. "Does Studying Economics Inhibit Cooperation?" *Journal of Economic Perspectives* 7 (2): 159-71.

Frankena, W. 1963. *Ethics.* Englewood Cliffs, NJ: Prentice Hall.

Freeman, Christopher. 1982. *The Economics of Industrial Innovation.* 2nd ed. London: Francis Pinter.

Fried, Vance, and Benjamin Oviatt. 1989. "Michael Porter's Missing Chapter: The Risk of Antitrust Allegations." *Academy of Management Executive* 3 (1): 49-56.

Friedman, Milton. 1953. *Essays in Positive Economics.* Chicago: University of Chicago Press.

———. 1996. "Foreword." Pp. vii-viii in J. Gwartney, R. Lawson, and W. Block, *Economic Freedom of the World: 1975-1995.* Vancouver, British Columbia, Canada: Fraser Institute.

Fukuyama, Francis. 1995. *Trust: The Social Virtues and the Creation of Prosperity.* New York: Free Press.

Gale, Bradley T., and Ben S. Branch. 1982. "Concentration versus Market Share: Which Determines Performance and Why Does It Matter?" *The Antitrust Bulletin* 27 (Spring): 83-103.

Gambetta, D. 1988. *Trust: Making and Breaking Cooperative Relationships.* New York: Basil Blackwell.

Gardner, John W. 1965. *Self Renewal: The Individual and the Innovative Society.* New York: Harper and Row.

Garrison, Roger. 1979. "Waiting in Vienna." Pp. 215-26 in M. J. Rizzo, ed., *Time, Uncertainty, and Disequilibrium.* Lexington, MA: Lexington Books.

Gastil, Raymond D. 1991. "The Comparative Survey of Freedom: Experiences and Suggestions." In A. Inkeles, ed., *On Measuring Democracy.* New Brunswick, NJ: Transaction Publishers.

Gerlach, Michael L. 1992a. *Alliance Capitalism: The Social Organization of Japanese Business.* Berkeley: University of California Press.

———. 1992b. "The Japanese Corporate Network: A Blockmodel Approach." *Administrative Science Quarterly* 37: 105-39.

Ghemawat, Pankaj. 1986. "Sustainable Advantage." *Harvard Business Review* 86 (July-Aug.): 53-58.

Ghoshal, Sumantra, and Peter Moran. 1996. "Bad for Practice: A Critique of the Transaction Cost Theory." *Academy of Management Review* 21 (1): 13-47.

Glazer, Rashi. 1991. "Marketing in an Information-Intensive Environment: Strategic Implications of Knowledge as an Asset." *Journal of Marketing* 55 (Oct.): 1-19.

Goldman, Marshall I. 1960. "Product Differentiation and Advertising: Some Lessons from Soviet Experience." *Journal of Political Economy* 68: 346-57.

———. 1971. *Comparative Economic Systems: A Reader.* New York: Random House.

Gomulka, Stanislaw, and Mark Schaffer. 1991. "A New Method of Long-Run Growth Accounting, with Applications to the Soviet Economy, 1928-87, and the U.S. Economy, 1949-78." Centre for Economic Performance Discussion Paper No. 14. London: London School of Economics and Political Science.

Goold, Michael, and Kathleen Luchs. 1993. "Why Diversify? Four Decades of Management Thinking." *Academy of Management Executive* 7 (3): 7-25.

Gordon, Wendell C., and John Adams. 1989. *Economics as Social Science: An Evolutionary Approach.* Riverdale, MD: Riverdale.

Gould, John P., and Edward P. Lazear. 1989. *Microeconomic Theory.* Homewood, IL: Richard D. Irwin.

Granger, C. W. J. 1969. "Investigating Causal Relationships by Econometric Models and Cross-Spectral Methods." *Econometrica* 37: 424-38.

Granovetter, Mark. 1985. "Economic Action and Social Structure: The Problem of Embeddedness." *American Journal of Sociology* 91 (3): 481-510.

———. 1990. "The Old and New Economic Sociology: A History and Agenda." Pp. 89-112 in R. Frieland and A. F. Robertson, eds., *Beyond the Marketplace: Rethinking Economy and Society.* New York: Aldine de Gruyter.

———. 1994. "Business Groups." Pp. 453-75 in N. J. Smelser and R. Swedberg, eds., *The Handbook of Economic Sociology.* Princeton, NJ: Princeton University Press.

Grant, Robert M. 1991. "The Resource-Based Theory of Competitive Advantage: Implications for Strategy Formulation." *California Management Review* 33: 114-33.

Gronroos, Christran. 1996. "Relationship Marketing: Strategic and Tactical Implications." *Management Decision* 34 (3): 5-14.

Grossman, Gene, and Elthanon Helpman. 1991. *Innovation and Growth in the Global Economy.* Cambridge: MIT Press.

———, and ———. 1994. "Endogenous Innovation in the Theory of Growth." *Journal of Economic Perspectives* 8 (Winter): 23-44.

Gummesson, Evert. 1995. "Focus Shifts in Marketing: A New Agenda for the Third Millennium." Presentation at the 20th Anniversary Program of the Marketing Technology Center, Stockholm, Sweden.

Gwartney, James, and Robert Lawson. 1997. *Economic Freedom of the World 1997.* Vancouver, British Columbia, Canada: Fraser Institute.

Gwartney, James, Robert Lawson, and Walter Block. 1996. *Economic Freedom of the World: 1975-1995.* Vancouver, British Columbia, Canada: Fraser Institute.

Hagedoorn, John, and Jos Schakenraad. 1990a. "Inter-firm Partnerships and Co-operative Strategies in Core Technologies." Pp. 3-37 in C. Freeman and L. Soete, eds., *New Explorations in the Economics of Technical Change.* London: Pinter.

————, and ————. 1990b. "Strategic Partnering and Technological Co-operation." Pp. 171-87 in B. Dankbaar, J. Groenewegen, and H. Schenk, eds., *Perspectives in Industrial Organization.* Dordrect, The Netherlands: Kluwer Academic Publishers.

Hamel, Gary, and Aimé Heene. 1994. *Competence-Based Competition.* New York: John Wiley.

Hamel, Gary, and C. K. Prahalad. 1989. "Strategic Intent." *Harvard Business Review* (May-June): 63-76.

————, and ————. 1994a. *Competing for the Future.* Cambridge, MA: Harvard Business School Press.

————, and————. 1994b. "Competing for the Future." *Harvard Business Review* (July-Aug.): 122-28.

Hamilton, Walton H. 1932/1968. "Institution." Pp. 84-89 in E. R. A. Seligman and A. Johnson, eds., *Encyclopedia of the Social Sciences.* Vol. 8. Guilford, CT: Dushkin Publishing.

Hansen, Gary S., and Birger Wernerfelt. 1989. "Determinants of Firm Performance: The Relative Importance of Economic and Organizational Factors." *Strategic Management Journal* 10 (Sept.-Oct.): 399-411.

Harberger, A. 1954. "Monopoly and Resource Allocation." *American Economic Review* 44 (May): 77-87.

Harré, Rom. 1986. *Varieties of Realism.* Oxford, UK: Basil Blackwell.

Harrison, L. E. 1992. *Who Prospers?: How Cultural Values Shape Economic and Political Success.* New York: Basic Books.

Harrod, R. F. 1948. *Towards a Dynamic Economics.* London: Macmillan.

Haspeslagh, Philippe. 1982. "Portfolio Planning: Uses and Limits." *Harvard Business Review* 60 (Jan.-Feb.): 58-73.

Hayek, Friedrich A. 1935a. "The Nature and History of the Problem." Pp. 1-40 in F. A. Hayek, ed., *Collectivist Economic Planning.* London: Routledge. Reprinted 1948, pp. 119-47 in F. A. Hayek, ed., *Individualism and Economic Order.* Chicago: University of Chicago Press.

————. 1935b. "The State of the Debate." Pp. 201-43 in F. A. Hayek, ed., *Collectivist Economic Planning.* London: Routledge. Reprinted 1948, pp. 148-80 in F. A. Hayek, ed., *Individualism and Economic Order.* Chicago: University of Chicago Press.

————, ed. 1935c. *Collectivist Economic Planning: Critical Studies on the Possibilities of Socialism.* London: Routledge.

Hayek, Friedrich A. 1937. "Economics and Knowledge." *Economica* 4: 33-54. Reprinted 1948, pp. 33-56 in F. A. Hayek, ed., *Individualism and Economic Order.* Chicago: University of Chicago Press.

————. 1940. "The Competitive Solution." *Economica* 7: 125-49. Reprinted 1948, pp. 181-208 in F. A. Hayek, ed., *Individualism and Economic Order.* Chicago: University of Chicago Press.

————. 1945. "The Use of Knowledge in Society." *American Economic Review* 35: 519-30. Reprinted 1948, pp. 77-91 in F. A. Hayek, ed., *Individualism and Economic Order.* Chicago: University of Chicago Press.

————. 1948. *Individualism and Economic Order.* Chicago: University of Chicago Press.

————. 1952/1979. *The Counter-Revolution of Science.* Indianapolis, IN: Liberty Press.

————. 1960. *The Constitution of Liberty.* Chicago: University of Chicago Press.

———. 1978. *New Studies in Philosophy, Politics, Economics, and the History of Ideas.* Chicago: University of Chicago Press.

Hays, Laurie. 1994. "Blue Period: Gerstner Is Struggling as He Tries to Change Ingrained IBM Culture." *Wall Street Journal* (May 13): A1, A5.

Hechter, Michael. 1987. *Principles of Group Solidarity.* Berkeley: University of California Press.

Heene, Aimé, and Ron Sanchez. 1996. *Competence-Based Strategic Management.* New York: John Wiley.

Heilbroner, Robert L. 1970. *Between Capitalism and Socialism: Essays in Political Economics.* New York: Random House.

———. 1990. "Reflections after Communism." *New Yorker* (September 10): 91-100.

Herrigel, Gary. 1990. *Industrial Organization and the Politics of Industry: Centralized and Decentralized Production in Germany.* Ph.D. diss., Department of Political Science, MIT.

High, Jack. 1984-1985. "Bork's Paradox: Static vs. Dynamic Efficiency in Antitrust Analysis." *Contemporary Policy Issues* 3 (Winter): 21-34.

Hirschman, Albert O. 1970. *Exist, Voice and Loyalty: Responses to Decline in Firms, Organizations and States.* Cambridge, MA: Harvard University Press.

Hirshleifer, Jack. 1976. 2nd ed., 1980. *Price Theory and Application.* Englewood Cliffs, NJ: Prentice Hall.

———. 1982. "Evolutionary Models in Economics and Law." *Research in Law and Economics* 4: 1-60.

Hitt, Michael A., and R. D. Ireland. 1985. "Corporate Distinctive Competence, Strategy, Industry and Performance." *Strategic Management Journal* 6: 273-93.

———, and ———. 1986. "Relationships among Corporate Distinctive Competencies, Diversification Strategy, Corporate Structure and Performance." *Journal of Management Studies* 23: 401-16.

Hodgson, Geoffrey M. 1992. "The Reconstruction of Economics: Is There Still a Place for Neoclassical Theory?" *Journal of Economic Issues* 26 (3): 749-67.

———. 1993. *Economics and Evolution.* Ann Arbor: University of Michigan Press.

———. 1994. "The Return of Institutional Economics." Pp. 58-76 in N. J. Smelser and R. Swedberg, eds., *The Handbook of Economic Sociology.* Princeton, NJ: Princeton University Press.

Hodgson, Geoffrey M., Warren J. Samuels, and Marc R. Tool, eds. 1993. *Companion to Institutional and Evolutionary Economics.* Aldershot, UK: Edward Elgar.

Hofer, Charles, and Dan Schendel. 1978. *Strategy Formulation: Analytical Concepts.* St. Paul, MN: West.

Hofstadter, R. 1965. *The Paranoid Style in American Politics and Other Essays.* New York: Knopf.

Hofstede, G. 1980. *Culture's Consequences: International Differences in Work-Related Values.* Beverly Hills, CA: Sage.

Hooley, George J., J. E. Lynch, and J. Shepherd. 1990. "The Marketing Concept: Putting the Theory into Practice." *European Journal of Marketing* 24 (9): 7-23.

Houston, Franklin. 1986. "The Marketing Concept: What It Is and What It Is Not?" *Journal of Marketing* 50 (April): 81-87.

Hovenkamp, J. 1985. "Antitrust after Chicago." *Michigan Law Review* 84: 213-45.

Hunt, Shelby D. 1989. "Naturalistic, Humanistic, and Interpretive Inquiry: Challenges and Ultimate Potential." Pp. 185-98 in E. Hirschman, ed., *Interpretive Consumer Research.* Provo, UT: Association for Consumer Research.

———. 1990a. "Commentary on an Empirical Investigation of a General Theory of Ethics." *Journal of the Academy of Marketing Science* 18 (Spring): 173-77.

———. 1990b. "Truth in Marketing Theory and Research." *Journal of Marketing* 54: 1-15.

———. 1991a. *Modern Marketing Theory: Critical Issues in the Philosophy of Marketing Science.* Cincinnati, OH: South-Western.

————. 1991b. "Positivism and Paradigm Dominance in Consumer Research: Toward Critical Pluralism and Rapprochement." *Journal of Consumer Research* 18 (June): 32-44.

————. 1992. "For Reason and Realism in Marketing." *Journal of Marketing* 56 (April): 89-102.

————. 1993. "Objectivity in Marketing Theory and Research." *Journal of Marketing* 57 (April): 76-91.

————. 1994. "A Realist Theory of Empirical Testing: Resolving the Theory Ladenness/Objectivity Debate." *Journal of the Philosophy of the Social Sciences* 24 (June): 133-54.

————. 1995. "The Resource-Advantage Theory of Competition: Toward Explaining Productivity and Economic Growth." *Journal of Management Inquiry* 4 (Dec.): 317-32.

————. 1997a. "Competing through Relationships: Grounding Relationship Marketing in Resource Advantage Theory." *Journal of Marketing Management* 13: 431-45.

————. 1997b. "Evolutionary Economics, Endogenous Growth Models, and Resource-Advantage Theory." *Eastern Economic Journal* 23 (4): 425-39.

————. 1997c. "Resource-Advantage Theory: An Evolutionary Theory of Competitive Firm Behavior?" *Journal of Economic Issues* 31 (March): 59-77.

————. 1997d. "Resource-Advantage Theory and the Wealth of Nations." *Journal of Socio-Economics* 26 (4): 335-57.

————. 1998. "Productivity, Economic Growth, and Competition: Resource Allocation or Resource Creation?" *Business and the Contemporary World* 10 (3): 367-94.

————. 1999a. "The Competence-Based, Resource-Advantage, and Neoclassical Theories of Competition: Toward a Synthesis." In R. Sanchez and A. Heene, eds., *Competence-Based Strategic Management: Theory and Research.* Advances in Applied Business Strategy. Greenwich, CT: JAI Press.

————. 1999b. "The Strategic Imperative and Sustainable Competitive Advantage: Public Policy and Resource Advantage Theory." *Journal of Academy of Marketing Science* 27 (2): 144-59.

————. 1999c. "Synthesizing Resource-Based, Evolutionary and Neoclassical Thought: Resource-Advantage Theory as a General Theory of Competition." In N. J. Foss and P. Robertson, eds., *Resources, Technology, and Strategy.* London: Routledge.

Hunt, Shelby D., and Robert M. Morgan. 1995. "The Comparative Advantage Theory of Competition." *Journal of Marketing* 59 (April): 1-15.

————, and ————. 1996. "The Resource-Advantage Theory of Competition: Dynamics, Path Dependencies, and Evolutionary Dimensions." *Journal of Marketing* 60 (Oct.): 107-14.

————, and ————. 1997. "Resource-Advantage Theory: A Snake Swallowing Its Tail or a General Theory of Competition?" *Journal of Marketing* 61 (Oct.): 74-82.

Hunt, Shelby D., James A. Muncy, and Nina Ray. 1981. "Alderson's General Theory of Marketing: A Formalization." Pp. 267-72 in B. Enis and K. J. Roering, eds., *Review of Marketing: 1981.* Chicago: American Marketing Association.

Hunt, Shelby D., and Arturo Vasquez-Parraga. 1993. "Organizational Consequences, Marketing Ethics, and Salesforce Supervision." *Journal of Marketing Research* 30 (Feb.): 78-90.

Hunt, Shelby D., and Scott J. Vitell. 1986. "A General Theory of Marketing Ethics." *Journal of Macromarketing* 6 (Spring): 5-16.

————, and ————. 1993. "The General Theory of Marketing Ethics: A Retrospective and Revision." Pp. 775-84 in N. C. Smith and J. A. Quelch, eds., *Ethics in Marketing.* Homewood, IL: Richard D. Irwin.

Itoh, Motoshye. 1983. "Monopoly, Product Differentiation and Economic Welfare." *Journal of Economic Theory* 31: 88-104.

Jacobs, M. T. 1991. *Short-Term America: The Causes and Cures of Our Business Myopia.* Boston: Harvard Business School Press.

Jacobson, Robert. 1988. "Distinguishing among Competing Theories of the Market Share Effect." *Journal of Marketing* 52 (Oct.): 68-80.

————. 1992. "The 'Austrian' School of Strategy." *Academy of Management Review* 17 (4): 782-807.

Jacobson, Robert, and David A. Aaker. 1985. "Is Market Share All That It's Cracked Up to Be?" *Journal of Marketing* 49 (Fall): 11-22.

Jaworski, Bernard J., and Ajay K. Kohli. 1993. "Market Orientation: Antecedents and Consequences." *Journal of Marketing* 57 (July): 53-70.

Jensen, M. C., and W. H. Meckling. 1976. "Theory of the Firm: Managerial Behavior, Agency Costs, and Ownership Structure." *Journal of Financial Economics* 3 (4): 305-60. Reprinted 1986, pp. 214-75 in J. B. Barney and W. G. Ouchi, eds., *Organizational Economics*. San Francisco: Jossey-Bass.

Johnson, Bryan T., Kim R. Holmes, and Melanie Kirkpatrick. 1998. *The 1998 Index of Economic Freedom.* Washington, DC: Heritage Foundation and Dow Jones & Co.

Joskow, Paul F. 1988. "Asset Specificity and the Structure of Vertical Relationships: Empirical Evidence." *Journal of Law, Economics, and Organization* 4: 95-117.

Kanter, Rosabeth Moss, and Paul S. Myers. 1991. "Interorganizational Bonds and Intraorganizational Behavior: How Alliances and Partnerships Change the Organizations Forming Them." Pp. 329-44 in A. Etzioni and P. R. Lawrence, eds., *Socioeconomics: Toward a New Synthesis.* Armonk, NY: M. E. Sharpe.

Kapp, K. William. 1976. "The Nature and Significance of Institutional Economics." *Kyklos* 29: 209-32.

Katz, Michael L., and Carl Shapiro. 1985. "Network Externalities, Competition, and Compatability." *American Economic Review* 75 (3): 424-40.

Kay, John. 1995. *Why Firms Succeed.* Oxford, UK: Oxford University Press.

Keizer, W. 1989. "Recent Reinterpretations of the Socialist Calculation Debate." *Journal of Economic Studies* 16 (2): 63-83.

Keller, Kevin L. 1993. "Conceptualizing, Measuring, and Managing Customer-Based Brand Equity." *Journal of Marketing* 57 (1): 1-22.

———. 1998. *Strategic Brand Management: Building, Measuring, and Managing Brand Equity.* Upper Saddle River, NJ: Prentice Hall.

Keller, Mary Ann. 1993. *Collision: GM, Toyota, Volkswagen and the Race to Own the 21st Century.* New York: Currency Doubleday.

King, Robert G., and Ross Levine. 1993. "Finance, Entrepreneurship, and Growth: Theory and Evidence." *Journal of Monetary Economics* 32 (Dec.): 513-42.

Kirzner, Israel M. 1973. *Competition and Entrepreneurship.* Chicago: University of Chicago Press.

———. 1979. *Perception, Opportunity and Profit: Studies in the Theory of Entrepreneurship.* Chicago: University of Chicago Press.

———. 1982. *Method, Process, and Austrian Economics.* Lexington, MA: Lexington Books.

———. 1985. *Discovery and the Capitalist Process.* Chicago: University of Chicago Press.

———. 1988. "The Economic Calculation Debate: Lessons of Austrians." *Review of Austrian Economics* 2: 1-18.

———. 1992. *The Meaning of Market Process.* London: Routledge.

———. 1996. *Essays on Capital and Interest.* Cheltenham, UK: Edward Elgar.

Klein, B. 1988. "Vertical Integration as Organizational Ownership." *Journal of Law, Economics, and Organization* 4: 201-13.

Klein, Peter. 1996. "Economic Calculation and the Limits of Organization." *Review of Austrian Economics* 9 (2): 3-28.

Knack, Stephen, and Philip Keefer. 1995. "Institutions and Economic Performance: Cross-Country Tests Using Alternative Institutional Measures." *Economics and Politics* 7: 207-27.

Knight, Frank H. 1936. "The Place of Marginal Economics in a Collectivist System." *American Economic Review, Papers and Proceedings* 26: 255-66.

Kohli, Ajay K., and Bernard J. Jaworski. 1990. "Market Orientation: The Construct, Research Propositions, and Managerial Implications." *Journal of Marketing* 54 (April): 1-18.

Koopmans, Tjalling C. 1965. "On the Concept of Optimal Economic Growth." In *The Economic Approach to Development Planning*. Amsterdam: North Holland.

Krausz, Michael, and Jack W. Meiland. 1982. *Relativism: Cognitive and Moral*. Notre Dame, IN: University of Notre Dame Press.

Kravis, Irving B., Alan Heston, and Robert Summers. 1982. *World Product and Income: International Comparisons of Real Gross Product*. Baltimore: Johns Hopkins University Press.

Kuhn, Thomas S. 1962. *The Structure of Scientific Revolutions*. Chicago: University of Chicago Press.

Kuhn, W. E. 1970. *The Evolution of Economic Thought*. 2nd ed. Cincinnati, OH: South-Western.

Lach, Saul, and Mark Schankerman. 1989. "Dynamics of R&D and Investment in the Scientific Sector." *Journal of Political Economy* 97: 880-904.

Lachmann, L. M. 1986. *The Market as an Economic Process*. New York: Basil Blackwell.

Lado, Augustine A., Nancy Boyd, and Susan C. Hanlon. 1997. "Competition, Cooperation, and the Search for Economic Rents: A Syncretic Model." *Academy of Management Review* 22 (1): 110-41.

Lado, Augustine A., Nancy Boyd, and P. Wright. 1992. "A Competency-Based Model of Sustainable Competitive Advantage." *Journal of Management* 18: 77-91.

Lado, Augustine A., and M. C. Wilson. 1994. "Human Resources Systems and Sustained Competitive Advantage: A Competency-Based Perspective." *Academy of Management Review* 19: 699-727.

Lakatos, Imre. 1978. *The Methodology of Scientific Research Programmes*. Cambridge, UK: Cambridge University Press.

Lancaster, Kelvin J. 1966. "A New Approach to Consumer Theory." *Journal of Political Economy* 74: 132-57.

————. 1991. *Modern Consumer Theory*. Aldershot, UK: Edward Elgar.

Landauer, C. 1947. *Theory of National Economic Planning*. Berkeley: University of California Press.

Lande, Robert H. 1982. "Wealth Transfers as the Original and Primary Concern of Antitrust: The Efficiency Interpretation Challenged." *Hastings Law Journal* 34: 65-85.

————. 1988. "The Rise and (Coming) Fall of Efficiency as the Ruler of Antitrust." *Antitrust Bulletin* 33 (Fall): 429-65.

————. 1993. "Chicago Takes It on the Chin: Imperfect Information Could Play a Crucial Role in the Post-*Kodak* World." *Antitrust Law Journal* 62: 193-201.

Landes, David S. 1998. *The Wealth and Poverty of Nations: Why Some Are So Rich and Some Are So Poor*. New York: Norton.

Lange, Oskar R., and Fred M. Taylor. 1936. "On the Economic Theory of Socialism." Reprinted 1964, pp. 55-143 in B. E. Lippincott, ed., *On the Economic Theory of Socialism*. New York: McGraw-Hill.

————, and ————. 1938. "On the Economic Theory of Socialism." In B. E. Lippincott, ed., *On the Economic Theory of Socialism*. Minneapolis: University of Minnesota Press.

————. 1967. "The Computer and the Market." In C. H. Feinstein, ed., *Socialism, Capitalism, and Economic Growth: Essays Presented to Maurice Dobb*. New York: Cambridge University Press.

Langlois, Richard N., ed. 1986. *Economics as a Process: Essays in the New Institutional Economics*. Cambridge, UK: Cambridge University Press.

Langlois, Richard N., and P. L. Robertson. 1995. *Firms, Markets and Economic Change: A Dynamic Theory of Business Institutions*. London: Routledge.

Lavin, Douglas. 1994. "Chrysler Is Now Lowest-Cost Producer in Auto Industry, Harbour Report Says." *Wall Street Journal* (June 23): B3.

Laverty, Kevin J. 1996. "Economic 'Short-Termism': The Debate, the Unresolved Issues, and the Implications for Management Practice and Research." *Academy of Management Review* 21 (3): 825-60.

Lavoie, Don. 1985. *Rivalry and Central Planning: The Socialist Calculation Debate Reconsidered.* Cambridge, UK: Cambridge University Press.

Learned, E. P., C. R. Christensen, K. R. Andrews, and W. D. Guth. 1965. *Business Policy: Text and Cases.* Homewood, IL: Richard D. Irwin.

Lekachman, Robert. 1959. *A History of Economic Ideas.* New York: Harper.

Leontief, Wassily. 1970. "Theoretical Assumptions and Nonobservable Facts." Reprinted 1985 in W. Leontief, 1985, *Essays in Economics.* New Brunswick, NJ: Transaction Books.

———. 1982. "Academic Economics." *Science 9* (July): xii.

Leplin, J., ed. 1984. *Scientific Realism.* Berkeley: University of California Press.

Lerner, A. P. 1934. "Economic Theory of Socialist Economy." *Review of Economic Studies* 2: 51-61.

———. 1936. "A Note on Socialist Economics." *Review of Economic Studies* 4: 72-76.

———. 1937. "Statics and Dynamics in Socialist Economics." *Economic Journal* 47: 253-70.

———. 1938. "Theory and Practice in Socialist Economics." *Review of Economic Studies* 6: 71-75.

Levine, A. L. 1980. "Increasing Returns, the Competitive Model, and the Enigma of Alfred Marshall." *Scottish Journal of Political Economy* 27: 260-75.

Levine, Ross, and David Renelt. 1991. "Cross Country Studies of Growth and Policy: Some Methodological, Conceptual, and Statistical Problems." World Bank Working Paper Series No. 608. New York: World Bank.

———, and ———. 1992. "A Sensitivity Analysis of Cross-Country Growth Regressions." *American Economic Review* 82 (Sept.): 942-63.

Levy, G. B. 1996. "Theory Choice and the Comparison of Rival Theoretical Perspectives in Political Sociology." *Journal of Philosophy of the Social Sciences 26* (March): 26-60.

Liebowitz, S. J., and Margolis, S. E. 1990. "The Fable of the Keys." *Journal of Law and Economics* 33 (April): 1-25.

———, and ———. 1994. "Network Externality: An Uncommon Tragedy." *Journal of Economic Perspectives* 8 (12): 133-50.

———, and ———. 1995. "Path Dependence, Lock-in, and History." *Journal of Law, Organization and History* 74: 205-26.

———, and ———. 1996. "Typing Errors." *Reason* (June): 29-35.

Lincoln, James R., M. L. Gerlach, and C. L. Ahmadjian. 1996. "Keiretsu Networks and Corporate Performance in Japan." *American Sociological Review* 61: 67-88.

Lincoln, Yvonna S., and Guba, Egon G. 1985. *Naturalistic Inquiry.* Beverly Hills, CA: Sage.

Lippman, S. A., and R. P. Rumelt. 1982. "Uncertain Imitability." *Bell Journal of Economics* 13: 418-38.

Lipsey, Richard G., and Peter Steiner. 1975. *Economics.* 4th ed. New York: Harper and Row.

Lipsey, Robert, and Irving Kravis. 1987. *Saving and Economic Growth: Is the United States Really Falling Behind?* New York: Conference Board.

Little, Ian M. D. 1950. *A Critique of Welfare Economics.* Oxford, UK: Clarendon Press.

Little, Ian M. D. 1957. *A Critique of Welfare Economics.* 2nd. ed. Oxford, UK: Clarendon Press.

Loasby, Brian. 1991a. *Equilibrium and Evolution.* Manchester, UK: University of Manchester Press.

Loasby, Brian. 1991b. "Joan Robinson's 'Wrong Turning.' " Pp. 34-48 in I. H. Rima, ed., *The Joan Robinson Legacy.* London: M. E. Sharpe.

Lucas, Robert E. 1988. "On the Mechanics of Economic Development." *Journal of Monetary Economics* 22 (July): 3-42.

———. 1993. "Making a Miracle." *Econometrica* 61: 251-72.

Maddison, Angus. 1989. *The World Economy in the 20th Century.* Paris: Development Center of the Organization for Economic Co-operation and Development.

———. 1991. *Dynamic Forces in Capitalist Development: A Long-Run Comparative View.* Oxford, UK: Oxford University Press.

————. 1994. "Explaining the Economic Performance of Nations, 1820-1989." Pp. 20-61 in W. Baumol, R. R. Nelson, and E. N. Wolff, eds., *Convergence of Productivity*. New York: Oxford University Press.

Madhok, Anoop. 1997. "Cost, Value, and Foreign Market Entry Mode: The Transaction and the Firm." *Strategic Management Journal* 18 (1): 39-62.

Mahoney, Joseph T., and J. Rojendran Pandian. 1992. "The Resource Based View within the Conversation of Strategic Management." *Strategic Management Journal* 13: 363-80.

Manicas, Peter T. 1987. *A History and Philosophy of the Social Sciences*. New York: Basil Blackwell.

Mankiw, N. Gregory. 1998. *Principles of Economics*. New York: Dryden Press, Harcourt Brace College Publishers.

Mankiw, N. Gregory, David Romer, and David N. Weil. 1992. "A Contribution to the Empirics of Economic Growth." *Quarterly Journal of Economics* 107 (May): 407-37.

Margolis, Howard. 1982. *Selfishness, Altruism and Rationality: A Theory of Social Choice*. Cambridge, UK: Cambridge University Press.

Marshall, Alfred. 1890/1949. *Principles of Economics*. London: Macmillan.

Marwell, Gerald, and Ruth E. Ames. 1981. "Economists Free Ride: Does Anyone Else?" *Journal of Public Economics* 15: 295-310.

Masland, T., R. Norland, M. Liu, and J. Contreras. 1992. "Slavery." *Newsweek* (May 4): 30-39.

Mason, E. S. 1939. "Price and Production Policies of Large Scale Enterprises." *American Economic Review* 29: 61-74.

Mauri, Alfredo, and Max P. Michaels. 1998. "Firm and Industry Effects within Strategic Management." *Strategic Management Journal* 19: 211-21.

Mayhew, Anne. 1987. "Culture: Core Concept Under Attack." *Journal of Economic Issues* 21 (2): 587-603.

Mayo, Michael A., and Lawrence J. Marks. 1990. "An Empirical Investigation of a General Theory of Marketing Ethics." *Journal of the Academy of Marketing Science* 18 (Spring): 163-72.

McCarthy, E. Jerome. 1960. *Basic Marketing: A Managerial Approach*. Homewood, IL: Richard D. Irwin.

McGahan, A. M., and M. Porter. 1997. "How Much Does Industry Matter, Really?" *Strategic Management Journal* 18 (Summer Special Issue): 15-30.

McGee, John S. 1958. "Predatory Price Cutting: The Standard Oil (N.J.) Case." *Journal of Law and Economics* 1: 137-69.

McGrath, R. C., I. C. MacMillan, and S. Venkataramen. 1995. "Defining and Developing Competence." *Strategic Management Journal* 16: 251-76.

McKay, Edward S. 1954. "How to Set Up Your Marketing Program." Pp. 5-20 in *A Blueprint for an Effective Marketing Program: Marketing Series 91*. New York: American Management Association.

McKitterick, J. B. 1957. "What Is the Marketing Management Concept?" Pp. 71-81 in F. M. Bass, ed., *The Frontiers of Marketing Thought and Practice*. Chicago: American Marketing Association.

McMullin, Ernan. 1984. "A Case for Scientific Realism." Pp. 8-40 in J. Leplin, ed., *Scientific Realism*. Berkeley: University of California Press.

McNeill, William H. 1963. *The Rise of the West: A History of the Human Community*. Chicago: University of Chicago Press.

McNulty, P. J. 1968. "Economic Theory and the Meaning of Competition." *Quarterly Journal of Economics* 82: 639-56.

Mehra, A. 1994. "Strategic Groups: A Resource-Based Approach." *Journal of Socio-Economics* 23 (4): 425-39.

Menguc, Bulent. 1997. "Organizational Consequences, Marketing Ethics, and Salesforce Supervision: Further Empirical Evidence." *Journal of Business Ethics* 16: 1-20.

Merton, Robert. 1949. *Social Theory and Social Structure*. New York: Free Press.

Metcalfe, J. S., and P. P. Saviotti. 1991. *Evolutionary Theories of Economic and Technological Change.* Chur, UK: Harwood Academic Publishers.

Miller, Danny, and Jamal Shamsie. 1996. "The Resource-Based View of the Firm in Two Environments: The Hollywood Studios from 1936 to 1965." *Academy of Management Journal* 39 (3): 519-43.

Mintzberg, Henry. 1987. "Crafting Strategy." *Harvard Business Review* (July-Aug.): 66-75.

———. 1994. *The Rise and Fall of Strategic Planning.* New York: Free Press.

Mirowski, P. 1983. "An Evolutionary Theory of Economic Change: A Review Article." *Journal of Economic Issues* 17 (3): 757-68.

Mises, Ludwig von. 1920. "Economic Calculation in Socialist Commonwealth." S. Adler, Trans. *Archiv fur Sozialwissenschaft and Sozialpolitik* 47. Reprinted 1935, pp. 87-130 in F. A. Hayek, ed., *Collectivist Economic Planning: Critical Studies on the Possibilities of Socialism.* London: Routledge.

———. 1922/1951. *Socialism: An Economic and Sociological Analysis.* J. Kahane, Trans. London: Jonathan Cape. German ed. 1922; 1st English ed. 1936; 2nd English ed. 1951.

———. 1947. *Planned Chaos.* Irvington-on-Hudson, NY: Foundation for Economic Education. Reprinted 1981, as "Epilogue" to L. von Mises, *Socialism: An Economic and Sociological Analysis.* Indianapolis, IN: Liberty *Classics.*

———. 1949. *Human Action: A Treatise on Economics.* New Haven, CT: Yale University Press.

———. 1969. *The Historical Setting of the Austrian School.* New Rochelle, NY: Arlington House.

Mongiovi, Gary. 1992. "Review of *The John Robinson Legacy.*" *Economic Journal* 102 (July): 963-65.

Montgomery, Cynthia A., ed. 1995. *Resource-Based and Evolutionary Theories of the Firm: Towards a Synthesis.* Norwell, MA: Kluwer Academic Publishers.

Montgomery, Cynthia A., and Michael E. Porter. 1991. *Strategy: Seeking and Securing Competitive Advantage.* Boston: Harvard Business School Publishing.

Moran, Peter, and Sumantra Ghoshal. 1996. "Theories of Economic Organization: The Case for Realism and Balance." *Academy of Management Review* 21 (1): 58-72.

Morgan, Robert A., and Shelby D. Hunt. 1994. "The Commitment-Trust Theory of Relationship Marketing." *Journal of Marketing* 58 (July): 20-38.

Mowery, David C., and Nathan Rosenberg. 1989. *Technology and the Pursuit of Economic Growth.* Cambridge, UK: Cambridge University Press.

Myers, James H. 1996. *Segmentation and Positioning Strategies for Marketing Decisions.* Chicago: American Marketing Association.

Narver, John C., and Stanley F. Slater. 1990. "The Effect of Market Orientation on Business Profitability." *Journal of Marketing* 54 (Oct.): 20-35.

Nayyan, Praveen, and Karen Bantel. 1994. "Competitive Agility = A Source of Competitive Advantage Based on Speed and Variety." *Advances in Strategic Management* 10A: 193-222.

Neale, Walter C. 1987. "Institutions." *Journal of Economic Issues* 21 (3): 1177-1206.

Nelson, Phillip. 1970. "Information and Consumer Behavior." *Journal of Political Economy* 78: 311-29.

Nelson, Richard R. 1991. "Why Do Firms Differ, and How Does It Matter?" *Strategic Management Journal* 12: 61-74.

———. 1995. "Recent Evolutionary Theorizing about Economic Change." *Journal of Economic Literature* 33 (March): 48-90.

Nelson, Richard R., and Sidney G. Winter. 1982. *An Evolutionary Theory of Economic Change.* Cambridge, MA: Belknap Press.

North, Douglass C. 1981. *Structure and Change in Economic History.* New York: Norton.

———. 1986. "The New Institutional Economics." *Journal of Institutional and Theoretical Economics* 142: 230-37.

———. 1990. *Institutions, Institutional Change, and Economic Performance.* Cambridge, UK: University of Cambridge Press.

————. 1991. "Institutions." *Journal of Economic Perspectives* 5 (1): 97-112.

Ofer, Gur. 1987. "Soviet Economic Growth: 1928-85." *Journal of Economic Literature* 25 (4, Dec.): 1767-1833.

O'Keeffe, Michael, Felix Mavondo, and William Schroder. 1996. *The Resource-Advantage Theory of Competition: Implications for Australian Competition.* Melbourne, Australia: Monash University Agriculture Research Unit.

Ortony, Andrew. 1979. *Metaphor and Thought.* Cambridge, UK: Cambridge University Press.

Parsons, Talcott, and Neil Smelser. 1956. *Economy and Society: A Study in the Integration of Economic and Social Theory.* Glencoe, IL: Free Press.

Parvatiyar, Atul, Jagdish N. Sheth, and F. Brown Whittington, Jr. 1992. "Paradigm Shift in Interfirm Marketing Relationships: Emerging Research Issues." Working Paper. Atlanta, GA: Emory University Marketing Department.

Pelikan, P. 1988. "Can the Imperfect Innovation System of Capitalism Be Outperformed?" In G. Dosi, C. Freeman, R. Nelson, G. Silverberg, and L. Soite, eds., *Technical Change and Economic Theory.* London: Pinter.

————. 1989a. "Evolution, Economic Competence and Corporate Control." *Journal of Economic Behavior and Organization* 12: 279-303.

————. 1989b. "Markets as Instruments of Evolution of Structures." Working Paper No. 237. Stockholm: Industrial Institute for Economic and Social Research.

Penrose, Edith T. 1959. *The Theory of the Growth of the Firm.* London: Basil Blackwell and Mott.

Perrow, Charles. 1981. "Markets, Hierarchies and Hegemony." Pp. 371-86, 403-4 in A. H. Van De Ven and W. F. Joyce, eds., *Perspectives on Organization Design and Behavior.* New York: John Wiley.

————. 1986. *Complex Organizations.* New York: Random House.

Peteraf, Margaret A. 1993. "The Cornerstones of Competitive Advantage: A Resource-Based View." *Strategic Management Journal* 14 (3): 179-91.

Phelps, E. S. 1975. *Altruism, Morality, and Economic Theory.* New York: Russell Sage Foundation.

Pigou, A. C. 1928. "An Analysis of Supply." *Economic Journal* 38: 387-404.

Podolny, Joel M., T. E. Stuart, and M. T. Hannan. 1996. "Networks, Knowledge, and Niches: Competition in the Worldwide Semiconductor Industry." *American Journal of Sociology* 102: 659-89.

Poirot, C. S., Jr. 1993. "Institutions and Economic Evolution." *Journal of Economic Issues* 28 (3): 887-907.

Polanyi, Michael. 1957. *Personal Knowledge: Towards a Post-Critical Philosophy.* London: Routledge and Kegan Paul.

————. 1966. *The Tacit Dimension.* Garden City, NY: Doubleday.

Porter, Michael E. 1980. *Competitive Advantage.* New York: Free Press.

————. 1985. *Competitive Strategy.* New York: Free Press.

————. 1987. "From Competitive Advantage to Corporate Strategy." *Harvard Business Review* 65 (May-June): 43-59.

————. 1990. *The Competitive Advantage of Nations.* New York: Free Press.

————. 1991. "Towards a Dynamic Theory of Strategy." *Strategic Management Journal* 12: 95-117.

————. 1992a. *Capital Choices: Changing the Way America Invests in Industry.* Washington, DC: Council on Competitiveness.

————. 1992b. "Capital Disadvantage: America's Failing Capital Investment System." *Harvard Business Review* 70 (July-Aug.): 65-82.

Posner, Richard A. 1976. *Antitrust Law.* Chicago: University of Chicago Press.

————. 1979. "The Chicago School of Antitrust Analysis." *University of Pennsylvania Law Review* 127: 925-33.

————. 1986. *Economic Analysis of Law.* Boston: Little, Brown.

Powell, Walter W. 1993. "The Social Construction of an Organizational Field: The Case of Biotechnology." Paper presented at Conference on Strategic Change at Warwick Business School, Warwick, UK.

Powell, Walter W., and Paul J. DiMaggio, eds. 1991. *The New Institutionalism in Organizational Analysis.* Chicago: University of Chicago Press.

Powell, Walter W., and Laurel Smith-Doerr. 1994. "Networks and Economic Life." Pp. 368-402 in N. J. Smelser and R. Swedberg, eds., *The Handbook of Economic Sociology.* Princeton, NJ: Princeton University Press.

Prahalad, C. K., and Gary Hamel. 1990. "The Core Competence of the Corporation." *Harvard Business Review* (May-June): 79-91.

———, and ———. 1993. "Strategy as Stretch and Leverage." *Harvard Business Review* (March/April): 63-76.

Pringle, Charles D., and Mark J. Kroll. 1997. "Why Trafalgar Was Won Before It Was Fought: Lessons from Resource-Based Theory." *Academy of Management Executive* 11 (4): 73-89.

Prychitko, David L. 1994. "Praxeology." Pp. 77-83 in P. Boettke, ed., *The Elgar Companion to Austrian Economics.* Brookfield, VT: Edward Elgar.

Putnam, Robert D. 1995. "Bowling Alone: America's Declining Social Capital." *Journal of Democracy* 6 (1): 65-78.

Ranson, B. 1987. "The Institutionalist Theory of Capital Formation." *Journal of Economic Issues* 21 (Sept.): 1265-78.

Ravenscraft, David J. 1983. "Structure-Profit Relationships at the Line of Business and Industry Level." *Review of Economics and Statistics* 65 (Feb.): 22-31.

Reed, Richard, and Robert J. DeFillippi. 1990. "Causal Ambiguity, Barriers to Imitation, and Sustainable Competitive Advantage." *Academy of Management Review* 15 (Jan.): 88-117.

Reekie, Donald, and Ronald Savitt. 1982. "Marketing Behavior and Entrepreneurship: A Synthesis of Alderson and Austrian Economics." *European Journal of Marketing* 16 (7): 55-66.

Rindfleisch, Aric, and Jan B. Heide. 1997. "Transaction Cost Analysis: Past, Present and Future Applications." *Journal of Marketing* 61 (4): 30-54.

Robbins, Lionel. 1932. 3rd ed., 1984. *The Nature and Significance of Economic Science.* London: Macmillan.

———. 1934. *The Great Depression.* New York: Macmillan.

Robertson, Thomas S., and Harold H. Kassarjian. 1991. *Handbook of Consumer Behavior.* Englewood Cliffs, NJ: Prentice Hall.

Robinson, Joan. 1933. *The Economics of Imperfect Competition.* London: Macmillan.

———. 1951. *Collected Economic Papers, Vol. 1.* Oxford, UK: Basil Blackwell.

———. 1954. "The Impossibility of Competition." Pp. 245-54 in E. Chamberlin, ed., *Monopoly and Competition and Their Regulation.* London: Macmillan.

———. 1979. *Collected Economic Papers, Vol. 5.* Oxford, UK: Basil Blackwell.

———. 1980. *Further Contributions to Modern Economics.* Oxford, UK: Basil Blackwell.

Roehl, Tom. 1996. "The Role of International R&D in the Competence-Building Strategies of Japanese Pharmaceutical Firms." Pp. 377-96 in R. Sanchez, A. Heene, and H. Thomas, *Dynamics of Competence-Based Competition.* New York: Elsevier Science.

Romer, Paul M. 1986. "Increasing Returns and Long-Run Growth." *Journal of Political Economy* 94 (Oct.): 1002-37.

———. 1987a. "Crazy Explanations for the Productivity Slowdown." Pp. 163-202 in S. Fischer, ed., *NBER Macroeconomics Annual.* Cambridge: MIT Press.

———. 1987b. "Growth Based on Increasing Returns Due to Specialization." *American Economic Review* 77 (2): 55-62.

———. 1990. "Endogenous Technological Change." *Journal of Political Economy* 98: 71-102.

———. 1993a. "Idea Gaps and Object Gaps in Economic Development." *Journal of Monetary Economics* 32: 543-73.

―――. 1993b. "Two Strategies for Economic Development: Using Ideas and Promoting Ideas." Pp. 63-91 in *Proceedings of the World Bank Annual Conferences on Development Economics 1992*. New York: World Bank.

―――. 1994. "The Origins of Endogenous Growth." *Journal of Economic Perspectives* 8 (Winter): 3-22.

Roquebert, Jaime A., Robert L. Phillips, and Peter A. Westfall. 1996. "Markets versus Management: What 'Drives' Profitability?" *Strategic Management Journal* 17: 653-64.

Rosenberg, Alexander. 1992. *Economics: Mathematical Politics or Science of Diminishing Returns?* Chicago: University of Chicago Press.

Rosenberg, Nathan. 1963. "Technological Change in the Machine Tool Industry: 1840-1910." *Journal of Economic History* 23 (Dec.): 414-46.

Rosenberg, Nathan, and L. E. Birdzell, Jr. 1986. *How the West Grew Rich*. New York: Basic Books.

Rothbard, Murray. 1962. *Man, Economy, and State*. 2 vols. Princeton, NJ: Van Nostrand.

―――. 1976. "Ludwig von Mises and Economic Calculation under Socialism." Pp. 67-77 in L. S. Moss, ed., *The Economics of Ludwig von Mises: Toward a Critical Reappraisal*. Kansas City, MO: Sheed and Ward.

―――. 1987. "Breaking Out of the Walrasian Box: Schumpeter and Hansen." *Review of Austrian Economics* 1: 97-108.

Rumelt, Richard P. 1984. "Toward a Strategic Theory of the Firm." Pp. 556-70 in R. Lamb, ed., *Competitive Strategic Management*. Englewood Cliffs, NJ: Prentice Hall.

―――. 1991. "How Much Does Industry Matter?" *Strategic Management Journal* 12: 167-85.

Sabel, Charles F. 1989. "Flexible Specialisation and the Re-emergence of Regional Economies." Pp. 17-70 in P. Hirst and J. Zeitlin, eds., *Reversing Industrial Decline?* London: Berg.

Sabel, Charles F., H. Kern, and G. Herrigel. 1991. "Kooperative Prodktion: Neue Formen der Zusammenarbeit zwischen Endfertigern und Zulieferern in der Automobilindustrie und die Neuordnung der Firma." Pp. 203-27 in H. G. Mendius and U. Wendeling-Schroder, eds., *Zuliefere im Netz: Neustrukturierung der Logistik am Beispiel der Automobilzulieferung*. Cologne, Germany: Bund Vergag.

Samuelson, Paul A. 1947. 1983 enlarged ed. *Foundations of Economic Analysis*. Cambridge: MIT Press.

Samuelson, Paul A., and W. D. Nordhaus. 1989. *Economics*. 13th ed. Englewood Cliffs, NJ: Prentice Hall.

―――, and ―――. 1995. *Economics*. 15th ed. Englewood Cliffs, NJ: Prentice Hall.

Sanchez, Ron, and Aimé Heene. 1997. *Strategic Learning and Knowledge Management*. New York: John Wiley.

Sanchez, Ron, Aimé Heene, and Howard Thomas. 1996. *Dynamics of Competence-Based Competition*. New York: Elsevier Science.

Saxenian, Anna Lee. 1994. *Regional Networks: Industrial Adaptation in Silicon Valley and Route 128*. Cambridge, MA: Harvard University Press.

Schendel, Don. 1994. "Introduction to Competitive Organizational Behavior: Toward an Organizationally-Based Theory of Competitive Advantage." *Strategic Management Journal* 15: 14.

Scherer, R. 1977. "The Posnerian Harvest: Separating Wheat from Chaff." *Yale Law Journal* 86: 974, 976-79.

Schmalensee, Robert. 1985. "Do Markets Differ Much?" *American Economic Review* 75 (3): 341-50.

Schmookler, Jacob. 1966. *Invention and Economic Growth*. Cambridge, MA: Harvard University Press.

Schoemaker, P. J. H., and R. Amit. 1994. "Investment in Stratregic Assets: Industry and Firm-Level Perspectives." Pp. 3-33 in P. Shrivastava, A. S. Huff, and J. E. Dutton, eds., *Advances in Strategic Management*. Vol. 10A. Greenwich, CT: JAI Press.

Schotter, Andrew. 1981. *The Economic Theory of Social Institutions.* New York: Cambridge University Press.

Schultz, Theodore. 1961. "Investment in Human Capital." *American Economic Review* 51 (March): 1-17.

Schulze, William S. 1994. "The Two Schools of Thought in Resource-Based Theory." Pp. 127-51 in P. Shrivastava, A. S. Huff, and J. E. Dutton, eds., *Advances in Strategic Management.* Vol. 10A. Greenwich, CT: JAI Press.

Schumpeter, Joseph A. 1934/1961/1983. *The Theory of Economic Development.* Cambridge, MA: Harvard University Press.

———. 1950. *Capitalism, Socialism, and Democracy.* New York: Harper and Row.

———. 1954. *History of Economic Analysis.* New York: Oxford University Press.

Scott, Allen J. 1990. "The Technopoles of Southern California." *Environment and Planning A* 22: 1575-1605.

Scott, W. Richard. 1995. *Institutions and Organizations.* Thousand Oaks, CA: Sage.

Segerstrom, Paul S., T. C. A. Anant, and Elias Dinopoulous. 1990. "A Schumpeterian Model of the Product Life Cycle." *American Economic Review* 80 (Dec.): 1077-91.

Sellars, W. 1963. *Science, Perception and Reality.* New York: Humanities Press.

Selznick, P. 1957. *Leadership in Administration.* New York: Harper and Row.

Shand, Alexander. 1984. *The Capitalist Alternative: An Introduction to Neo-Austrian Economics.* New York: New York University Press.

Shepherd, William G. 1982. "Causes of Increased Competition in the U.S. Economy, 1939-1980." *Review of Economics and Statistics* 64 (Nov.): 613-26.

Sherwood, Robert M. 1990. *Intellectual Property and Economic Development.* Boulder, CO: Westview Press.

Sheth, Jagdish N., and Atal Parvatiyar. 1995a. "The Evolution of Relationship Marketing." *International Business Review* 4: 397-418.

———, and ———. 1995b. "Relationship Marketing in Consumer Markets: Antecedents and Consequences." *Journal of the Academy of Marketing Science* 23 (4): 255-71.

Siegel, H. 1987. *Relativism Refuted.* Dordrecht, The Netherlands: D. Reidel.

Siegfried, J. J., and T. K. Tieman. 1974. "The Welfare Cost of Monopoly: An Inter-industry Analysis." *Economic Inquiry* 12 (June): 190-202.

Simon, Herbert A. 1959. "The Theories of Decision Making in Economics and Behavioral Science." *American Economic Review* 49 (June): 253-83.

———. 1979. "Rational Decision Making in Business Organizations." *American Economic Review* 69 (Sept.): 493-512.

Simon, Julian. 1981. *The Ultimate Resource.* Princeton, NJ: Princeton University Press.

Sims, Christopher A. 1972. "Money, Income and Causality." *American Economic Review* 42 (4): 540-52.

Singhapakdi, Anusorn, and Scott J. Vitell, Jr. 1990. "Marketing Ethics: Factors Influencing Perceptions of Ethical Problems and Alternatives." *Journal of Macromarketing* 10 (Spring): 4-18.

———, and ———. 1991. "Research Note: Selected Factors Influencing Marketers' Deontological Norms." *Journal of the Academy of Marketing Science* 19 (Winter): 37-42.

Sinnett, M. W. 1987. "Method versus Methodology: The Ultimate Resource." *Review of Austrian Economics* 1: 207-23.

Slater, Stanley F., and John C. Narver. 1994. "Does Competitive Environment Moderate the Market Orientation-Performance Relationship?" *Journal of Marketing* 58 (Jan.): 46-55.

———, and ———. 1995. "Market Orientation and the Learning Organization." *Journal of Marketing* 59 (July): 63-74.

Smelser, Neil J., and Richard Swedberg. 1994. *The Handbook of Economic Sociology.* Princeton, NJ: Princeton University Press.

Smith, Adam. 1776/1937. *Wealth of Nations.* Modern Library Edition. New York: Random House.

Smith, Wendell. 1956. "Product Differentiation and Market Segmentation as Alternative Marketing Strategies." *Journal of Marketing* 21 (July): 3-8.

Snow, Charles C., and Lawrence Hrebiniak. 1980. "Strategy, Distributive Competence, and Organizational Performance." *Administrative Science Quarterly* 25 (June): 317-36.

Solow, Robert M. 1956. "A Contribution to the Theory of Economic Growth." *Quarterly Journal of Economics* 70 (Feb.): 65-94.

———. 1957. "Technical Change and the Aggregate Production Function." *Review of Economics and Statistics* 39: 312-20.

———. 1990. *The Labor Market as a Social Institution.* Oxford, UK: Basil Blackwell.

———. 1994. "Perspectives on Growth Theory." *Journal of Economic Perspectives* 8 (Winter): 45-54.

Sparks, John R., and Shelby D. Hunt. 1998. "Marketing Researcher Ethical Sensitivity." *Journal of Marketing* 62 (2): 92-109.

Spence, Michael. 1976. "Product Differentiation and Welfare." *American Economic Review* 66 (Papers and Proceedings): 407-14.

Steiner, G. A. 1969. *Top Management Planning.* New York: Macmillan.

———. 1979. *Strategic Planning: What Every Manager Should Know.* New York: Free Press.

Stigler, George J. 1949. *Five Lectures on Economic Problems.* New York: Macmillan.

———. 1957. "Perfect Competition, Historically Contemplated." *Journal of Political Economy* 65 (1): 1-17.

———. 1961. "The Economics of Information." *Journal of Political Economy* 71 (June): 213-25.

———. 1966. *The Theory of Price.* 3rd ed. New York: Macmillan.

———. 1982. "Economists and the Problem of Monopoly." *American Economic Review* 72: 1-3.

Stokey, Nancy. 1991. "Human Capital, Product Quality, and Growth." *Quarterly Journal of Economics* 106 (May): 587-616.

Summers, Robert, and Alan Heston. 1991. "The Penn World Table (Mark 5): An Expanded Set of International Comparisons, 1950-1988." *Quarterly Journal of Economics* 106 (2, May): 327-68.

———, and ———. 1993. "Penn World Tables, Version 5.5." Available on diskette from the National Bureau of Economic Research, Cambridge, MA.

Suppe, Frederic. 1977. *The Structure of Scientific Theories.* 2nd ed. Chicago: University of Illinois Press.

Suris, Oscar. 1996. "Chrysler Ranks Highest in Efficiency among Big Three, but All Trail Japan." *Wall Street Journal* (May 30): A2.

Swan, Trevor W. 1956. "Economic Growth and Capital Accumulation." *Economic Record* 32 (Nov.): 334-61.

Sweezy, A. 1936. "The Economist in a Socialist Economy." Pp. 422-33 in *Explorations in Economics: Notes and Essays Contributed in Honor of F. W. Taussig.* London: McGraw-Hill.

Sweezy, P. M. 1949. *Socialism.* New York: McGraw-Hill.

Sydow, Jorg. 1991. "On the Management of Strategic Networks." Institut fur Management Working Paper No. 67-91. Berlin, Germany: Freie Universitat.

Taylor, F. M. 1929. "The Guidance of Production in a Socialist State." *American Economic Review* 19 (1): 1-8. Reprinted 1964, pp. 41-54 in B. E. Lippincott, ed., *On the Economic Theory of Socialism.* New York: McGraw-Hill.

Taylor, Robert E. 1982a. "Antitrust Enforcement Will Be More Selective." *Wall Street Journal* (Jan. 11): 6.

———. 1982b. "A Talk with Antitrust Chief Baxter." *Wall Street Journal* (March 4): 28.

Taylor, Thomas C. 1980. *The Fundamentals of Austrian Economics.* San Francisco: Cato Institute.

Teece, David, and Gary Pisano. 1994. "The Dynamic Capabilities of Firms: An Introduction." *Industrial and Corporate Change* 3 (E): 537-56.

Teece, David, Gary Pisano, and Amy Shuen. 1997. "Dynamic Capabilities and Strategic Management." *Strategic Management Journal* 18 (7): 509-33.

Telser, Lester G. 1960. "Why Should Manufacturers Want Fair Trade?" *Journal of Law and Economics* 3: 86-105.

Thorelli, Hans B. 1986. "Networks: Between Markets and Hierarchies." *Strategic Management Journal* 7: 37-51.

Triffin, Robert. 1940. *Monopolistic Competition and General Equilibrium Theory.* Cambridge, MA: Harvard University Press.

United Nations. 1985. *International Comparisons of Prices and Purchasing Power in 1980.* New York: United Nations.

Uzzi, Brian. 1996. "The Sources and Consequences of Embeddedness for the Economic Performance of Organizations: The Network Effect." *American Sociological Review* 61: 674-98.

Varadarajan, P. Rajan, and Margaret H. Cunningham. 1995. "Strategic Alliances: A Synthesis of Conceptual Foundations." *Journal of the Academy of Marketing Science* 23 (4): 282-96.

Veblen, Thorstein B. 1899. *The Theory of the Leisure Class: An Economic Study of Institutions.* New York: Macmillan.

————. 1904. *The Theory of Business Enterprise.* New York: Charles Scribner's Sons.

————. 1914. *The Instinct of Workmanship, and the State of the Industrial Arts.* New York: Augustus Kelley. Reprinted 1990, with a new introduction by Murray G. Murphey and a 1964 introductory note by Joseph Dorfman. New Brunswick, NJ: Transaction Books.

————. 1919. *The Place of Science in Modern Civilization and Other Essays.* New York: Huebsch. Reprinted 1990, with a new introduction by W. J. Samuels. New Brunswick, NJ: Transaction Books.

Vitell, Scott J., and Shelby D. Hunt. 1990. "The General Theory of Marketing Ethics: A Partial Test of the Model." Pp. 237-65 in J. N. Sheth, ed., *Research in Marketing.* Vol. 10. Greenwich, CT: JAI Press.

Wall Street Journal. 1978. "Borden Ordered to Alter Pricing for ReaLemon" (Nov. 24): 8.

Walras, Leon. 1874/1954. *Elements of Pure Economics.* Translated 1954 by William Jaffe. Homewood, IL: Richard D. Irwin.

Weitzman, Martin L. 1990. "Comment." Pp. 339-42 in O. J. Blanchard and S. Fischer, eds., *NBER Macroeconomics Annual.* Cambridge: MIT Press.

Wernerfelt, Birger. 1984. "A Resource-Based View of the Firm." *Strategic Management Journal* 5: 171-80.

Williamson, Oliver E. 1968. "Economics as an Antitrust Defense: The Welfare Tradeoffs." *American Economic Review* 58 (March): 18-35.

————. 1975. *Markets and Hierarchies: Analysis and Anti-trust Implications.* New York: Free Press.

————. 1979. "Transaction-Cost Economics: The Governance of Contractual Relations." *Journal of Law and Economics* 22: 233-61.

————. 1981a. "The Economics of Organization: The Transaction Cost Approach." *American Journal of Sociology* 87 (Nov.): 548-77.

————. 1981b. "The Modern Corporation: Origins, Evolution, Attributes." *Journal of Economic Literature* 19 (Dec.): 1537-68.

————. 1983. "Credible Commitments: Using Hostages to Support Exchange." *American Economic Review* 73: 519-40.

————. 1985. *The Economic Institutions of Capitalism.* New York: Free Press.

————. 1989. "Transaction Cost Economics." Pp. 136-82 in R. Schmalensee and R. D. Willig, eds., *Handbook of Industrial Organization.* Amsterdam, The Netherlands: North Holland.

————. 1991a. "Comparative economic organization: The analysis of discrete structural alternatives." *Administrative Science Quarterly* 36: 269-96.

————. 1991b. "Economic Institutions: Spontaneous and Intentional Governance." *Journal of Law, Economics, and Organization* 7: 159-87.

————. 1993. "Opportunism and Its Critics." *Managerial and Decision Economics* 14: 94-107.

———. 1994. "Transaction Cost Economics and Organization Theory." Pp. 77-107 in N. J. Smelser and R. Swedberg, *The Handbook of Economic Sociology.* Princeton, NJ: Princeton University Press.

———. 1996. *The Mechanisms of Governance.* Oxford, UK: Oxford University Press.

Witt, Ulrich. 1992. "Evolutionary Concepts in Economics." *Eastern Economic Journal* (Fall): 405-19.

Yeager, Leland. 1987. "Why Subjectivism?" *Review of Austrian Economics* 1: 5-31.

Yergin, Daniel, and Joseph Stanislaw. 1998. *The Commanding Heights.* New York: Simon and Schuster.

Young, Alwyn. 1991. "Learning by Doing and the Dynamic Effects of International Trade." *Quarterly Journal of Economics* 106 (May): 369-406.

———. 1993. "Invention and Bounded Learning by Doing." *Journal of Political Economy* 101 (June): 443-72.

Young, Louis C., and Ian F. Wilkinson. 1989. "The Role of Trust and Co-operation in Marketing Channels: A Preliminary Study." *European Journal of Marketing* 23 (2): 109-22.

Zald, Mayer N. 1987. "Review Essay: The New Institutional Economics." *American Journal of Sociology* 93: 701-8.

Zukin, Sharon, and Paul DiMaggio, eds. 1990. *Structures of Capital: The Social Organization of the Economy.* Cambridge, UK: Cambridge University Press.

Author Index

285

Subject Index

About the Author

Shelby D. Hunt is the J. B. Hoskins and P. W. Horn Professor of Marketing at Texas Tech University, Lubbock, Texas. A past editor of the *Journal of Marketing* (1985-1987), and author of *Modern Marketing Theory: Critical Issues in the Philosophy of Marketing Science* (1991), he has numerous articles on competitive theory, macromarketing, ethics, channels of distribution, philosophy of science, and marketing theory. Three of his *Journal of Marketing* articles, "The Nature and Scope of Marketing" (1976), "General Theories and Fundamental Explananda of Marketing" (1983), and "The Comparative Advantage Theory of Competition" (1995), have won the Harold H. Maynard Award for the "best article on marketing theory." He received the 1986 Paul D. Converse Award from the American Marketing Association for his contributions to theory and science in marketing. He received the 1987 Outstanding Marketing Educator Award from the Academy of Marketing Science and the 1992 American Marketing Association/Richard D. Irwin Distinguished Marketing Educator Award.